13th Workshop on Multiword Expressions (MWE 2017)

Valencia, Spain
4 April 2017

ISBN: 978-1-5108-3868-0

MWE 2017

13th Workshop on Multiword Expressions

Proceedings of the Workshop

EACL 2017 Workshop
April 4, 2017
Valencia, Spain

Sponsors

Introduction

The 13th edition of the annual *Workshop on Multiword Expressions* (MWE 2017)[1] took place on April 4, 2017 in Valencia, Spain, in conjunction with the 15th Conference of the European Chapter of the Association for Computational Linguistics (EACL 2017). It was endorsed by the Special Interest Group on the Lexicon of the Association for Computational Linguistics (SIGLEX)[2] and by the European IC1207 COST Action PARSEME.[3] The workshop featured a dedicated track for the Shared Task on the Identification of Verbal Multiword Expressions.

The workshop has been held since 2001 in conjunction with major computational linguistics conferences (ACL, COLING, LREC, EACL). It attracts the attention of an ever-growing community working on a variety of languages and linguistic phenomena and represents an important venue for the community to interact, share resources and tools, and collaborate on efforts for advancing the computational treatment of multiword expressions.

In this 13th edition of the workshop, we have called for papers on major challenges in MWE processing, both from theoretical and computational viewpoints, focusing on research related (but not limited) to the following topics:

- Manually and automatically constructed lexical resources
- MWE representation in lexical resources
- MWE annotation in corpora and treebanks
- MWEs in non-standard language (e.g. tweets, forums, spontaneous speech)
- Original MWE discovery methods (e.g. using word embeddings, parallel corpora)
- Original MWE in-context identification methods (e.g. using deep learning, topic models)
- MWE processing in syntactic frameworks (e.g. HPSG, LFG, TAG, universal dependencies)
- MWE processing in semantic frameworks (e.g. WSD, semantic parsing)
- MWE processing in end-user applications (e.g. summarization, machine translation)
- Orchestration of MWE processing with respect to applications
- Evaluation of MWE processing techniques
- Models of first and second language acquisition of MWEs
- Theoretical and psycholinguistic studies on MWEs
- Crosslinguistic studies on MWEs

Submissions included both long and short papers. In total, 34 papers (22 short and 12 long) were submitted to the *main track* of the workshop. From those, 7 papers (4 short and 3 long) were accepted as oral presentations and 14 papers (11 short and 3 long) were accepted as posters. The overall acceptance rate is 62% including oral presentations and posters, short and long papers.

Additionally, 6 system description papers and 1 shared task description paper were submitted to the *shared task track*. The former were all selected as posters and the latter as an oral presentation. The reviewing modalities were different in this track, therefore we do not count these papers in the workshop acceptance rate.

In addition to the oral and poster sessions, the workshop featured an invited talk by Paul Cook, from the University of New Brunswick, Canada. The presentation was entitled *Exploiting multilingual lexical*

---

[1] http://multiword.sf.net/mwe2017
[2] http://www.siglex.org/
[3] http://parseme.eu/

resources to predict the compositionality of MWEs. The program also included a panel discussion on the future directions of the MWE community and the SIGLEX Section.

We would like to thank the members of the program committee for the timely reviews, authors for their valuable contributions, shared task organizers, annotators, and system developers for their hard work, and all involved participants for their interest in the workshop. We also want to thank the IC1207 COST Action PARSEME and SIGLEX for their endorsement and support, as well as the EACL 2017 organizers.

Stella Markantonatou, Carlos Ramisch, Agata Savary, and Veronika Vincze

Organizers:

Stella Markantonatou, Institute for Language and Speech Processing/RC "Athena" (Greece)
Carlos Ramisch, Aix Marseille University (France)
Agata Savary, Université François Rabelais Tours (France)
Veronika Vincze, Hungarian Academy of Sciences (Hungary)

Program Committee - Main Track:

Iñaki Alegria, University of the Basque Country (Spain)
Anna Anastassiadis-Symeonidis, Aristotle University of Thessaloniki (Greece)
Dimitra Anastasiou, Luxemburg Institute of Science and Technology (Luxembourg)
Doug Arnold, University of Essex (UK)
Timothy Baldwin, The University of Melbourne (Australia)
Eduard Bejček, Charles University (Czech Republic)
Francis Bond, Nanyang Technological University (Singapore)
Antonio Branco, University of Lisbon (Portugal)
Miriam Butt, Universität Konstanz (Germany)
Marie Candito, Paris Diderot University (France)
Fabienne Cap, Uppsala University (Sweden)
Marine Carpuat, University of Maryland (USA)
Helena Caseli, Federal University of São Carlos (Brazil)
Anastasia Christofidou, Academy of Athens (Greece)
Ken Church, IBM Watson (USA)
Matthieu Constant, Université de Lorraine (France)
Silvio Cordeiro, Aix Marseille University (France) and Federal University of Rio Grande do Sul (Brazil)
Béatrice Daille, Nantes University (France)
Koenraad de Smedt, University of Bergen (Norway)
Mona Diab, The George Washington University (USA)
Gaël Dias, University of Caen Basse-Normandie (France)
Ismail El Maarouf, Adarga Ltd (UK)
Gülşen Eryiğit , Istanbul Technical University (Turkey)
Stefan Evert, FAU Erlangen-Nürnberg (Germany)
Meghdad Farahmand, University of Geneva (Switzerland)
Joaquim Ferreira da Silva, New University of Lisbon (Portugal)
Dan Flickinger, Stanford University (USA)
Angeliki Fotopoulou, Institute for Language and Speech Processing/RC "Athena" (Greece)
Voula Giouli, Institute for Language and Speech Processing/RC "Athena" (Greece)
Antton Gurrutxaga, Elhuyar Foundation (Basque Country, Spain)
Chikara Hashimoto, Yahoo!Japan (Japan)
Kyo Kageura, University of Tokyo (Japan)
Philipp Koehn, John Hopkins University (USA)
Dimitris Kokkinakis, University of Gothenburg (Sweden)
Yannis Korkontzelos, Edge Hill University (UK)
Brigitte Krenn, Austrian Research Institute for Artificial Intelligence (Austria)
Cvetana Krstev, University of Belgrade (Serbia)
Eric Laporte, University Paris-Est Marne-la-Vallee (France)
Evita Linardaki, Hellenic Open University (Greece)

Hector Martínez Alonso, INRIA (France)
Diana McCarthy, University of Cambridge (UK)
Johanna Monti, "L'Orientale" University of Naples (Italy)
Preslav Nakov, Qatar Computing Research Institute, HBKU (Qatar)
Joakim Nivre, Uppsala University (Sweden)
Diarmuid Ó Séaghdha, Apple (UK)
Michael Oakes, University of Wolverhampton (UK)
Jan Odijk, University of Utrecht (The Netherlands)
Petya Osenova, Bulgarian Academy of Sciences (Bulgaria)
Haris Papageorgiou, Institute for Language and Speech Processing/RC "Athena" (Greece)
Yannick Parmentier, Université d'Orléans (France)
Carla Parra Escartín, ADAPT Centre, Dublin City University (Ireland)
Agnieszka Patejuk, Institute of Computer Science, Polish Academy of Sciences (Poland)
Pavel Pecina, Charles University (Czech Republic)
Scott Piao, Lancaster University (UK)
Thierry Poibeau, CNRS and École Normale Supérieure (France)
Martin Riedl, University of Hamburg (Germany)
Mike Rosner, University of Malta (Malta)
Manfred Sailer, Goethe-Universität Frankfurt am Main (Germany)
Magali Sanches Duran, University of São Paulo (Brazil)
Federico Sangati, Independent researcher (Italy)
Nathan Schneider, Georgetown University (USA)
Sabine Schulte im Walde, University of Stuttgart (Germany)
Serge Sharoff, University of Leeds (UK)
Kiril Simov, Bulgarian Academy of Sciences (Bulgaria)
Sara Stymne, Uppsala University (Sweden)
Stan Szpakowicz, University of Ottawa (Canada)
Beata Trawinski, Institut für Deutsche Sprache Mannheim (Germany)
Yulia Tsvetkov, Stanford University (USA)
Yuancheng Tu, Microsoft (USA)
Ruben Urizar, University of the Basque Country (Spain)
Lonneke van der Plas, University of Malta (Malta)
Gertjan van Noord, University of Groningen (The Netherlands)
Aline Villavicencio, Federal University of Rio Grande do Sul (Brazil)
Tom Wasow, Stanford University (USA)
Marion Weller-Di Marco, University of Stuttgart (Germany)
Shuly Wintner, University of Haifa (Israel)

Program Committee - Shared Task Track:

Verginica Barbu Mititelu, ICIA, Romanian Academy (Romania)
Eduard Bejček, Charles University (Czech Republic)
Marie Candito, Paris Diderot University (France)
Fabienne Cap, Uppsala University (Sweden)
Matthieu Constant, Université de Lorraine (France)
Silvio Cordeiro, Aix Marseille University (France) and Federal University of Rio Grande do Sul (Brazil)
Koenraad De Smedt, University of Bergen (Norway)
Gaël Dias, University of Caen Basse-Normandie (France)
Ismail El Maarouf, Adarga Ltd (UK)
Gülşen Eryiğit, Istanbul Technical University (Turkey)

Voula Giouli, Institute for Language and Speech Processing/RC "Athena" (Greece)
Natalia Klyueva, Charles University (Czech Republic)
Yannis Korkontzelos, Edge Hill University (UK)
Johanna Monti, "L'Orientale" University of Naples (Italy)
Luka Nerima, University of Geneva (Switzerland)
Michael Oakes, University of Wolverhampton (UK)
Carla Parra Escartín, ADAPT Centre, Dublin City University (Ireland)
Federico Sangati, Independent researcher (Italy)
Nathan Schneider, Georgetown University (USA)
Katalin Ilona Simkó, University of Szeged (Hungary)
Kiril Simov, Bulgarian Academy of Sciences (Bulgaria)
Lonneke van der Plas, University of Malta (Malta)

Invited Speaker:

Paul Cook, University of New Brunswick (Canada)

ParaDi: Dictionary of Paraphrases of Czech Complex Predicates with Light Verbs

Petra Barančíková and **Václava Kettnerová**
Institute of Formal and Applied Linguistics,
Faculty of Mathematics and Physics, Charles University,
Malostranské náměstí 25, 118 00, Praha, Czech Republic,
barancikova@ufal.mff.cuni.cz, kettnerova@ufal.mff.cuni.cz

Abstract

We present a new freely available dictionary of paraphrases of Czech complex predicates with light verbs, *ParaDi*. Candidates for single predicative paraphrases of selected complex predicates have been extracted automatically from large monolingual data using *word2vec*. They have been manually verified and further refined. We demonstrate one of many possible applications of *ParaDi* in an experiment with improving machine translation quality.

1 Introduction

Multiword expressions (MWEs) pose a serious challenge for both foreign speakers and many NLP tasks (Sag et al., 2002). From various multiword expressions, those that involve verbs are of great significance as verbs represent the syntactic center of a sentence.

In this paper, we focus on one particular type of Czech multiword expressions – on complex predicates with light verbs (CPs). CPs consist of a light verb and another predicative element – a predicative noun, an adjective, an adverb or a verb; the pairs function as single predicative units. As such, most CPs have their single predicative counterparts by which they can be paraphrased, e.g. the CPs *dát polibek* and *dát pusu* 'give a kiss' can be both paraphrased by *políbit* 'to kiss'.

In contrast to their single predicative paraphrases, CPs manifest much greater flexibility in their modification, c.f. adjectival modifiers of the CP *dát polibek* 'give a kiss' and the corresponding adverbial modifiers of its single verb paraphrase *políbit* 'to kiss' in *dát vášnivý/něžný/letmý/manželský/májový/smrtící polibek* 'give a passionate/tender/fleeting/marriage/May/fatal

kiss' vs. *vášnivě/něžně/letmo/*manželsky/*májově/*smrtelně políbit* 'kiss passionately/tenderly/fleetingly/*marriagely/*Mayly/?fatally'. Easier modification of CPs is usually considered as the main motivation for their widespread use (Brinton and Akimoto, 1999).

In this paper, we present *ParaDi*, a dictionary of single predicative verb paraphrases of Czech CPs. We restricted the dictionary only to CPs that consist of light verbs and predicative nouns, which represent the most frequent and central type of CPs in the Czech language.

ParaDi was built on a semi-automatic basis. First, candidates for single verb paraphrases of selected CPs have been automatically identified in large monolingual data using *word2vec*, a shallow neural network. The list of these candidates has been then manually checked and further refined. In many cases, if CPs are to be correctly paraphrased by the identified single predicative verbs, these verbs require certain semantic and/or syntactic modifications.

It has been widely acknowledged that many NLP applications – let us mention, e.g. information retrieval (Wallis, 1993), question answering, machine translation (Madnani and Dorr (2013); Callison-Burch et al. (2006); Marton et al. (2009)) or machine translation evaluation (Kauchak and Barzilay (2006); Zhou et al. (2006); Barančíková et al. (2014)) – can benefit from paraphrases.

Here we show how the dictionary providing high quality data can be integrated into an experiment with improving statistical machine translation quality. If translated separately, CPs often cause errors in machine translation. In our experiment, we use the dictionary to simplify Czech source sentences before translation by replacing CPs with their respective single predicative verb paraphrases. Human annotators have evaluated quality of the translated simplified sen-

1

Proceedings of the 13th Workshop on Multiword Expressions (MWE 2017), pages 1–10,
Valencia, Spain, April 4. ©2017 Association for Computational Linguistics

tences higher than of the original sentences contain CPs.

This paper is structured as follows. First, related work on CPs generally and on their paraphrases is introduced (Section 2). Second, the paraphrasing model for CPs is thoroughly described, especially the selection of CPs, an automatic extraction of candidates for their paraphrases and their manual evaluation (Section 3). Third, the resulting data and the structure of the lexical space of the dictionary are discussed (Section 4). Finally, in order to present one of many practical applications of this dictionary, a random sample of paraphrases from the *ParaDi* dictionary is used in a machine translation experiment (Section 5).

2   Related Work

A theoretical research on CPs with light verbs has a long history, which can be traced back to Jespersen (1965). An ample literature devoted to this language phenomenon so far is characterized by an enormous diversity in used terms and analyses, see esp. (Amberber et al., 2010) and (Alsina et al., 1997). Here we use the term *CP with the light verb* for a collocation within which the verb – not retaining its full semantic content – provides rather grammatical functions (incl. syntactic structure) and to which individual semantic properties are primarily contributed by the noun (Algeo, 1995).

The information on CPs is a part of several lexical resources containing manually annotated data. For instance, CPs are represented in syntactically rich annotated corpora from the family of the Prague Dependency Treebanks: the Prague Dependency Treebank 3.0 (PDT)[1] and the Prague Czech-English Dependency Treebank 2.0[2], see (Bejček et al., 2013) and (Hajič et al., 2012). Further, the PropBank[3] project has been recently enhanced with the information on CPs; the annotation scheme of CPs in PropBank is thoroughly described in (Hwang et al., 2010). Finally, the Hungarian corpus of CPs based on the data from the Szeged Treebank has been built (Vincze and Csirik, 2010).

At present, one of trending topics in NLP community is an automatic identification of CPs. In this task, various statistical measures often combined with information on syntactic and/or semantic properties of CPs are employed (e.g. Bannard (2007), Fazly et al. (2005)). The automatic detection benefits especially from parallel corpora representing valuable sources of data in which CPs can be automatically recognized via word alignment, see e.g. (Chen et al., 2015), (de Medeiros Caseli et al., 2010), (Sinha, 2009), (Zarrießand Kuhn, 2009).

Work on paraphrasing CPs is still not extensive. A paraphrasing model has been proposed within the Meaning↔Text Theory(Žolkovskij and Mel'čuk, 1965). Its representation of CPs by means of lexical functions and rules applied in the paraphrasing model are thoroughly described in (Alonso Ramos, 2007). Further, Fujita et al. (2004) present a paraphrasing model which takes advantage of semantic representation of CPs by lexical conceptual structures. Similarly as our proposed dictionary of paraphrases, this model also takes into account changes in the grammatical category of voice and changes in morphological cases of arguments, which have appeared to be highly relevant for the paraphrasing task.

3   Paraphrase Model

In this section, the process of paraphrase extraction is described in detail. First, we present the selection of CPs (Section 3.1). For their paraphrasing, we had initially intended to use some of existing sources of paraphrases, however, they turned out to be completely unsatisfactory for our task.[4]

Word2vec is a group of shallow neural networks generating representations of words in a continuous vector space depending on contexts they appear in (Mikolov et al., 2013). In line with distributional hypothesis (Harris, 1954), semantically

---

[1] http://ufal.mff.cuni.cz/pdt3.0

[2] http://ufal.mff.cuni.cz/pcedt2.0/en/index.html

[3] https://verbs.colorado.edu/~mpalmer/projects/ace.html

[4] We used the *ParaPhrase DataBase* (PPDB), (Ganitkevitch and Callison-Burch, 2014; Ganitkevitch et al., 2013) the largest paraphrase database available for the Czech language. PPDB has been created automatically from large parallel data and it comes in several sizes ranging from S to XXL. However, the bigger its size, the bigger the amount of noise. We chose the size L as a reasonable trade-off between quality and quantity. We combined the phrasal paraphrases, many-to-one and one-to-many. We lemmatized and tagged the collection of PPDB using the state-of-the-art POS tagger *Morphodita* (Straková et al., 2014). Even though this collection contains almost 400k lemmatized paraphrases in total, it contained only 54 candidates for single predicative verb paraphrases of CP. Only 2 of these 45 candidates these candidates have been detected correctly, the rest was noise in PPDB. As a result, we chose not to use parallel data in our task but we have adopted another approach applying *word2vec*, a neural network based model to large monolingual data.

similar words are mapped close to each other (measured by the cosine similarity) so we can expect CPs and their single verb paraphrases to have similar vector space distribution.

Word2vec computes vectors for single tokens. As CPs represent MWEs, their preprocessing was necessary: CPs have to be first identified and connected into a single token (Section 3.2).

Particular settings of our model for an automatic extraction of candidates for single predicative verb paraphrases are presented in Section 3.3. Finally, a manual evaluation of the extracted candidates, including their further annotation with semantic and syntactic information, is described (Section 3.4).

3.1 CPs Selection

Two different datasets of CPs, containing together 2,257 unique CPs, have been used. As both these datasets have been manually created, they allow us to achieve the desired quality of the resulting data.

The first dataset resulted from the experiment examining the native speakers' agreement on the interpretation of light verbs (Kettnerová et al., 2013). CPs in this dataset consist of collocations of light verbs and predicative nouns expressed by a prepositionless case (e.g., *položit otázku* 'put a question'), by a simple prepositional case (e.g., *dát do pořádku* 'put in order'), and by a complex prepositional group (e.g., *přejít ze smíchu do pláče* 'go from laughing to crying').

The second dataset resulted from a project aiming to enhance the high coverage valency lexicon of Czech verbs, VALLEX,[5] with the information on CPs (Kettnerová et al., 2016). In this case, only the nominal collocates expressed in the prepositionless accusative were selected as they represent the central type of Czech CPs. As the frequency and saliency have been taken as the main criteria for their selection, the resulting set represents a valuable source of CPs for Czech.

The overall number of CPs in the datasets is presented in Table 1. The union of CPs from these datasets – 2,257 CPs in total – has been used in the paraphrase candidates extraction task.

3.2 Data Preprocessing

For *word2vec* training, only monolingual data – generally easily obtainable in a large amount – is necessary. We have used large lemmatized corpora

---

[5]http://ufal.mff.cuni.cz/vallex/3.0/

	CPs	Verbs	Nouns
First dataset	726	49	612
Second dataset	1640	126	699
Union	2257	154	1061

Table 1: The number of unique CPs, light verbs and predicative nouns from two datasets. Their union has been used in the paraphrase extraction task.

Corpus	Sentences	Tokens
CNK2000	2.78	121.81
CNK2005	7.95	122.99
CNK2010	8.18	122.48
Czeng 1.0	14.83	206.05
Czech Press	258.40	4018.89
Total	292.14	4592.22

Table 2: Basic statistics of datasets (numbers in millions of units).

of Czech texts: SYN2000 (Čermák et al., 2000), SYN2005 (Čermák et al., 2005), SYN2010 (Křen et al., 2010) and CzEng 1.0 (Bojar et al., 2011). As these four large corpora with almost 600 million tokens in total have turned out to be insufficient, they have been extended with the data from the Czech Press – a large collection of contemporary news texts containing more than 4,000 million tokens. The overall statistics on all datasets is presented in Table 2.

To generate CPs paraphrases, all the selected CPs (Section 3.1) had to be automatically identified in the given corpora. For the identification of the CPs, we proceeded from light verbs. First, all verbs in the corpora were detected. From these verbs, only those verbs that represent light verbs as parts of the selected CPs were further processed.

For each identified light verb, each noun phrase in the context $\pm$ 4 words from the given light verb was extracted in case the verb and the given noun phrase can combine in some of the selected CPs.

Further, as *word2vec* generates representations of single word units, every detected noun phrase was connected with its respective light verb into a single word unit. In case that some light verb could combine with more than one noun phrase into CPs, or in case that one noun phrase could be connected with more than one light verb, we have followed the principle that every verb should be connected to at least one candidate in order to maximize a number of identified CPs.

rank	CP	frequency
1.	*mít problém* 'have a problem'	319,791
2.	*mít možnost* 'have a possibility'	300,330
3.	*mít šanci* 'have a chance'	292,340
...	...	...
998.	*vznést žalobu* 'bring charges'	535
...	...	...
1775.	*vést k sebevyvrácení* 'lead to self-refutation'	1
1776.	*dojít k flagelantství* 'flagellation takes place'	1

Table 3: The ranking of the CPs identified in the corpora, based on their frequency.

For example, if there were two light verbs v_1 and v_2 in a sentence and v_1 had a candidate c_1, while v_2 had two candidates c_1 and c_2, v_1 was connected with c_1 and v_2 with c_2. In case this principle was not sufficient, the light verb was assigned the closest noun phrase on the basis of word order.

When each noun phrase was connected maximally with one light verb and each light verb was connected maximally with one noun phrase, we have joined the noun phrases to their respective light verbs into single word units with the underscore character and erase the noun phrases from their original position in sentences.

For example, after identifying the light verb *mít* 'have' in a sentence and the prepositionless noun phrase *problém* 'problem' in its context on the above principles, the given light verb and the given noun phrase have been connected into the resulting single word unit *mít_problém*; this whole unit then replaced the verb *mít* 'have' in the sentence, while the noun phrase *problém* 'problem' was deleted from the sentence.

On this basis, almost 8.5 million instances of CPs were identified in the corpora, 99,9% of them has frequency more than 100 occurrences in the corpora. However, only 1,776 unique CPs were detected – almost 500 CPs from the selected datasets (Section 3.1) did not occur even once. The rank and frequency of selected CPs identified in the corpora is presented in Table 3.

3.3 Word2vec Model

To the resulting data, we have applied *gensim*, a freely available *word2vec* implementation (Řehůřek and Sojka, 2010). In particular, we have used a model of vector size 500 with continuous bag of word (CBOW) training algorithm and negative sampling.

As it is impossible for the model to learn anything about a rarely seen word, we have set a minimum number of word occurrences to 100 in order to limit the size of the vocabulary to reasonable words. This requirement filtered also uncommonly used CPs from the identified CPs in the corpora: from 1,776 CPs only 1,486 CPs fulfilled the given limit.

After training the model, for each of 1,486 CPs we have extracted 30 words with the most similar vectors. From these 30 words, we have selected up to ten single verbs closest to the given CP. These verbs were taken as candidates for single predicative verb paraphrases of the given CP.

As a result, 8,921 verbs in total corresponding to 3,735 unique verb lemmas have been selected as candidates for single predicative verb paraphrases of the given 1,486 CPs.

3.4 Annotation Process

In this section, the annotation process of the extracted 8,921 candidates for single predicative verb paraphrases of CPs is thoroughly described. Manual processing of the extracted single verbs allowed us to evaluate the results of the adopted method.

Let us repeat that *word2vec* generates semantically similar words depending on their contexts they appear in. However, not only words having the same meaning can have similar space representation. Words with the opposite meaning (e.g. 'finish' vs 'start'), more specific meaning ('finish' vs. 'graduate') or even different meaning can be extracted as they can appear in similar contexts as well. Manual evaluation of the extracted candidates for single verb paraphrases is thus necessary.

In the manual evaluation, two annotators have been asked to indicate for each instance of the extracted candidates for single verb paraphrases of a CP whether it represents the paraphrase of the given CP, or not. For example, the single verbs *upřednostňovat* and *preferovat* 'to prefer' are the paraphrase of the CP *dávat přednost* 'to give a preference' while the verb *srazit* 'to run down' not.

Moreover, single verbs antonymous with the respective CPs have been indicated as well as in particular context they can also function as a paraphrase. For example, depending on contexts both extracted single verbs *stoupnout* 'to rise' and *poklesnout* 'to drop' can function as paraphrases of the CP *zaznamenat propad* 'to experience a drop', while the first one has the meaning synonymous with the given CP, the meaning of the latter is antonymous.

Further, when the annotators have determined a certain candidate as the single verb paraphrase of a CP, they have taken the following three morphological, syntactic and semantic aspects into account.

First, they had to pay special attention to the morphological expression of arguments. Changes in their morphological expression reflect different syntactic perspectives from which the action denoted by the given CP and its single verb paraphrase is viewed. For example, the single verb *potrestat* 'to punish' can serve as the paraphrase of the CP *dostat trest* 'to get a punishment' in a sentence, however, the semantic roles of the subject and the object are switched.

Second, in some cases the reflexive morpheme *se/si*, reflecting the inchoative meaning, had to be added to single predicative verb paraphrases so that their meaning corresponds to the meaning of their respective CPs. For example, the CP *mít problém* 'have a problem' can be paraphrased by the verb *trápit* only on the condition that the reflexive morpheme is attached to the verb lemma *trápit se* 'to worry'.

Third, some single predicative verbs function as paraphrases of particular CPs only if nouns in these CPs have certain adjectival modifications. These paraphrases have been assigned the given adjectives during the annotation.

As the above given three features are not mutually exclusive, they can combine. For example, the verb *zaměstnat* 'to hire' is a paraphrase of the CP *nalézt uplatnění* 'to find an use' but both the reflexive morpheme *se* and a modification by the adverb *pracovní* 'working' is required.

To summarize, for each identified single predicative verb paraphrase v of a CP l, the annotators have chosen from the following options:

- v is a synonymous paraphrase of l (without any modification of the context)

	synonyms	antonyms
no constrains	1607	51
+ reflexive morpheme	353	2
+ voice change	173	5
+ an adjective	53	–
total	2177	58

Table 4: The basic statistics on the annotation. The *synonyms* column does not add up as the conditions are not mutually exclusive as mentioned earlier.

  e.g., *mít zájem* 'to be interested' and *chtít* 'to want'

- v is an antonym of l (the modification of the context is necessary)
  e.g., *zaznamenat propad* 'to experience a drop' and *stoupnout* 'to rise'

- v is a paraphrase of l but changes in the morphological expression of arguments are necessary
  e.g., *dostat nabídku* 'to get an offer' and *nabídnout* 'to offer'

- v is a paraphrase of l but the reflexive morpheme *se/si* has to be added (the modification of verb lemma is necessary)
  e.g., *nést název* 'to be called' and *nazývat se* 'to be called'

- v is a paraphrase of l with a particular adjectival modification (the adjective modifier of the noun should be present)
  e.g., *podat oznámení* 'to make an announcement' can be paraphrased as *žalovat* 'to sue' only if the noun *oznámení* is modified with the adjective *trestní* 'criminal'

- v is a not a paraphrase of l

As a result of the annotation process, the total number of the indicated single verb paraphrases of CPs was 2,177. For 999 CPs at least one single verb paraphrase has been found. The highest number of single verb paraphrases indicated for one CP has been eight; it has been the CP *vznést dotaz* 'to ask a question'. Figure 1 shows the number of paraphrases per CPs.

Table 4 presents more detailed results of the annotation. It shows frequency of additional morphological, syntactic and semantic features.

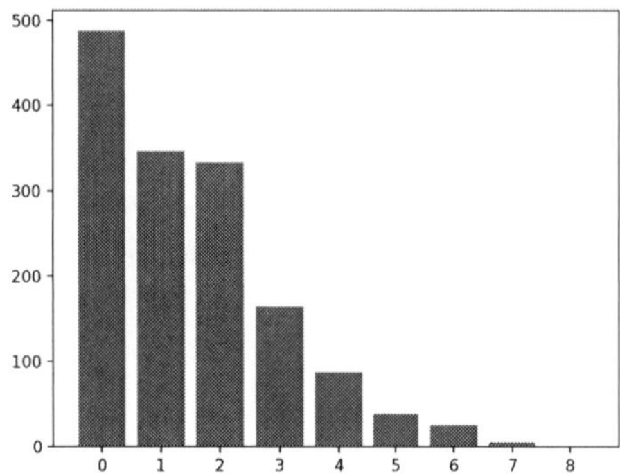

Figure 1: The number of single predicative verb paraphrases and antonymous verbs per CPs in the *ParaDi* dictionary.

4 Dictionary of Paraphrases

2,235 single predicative verbs indicated by the annotators as synonymous or antonymous verbs of 999 CPs (Section 3.4) form the lexical stock of *ParaDi*, a dictionary of single verb paraphrases of Czech CPs. The format of the *ParaDi* dictionary has been designed with respect to both human and machine readability. The dictionary is represented in JSON, as it is flexible and language-independent data format.

The lexical entries in the dictionary describe individual light verbs. Under light verb keys, all predicative nouns constituting CPs with the given light verb are listed. The predicative nouns are lemmatized; the information on their morphology is included under their *morph* keys the value of which are prepositionless and prepositional cases.

Each CP in the lexical entry might be assigned one or two lists of single predicative verbs: one for synonymous paraphrases and the other for antonymous verbs. Paraphrases in the lists are sorted based on the distance from their respective LVC in the vector space. Moreover, each verb may be assigned one or more following features:

- *voice_change* – indicating changes in the morphosyntactic expression of arguments,

- *adjective* – indicating necessary adjectival modification,

- *reflexive* – indicating that reflexive morpheme is necessary,

```
'lverb': 'zaznamenat',
[{'noun': 'propad',
'morph': '4',
'synonyms': [
{'lemma': 'poklesnout'},
{'lemma': 'klesnout'},
{'lemma': 'propadnout',
 'reflexive': 'se'}
],
'antonyms': [
{'lemma': 'stoupnout'}
],
...
]
}
```

Figure 2: The lexical representation of the CP *zaznamenat propad* 'to record a slump'.

An illustrative example of the lexical representation of paraphrases in *ParaDi* is presented in Figure 2. It displays the lexical entry of the CP *zaznamenat propad* 'to record a slump'. Under the light verb *zaznamenat* 'to record', there is a list of nouns that combine with this light verb into CPs. In case of the noun *propad* 'slump', the noun is expressed by the prepositionless accusative. This CP has three single verb paraphrases (*poklesnout* 'to decrease', *klesnout* 'to drop', *propadnout se* 'to slump') and one antonymous verb (*stoupnout* 'to increase'). The paraphrase *propadnout* 'to slump' needs to have the reflexive morpheme *se*.

ParaDi is freely available at the following URL: `http://hdl.handle.net/11234/1-1969`

5 Machine Translation Experiment

We have taken advantage of the *ParaDi* dictionary in a machine translation experiment in order to verify its benefit for one of key NLP tasks. We have selected 50 random CPs from the dictionary. For each of them, we have randomly extracted one sentence from our data containing the given CP. This set of sentences is referred to as BEFORE. By substituting a CP for its first (i.e. closest in the vector space) paraphrase on the basis of the dictionary, we have created a new dataset AFTER.

We have translated both these datasets – BEFORE and AFTER – using two freely avail-

Source	Moses	GT
BEFORE	30%	33%
AFTER	45%	44%
TIE	25%	23%

Table 5: Results of the experiment. First column shows a source of better ranked sentence from the pairwise comparison or whether they tied.

able MT systems – *Google Translate*[6] (GT) and *Moses*[7] in the Czech to English setting.

We have used crowdsourcing for evaluation of the resulting translations. Both options were presented in a randomized order and the annotators were instructed to choose whether one translation is better or they have the same quality.

We have collected almost 300 comparisons. We measured inter-annotator agreement using Krippendorff's alpha (Krippendorff, 2007), a reliability coefficient developed to measure the agreement between judges. The inter-annotator agreement has achieved 0.58, i.e. moderate agreement.

The results (see Table 5) are very promising: in most cases the annotators clearly preferred translations of AFTER (i.e. with single predicative verbs) to BEFORE (i.e. with CPs). The results are consistent for both translation systems.

However, it is clear from the example in Table 6 that even though the change in the source sentence was minimal, the translations changed substantially as both the translation models are phrase-based. Based on this fact, we can expect that not only difference in quality between translations of CPs and their respective synonymous verbs was evaluated. This low quality translation inevitably reflected in lower inter-annotator agreement, typical for machine translation evaluation (Bojar et al., 2013).

6 Conclusion

We have presented *ParaDi*, a semiautomatically created dictionary of single verb paraphrases of Czech complex predicates with light verbs. We have shown that such paraphrases are automatically obtainable from large monolingual data with a manual verification. *ParaDi* represents a core of such dictionary, which can be further enriched. We have demonstrated one of its possible applica-

---

tions, namely an experiment with improving machine translation quality. However, the dictionary can be used in many other NLP tasks (text simplification, information retrieval, etc.) and can be similarly created for other languages.

Acknowledgments

The research reported in this paper has been supported by the Czech Science Foundation GA ČR, grant No. GA15-09979S. This work has been using language resources developed and/or stored and/or distributed by the LINDAT-Clarin project of the Ministry of Education, Youth and Sports of the Czech Republic, project No. LM2015071.

References

John Algeo. 1995. Having a look at the expanded predicate. In B. Aarts and Ch. F. Meyer, editors, *The Verb in Contemporary English: Theory and Description*, pages 203–217. Cambridge University Press, Cambridge.

Margarita Alonso Ramos. 2007. Towards the synthesis of support verb constructions: Distribution of syntactic actants between the verb and the noun. In L. Wanner and I. A. Mel'čuk, editors, *Selected Lexical and Grammatical Issues in the Meaning-Text Theory*, pages 97–137. John Benjamins Publishing Company, Amsterdam, Philadelphia.

Alex Alsina, Joan Bresnan, and Peter Sells, editors. 1997. *Complex Predicates*. CSLI Publications, Stanford.

Mengistu Amberber, Brett Baker, and Mark Harvey, editors. 2010. *Complex Predicates in Cross-Linguistic Perspective*. Cambridge University Press, Cambridge.

Colin Bannard. 2007. A measure of syntactic flexibility for automatically identifying multiword expressions in corpora. In *Proceedings of the Workshop on a Broader Perspective on Multiword Expressions*, MWE '07, pages 1–8, Stroudsburg, PA, USA. Association for Computational Linguistics.

Petra Barančíková, Rudolf Rosa, and Aleš Tamchyna. 2014. Improving Evaluation of English-Czech MT through Paraphrasing. In Nicoletta Calzolari, Khalid Choukri, Thierry Declerck, Hrafn Loftsson, Bente Maegaard, and Joseph Mariani, editors, *Proceedings of the 9th International Conference on Language Resources and Evaluation (LREC 2014)*, pages 596–601, Reykjavík, Iceland. European Language Resources Association.

Eduard Bejček, Eva Hajičová, Jan Hajič, Pavlína Jínová, Václava Kettnerová, Veronika Kolářová, Marie Mikulová, Jiří Mírovský, Anna Nedoluzhko,

---

Source	BEFORE	Fotbalisté	Budějovic	opět	**nedali**	**branku**
		Football players	Budějovice	again	did not give	gate
		Football players of Budějovice didn't make a goal again				
	AFTER	Fotbalisté	Budějovic	opět	**neskórovali**	
		Football players	Budějovice	again	did not score	
		Football players of Budějovice didn't score again				
GT	BEFORE	Footballers Budejovice again not given goal				
	AFTER	Footballers did not score again Budejovice				
Moses	BEFORE	Footballers Budějovice again gave the gate				
	AFTER	Footballers Budějovice score again				

Table 6: An example of the translated sentences. The judges unanimously agreed that AFTER translations are better than BEFORE. Moses translated the CP *dát branku* literally word by word and the meaning of this translation is far from the meaning of the source sentence.

Jarmila Panevová, Lucie Poláková, Magda Ševčíková, Jan Štěpánek, and Šárka Zikánová. 2013. Prague dependency treebank 3.0.

Ondřej Bojar, Zdeněk Žabokrtský, Ondřej Dušek, Petra Galuščáková, Martin Majliš, David Mareček, Jiří Maršík, Michal Novák, Martin Popel, and Aleš Tamchyna. 2011. Czech-english parallel corpus 1.0 (CzEng 1.0). LINDAT/CLARIN digital library at Institute of Formal and Applied Linguistics, Charles University in Prague.

Ondřej Bojar, Christian Buck, Chris Callison-Burch, Christian Federmann, Barry Haddow, Philipp Koehn, Christof Monz, Matt Post, Radu Soricut, and Lucia Specia. 2013. Findings of the 2013 Workshop on Statistical Machine Translation. In *Proceedings of the Eighth Workshop on Statistical Machine Translation*, pages 1–44, Sofia, Bulgaria, August. Association for Computational Linguistics.

Laurel Brinton and Minoji Akimoto, editors. 1999. *Collocational and Idiomatic Aspects of Composite Predicates in the History of English*. John Benjamins Publishing Company, Amsterdam, Philadelphia.

Chris Callison-Burch, Philipp Koehn, and Miles Osborne. 2006. Improved Statistical Machine Translation Using Paraphrases. In *Proceedings of the Main Conference on Human Language Technology Conference of the North American Chapter of the Association of Computational Linguistics*, HLT-NAACL '06, pages 17–24, Stroudsburg, PA, USA. Association for Computational Linguistics.

František Čermák, Renata Blatná, Jaroslava Hlaváčová, Jan Kocek, Marie Kopřivová, Michal Křen, Vladimír Petkevič, and Michal Schmiedtová, Věra Šulc. 2000. SYN2000: balanced corpus of written Czech. LINDAT/CLARIN digital library at Institute of Formal and Applied Linguistics, Charles University in Prague.

František Čermák, Jaroslava Hlaváčová, Milena Hnátková, Tomáš Jelínek, Jan Kocek, Marie Kopřivová, Michal Křen, Renata Novotná, Vladimír Petkevič, Věra Schmiedtová, Hana Skoumalová, Johanka Spoustová, Michal Šulc, and Zdeněk Velíšek. 2005. SYN2005: balanced corpus of written Czech. LINDAT/CLARIN digital library at Institute of Formal and Applied Linguistics, Charles University in Prague.

Wei-Te Chen, Claire Bonial, and Martha Palmer. 2015. English light verb construction identification using lexical knowledge. In *Proceedings of the Twenty-Ninth AAAI Conference on Artificial Intelligence*, AAAI'15, pages 2375–2381. AAAI Press.

Helena de Medeiros Caseli, Carlos Ramisch, Maria das Graças Volpe Nunes, and Aline Villavicencio. 2010. Alignment-based extraction of multiword expressions. *Language Resources and Evaluation*, 44(1-2):59–77.

Afsaneh Fazly, Ryan North, and Suzanne Stevenson. 2005. Automatically distinguishing literal and figurative usages of highly polysemous verbs. In *Proceedings of the ACL-SIGLEX Workshop on Deep Lexical Acquisition*, DeepLA '05, pages 38–47, Stroudsburg, PA, USA. Association for Computational Linguistics.

Atsushi Fujita, Kentaro Furihata, Kentaro Inui, Yuji Matsumoto, and Koichi Takeuchi. 2004. Paraphrasing of japanese light-verb constructions based on lexical conceptual structure. In *Proceedings of the Workshop on Multiword Expressions: Integrating Processing*, MWE '04, pages 9–16, Stroudsburg, PA, USA. Association for Computational Linguistics.

Juri Ganitkevitch and Chris Callison-Burch. 2014. The Multilingual Paraphrase Database. In *The 9th edition of the Language Resources and Evaluation Conference*, Reykjavik, Iceland, May. European Language Resources Association.

Juri Ganitkevitch, Benjamin Van Durme, and Chris Callison-Burch. 2013. PPDB: The Paraphrase Database. In *Proceedings of the 2013 Conference of* the *North American Chapter of the Association for Computational Linguistics: Human Language Technologies*, pages 758–764, Atlanta, Georgia, June. Association for Computational Linguistics.

Jan Hajič, Eva Hajičová, Jarmila Panevová, Petr Sgall, Ondřej Bojar, Silvie Cinková, Eva Fučíková, Marie Mikulová, Petr Pajas, Jan Popelka, Jiří Semecký, Jana Šindlerová, Jan Štěpánek, Josef Toman, Zdeňka Urešová, and Zdeněk Žabokrtský. 2012. Announcing prague czech-english dependency treebank 2.0. In *Proceedings of the 8th International Conference on Language Resources and Evaluation (LREC 2012)*, pages 3153–3160, İstanbul, Turkey. ELRA, European Language Resources Association.

Zellig Harris. 1954. Distributional structure. *Word*, 10(23):146–162.

Jena D. Hwang, Archna Bhatia, Claire Bonial, Aous Mansouri, Ashwini Vaidya, Nianwen Xue, and Martha Palmer. 2010. PropBank Annotation of Multilingual Light Verb Constructions. In *Proceedings of the Fourth Linguistic Annotation Workshop*, pages 82–90, Uppsala, Sweden, July. Association for Computational Linguistics.

Otto Jespersen. 1965. *A Modern English Grammar on Historical Principles VI., Morphology*. A Modern English Grammar on Historical Principles. George Allen & Unwin Ltd., London.

David Kauchak and Regina Barzilay. 2006. Paraphrasing for Automatic Evaluation. In *Proceedings of the Main Conference on Human Language Technology Conference of the North American Chapter of the Association of Computational Linguistics*, HLT-NAACL '06, pages 455–462, Stroudsburg, PA, USA. Association for Computational Linguistics.

Václava Kettnerová, Markéta Lopatková, Eduard Bejček, Anna Vernerová, and Marie Podobová. 2013. Corpus Based Identification of Czech Light Verbs. In Katarína Gajdošová and Adriána Žáková, editors, *Proceedings of the Seventh International Conference Slovko 2013; Natural Language Processing, Corpus Linguistics, E-learning*, pages 118–128, Lüdenscheid, Germany. Slovak National Corpus, Ľ. Štúr Institute of Linguistics, Slovak Academy of Sciences, RAM-Verlag.

Václava Kettnerová, Petra Barančíková, and Markéta Lopatková. 2016. Lexicographic Description of Czech Complex Predicates: Between Lexicon and Grammar. In *Proceedings of the XVII EURALEX International Congress*.

Michal Křen, Tomáš Bartoň, Václav Cvrček, Milena Hnátková, Tomáš Jelínek, Jan Kocek, Renata Novotná, Vladimír Petkevič, Pavel Procházka, Věra Schmiedtová, and Hana Skoumalová. 2010. SYN2010: balanced corpus of written Czech. LINDAT/CLARIN digital library at Institute of Formal and Applied Linguistics, Charles University in Prague.

Klaus Krippendorff. 2007. Computing Krippendorff's Alpha Reliability. Technical report, University of Pennsylvania, Annenberg School for Communication.

Nitin Madnani and Bonnie J. Dorr. 2013. Generating Targeted Paraphrases for Improved Translation. *ACM Trans. Intell. Syst. Technol.*, 4(3):40:1–40:25, July.

Yuval Marton, Chris Callison-Burch, and Philip Resnik. 2009. Improved Statistical Machine Translation Using Monolingually-derived Paraphrases. In *Proceedings of the 2009 Conference on Empirical Methods in Natural Language Processing: Volume 1 - Volume 1*, EMNLP '09, pages 381–390, Stroudsburg, PA, USA. Association for Computational Linguistics.

Tomas Mikolov, Kai Chen, Greg Corrado, and Jeffrey Dean. 2013. Efficient estimation of word representations in vector space. *CoRR*, abs/1301.3781.

Radim Řehůřek and Petr Sojka. 2010. Software Framework for Topic Modelling with Large Corpora. In *Proceedings of the LREC 2010 Workshop on New Challenges for NLP Frameworks*, pages 45–50, Valletta, Malta, May. ELRA.

Ivan A. Sag, Timothy Baldwin, Francis Bond, Ann Copestake, and Dan Flickinger. 2002. Multiword Expressions: A Pain in the Neck for NLP. In *In Proc. of the 3rd International Conference on Intelligent Text Processing and Computational Linguistics (CICLing-2002*, pages 1–15.

R. Mahesh K. Sinha. 2009. Mining Complex Predicates in Hindi Using a Parallel Hindi-English Corpus. In *Proceedings of the Workshop on Multiword Expressions: Identification, Interpretation, Disambiguation and Applications*, MWE '09, pages 40–46, Stroudsburg, PA, USA. Association for Computational Linguistics.

Jana Straková, Milan Straka, and Jan Hajič. 2014. Open-Source Tools for Morphology, Lemmatization, POS Tagging and Named Entity Recognition. In *Proceedings of 52nd Annual Meeting of the Association for Computational Linguistics: System Demonstrations*, pages 13–18, Baltimore, Maryland, June. Association for Computational Linguistics.

Veronika Vincze and János Csirik. 2010. Hungarian Corpus of Light Verb Constructions. In *Proceedings of the 23rd International Conference on Computational Linguistics*, COLING '10, pages 1110–1118, Stroudsburg, PA, USA. Association for Computational Linguistics.

Alexander K. Žolkovskij and Igor A. Mel'čuk. 1965. O vozmožnom metode i instrumentax semantičeskogo sinteza. *Naučno-texničeskaja informacija*, (6).

Peter Wallis. 1993. Information Retrieval based on Paraphrase.

Sina Zarrießand Jonas Kuhn. 2009. Exploiting Translational Correspondences for Pattern-independent MWE Identification. In *Proceedings of the Workshop on Multiword Expressions: Identification, Interpretation, Disambiguation and Applications*, MWE '09, pages 23–30, Stroudsburg, PA, USA. Association for Computational Linguistics.

Liang Zhou, Chin-Yew Lin, and Eduard Hovy. 2006. Re-evaluating Machine Translation Results with Paraphrase Support. In *Proceedings of the 2006 Conference on Empirical Methods in Natural Language Processing*, EMNLP '06, pages 77–84, Stroudsburg, PA, USA. Association for Computational Linguistics.

Multi-word Entity Classification in a Highly Multilingual Environment

Sophie Chesney[*,†], Guillaume Jacquet[†], Ralf Steinberger[†] and
Jakub Piskorski[†]

[†]Text and Data Mining Unit, Joint Research Centre, European Commission, Ispra, Italy
[*]Cognitive Science Research Group, School of Electronic Engineering and Computer Science,
Queen Mary University of London, UK
`s.chesney@qmul.ac.uk`
`{firstname.lastname}@jrc.ec.europa.eu`

Abstract

This paper describes an approach for the classification of millions of existing multi-word entities (MWEntities), such as organisation or event names, into thirteen category types, based only on the tokens they contain. In order to classify our very large in-house collection of multilingual MWEntities into an application-oriented set of entity categories, we trained and tested distantly-supervised classifiers in 43 languages based on MWEntities extracted from BabelNet. The best-performing classifier was the multi-class SVM using a TF.IDF-weighted data representation. Interestingly, one unique classifier trained on a mix of all languages consistently performed better than classifiers trained for individual languages, reaching an averaged F1-value of 88.8%. In this paper, we present the training and test data, including a human evaluation of its accuracy, describe the methods used to train the classifiers, and discuss the results.

1 Introduction

Named Entities (NEs) such as persons, organisations, locations or events are crucial bearers of information as they are often the answers to major text understanding questions. Software to carry out Named Entity Recognition (NER) in free text needs to recognise the relevant strings in text and disambiguate the broad entity types (e.g. *Paris Hilton* is a person rather than a location), justifying the term Named Entity Recognition and Classification (NERC). In this paper we focus on MWEntity classification, thereby placing NERC in the context of the study of MWExpressions.

Our work is carried out in a highly multilingual environment, and as a result, suitable training corpora are difficult to source. Motivated by this, in addition to a method of MWEntity classification, we also present a technique for automatically generating a silver-standard annotated resource of 3.8 million entities for use as training data. This resource incorporates data from 43 different languages, covering multiple language families. MWEntities are often not translated, so it is rather common to find names from one language in amongst entities from another (e.g. French MWEntity 'institut polytechnique des sciences avancées' found in the Arabic dataset).

It is important to specify that our classification work is exclusively based on internal features of the names; that is, the tokens contained within each MWEntity. No additional external features were extracted. This is due in part to the fact that the contexts of our historically accumulated MWEntities are no longer known. We therefore aim at developing a system that can be widely applied to data sets that do not include, or give access to, such contextual information.

The paper begins with a section on related work (2) and is followed by a section describing the starting point and the objective of our work: the target entity hierarchy (3.1); the set of entities extracted from the BabelNet resource (Navigli and Ponzetto, 2012) and the method used for the extraction (3.2); and an evaluation of this BabelNet silver-standard including inter-annotator agreement data (3.3). In Section 4, we present the classification methods we tested, i.e. a baseline approach and two variants of Support Vector Machines. Experiments and results achieved are presented in Section 5, together with a discussion of the results. We conclude with a short summary and a pointer to future work.

Proceedings of the 13th Workshop on Multiword Expressions (MWE 2017), pages 11–20,
Valencia, Spain, April 4. ©2017 Association for Computational Linguistics

2   Related Work

In this task, we work exclusively on the classification of MWEntities, which are subject to their own idiosyncrasies and difficulties. Though many of the papers discussed below do not necessarily exclude multi-word units in their NERC systems, none of them explicitly focus on MWEntities. Furthermore, although a large body of work exists on the study of multi-word expressions more generally, including idioms (Villada Moirón and Tiedemann, 2006; Gharbieh et al., 2016), fixed expressions such as 'in short' and compound nominals such as 'car park', work focusing exclusively on multi-word named entities is less prominent in the literature. Here, we are interested in this subset of MWExpressions in the task of Named Entity Classification (NEC), particularly as they tend to be richer in word-internal features, upon which our systems are based.

Early NERC systems began emerging during the 1990s, favouring handcrafted rule-based approaches. Due to the fact that these systems offer control over results and straight-forward fine-tuning, many industrial NERC systems continue to be rule-based, at least to some extent (Steinberger, 2012). In an academic context, however, machine learning approaches to automatically detecting such rules have become more popular in recent work. The majority of recent NERC systems use supervised learning, relying on large, often manually annotated corpora from which to extract and learn positive and negative features for a particular class of entity. Since such corpora are costly, attention has also turned to distant-supervision, which utilises existing structured resources (e.g. WordNet (Fellbaum, 1998), DBPedia (Auer et al., 2007), Freebase (Bollacker et al., 2008), BabelNet (Navigli and Ponzetto, 2012), among others) to automatically generate 'silver-standard' annotated corpora, without incurring the cost associated with gaining access to manually annotated corpora (e.g. Fleischman and Hovy (2002), Ling and Weld (2012), Nothman et al. (2013)). We follow this general approach with the production of a large-scale automatically-created MWEntity resource extracted from BabelNet, used to distantly supervise our classifiers. Similarly, weakly-supervised systems use a bootstrapping technique to approach the same issue, starting with a few annotated examples and automatically expanding the corpus based on these 'seed' terms (e.g. Pasca et

al. (2006), Ratinov and Roth (2009)).

In this work, we are interested in drawing a distinction between the recognition of named entities and, most relevant to us, their classification. The task of entity classification has been approached largely through machine learning techniques, utilising both word-internal features (Durrett and Klein, 2014) and additional contextual information, such as dictionary definitions (Gangemi et al., 2012) and 'lexical expansions' (e.g. synonyms and derivationally related forms) extracted from WordNet, as well as co-occurrence statistics from external corpora (Del Corro et al., 2015).

Very recent work has also moved towards multi-source learning, automatically retrieving additional semi-structured contextual information, such as webpage titles and URLs, through Web search (Vexler and Minkov, 2016).

Much of the early work in the area of NERC was monolingual, often working on English data. As approaches have advanced, multilingual named entities have received more attention, though the reliance on large corpora often limits the possible coverage. In an attempt to overcome this bottleneck, Nothman et al. (2013) automatically classify Wikipedia articles into named entity types, exploiting the links between in-text entities and their corresponding Wikipedia pages. The authors therefore engineer a silver-standard annotated corpus of named entities in nine languages (English, German, French, Polish, Italian, Spanish, Dutch, Portuguese and Russian), for use as training data for NERC systems. In this work, we approach large-scale multi-word entity classification in 43 languages, developing a highly multilingual NE classification system tailored specifically for MWEntities, using distant-supervision.

3   Extraction of a Multi-Word Entity Silver-Standard Resource from BabelNet

When addressing the MWEntity recognition task, some approaches are based on methods that make the classification of recognised MWEntities difficult. This is the case for approaches using co-occurrences of MWEntities and their acronyms (Jacquet et al., 2016), or those derived from n-gram methods (Ekbal and Saha, 2013). In both cases, the method is able to extract MWEntities from text and consider them as one expression, but cannot provide an entity type for these expressions. Also, although many publicly available entity resources exist, they often are difficult to use in a specific application for a variety of reasons. For example, the provided entity types may not correspond to what is required for the specific application, may be too specific or too coarse-grained, or not provided at all. In these cases, there is a strong need to (re-)annotate an existing resource of MWEntities. To address this goal, we propose a method of creating a silver-standard data set from BabelNet. We defined the required annotation types for our specific application and extracted the entities and their variants which have the hypernyms corresponding to these annotation types from BabelNet. We conducted a partial manual evaluation of the obtained resource, discussed in Section 3.3.

3.1 Named Entity Type Hierarchy

Related to Sekine's (2002) Extended Named Entity (ENE) Hierarchy[1], our own in-house entity hierarchy contains nine major classes (person, organisation, location, event, product, identifier, time, number and Other) with altogether almost fifty sub-classes.

In our existing text processing system, many of these NE categories are already recognised and classified (e.g. persons, cities, email addresses, date expressions), so these are not considered here. In this paper, we focus on classifying MWEntities according to a subset of thirteen categories shown in Table 1, corresponding to the types requiring more fine-grained annotation in our system.

3.2 Automatically-Created Annotated Resource from BabelNet

For the sake of creating resources for each of the named-entity types listed in Table 1, we have exploited BabelNet (Navigli and Ponzetto, 2012), a large multilingual encyclopaedic dictionary and semantic network, created by merging various publicly available linguistic resources, e.g. WordNet and Wikipedia. BabelNet contains circa 7.7 million NE-related synsets. In order to extract sought-after entities, we used the BabelNet API[2]. Since the NE-related BabelNet synsets are not tagged with a specific NE tag, the NE type was inferred by using the hypernym information provided in BabelNet (i.e. using WordNet hypernyms

[1]http://nlp.cs.nyu.edu/ene/version7_1_0Beng.html

[2]http://babelnet.org/guide

ORGANISATION		
Subtype	**Example**	**Encoding**
POLITICAL-PUBLIC	Democratic Party	ORG-PP
COMMERCIAL	Microsoft Inc.	ORG-CO
SPORT	FC Barcelona	ORG-SP
EDUC-RESEARCH	University of Lugano	ORG-ER
LOCATION		
Subtype	**Example**	**Encoding**
FACILITY	Schiphol Airport	LOC-FA
OTHER	Mount Everest	LOC-OT
PRODUCT		
Subtype	**Example**	**Encoding**
ELECTRONICS	Commodore 64	PRO-EL
WEAPON	AGM-1 Carbine	PRO-WE
VEHICLE	Mitsubishi Pajero	PRO-VE
ART	Star Wars	PRO-AR
EVENT		
Subtype	**Example**	**Encoding**
INCIDENT	Chernobyl Disaster	EVT-IN
NATURAL	Hurricane Katrina	EVT-NA
OCCASION	Nobel Prize Awards	EVT-OC

Table 1: Types used for NE-classification task.

and Wikipedia categories). To be more precise, based on hypernym frequency information for the entire set of named entities contained in BabelNet, for each NE type a list of *positive* and *negative* hypernyms was manually created. These lists were subsequently used to extract entities of each particular type. A given NE-related synset was extracted if: (a) there was at least one hypernym for the main sense of the synset in the list of positive hypernyms, and (b) no hypernym for the main sense of the synset was on the list of negative hypernyms. For instance, the full list of positive and negative hypernyms for extracting commercial organisation names (ORG-CO) is given in Table 2.

positive hypernyms	negative hypernyms
company, periodical, magazine, record_company, publisher, airline, enterprise, corporation, bank, brewery, automobile_manufacturer, film_production_company, limited_company, joint-stock_company, holding_company telephone_company, drug_company, investment_company, shipping_company, oil_company, electric_company, train_operating_company, telecommunication_company, bank_holding_company, consulting_company, moving_company, transport_company, consultancy, factory, private_bank	city, City, settlement, town, metropolis, municipality, village, commune, park, capital, earthquake, tsunami, fire, avalanche, hurricane, flood, port, mountain, person

Table 2: The list of positive and negative hypernyms for the extraction of commercial organisation names (ORG-CO).

The main drive behind the usage of a negative hypernym list was to filter out potentially ambiguous named entity candidates, e.g. the same name might refer to a person, organisation and a location. The list of positive/negative hypernyms for each of the 13 categories varied. However, no list contained more than 100 items.

In total, we obtained circa 3.8 million named entities from BabelNet after expanding each extracted NE-related synset. The left-hand columns in Table 3 provide a breakdown of the number of extracted entities per type.

Entity Type	#Extracted Entities	#Filtered Entities
ORG-PP	214 056	100 373
ORG-CO	440 522	158 502
ORG-SP	285 312	139 578
ORG-ER	271 486	144 137
LOC-FA	1 182 857	469 633
LOC-OT	782 578	207 053
PRO-EL	33 053	8 817
PRO-WE	29 044	10 238
PRO-VE	55 494	17 617
PRO-AR	363 356	141 541
EVT-IN	68 647	38 139
EVT-NA	14 292	7 920
EVT-OC	94 908	54 256
TOTAL	3 835 605	1 497 804

Table 3: Number of entities extracted from Babel-Net before and after filtering (see Section 5.2).

3.3 Manual Evaluation of the Automatically-Created Resource from BabelNet

A crucial element of our work consisted of evaluating the quality of the automatically generated annotated resource from BabelNet. To justify its use as a gold (or 'silver') standard resource for this supervised classification task, we conducted a small manual evaluation, shown in Table 5, with native speakers of five different languages (German, French, Polish, English and Swedish), evaluating both the quality of the automatic annotations as well as inter-annotator agreement for English across four annotators (one of whom is a native English speaker).

Each annotator was trained on a trial set of 100 randomly extracted English MWEntities, then tested on a further 200 randomly extracted multiword entities for their own native language, and an additional 200 for English. The annotators were asked to provide two separate sets of annotations: first, the annotators provided 'offline' annotations for each of the entities, selecting from a set of 13 possible entity types (corresponding to the types described in Table 1). The no-guess tag ('NG')

MWEntity	Ref annot.	Manual annot.
Examples of full agreement (167 MWEntities over 200)		
lisnagarvey high school	ORG-ER	ORG-ER
teeside mohawks	ORG-SP	ORG-SP
grand château dansembourg	LOC-FA	LOC-FA
a writers nightmare	PRO-AR	PRO-AR
maritsa hotel	LOC-FA	LOC-FA
slaughter grüning and company	ORG-CO	ORG-CO
At least 3 different annotations from 4 annotators (8 MWEntities over 200)		
vic urban	ORG-CO	...
st marys badley	LOC-FA	...
go gaia	ORG-CO	...
tarnobrzeg voivodship	ORG-PP	...
rez quad	ORG-ER	...
janet jeffrey carlile harris carillon	LOC-FA	...
lindley court	ORG-ER	...
the church on brady	LOC-FA	...
All annotators agreed, but disagreed with ref. (6 MWEntities over 200)		
colt revolver	ORG-CO	PRO-WE
rip mountain	LOC-FA	LOC-OT
accademia florence	ORG-ER	LOC-FA
childrens champion awards	ORG-CO	EVT-OC
1999 nato bombing of valjevo	ORG-CO	EVT-IN
buffalo rochester and pittsburgh railroad	ORG-CO	LOC-FA

Table 4: Some example of MWEntities to be annotated.

was used when an annotation decision could not be made with certainty, or when an entity appeared to belong in a category not included in the possible list of tags. Secondly, the annotators were permitted to research their secondary guess 'online'. For consistency, the BabelNet labels were hidden throughout.

Table 5 shows that the 'offline' annotation results are quite heterogeneous among annotators, with a precision between 81.6% and 92.4%, and a recall between 66.5% and 81.0%. On the other hand, the 'online' annotation results are much more homogeneous, for the same language between different annotators, and also across languages: precision varied between 87.6% and 92.5%, and recall between 85.0% and 90.5%. The averaged kappa across the 4 English annotators is 0.848, and among the 200 annotated MWEntities, 159 were annotated with full inter-annotator agreement, including only 6 which differed from the automatically-generated BabelNet annotation (listed in Table 4). 10 were annotated with the same type by 3 of 4 annotators. The remaining 31 MWEntities, where only two annotators agreed,

Languages	'offline' annotation			'online' annotation			SVM_tfidf (lang. indep.)		
	P	R	F1	P	R	F1	P	R	F1
ENGLISH									
a1 (Nat.)	83.9%	75.5%	79.5%	92.5%	86.5%	89.4%	87.5%	87.5%	87.5%
a2	92.4%	66.5%	77.3%	91.3%	89.0%	90.1%			
a3	86.7%	72.0%	78.7%	88.7%	86.5%	87.6%			
a4	82.5%	80.0%	81.2%	91.1%	87.5%	89.3%			
FRENCH	89.9%	80.5%	85.0%	91.9%	90.5%	91.2%	91.5%	91.5%	91.5%
POLISH	81.6%	75.5%	78.4%	90.7%	87.5%	89.1%	85.5%	85.5%	85.5%
GERMAN	83.2%	77.0%	80.0%	87.6%	85.0%	86.3%	84.0%	84.0%	84.0%
SWEDISH	86.6%	81.0%	83.7%	90.7%	87.5%	89.1%	77.0%	77.0%	77.0%

Table 5: Manual annotations on 200 MWEntities randomly extracted for 5 languages from the created resource, compared with the best-performing system (right-most column).

highlight the difficulty of the task: some MWEntities are ambiguous, and could easily be annotated with different types. For example, *'buffalo rochester and pittsburgh railroad'* could be annotated both as a company or a facility. This manual evaluation aims to show that, although the resource we extracted from BabelNet is not perfect, it is consistent enough across annotators and languages to consider it a silver-standard in our experiments.

4 MWEntity Classification Approaches

We present two main approaches to the multiclass MWEntity classification problem described above: a baseline using cosine similarity, and two variations of (distantly) supervised Support Vector Machines. We use Scikit-learn (Pedregosa et al., 2011), the machine learning library for Python, for implementing the different approaches.

4.1 Baseline Approach: CoSSIM

The baseline approach adopted in this classification task, hereafter referred to as the COSSIM system, is modelled on a simple search engine, where query word vectors are compared with document vectors through cosine similarity. In our case, a query word vector is analogous to the expression to be classified, while the document vectors are analogous to vectors representing each category in the training set. The type associated with the category vector most similar to the query vector is selected as the classification for the query expression. For each category, using a TF.IDF vectorisation process, we generate a ranking in the importance of terms that can be considered a type of 'topic signature' (Fleischman and Hovy, 2002) for this category, since words more strongly associated with a particular category receive higher TF.IDF scores. When no token in the to-be-classified multi-word entity occurs in the training data for a given category, this expression will receive a cosine similarity score of 0 with this category. If this is the case for all categories, COSSIM is unable to classify the expression and instead outputs a no-guess label ('NG'). Both the training and test expressions are vectorised with a TF.IDF vectoriser (Pedregosa et al., 2011), with standard L2 normalisation (to normalise for variation in the number of expressions found in each category) and sublinear TF calculations (which log-scales the TF counts).

4.2 SVM Approaches: SVM_TFIDF & SVM_COUNTS

We develop two supervised Support Vector Machine (SVM) classifiers which differ only in the vectorisation method adopted: SVM_TFIDF utilises the same TF.IDF vectoriser as COSSIM, while SVM_COUNTS uses a simple count vectoriser. We therefore follow a simple bag-of-words (BoW) model for extracting TF.IDF and count-based features from the tokens contained within each MWEntity. Classification is 'pairwise (One-Versus-One; OVO), meaning that a binary classifier is trained for each pair of classes and the class which receives most votes (highest count) is selected. This method of multi-class classification was favoured over One-Versus-Rest classification to minimise training time, following Hsu and Lin (2002). This is implemented using Scikit-learn's LinearSVC SVM classifier with the One-Versus-One wrapper (Pedregosa et al., 2011). We chose an SVM classification approach following its widely-acknowledged strong performance on text classification tasks (Joachims, 1998; Yang and Liu, 1999; Qin and Wang, 2009; Ye et al., 2009).

4.3 Confidence Thresholds

We were interested in whether we could utilise the scores of the CosSim, SVM_TFIDF, and SVM_COUNTS as parameters for maximising for precision or recall in the classification task, as this is particularly relevant in the context of our specific application. We therefore define 5 threshold levels corresponding to the lower percentiles of the scores at 5% intervals (0, 5, 10, 15 and 20%) in order to evaluate whether this method has the desired effect, and calculate the exact score thresholds using `numpy.percentile()` [3]. For each classification with a confidence or similarity score below the threshold, the expression in question is re-classified with the no-guess tag ('NG').

Both SVM systems *always* attempt to classify an expression, so at the 0% threshold there will be no 'NG' classifications; however, as detailed in Section 4.1, CosSim does not classify an expression if it has a similarity score of 0 with all possible categories, instead classifying with 'NG' also at the 0% threshold.

5 Evaluations

This section provides a brief discussion of the method of cross-validation used in this work and an overview of the preprocessing carried out on the resource automatically generated from BabelNet, before turning to the experimental method and results of the experiments.

5.1 Cross-Validation

The automatically annotated resource from BabelNet is separated into 43 languages, varying in coverage. We use 10-fold shuffle-split cross-validation, split 75% training and 25% testing for all experiments detailed below. The general approach was as follows (any discrepancies from this will be explicitly detailed later where necessary): the data for each language is randomly shuffled (with a constant random state initialisation value for reproducibility) 10 times, and each shuffled version is then separated for training and testing. With this method, it is not guaranteed that each fold will be different, but it is likely with sizeable data sets; nonetheless, we favour this technique over k-fold cross-validation as it maximises the training data available, even for the smallest languages in the resource.

<hr>

[3] http://www.numpy.org/

5.2 Preprocessing

When preparing the automatically generated resource from BabelNet for use in the MWEntity classification task, we considered only those entities that consist of at least two tokens, and additionally removed some potentially problematic entries (i.e. entities containing only two tokens including one with a single character).

In addition, we excluded non-alphanumerical strings and removed all duplicates within each entity category. We did not exclude entities which occurred in more than one category, as we argue that removing such cases would lead to a bias in the results.

Following this method of filtering, approximately 1.5 million entries were retained for the experiments. Table 3 provides a breakdown of the initial number of extracted entities per type and the final number of entities that were used for the purpose of carrying out the MWEntity classification experiments.

We also experimented with replacing all numerical characters with the same token ('0'), after observing that certain classes contain many similarly formatted numerical tokens, such as dates. In these tests, we chose to replace each number character individually, in order to retain some distinctions between classes: for example, taken from the Swedish data set, 'EVT-NA' contains a large number of dates ('2004 asiatiske tsunami' → '0000 asiatiske tsunami'), while 'PRO-WE' contains mixed alphanumerical strings ('mp40 schmeisser' → 'mp00 schmeisser'). Despite the intuition that replacing numerical characters in this way would create more generalised features for the classes in question, this in fact had little or no positive effect in the classification task using the SVM_TFIDF method, and a significantly negative effect with the CosSim method. Consequently, it was not adopted in the full-scale experiments described below.

5.3 Experiments

During development, we compared the performance of the two SVM systems, SVM_TFIDF and SVM_COUNTS. In line with the expectation that TF.IDF vectorisation would provide more informative features in the task of differentiating between categories, we found SVM_TFIDF performed marginally better overall. In the following full-scale experiments, we therefore will only dis-

Excluded	Language dependent			Language independent		
percentile	P	R	F1	P	R	F1
CosSim						
0%	81.8%	61.5%	66.3%	81.3%	62.8%	67.0%
5%	83.2%	59.8%	65.0%	82.8%	59.9%	65.1%
10%	84.1%	56.7%	63.1%	83.7%	56.6%	62.5%
15%	85.1%	53.6%	60.6%	84.1%	53.4%	59.7%
20%	85.9%	50.4%	58.0%	85.0%	50.2%	56.9%
SVM_TFIDF						
0%	87.8%	87.5%	87.5%	**88.9%**	**88.8%**	**88.8%**
5%	90.0%	85.4%	87.4%	**91.6%**	**86.6%**	**88.6%**
10%	91.8%	82.6%	86.6%	**92.6%**	**83.3%**	**87.5%**
15%	93.0%	79.0%	84.9%	**93.4%**	**79.5%**	**85.5%**
20%	93.6%	75.0%	82.8%	**94.2%**	**75.4%**	**83.3%**

Table 6: Average results across the 43 tested languages, with language-dependent or independent approaches, for the 5 tested percentile thresholds.

cuss the comparison between SVM_TFIDF and the baseline approach, CosSim.

The main task compared the performance of language-dependent and language-independent training for the two classification methods, when applied across 43 languages at 5 different threshold levels (see Section 4.3 for threshold definitions). The 43 languages correspond mostly to European languages including Russian, plus Arabic.

5.3.1 Language-Dependent Training

For each of the classification methods, SVM_TFIDF and CosSim, a language-specific classifier is built for each of the 43 languages in the resource. Using the method of 10-fold cross-validation described in Section 5.1, the data for each language is separated for training and testing, to allow for a language-by-language comparison on the performance of each classification method. We compare the performance of SVM_TFIDF with the baseline CosSim across each of the 5 threshold levels for all 43 languages.

5.3.2 Language-Independent Training

In order to fairly compare the performance of a language-independent classifier with those with language-dependent training, testing is still carried out language-dependently (we use the same test sets in both experiments). We create a language-independent training corpus by concatenating each of the language-specific training sets from the previous experiment, and importantly, excluding any duplicate MWEntities, so as to remove any overlap between training and testing data. Once again, we compare the performance of SVM_TFIDF with the baseline CosSim across each of the 5 threshold levels for all 43 languages.

5.4 Results

As Table 6 shows, in both experiments, SVM_TFIDF is the best-performing classification method in precision, recall and F1, across all percentile thresholds. The baseline, CosSim, performs marginally worse in terms of precision, but significantly worse in terms of recall (across all thresholds and both training methods). We exclude a higher percentage of low-scoring classifications in the threshold experiments, leading to a distinct improvement in precision, in the best case increasing by over 5.7% in SVM_TFIDF. This supports the intuition that the scores assigned by both the SVM systems and the CosSim system correlate to the accuracy of the chosen label. This can therefore be viewed as a means of tweaking or prioritising precision over recall or vice versa. Maximising precision with the 20% threshold, when averaged across all languages, we achieve precision of over 94% with the language-independent SVM_TFIDF classifier. More specifically, we see precision of over 95% in 16 of the 43 languages tested.

The best system overall is the language-independent SVM_TFIDF classifier, significantly outperforming the CosSim system when trained on both language-dependent and independent data, especially in terms of recall and F1. At its peak, we see a marked difference of over 26% between the two systems in terms of recall, both trained on language-independent data. We also see consistent improvements in precision, recall and F1 across all percentile thresholds from SVM_TFIDF trained on language-dependent to independent data.

In particular, Table 7 shows a significant boost

Selected languages	Support	Description	Language dependent			Language independent		
			P	**R**	**F1**	**P**	**R**	**F1**
Romanian	23588	best	94%	94%	94%	96%	96%	96%
English	713656	largest	88%	88%	88%	88%	88%	88%
Faroese	120	smallest/worst	56%	55%	50%	74%	68%	67%
Arabic	16520	non-Latin	87%	87%	87%	88%	88%	88%
Russian	43936	non-Latin	86%	85%	85%	87%	87%	87%

Table 7: Results for some specific languages of the 43 tested, with language-dependent or independent approaches, with SVM_TFIDF method at the 0% percentile threshold.

Selected classes	Support	Description	Language dependent			Language independent		
			P	**R**	**F1**	**P**	**R**	**F1**
EVT-NA	7920	best	96.4%	91.4%	93.6%	96.8%	94.4%	95.6%
LOC-FA	469633	largest	89.9%	93.4%	91.7%	90.6%	94.4%	92.1%
ORG-CO	158502	worst prec.	76.9%	80.6%	78.5%	81.3%	81.4%	81.4%
PRO-EL	8817	worst recall	83.5%	58.6%	67.8%	82.8%	65.3%	72.8%

Table 8: Results for some specific type classes, with language-dependent or independent approaches, with SVM_TFIDF method at the 0% percentile threshold.

in performance in Faroese, the smallest language in the data set (from an F1 of 50% to 67%), with little or no impact on English, the largest portion of the resource. Similar improvements are seen in the other under-represented languages in the resource: Ladino (F1 67% to 88%), Luxembourgish (F1 77% to 88%) and, to a lesser extent, Romansh (F1 81% to 82%). This suggests that utilising cross-linguistic data to supplement the training data for the smaller languages is beneficial.

At the 0% percentile threshold, the language achieving the best results is Romanian, with precision, recall and F1 well above the 88% average for this system, at 96%. Furthermore, we also see minor improvements on languages not using the Latin alphabet, such as Arabic and Russian, suggesting that language-independent training can even improve performance in cases where we would expect that language-specific features would be most useful. This is likely due to the fact that a single-language corpus often contains some portion of international terms.

Table 8 shows that language-independent training also causes a small boost in performance across individual class types. In particular, a marked improvement is made in the 'PRO-EL' class, which achieves the worst recall value with language-dependent training, improving by 6.7%. In general, Table 8 demonstrates that performance varies across classes, with a particularly striking difference in recall between the best-performing class ('EVT-NA') and the worst ('PRO-EL'). Given that these two classes are relatively close in size, this suggests class size is not the unique driv-

ing factor in performance and that different NE categories are linguistically diverse.

6 Conclusion and Future Work

We presented an approach to automatically classify MWEntities based only on their internal features. We described how to construct a silver-standard resource of MWEntities from BabelNet adapted to an application-driven type hierarchy. The classifiers were applied in a highly multilingual environment, 43 languages, and we showed how they perform better when trained on all languages combined, with a language-independent training set. With the SVM_TFIDF approach, using 10-fold shuffle-split cross-validation on a 1.5 million MWEntity data set, we obtained a precision/recall of 88.9%/88.8% when all expressions are classified, and 94.2%/75.4% when we filter the 20% least confident classifications. We also showed that these results are reasonably stable across languages, being more sensitive to the number of expressions available to train this language than to its scripting. In addition, we demonstrated that, despite the fuzzy delimitation between entity types, for instance between facilities and organisations, the classifiers perform reasonably well for all entity types.

We now plan to explore one more method: using the best-performing classifier (training all languages combined using SVM and a TF.IDF-weighted data representation) on character n-grams. We hope that this may help to capture words that are similar across languages, but not identical (e.g. *national / nazionale / nacional / nationaal*).

We will then apply the best-performing classifier to our vast and equally highly multilingual in-house collections of MWEntities. As our in-house collections also contain MWExpressions that are not entities (e.g. *Chief Executive Officer, kilometres per hour*), we will have to face the challenge of having to identify the expressions that are not covered by the classes we have trained. We hope that the thresholds to exclude the least confident classifications will be efficient at that task.

7 Acknowledgement

This work was carried out while the first author was a member of the Text and Data Mining Unit of the Joint Research Centre, European Commission. The author is now based in the Cognitive Science Research Group at Queen Mary University of London.

References

Sören Auer, Christian Bizer, Georgi Kobilarov, Jens Lehmann, Richard Cyganiak, and Zachary Ives. 2007. Dbpedia: A nucleus for a web of open data. In *Proceedings of the 6th International The Semantic Web and 2Nd Asian Conference on Asian Semantic Web Conference*, ISWC'07/ASWC'07, pages 722–735, Berlin, Heidelberg. Springer-Verlag.

Kurt Bollacker, Colin Evans, Praveen Paritosh, Tim Sturge, and Jamie Taylor. 2008. Freebase: A collaboratively created graph database for structuring human knowledge. In *Proceedings of the 2008 ACM SIGMOD International Conference on Management of Data*, SIGMOD '08, pages 1247–1250, New York, NY, USA. ACM.

Luciano Del Corro, Abdalghani Abujabal, Rainer Gemulla, and Gerhard Weikum. 2015. Finet: Context-aware fine-grained named entity typing. In *Proceedings of the 2015 Conference on Empirical Methods in Natural Language Processing*, pages 868–878. Association for Computational Linguistics.

Greg Durrett and Dan Klein. 2014. A joint model for entity analysis: Coreference, typing, and linking. *Transactions of the Association of Computational Linguistics*, 2:477–490.

Asif Ekbal and Sriparna Saha. 2013. Stacked ensemble coupled with feature selection for biomedical entity extraction. *Knowledge-Based Systems*, 46:22–32.

Christiane Fellbaum. 1998. *WordNet: An Electronic Lexical Database*. Bradford Books.

Michael Fleischman and Eduard Hovy. 2002. Fine grained classification of named entities. In *COLING 2002: The 19th International Conference on Computational Linguistics*.

Aldo Gangemi, Andrea Giovanni Nuzzolese, Valentina Presutti, Francesco Draicchio, Alberto Musetti, and Paolo Ciancarini. 2012. Automatic typing of dbpedia entities. In *International Semantic Web Conference*, pages 65–81. Springer.

Waseem Gharbieh, Virendra Bhavsar, and Paul Cook, 2016. *Proceedings of the 12th Workshop on Multiword Expressions*, chapter A Word Embedding Approach to Identifying Verb-Noun Idiomatic Combinations, pages 112–118. Association for Computational Linguistics.

Chih-Wei Hsu and Chih-Jen Lin. 2002. A comparison of methods for multiclass support vector machines. *IEEE transactions on Neural Networks*, 13(2):415–425.

Guillaume Jacquet, Maud Ehrmann, Ralf Steinberger, and Jaakko Väyrynen. 2016. Cross-lingual linking of multi-word entities and their corresponding acronyms. In *Proceedings of the 10th Language Resources and Evaluation Conference*, Portorož, Slovenia.

Thorsten Joachims. 1998. Text categorization with support vector machines: Learning with many relevant features. In *European conference on machine learning*, pages 137–142. Springer.

Xiao Ling and Daniel S Weld. 2012. Fine-grained entity recognition. In *AAAI*.

Roberto Navigli and Simone Paolo Ponzetto. 2012. BabelNet: The automatic construction, evaluation and application of a wide-coverage multilingual semantic network. *Artificial Intelligence*, 193:217–250.

Joel Nothman, Nicky Ringland, Will Radford, Tara Murphy, and James R Curran. 2013. Learning multilingual named entity recognition from wikipedia. *Artificial Intelligence*, 194:151–175.

Marius Pasca, Dekang Lin, Jeffrey Bigham, Andrei Lifchits, and Alpa Jain. 2006. Organizing and searching the world wide web of facts-step one: the one-million fact extraction challenge. In *AAAI*, volume 6, pages 1400–1405.

Fabian Pedregosa, Gal Varoquaux, Alexandre Gramfort, Vincent Michel, Bertrand Thirion, Olivier Grisel, Mathieu Blondel, Peter Prettenhofer, Ron Weiss, Vincent Dubourg, Jake Vanderplas, Alexandre Passos, David, Cournapeau, Matthieu Brucher, Matthieu Perrot, and douard Duchesnay. 2011. Scikit-learn: Machine learning in Python. *Journal of Machine Learning Research*, 12:2825–2830.

Yu-ping Qin and Xiu-kun Wang. 2009. Study on multi-label text classification based on svm. In *Fuzzy Systems and Knowledge Discovery, 2009. FSKD'09. Sixth International Conference on*, volume 1, pages 300–304. IEEE.

Lev Ratinov and Dan Roth, 2009. *Proceedings of the Thirteenth Conference on Computational Natural Language Learning (CoNLL-2009)*, chapter Design Challenges and Misconceptions in Named Entity Recognition, pages 147–155. Association for Computational Linguistics.

Satoshi Sekine, Kiyoshi Sudo, and Chikashi Nobata. 2002. Extended named entity hierarchy. In *LREC*.

Ralf Steinberger. 2012. A survey of methods to ease the development of highly multilingual text mining applications. *Language Resources and Evaluation*, 46(2):155–176.

Reuth Vexler and Einat Minkov, 2016. *Proceedings of the Sixth Named Entity Workshop*, chapter Multi-source named entity typing for social media, pages 11–20. Association for Computational Linguistics.

Begoña Villada Moirón and Jörg Tiedemann, 2006. *Proceedings of the Workshop on Multi-word-expressions in a multilingual context*, chapter Identifying idiomatic expressions using automatic word-alignment.

Yiming Yang and Xin Liu. 1999. A re-examination of text categorization methods. In *Proceedings of the 22nd annual international ACM SIGIR conference on Research and development in information retrieval*, pages 42–49. ACM.

Qiang Ye, Ziqiong Zhang, and Rob Law. 2009. Sentiment classification of online reviews to travel destinations by supervised machine learning approaches. *Expert Systems with Applications*, 36(3):6527–6535.

Using bilingual word-embeddings for multilingual collocation extraction

Marcos Garcia, Marcos García-Salido and **Margarita Alonso-Ramos**
Universidade da Coruña, Departamento de Galego-Português, Francés e Lingüística
Facultade de Filoloxía, Campus da Zapateira, 15701 — A Coruña, Galicia, España
{marcos.garcia.gonzalez,marcos.garcias,margarita.alonso}@udc.gal

Abstract

This paper presents a new strategy for multilingual collocation extraction which takes advantage of parallel corpora to learn bilingual word-embeddings. Monolingual collocation candidates are retrieved using Universal Dependencies, while the distributional models are then applied to search for equivalents of the elements of each collocation in the target languages. The proposed method extracts not only collocation equivalents with direct translation between languages, but also other cases where the collocations in the two languages are not literal translations of each other. Several experiments —evaluating collocations with three syntactic patterns— in English, Spanish, and Portuguese show that our approach can effectively extract large pairs of bilingual equivalents with an average precision of about 90%. Moreover, preliminary results on comparable corpora suggest that the distributional models can be applied for identifying new bilingual collocations in different domains.

1 Introduction

Even though there is no universal definition of collocation, there is a general tendency to consider any syntactically related frequent pair of words to be a collocation (Smadja, 1993; Evert and Kermes, 2003; Kilgarriff, 2006). In the Firthian tradition of the term "collocation", not even a syntactic relation between the members is necessary, but in the phraseological tradition, not only the syntactic relation is a condition but also a lexical restriction.[1]

From this phraseological point of view, a collocation is a restricted binary co-occurrence of lexical units (LUs) between which a syntactic relation holds, and that one of the LUs (the *base*) is chosen according to its meaning as an isolated LU, while the other (the *collocate*) is chosen depending on the base and the intended meaning of the co-occurrence as a whole, rather than on its meaning as an isolated LU (Mel'čuk, 1998). Thus, a noun in English such as "picture" requires the verb "to take" (and not "to do", or "to make") in the phrase "take a picture", while "statement" selects "to make" ("make a statement").

In a bilingual (or multilingual) scenario, equivalent collocations are needed to produce more natural utterances in the target language(s). In this regard, the referred noun "picture" would select the verb "tirar" in Portuguese —"to remove"— ("tirar uma fotografia"). Similarly the Spanish "vino" ("wine") would require the adjective "tinto" ("vino tinto"), which is not the main translation of "red" ("red wine").

The unpredictability of these structures involves problems for tasks such as machine translation, whose performance can benefit from lists of multilingual collocations (or transfer rules for these units) (Orliac and Dillinger, 2003). In areas like second language learning, it has been shown that even advanced learners need to know which word combinations are allowed in a specific linguistic variety (Altenberg and Granger, 2001; Alonso-Ramos et al., 2010). Thus, obtaining resources of multilingual equivalent collocations could be useful for different applications such as those mentioned above. However, this kind of resources is scarce, and constructing them manually requires a large effort of expert lexicographers.

In the last years, several approaches were implemented aimed at extracting bilingual collocations, both from parallel corpora (Kupiec, 1993;

---

[1] An overview of different visions on collocations —both from theoretical and practical perspectives— can be found in Seretan (2011).

Proceedings of the 13th Workshop on Multiword Expressions (MWE 2017), pages 21–30,
Valencia, Spain, April 4. ©2017 Association for Computational Linguistics

Smadja et al., 1996; Wu and Chang, 2003), and from comparable or even from non-related monolingual resources (Lü and Zhou, 2004; Rivera et al., 2013), often combining statistical approaches with the use of bilingual dictionaries to find equivalents of each *base*.

In this paper we explore the use of distributional semantics (by means of bilingual word-embeddings) for identifying bilingual equivalents of monolingual collocations: On one hand, monolingual collocation candidates are extracted using a harmonized syntactic annotation —provided by Universal Dependencies (UD)[2]—, as well as standard association measures. On the other hand, bilingual word-embeddings are trained using lemmatized versions of noisy parallel corpora. Finally, these bilingual models are employed to search for semantic equivalents of both the *base* and the *collocate* of each collocation.

Several experiments —using the OpenSubtitles2016 parallel corpora in English, Portuguese, and Spanish (Lison and Tiedemann, 2016)— show that the proposed method successfully identifies bilingual collocations with different patterns: *adjective-noun*, *noun-noun*, and *verb-object*. Furthermore, preliminary results in comparable corpora suggest that the same strategy can be applied in this kind of resources to extract new pairs of bilingual collocations.

Section 2 includes some related work on collocation extraction, specially on papers dealing with bilingual resources. Then, our method is presented and evaluated in Sections 3 and 4, respectively. Finally, some conclusions and further work are drawn in Section 5.

2 Related work

Several approaches were employed in order to automatically identify monolingual collocations (and other multiword expressions) from corpora. Most strategies use statistical association measures on windows of *n-grams* with different sizes (Church and Hanks, 1990; Smadja, 1993). Other methods, such as the one presented in Lin (1999), started to apply dependency parsing aimed at better identifying combinations of words which occur in actual syntactic relations. More recently, the large availability of better parsers allowed researchers to combine automatically obtained syntactic information with statistical methods to extract collocations more accurately (Evert, 2008; Seretan, 2011).

A different perspective on collocation extraction focuses not only on their retrieval, but on semantically classifying the obtained collocations, in order to make them more useful for NLP applications (Wanner et al., 2006; Wanner et al., 2016).

Concerning the extraction of bilingual collocations, most works rely on parallel corpora to find the equivalent of a collocation in a target language. In this respect, Smadja (1992; 1996) first identifies monolingual collocations in English (the source language), and then uses *mutual information* (MI) and the *Dice coefficient* (respectively) to find French equivalents of the source collocations.

Kupiec (1993) also uses parallel corpora to find noun phrase equivalents between English and French. The method consist in applying an expectation maximization (EM) algorithm to previously extracted monolingual collocations.

Similarly, Haruno et al. (1996) obtain Japanese-English chunk equivalents by computing their MI scores and taking into account their frequency and position in the aligned corpora.

Another work which uses parallel corpora is presented in Wu and Chang (2003). The authors extract Chinese and English *n-grams* from aligned sentences by computing their *log-likelihood* ratio. Then, the *competitive linking algorithm* is used to decide whether each bilingual pair actually corresponds to a translation equivalent.

More recently, Seretan and Wehrli (2007) took advantage of syntactic parsing to extract bilingual collocations from parallel corpora. The strategy consist in first extracting monolingual collocations using *log-likelihood*, and then searching for equivalents of each *base* using bilingual dictionaries. The method also uses the position of the collocation in the corpus, and relies on the syntactic analysis by assuming that equivalent collocations will occur in the same syntactic relation in both languages.

Rivera et al. (2013) present a framework for bilingual collocation retrieval which can be applied —with different modules— in parallel and in comparable corpora. As in other works, monolingual collocations (based on *n-grams*) are extracted in a first step, and then bilingual dictionaries (or WordNet, in the comparable corpora scenario) are used to find the equivalents of the *base* in the aligned sentence (or in a small window of

---

[2]http://universaldependencies.org/

adjacent sentences) of the source collocation.

A different approach, which uses non-related monolingual corpora for finding bilingual collocations, was presented in Lü and Zhou (2004). Here, the authors apply dependency parsing and the *log-likelihood* ratio for obtaining English and Chinese collocations. Then, they search for translations using word translation equivalents with the same dependency relation in the target language (using the EM algorithm and a bilingual dictionary).

Although not focused on collocations, Pascale Fung applied methods based on distributional semantics to build bilingual lexica from comparable corpora (Fung, 1998, among others). This approach takes into account that in this type of resources the position and the frequency of the source and target words are not comparable, and also that the translations of the source words might not exist in the target document.

Similarly, the approach presented in this paper leverages noisy parallel corpora for building bilingual word-embeddings. However, with a view to applying it in other scenarios (such as comparable corpora), it does not need information about the position of the collocations in the corpora, — neither their comparative frequency— to identify the equivalents. Furthermore, it does not take advantage of external resources such as bilingual dictionaries, so the method can be easily applied to other languages.

3 Bilingual collocation extraction

This section presents our method for automatically extracting bilingual collocations from corpora. First, we briefly describe the approach for identifying candidates of monolingual collocations using syntactic dependencies. Then, the process of creating the bilingual word-embeddings is shown, followed by the strategy for discovering the collocation equivalents between languages.

3.1 Monolingual dependency-based collocation extraction

Early works on *n-gram* based collocation extraction already pointed out the need for using syntactic analysis for better identifying collocations from corpora (Smadja, 1993; Lin, 1999). Syntactic analysis can, on the one hand, avoid the extraction of syntactically unrelated words which occur in a small context windows. On the other hand, it can effectively identify the syntactic relation be-

tween lexical items occurring in long-distance dependencies (Evert, 2008).

Besides, and even though it is not always the case (Lü and Zhou, 2004), our method assumes that most bilingual equivalent of collocations bear the same syntactic relation in both the source and the target languages.

In order to better capture the syntactic relations between the *base* and the *collocate* of each collocation, our method uses state-of-the-art dependency parsing. Apart from that, and aimed at obtaining harmonized syntactic information between languages, we rely on *universal dependencies* annotation, which permits the use of the same strategy for extracting and analyzing the collocations in multiple languages.[3]

Preprocessing: Before extracting the collocation candidates from each corpus, we apply a pipeline of NLP tools in order to annotate the text with the desired information. Thus, the output of this process consists of a parsed corpus in a CoNLL-U format, where for each word we have its surface form, its lemma, its POS-tag and morphosyntactic features, its syntactic head as well as the *universal* relation the word has in this context.[4]

From this analyzed corpus, we extract the word pairs belonging to the desired relations (collocation candidates). On the one hand, we keep their surface forms, POS-tags, and other syntactic dependents which may be useful for the identification of potential collocations. On the other hand, in order to apply association measures, we retain a list of triples containing (a) the syntactic relation, (b) the head, and (c) the dependent (using their lemmas together with the POS-tags). Thus, from a sentence such as "John took a great responsibility", we obtain (among others) the following triples:

$nsubj$(take$_{\text{VERB}}$,John$_{\text{PROPN}}$)
$amod$(responsibility$_{\text{NOUN}}$,great$_{\text{ADJ}}$)
$dobj$(take$_{\text{VERB}}$,responsibility$_{\text{NOUN}}$)

This information (and also the corpus size and the frequency of the different elements of the potential collocations) is saved in order to rank the candidates.

Collocation patterns: At the moment, we are focused on extracting three different syntactic pat-

---

[3] http://universaldependencies.org/u/dep/all.html
[4] http://universaldependencies.org/format.html

terns of collocations in three languages (Spanish —*es*—, Portuguese —*pt*—, and English —*en*):

Adjective—Noun (amod): these candidates are pairs of adjectives (*collocate*) and nouns (*base*) where the former syntactically depends of the latter in a *amod* relation. Example: $killer_{base}; serial_{collocate}$.

Noun—Noun (nmod): this collocation pattern consists of two common nouns related by the *nmod* relation, where the head is the *base* and the dependent is the *collocate* (optionally with a *case* marking dependent preposition: "of" in English, "de" in Portuguese and Spanish). Example: $rage_b; fit_c$.[5]

Verb—Object (vobj): *verb-object* collocations consists of a verb (the *collocate* and a common noun (the *base*) occurring in a *dobj* relation. Example: $care_b; take_c$.

Identification of candidates: For each of the three patterns of collocations, we extract a list of potential candidates for the three languages. After that, the candidates are ranked using standard association measures that have been widely used in collocation extraction (*MI, t-score, z-score, Dice, log-likelihood*, etc.) (Evert, 2008).

In the current experiments, we selected two statistical measures whose results complement each other: *t-score* (which prefers frequent dependency pairs, and has been proved useful for collocation extraction (Krenn and Evert, 2001)), and *mutual information* (which is useful for a large corpus (Pecina, 2010), even if it tends to assign high scores to candidates with very low-frequency).

The output of both association measures is merged in a final list for each language and collocation pattern, defining thresholds of *t-score=>2* and *MI=>3* (Stubbs, 1995), and extracting only collocations with a frequency of *f=>10* (a relatively large value for reducing the extraction of incorrect entries from a noisy corpus and from potential errors of the automatic analysis).

It must be noted that, since these lists of monolingual collocations have been built based on statistical measures of collocability, their members need not be *bona fide* collocations in the phraseological meaning. Thus, the lists can include id-

---

[5]Note that some collocations belonging to this pattern are analyzed in UD —mainly in English— using the *compound* relation, so they are not extracted in the experiments performed in this paper.

ioms (e.g., "kick the bucket"), quasi-idioms (e.g., "big deal") (Mel'čuk, 1998), or free combinations (e.g., "buy a drink").

3.2 Bilingual word-embeddings

Word-embeddings are low-dimensional vector representations of words which capture their distributional context in corpora. Even though distributional semantics methods have been largely used in previous years, approaches based on word-embeddings have gained in popularity recently, since the publication of *word2vec* (Mikolov et al., 2013).

Based on the *Skip-gram* model of *word2vec*, Luong et al. (2015) proposed *BiSkip*, a word-embeddings model which learns learns bilingual representations using aligned corpora, thus being able to predict words crosslinguistically.

As our approach for collocation extraction uses lemmas (instead of surface forms) to identify the candidates, the bilingual models are also trained on lemmatized corpora. Therefore, we convert the raw parallel corpora in lemmatized resources (with any other information) keeping the original sentence alignment.

Once we have the lemma version of the corpora, the bilingual models are built using MultiVec, an implementation of *word2vec* and *BiSkip* (Berard et al., 2016). As we work with three different languages, we need three different bilingual models: *es–en*, *es–pt*, and *pt–en*.

As it will be shown, the obtained models can predict the similarity between words in bilingual scenarios by computing the cosine distance between their vectors. As the models learn the distribution of single words (lemmas), they deal with different semantic phenomena such as polysemy or homonymy. Concerning collocations, this means that, ideally, the bilingual models could predict not only the equivalents of a *base*, but also to capture the (less close) semantic relation between the bilingual *collocates*, if they occur an enough number of times in the corpora.

3.3 Bilingual collocation alignment

In order to identify the bilingual equivalent (in a target language) of a collocation, our method needs (a) monolingual collocations (ideally obtained from similar resources), and (b) a bilingual *source-target* model of word-embeddings.

With these resources, the following strategy is applied: For each collocation in the source language (e.g., *lío_b;tremendo_c*, in Spanish) we select its *base* and obtain —using the bilingual model— the *n* most similar lemmas in the target language (where *n=5* in our experiments): "trouble", "mess", etc. Then, starting from the most similar lemma, we search in the target list for collocations containing the equivalents of the *base* (*trouble_b;little_c*, *trouble_b;deep_c*, *mess_b;huge_c*, *mess_b;fine_c*, etc.). If a collocation with a *base* equivalent is found, we compute the cosine distance between both *collocates* ("tremendo" *versus* "little", "deep", "huge", and "fine") and select them as potential candidates if their similarity is higher than a threshold (empirically defined in this paper as 0.65), and if the target candidate is among the *n* most similar words of the source *collocate* (again, *n=5*). Finally, if these conditions are met, we align the source and target collocations, assigning the average distance between the *bases* and the *collocates* as a confidence value: *es-en:lío_b;tremendo_c=mess_b;huge_c;0.721*.

4 Experiments

This section presents the experiments carried out in order to evaluate the proposed method (henceforth DIS) in the three analyzed languages, using the three collocation patterns defined in Section 3.1. Our approach is compared against a baseline system (BAS) which uses hand-crafted bilingual dictionaries.[6]

Corpora: Monolingual collocations were extracted from a subset of the OpenSubtitles2016 corpus (Lison and Tiedemann, 2016), which contains parallel corpora from TV and Movie subtitles. We selected this resource because it is a large and multilingual parallel corpus likely to contain different collocations types (also from an informal register) to those present in other corpora, thus being useful for comparative studies.[7]

From the *en*, *es* and *pt* corpora, we selected those sentences which appear in the three languages (a total of $13,017,016$). They were tokenized, lemmatized and POS-tagged with a multilingual NLP pipeline (Garcia and Gamallo, 2015), obtaining three corpora of $\approx 91M$ (*es* and *pt*), and $\approx 98M$ (*en*) tokens. The resulting data were

Lg	amod		nmod		vobj	
es	480k	13,870	1.6M	5,673	430k	17,723
pt	420k	12,967	1.7M	5,643	560k	20,984
en	460k	14,175	1.6M	3,133	490k	15,492

Table 1: Number of unique input dependencies for each syntactic pattern, and final monolingual collocation candidates.

enriched with syntactic annotation using statistical models trained with MaltParser (Nivre et al., 2007) and the 1.4 version of the UD treebanks (Nivre et al., 2016).

Collocations: From each corpus, three patterns of collocations candidates were extracted: *amod*, *nmod*, and *vobj*. For each language and pattern, we obtained a single list of collocations by merging the *MI* and *t-score* outputs as explained in Section 3.1. Table 1 shows the number of filtered collocations in each case.

Another version of the corpora was created only with the lemma of each token, keeping the original sentence alignments. These corpora were used for training three bilingual word-embeddings models with MultiVec (with 100 dimensions and a window-size of 8 words): *es–en*, *es–pt*, and *pt–en*.[8]

Baseline (BAS): The performance of the method described in Section 3.3 was compared to a baseline which follows the same strategy, but using bilingual dictionaries instead of the word-embeddings models. Thus, the BAS method obtains the equivalents of both the *base* and the *collocate* of a source collocation, and verifies whether exists a target collocation with the translations. The bilingual dictionaries provided by the *apertium* project (SVN revision 75,477) were used for these experiments (Forcada et al., 2011).[9]

The *es-pt* dictionary has $14,364$ entries, while the *es-en* one contains $34,994$. The *pt-en* dictionary (not provided by *apertium*) was automatically obtained by transitivity from the two other lexica, with a size of $9,160$ pairs.

4.1 Results

With a view to knowing the performance of both BAS and DIS in the different scenarios, 100 bilingual collocation pairs were randomly selected

---

[6]The extractions of both methods are available at http://www.grupolys.org/~marcos/pub/mwe17.tar.bz2

[7]Note, however, that OpenSubtitles2016 includes non-professional translations with some noisy elements such as typos or case inconsistencies, among others.

[8]These models are available at http://www.grupolys.org/~marcos/pub/mwe17_models.tar.bz2

[9]https://svn.code.sf.net/p/apertium/svn/

Lg	amod		nmod		vobj	
Pair	BAS	DIS	BAS	DIS	BAS	DIS
es-pt	657	9,464	320	3,867	529	12,887
es-en	248	7,778	32	890	183	8,865
pt-en	213	7,083	43	917	241	9,206

Table 2: Number of bilingual extractions of the baseline and DIS systems.

from each language and pattern,[10] creating a total of 18 lists (9 from BAS and 9 from DIS).

Two reviewers labeled each bilingual collocation pair as (a) correct, (b) incorrect, or (c) dubious (which includes pairs where the translation might be correct in some contexts even if they were not considered faithful translations).[11] Correct collocation equivalents are those pairs where the monolingual extractions were considered correct (both in terms of co-occurrence frequency and of collocational pattern classification), and that their translations were judged as potential translations in a real scenario. The reviewers achieved 92% and 83% inter-annotator agreement in BAS and DIS outputs, respectively. Those pairs with correct/incorrect disagreement were discarded for the evaluation. Those with at least one dubious label were checked by a third annotator, deciding in each case whether they were correct, incorrect, o dubious.

From these data, we obtained the precision values for each case by dividing the number of correct collocation equivalents by the number of correct, incorrect, and dubious cases (so dubious cases were considered incorrect). Recall was obtained by multiplying the precision values for the number of extracted equivalents, and dividing the result by the smallest number of input collocations for each pair (Table 2).[12] Finally, we obtained F-score values (the harmonic mean between precision and recall) for each case, and calculated the macro-average results for each language, pattern,

___

[10] Except for those baseline extractions with less than 100 elements, where all of them were selected.

[11] Some of these dubious equivalents are actual translations in the original corpus, such as the *es-en* "copa de champaña" ("champagne cup") — "cup of wine", even if they are semantically different.

[12] Note that these recall results assume that every collocation in the shortest input list of each pair has an equivalent on the other language, which is not always the case. Thus, more realistic recall values (which would need an evaluation of every extracted pair) will be higher than the obtained in our experiments.

and approach.

Table 2 contains the bilingual collocation equivalents extracted by each method in the 9 settings, from the input lists of monolingual data (Table 1). These results clearly show that the baseline approach extract a lower number of bilingual equivalents. This might have happened due to the size of the dictionaries and because of the internal properties of the collocations, where the *collocates* may not be direct translations of each other. Moreover, it is worth noting that in both BAS and DIS results, the bilingual extractions including English are smaller than the *es-pt* ones.

Concerning the performance of the two approaches, Tables 3 (baseline) and 4 (DIS) contain the precision, recall and f-score for each language pair and collocation pattern.

BAS obtains high-precision results in every language and collocation pattern (91.7% in the worst scenario), with a macro-average value of 97%. These results are somehow expected due to the quality of the hand-crafted dictionaries. However, because of the poor recall numbers, the general performance of BAS is low, achieving f-score results of $\approx 4.7\%$. Interestingly, the size of the dictionary does not seem crucial to the results of the baseline. In this respect, the *es-pt* results are much higher (specially in recall) than *es-en*, whose dictionary size is more than the double. Also, the *pt-en* results are slightly better than the *es-pt* ones, the latter being obtained using a dictionary built by transitivity.

About DIS model, its precision is lower than the baseline, with results between 83.9% (*pt-en:vobj*) and 92.9% (*es-pt:amod*). However, this approach finds much more bilingual equivalents than the bilingual dictionaries, so recall values increase to an average of almost 50%. Unlike BAS (whose results are more homogeneous along the collocation patterns), DIS model obtains more variable numbers in each setting. Noticeably, the *nmod* extractions of the pairs including English have very low recall when compared to the other results, maybe derived from not having extracted nouns analyzed as *compound* (Section 3.1). As in the baseline, the DIS *es-pt* results are better than the two other pairs, so the linguistic distance seems to play an important role on bilingual collocation extraction.

The method proposed in this paper assigns a confidence value (obtained from the cosine distance between the vectors of the *base* and the *col-*

Lang	amod			nmod			vobj			avg		
Pair	*Prec*	*Rec*	*F1*	*Prec*	*Rec*	*F1*	*Prec*	*Rec*	*F1*	*Prec*	*Rec*	*F1*
es–pt	99.0	5.0	9.6	97.8	5.5	10.5	98.7	3.0	5.7	98.5	4.5	8.6
es–en	95.8	1.7	3.4	100	1.0	2.0	100	1.2	2.3	98.6	1.3	2.6
pt–en	97.9	1.6	3.2	91.7	1.3	2.5	92.1	1.4	2.8	93.9	1.4	2.8
avg	97.6	2.8	5.4	96.5	2.6	5.1	96.9	1.9	3.6	97.0	1.8	4.7

Table 3: Precision, recall and f-score of the baseline (BAS) system (*avg* is macro-average).

Lang	amod			nmod			vobj			avg		
Pair	*Prec*	*Rec*	*F1*	*Prec*	*Rec*	*F1*	*Prec*	*Rec*	*F1*	*Prec*	*Rec*	*F1*
es–pt	92.9	67.8	78.4	93.8	64.3	76.3	90.1	66.0	76.5	92.5	66.0	77.1
es–en	92.0	51.6	64.3	88.0	25.0	38.9	84.0	48.1	61.2	87.5	41.6	56.4
pt–en	90.5	49.5	64.0	90.0	26.3	40.1	83.9	49.9	62.6	88.2	41.9	56.8
avg	91.8	56.3	68.9	90.6	38.5	51.9	86.2	54.7	66.7	89.5	49.8	63.4

Table 4: Precision, recall and f-score of DIS system (*avg* is macro-average).

locate equivalents) to each bilingual pair of collocations. In this respect, Figure 1 plots the average performance and confidence curves versus the total number of extracted pairs. This figure shows that using a high confidence value ($> 90\%$), it is possible to extract $\approx 35,000$ bilingual pairs with high-precision. Besides, it is worth mentioning that filtering the extraction with confidence values higher than 90% does not increase the precision of the system, so we can infer that the errors produced in the most confident pairs arise due factors other than the semantic similarity (e.g. different degrees of compositionality). However, as the confident value decreases the precision of the extraction also gets worse, despite the rise in the number of extractions which involves higher recall and consequently better f-score.

Finally, all the bilingual collocations extracted by DIS were merged into a single list with the three languages, thus obtaining new bilingual equivalents (not extracted directly by the system) by transitivity.[13] This final multilingual resource has $31,735$ collocations, $8,747$ of them with translations in the three languages.

4.2 Error analysis

The manually annotated lists of bilingual collocations were used to perform an initial error analysis of our approach. These errors were classified, due to its origin, in the following types:

---

[13] The merging process obtained $3,352$ new bilingual collocation equivalents not present in the original extractions.

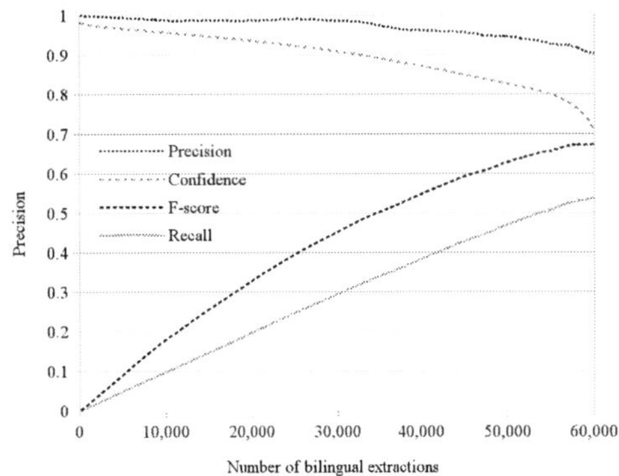

Figure 1: Average precision, recall, f-score, and confidence curves (from 0 to 1) versus total number of extractions of the DIS model.

Preprocessing: Several errors derived from issues produced by the NLP pipeline, such as POS-tagging or dependency parsing: e.g., "pain$_{Noun}$, end$_{Verb}$" was labeled as *dobj* (instead of *nsubj*).

Bilingual model: The bilingual word-embeddings approach, though useful, produces some errors such as the identification of antonyms (with similar distribution), which can align opposite collocation equivalents (such as *pt-en:tecido$_b$;vivo$_c$=tissue$_b$;dead$_c$*) where the extracted equivalent of the *collocate* "vivo" ("alive", in *pt*) was "dead". In most cases, however, the system obtained similar (but not synonym) collocations: *pt-en:chá$_b$;preto$_c$=coffee$_b$;black$_c$* ("black tea, black coffee").

Lemmatization and gender: The lemmatization of some words differs from language to language, so working with lemmas instead of tokens also might involve some errors. For instance, the word "hija" ("daughter", in Spanish) is lemmatized as "hijo" ("son") in Spanish and Portuguese ("filha, filho"), while in English "son" and "daughter" appear as different entries. Thus, some bilingual collocations differ in the gender of their *bases*: *es-en:hijo$_b$;encantador$_c$=daughter$_b$;lovely$_c$*

Monolingual extraction: The extraction of *base* and *collocate* pairs produced incorrect collocations such as *plan$_b$;figure$_c$*, instead of obtaining the phrasal verb "figure out" as *collocate*.

Other errors: Some other errors were produced by mixed languages in the original corpus (e.g., the verb form "are", in English, was analyzed as a verb form of the verb "arar" —"to plow"—, in Spanish) and from noise and misspellings in the corpora (proper nouns with lower case letters, etc.).

4.3 Comparable corpora

A final experiment was carried out in order to know (a) whether the bilingual word-embeddings —trained in the same parallel corpora as those used for extracting the collocations— could be successfully applied for aligning collocations obtained from different resources, and (b) the performance of the proposed method in comparable corpora.

So we applied the same strategy for monolingual collocation extraction in the Spanish and Portuguese *Wikipedia Comparable Corpus 2014*,[14] and calculated the semantic similarity between the collocations using the same word-embeddings models as in the previous experiments.

From these corpora, we obtained filtered lists of $73,291$ and $119,311$ candidate collocations in Portuguese and Spanish, respectively (from 140M and 80M of tokens). From the $51,183$ bilingual collocations obtained by the DIS approach, we randomly selected and evaluated 100 *es-pt* pairs.

The precision of the extraction was 88.9%, with a recall of 62.1% (again computed using the whole set of monolingual collocations), and 73.1% f-score. These results are in line with those obtained in the OpenSubtitles *es-pt* pair ($\approx 3\%$ lower), so

the method works well in different corpora and domains. It is worth noting that $43,025$ of the extracted collocation equivalents (84%) had not been retrieved from the OpenSubtitles corpus.

This last experiment shows that (a) the bilingual word-embeddings can be used for identifying collocation equivalents in different corpora than those used for training, and that (b) they can also be applied in corpora of different domains to obtain previously unseen multilingual collocations.

5 Conclusions and further work

In this paper we have presented a new strategy to automatically discover multilingual collocation equivalents from corpora.

First, three different patterns of monolingual collocations were extracted using syntactic analysis provided by harmonized UD annotation, together with a combination of standard association measures.

Besides, bilingual word-embeddings were trained in parallel corpora that had been previously lemmatized. These bilingual models were then used to find distributional equivalents of both the *base* and the *collocate* of each source collocation in the target language.

The performed experiments, using noisy parallel corpora in three languages, showed that the proposed method achieves an average precision in the bilingual alignment of collocations of about 90%, with reasonable recall values. Furthermore, the evaluation pointed out that using a confidence value for setting up a threshold is useful for retaining only high-precise bilingual equivalents, which could benefit different work on multilingual lexicography.

Finally, a preliminary test using comparable corpora suggested that the bilingual word-embeddings can be efficiently applied in different corpora than those used for learning, discovering new bilingual collocations not present in the original resources.

In further work, the results of the error analysis should be taken into account in order to reduce both the errors produced by the NLP pipeline, and those which arise from the word-embedding models. In this respect, it could be interesting to evaluate other approaches for the alignment of bilingual collocations which make use of better compositionality models and which effectively learn the semantic distribution of collocations.

---

[14] http://linguatools.org/tools/corpora/wikipedia-comparable-corpora/

Acknowledgments

This work has been supported by the Spanish Ministry of Economy, Industry and Competitiveness (MINECO) trough the projects with reference FFI2016-78299-P and FFI2014-51978-C2-1-R, by a *Juan de la Cierva formación* grant (FJCI-2014-22853), and by a postdoctoral fellowship granted by the Galician Government (POS-A/2013/191).

References

Margarita Alonso-Ramos, Leo Wanner, Orsolya Vincze, Gerard Casamayor del Bosque, Nancy Vázquez Veiga, Estela Mosqueira Suárez, and Sabela Prieto González. 2010. Towards a Motivated Annotation Schema of Collocation Errors in Learner Corpora. In Nicoletta Calzolari (Conference Chair), Khalid Choukri, Bente Maegaard, Joseph Mariani, Jan Odijk, Stelios Piperidis, Mike Rosner, and Daniel Tapias, editors, *Proceedings of the Seventh conference on International Language Resources and Evaluation (LREC 2010)*, pages 3209–3214, Paris. European Language Resources Association (ELRA).

Bengt Altenberg and Sylviane Granger. 2001. The grammatical and lexical patterning of MAKE in native and non-native student writing. *Applied linguistics*, 22(2):173–195.

Alexandre Berard, Christophe Servan, Olivier Pietquin, and Laurent Besacier. 2016. MultiVec: a Multilingual and Multilevel Representation Learning Toolkit for NLP. In Nicoletta Calzolari (Conference Chair), Khalid Choukri, Thierry Declerck, Sara Goggi, Marko Grobelnik, Bente Maegaard, Joseph Mariani, Helene Mazo, Asuncion Moreno, Jan Odijk, and Stelios Piperidis, editors, *Proceedings of the Tenth International Conference on Language Resources and Evaluation (LREC 2016)*, pages 4188–4192, Paris. European Language Resources Association (ELRA).

Kenneth Ward Church and Patrick Hanks. 1990. Word association norms, mutual information, and lexicography. *Computational linguistics*, 16(1):22–29.

Stefan Evert and Hannah Kermes. 2003. Experiments on candidate data for collocation extraction. In *Proceedings of the Tenth Conference on European Chapter of the Association for Computational Linguistics (EACL 2003)*, volume 2, pages 83–86, Budapest. Association for Computational Linguistics.

Stefan Evert. 2008. Corpora and collocations. In Anke Lüdeling and Merja Kytö, editors, *Corpus Linguistics. An International Handbook*, volume 2, pages 1212–1248. Mouton de Gruyter, Berlin.

Mikel L. Forcada, Mireia Ginestí-Rosell, Jacob Nordfalk, Jim O'Regan, Sergio Ortiz-Rojas, Juan Antonio Pérez-Ortiz, Felipe Sánchez-Martínez, Gema Ramírez-Sánchez, and Francis M. Tyers. 2011. Apertium: a free/open-source platform for rule-based machine translation. *Machine translation*, 25(2):127–144.

Pascale Fung. 1998. A statistical view on bilingual lexicon extraction: from parallel corpora to non-parallel corpora. In *Proceedings of the Third Conference of the Association for Machine Translation in the Americas. Machine Translation and the Information Soup (AMTA 1998)*, pages 1–17, Langhorne, Pennsylvania. Association for Machine Translation in the Americas.

Marcos Garcia and Pablo Gamallo. 2015. Yet Another Suite of Multilingual NLP Tools. In José-Luis Sierra-Rodríguez and José Paulo Leal and Alberto Simões, editor, *Languages, Applications and Technologies. Communications in Computer and Information Science*, International Symposium on Languages, Applications and Technologies (SLATE 2015), pages 65–75.

Masahiko Haruno, Satoru Ikehara, and Takefumi Yamazaki. 1996. Learning bilingual collocations by word-level sorting. In *Proceedings of the 16th Conference on Computational Linguistics (COLING 1996)*, volume 1, pages 525–530, Copenhagen. Association for Computational Linguistics.

Adam Kilgarriff. 2006. Collocationality (and how to measure it). In Elisa Corino and Carla Marello and Cristina Onesti, editor, *Proceedings of the 12th EURALEX International Congress*, volume 2, pages 997–1004, Torino.

Brigitte Krenn and Stefan Evert. 2001. Can we do better than frequency? A case study on extracting PP-verb collocations. In *Proceedings of the ACL Workshop on Collocations*, pages 39–46, Toulouse. Association for Computational Linguistics.

Julian Kupiec. 1993. An algorithm for finding noun phrase correspondences in bilingual corpora. In *Proceedings of the 31st Annual Meeting on Association for Computational Linguistics (ACL 1993)*, pages 17–22, Columbus, Ohio. Association for Computational Linguistics.

Dekang Lin. 1999. Automatic Identification of Non-compositional Phrases. In *Proceedings of the 37th Annual Meeting of the Association for Computational Linguistics on Computational Linguistics (ACL 1999)*, pages 317–324, College Park, Maryland. Association for Computational Linguistics.

Pierre Lison and Jörg Tiedemann. 2016. OpenSubtitles2016: Extracting Large Parallel Corpora from Movie and TV Subtitles. In Nicoletta Calzolari (Conference Chair), Khalid Choukri, Thierry Declerck, Sara Goggi, Marko Grobelnik, Bente

Maegaard, Joseph Mariani, Helene Mazo, Asuncion Moreno, Jan Odijk, and Stelios Piperidis, editors, *Proceedings of the Tenth International Conference on Language Resources and Evaluation (LREC 2016)*, Paris. European Language Resources Association (ELRA).

Yajuan Lü and Ming Zhou. 2004. Collocation translation acquisition using monolingual corpora. In *Proceedings of the 42nd Annual Meeting on Association for Computational Linguistics (ACL 2004)*, pages 167–174, Barcelona. Association for Computational Linguistics.

Minh-Thang Luong, Hieu Pham, and Christopher D. Manning. 2015. Bilingual Word Representations with Monolingual Quality in Mind. In *Proceedings of the 1st Workshop on Vector Space Modeling for Natural Language Processing (VSM-NLP) at the 2015 Conference of the North American Chapter of the Association for Computational Linguistics – Human Language Technologies (NAACL HLT 2015)*, pages 151–159, Denver, Colorado. Association for Computational Linguistics.

Igor Mel'čuk. 1998. Collocations and Lexical Functions. In Anthony Paul Cowie, editor, *Phraseology. Theory, Analysis and Applications*, pages 23–53. Clarendon Press, Oxford.

Tomas Mikolov, Kai Chen, Greg Corrado, and Jeffrey Dean. 2013. Efficient estimation of word representations in vector space. In *Workshop Proceedings of the International Conference on Learning Representations (ICLR) 2013*, Scottsdale, Arizona. arXiv preprint arXiv:1301.3781.

Joakim Nivre, Johan Hall, Jens Nilsson, Atanas Chanev, Gülsen Eryigit, Sandra Kübler, Svetoslav Marinov, and Erwin Marsi. 2007. MaltParser: A language-independent system for data-driven dependency parsing. *Natural Language Engineering*, 13(02):95–135.

Joakim Nivre, Marie-Catherine de Marneffe, Filip Ginter, Yoav Goldberg, Jan Hajic, Christopher D. Manning, Ryan McDonald, Slav Petrov, Sampo Pyysalo, Natalia Silveira, Reut Tsarfaty, and Daniel Zeman. 2016. Universal Dependencies v1: A Multilingual Treebank Collection. In Nicoletta Calzolari (Conference Chair), Khalid Choukri, Thierry Declerck, Sara Goggi, Marko Grobelnik, Bente Maegaard, Joseph Mariani, Helene Mazo, Asuncion Moreno, Jan Odijk, and Stelios Piperidis, editors, *Proceedings of the Tenth International Conference on Language Resources and Evaluation (LREC 2016)*, pages 1659–1666, Paris. European Language Resources Association (ELRA).

Brigitte Orliac and Mike Dillinger. 2003. Collocation extraction for machine translation. In *Proceedings of Ninth Machine Translation Summit (MT Summit IX)*, pages 292–298, New Orleans, Lousiana.

Pavel Pecina. 2010. Lexical association measures and collocation extraction. *Language Resources and Evaluation*, 44(1-2):137–158.

Oscar Mendoza Rivera, Ruslan Mitkov, and Gloria Corpas Pastor. 2013. A Flexible Framework for Collocation Retrieval and Translation from Parallel and Comparable Corpora. In *Proceedings of the Workshop on Multi-word Units in Machine Translation and Translation Technology*, pages 18–25, Nice.

Violeta Seretan and Eric Wehrli. 2007. Collocation translation based on sentence alignment and parsing. In *Actes de la 14e conference sur le Traitement Automatique des Langues Naturelles (TALN 2007)*, pages 401–410, Toulouse.

Violeta Seretan. 2011. *Syntax-based collocation extraction*, volume 44 of *Text, Speech and Language Technology Series*. Springer Science & Business Media.

Frank Smadja, Kathleen R McKeown, and Vasileios Hatzivassiloglou. 1996. Translating collocations for bilingual lexicons: A statistical approach. *Computational linguistics*, 22(1):1–38.

Frank Smadja. 1992. How to compile a bilingual collocational lexicon automatically. In *Proceedings of the AAAI Workshop on Statistically-Based NLP Techniques*, pages 57–63, San Jose, CA.

Frank Smadja. 1993. Retrieving Collocations from Text: Xtract. *Computational linguistics*, 19(1):143–177.

Michael Stubbs. 1995. Collocations and semantic profiles: On the cause of the trouble with quantitative studies. *Functions of language*, 2(1):23–55.

Leo Wanner, Bernd Bohnet, and Mark Giereth. 2006. Making sense of collocations. *Computer Speech & Language*, 20(4):609–624.

Leo Wanner, Gabriela Ferraro, and Pol Moreno. 2016. Towards Distributional Semantics-Based Classification of Collocations for Collocation Dictionaries. *International Journal of Lexicography*. 10.1093/ijl/ecw002.

Chien-Cheng Wu and Jason S Chang. 2003. Bilingual Collocation Extraction Based on Syntactic and Statistical Analyses. In *Proceedings of the 15th Conference on Computational Linguistics and Speech Processing (ROCLING 2003)*, pages 1–20, Taiwan. Association for Computational Linguistics and Chinese Language Processing.

The PARSEME Shared Task on Automatic Identification of Verbal Multiword Expressions

Agata Savary
Université de Tours, France
`first.last@univ-tours.fr`

Carlos Ramisch
Aix Marseille Université
France

Silvio Ricardo Cordeiro
Aix Marseille Université
France

Federico Sangati
Independent researcher
Italy

Veronika Vincze
University of Szeged
Hungary

Behrang QasemiZadeh
University of Düsseldorf
Germany

Marie Candito
Université Paris Diderot
France

Fabienne Cap
Uppsala University
Sweden

Voula Giouli
Athena Research Center
Athens, Greece

Ivelina Stoyanova
Bulgarian Academy of Sciences
Sofia, Bulgaria

Antoine Doucet
University of La Rochelle
France

Abstract

Multiword expressions (MWEs) are known as a "pain in the neck" for NLP due to their idiosyncratic behaviour. While some categories of MWEs have been addressed by many studies, verbal MWEs (VMWEs), such as *to take a decision*, *to break one's heart* or *to turn off*, have been rarely modelled. This is notably due to their syntactic variability, which hinders treating them as "words with spaces". We describe an initiative meant to bring about substantial progress in understanding, modelling and processing VMWEs. It is a joint effort, carried out within a European research network, to elaborate universal terminologies and annotation guidelines for 18 languages. Its main outcome is a multilingual 5-million-word annotated corpus which underlies a shared task on automatic identification of VMWEs. This paper presents the corpus annotation methodology and outcome, the shared task organisation and the results of the participating systems.

1 Introduction

Multiword expressions (MWEs) are known to be a "pain in the neck" for natural language processing (NLP) due to their idiosyncratic behaviour (Sag et al., 2002). While some categories of MWEs have been addressed by a large number of NLP studies, verbal MWEs (VMWEs), such as *to **take** a **decision**, to **break** one's **heart** or to **turn off**[1], have been relatively rarely modelled. Their particularly challenging nature lies notably in the following facts:

1. Their components may not be adjacent (***turn it off***) and their order may vary (*the **decision** was hard to **take***);
2. They may have both an idiomatic and a literal reading (*to **take the cake***);
3. Their surface forms may be syntactically ambiguous (*on* is a particle in the verb-particle construction ***take on** the task* and a preposition in *to sit on the chair*);
4. VMWEs of different categories may share the same syntactic structure and lexical choices (*to **make** a **mistake*** is a light-verb construction, *to **make a meal*** is an idiom),
5. VMWEs behave differently in different languages and are modelled according to different linguistic traditions.

These properties are challenging for automatic identification of VMWEs, which is a prerequisite for MWE-aware downstream applications such as

---

[1]Henceforth, boldface will be used to highlight the lexicalised components of MWEs, that is, those that are always realized by the same lexemes.

Proceedings of the 13th Workshop on Multiword Expressions (MWE 2017), pages 31–47,
Valencia, Spain, April 4. ©2017 Association for Computational Linguistics

parsing and machine translation. Namely, challenge 1 hinders the use of traditional sequence labelling approaches and calls for syntactic analysis. Challenges 2, 3 and 4 mean that VMWE identification and categorization cannot be based on solely syntactic patterns. Challenge 5 defies cross-language VMWE identification.

We present an initiative aiming at boosting VMWE identification in a highly multilingual context. It is based on a joint effort, carried on within a European research network, to elaborate universal terminologies, guidelines and methodologies for 18 languages. Its main outcome is a 5-million-word corpus annotated for VMWEs in all these languages, which underlies a shared task on automatic identification of VMWEs.[2] Participants of the shared task were provided with training and test corpora, and could present systems within two tracks, depending on the use of external resources. They were encouraged to submit results for possibly many covered languages.

In this paper, we describe the state of the art in VMWE annotation and identification (§ 2). We then present the corpus annotation methodology (§ 3) and its outcome (§ 4). The shared task organization (§ 5), the measures used for system evaluation (§ 6) and the results obtained by the participating systems (§ 7) follow. Finally, we discuss conclusions and future work (§ 8).

2   Related Work

Annotation   There have been several previous attempts to annotate VMWEs. Some focus specifically on VMWEs and others include them among the linguistic phenomena to be annotated. Rosén et al. (2015) offer a survey of VMWE annotation in 17 treebanks, pointing out that, out of 13 languages in which phrasal verbs do occur, 8 have treebanks containing annotated phrasal verbs, and only 6 of them contain annotated light-verb constructions and/or verbal idioms. They also underline the heterogeneity of these MWE annotations. Nivre and Vincze (2015) show that this is also the case in the treebanks of Universal Dependencies (UD), despite the homogenizing objective of the UD project (McDonald et al., 2013). More recent efforts (Adalı et al., 2016), while addressing VMWEs in a comprehensive way, still suffer from missing annotation standards.

Heterogeneity is also striking when reviewing annotation efforts specifically dedicated to VMWEs, such as Estonian particle verbs (Kaalep and Muischnek, 2006; Kaalep and Muischnek, 2008), Hungarian light-verb constructions (Vincze and Csirik, 2010), and Arabic verb-noun and verb-particle constructions (Bar et al., 2014). The same holds for English resources, such as the Wiki50 corpus (Vincze et al., 2011), which includes both verbal and non-verbal MWEs. Resources for English also include data sets of selected sentences with positive and negative examples of light-verb constructions (Tu and Roth, 2011), verb-noun combinations (Cook et al., 2008), and verb-particle constructions (Tu and Roth, 2012). While most annotation attempts mentioned so far focus on annotating MWEs in running texts, there also exist lists of MWEs annotated with their degree of idiomaticity, for instance, German particle verbs (Bott et al., 2016) and English noun compounds (Reddy et al., 2011). In contrast to these seminal efforts, the present shared task relies on VMWE annotation in running text according to a unified methodology.

Identification   MWE identification is a well-known NLP task. The 2008 MWE workshop proposed a first attempt of an MWE-targeted shared task. Differently from the shared task described here, the goal of participants was to rank provided MWE candidate lexical units, rather than to identify them in context. True MWEs should be ranked towards the top of the list, whereas regular word combinations should be at the end. Heterogeneous datasets containing several MWE categories in English, German and Czech were made available. Two systems participated, using different combinations of features and machine learning classifiers. In addition to the shared task, the MWE 2008 workshop also focused on gathering and sharing lexical resources containing annotated candidate MWEs. This repository is available and maintained on the community website.[3]

The DiMSUM 2016 shared task (Schneider et al., 2016) challenged participants to label English sentences (tweets, service reviews, and TED talk transcriptions) both with MWEs and supersenses for nouns and verbs.[4]   The provided dataset is made of approximately 90,000 tokens containing 5,069 annotated MWEs, about 10% of which are

---

[2] http://multiword.sourceforge.net/sharedtask2017

[3] http://multiword.sf.net/

[4] http://dimsum16.github.io

discontinuous. They were annotated following Schneider et al. (2014b), and thus contain several VMWEs types on top of non-verbal MWEs.

Links between MWE identification and syntactic parsing have also long been an issue. While the former has often been treated as a pre-processing step before the latter, both tasks are now more and more often integrated, in particular for continuous MWE categories (Finkel and Manning, 2009; Green et al., 2011; Green et al., 2013; Candito and Constant, 2014; Le Roux et al., 2014; Nasr et al., 2015; Constant and Nivre, 2016). Fewer works deal with verbal MWEs (Wehrli et al., 2010; Vincze et al., 2013; Wehrli, 2014; Waszczuk et al., 2016).

3 Annotation Methodology

In order to bring about substantial progress in the state of the art presented in the preceding section, the European PARSEME network[5], dedicated to parsing and MWEs, proposed a shared task on automatic identification of VMWEs. This initiative required the construction of a large multilingual VMWE-annotated corpus.

Within the challenging features of linguistic annotation, as defined by Mathet et al. (2015), the VMWE annotation task is concerned by:

- *Unitising*, i.e. identifying the boundaries of a VMWE in the text;
- *Categorisation*, i.e. assigning each identified VMWE to one of the pre-defined categories (cf. Section 3.1).
- *Sporadicity*, i.e. the fact that not all text tokens are subject to annotation (unlike in POS annotation for instance);
- *Free overlap* (e.g. **take** a **walk** and then a long **shower**: 2 LVCs with a shared light verb);
- *Nesting*, both at the syntactic level (e.g. **take** the fact that I didn't **give up into account**) and at the level of lexicalized components (e.g. **let the cat out of the bag**).

Two other specific challenges are:

- *Discontinuities* (e.g. **take** this **into account**);
- *Multiword token* VMWEs, e.g. separable IReflVs or VPCs: (ES) **ab-stener/se** (lit. *abstain self*) 'abstain',

(DE) **auf/machen** (lit. *out/make*) 'open'.[6]

This complexity is largely increased by the multilingual nature of the task, and calls for efficient project management. The 21 participating languages were divided into four *language groups* (LGs): *Balto-Slavic*: Bulgarian (BG), Croatian (HR), Czech (CS), Lithuanian (LT), Polish (PL) and Slovene (SL); *Germanic*: English (EN), German (DE), Swedish (SV) and Yiddish (YI); *Romance*: French (FR), Italian (IT), Romanian (RO), Spanish (ES) and Brazilian Portuguese (PT); and *others*: Farsi (FA), Greek (EL), Hebrew (HE), Hungarian (HU), Maltese (MT) and Turkish (TR). Note that the 4 last are non-Indo-European. Corpus release was achieved for 18 of these languages, that is, all except HR, EN and YI, for which no sufficiently available native annotators could be found. The coordination of this large project included the definition of roles – project leaders, technical experts, language group leaders (LGLs), language leaders (LLs) and annotators – and their tasks.

3.1 Annotation Guidelines

The biggest challenge in the initial phase of the project was the development of the annotation guidelines[7] which would be as universal as possible but which would still allow for language-specific categories and tests. To this end, a two-phase pilot annotation in most of the participating languages was carried out. Some corpora were annotated at this stage not only by native but also by near-native speakers, so as to promote cross-language convergences. Each pilot annotation phase provided feedback from annotators and was followed by enhancements of the guidelines, corpus format and processing tools. In this way, the initial guidelines dramatically evolved, new VMWE categories emerged, and the following 3-level typology was defined:

1. *universal* categories, that is, valid for all languages participating in the task:

---

[6]Note that annotating separate syntactic words within such tokens would be linguistically more appropriate, and would avoid bias in inter-annotator agreement and evaluation measures (cf. Sections 4.2 and 6). However, we preferred to avoid token-to-word homogenising mainly for the reasons of compatibility. Namely, for many languages pre-existing corpora were used, and we wished VMWE annotations to rely on the same tokenization as the other annotation layers.

[7]Their final version, with examples in most participating languages, is available at http://parsemefr.lif.univ-mrs. fr/guidelines-hypertext/.

---

[5]http://www.parseme.eu

(a) light verb constructions (LVCs), e.g. *to give* a **lecture**

(b) idioms (ID), e.g. *to **call it a day***

2. *quasi-universal* categories, valid for some language groups or languages, but not all:

   (a) inherently reflexive verbs (IReflVs), e.g. (FR) *s'évanouir* 'to faint'

   (b) verb-particle constructions (VPCs), e.g. *to **do in*** 'to kill'

3. *other* verbal MWEs, not belonging to any of the categories above (due to not having a unique verbal head) e.g. *to **drink and drive**, to **voice act**, to **short-circuit***.

While we allowed for language-specific categories, none emerged during the pilot or final annotations. The guidelines consist of linguistic tests and examples, organised into decision trees, aiming at maximising the level of determinism in annotator's decision making. Most of the tests are generic, applying to all languages relevant to a given category, but some are language-specific, such as those distinguishing particles from prepositions and prefixes in DE, EN and HU. Once the guidelines became stable, language leaders added examples for most tests in their languages using a dedicated interface.

3.2 Annotation Tools

For this large-scale corpus construction, we needed a centralized web-based annotation tool. Its choice was based on the following criteria: (i) handling different alphabets, (ii) accounting for right-to-left scripts, and (iii) allowing for discontinuous, nested and overlapping annotations. We chose FLAT[8], a web platform based on FoLiA[9], a rich XML-based format for linguistic annotation (van Gompel and Reynaert, 2013). In addition to the required criteria, it enables token-based selection of text spans, including cases in which adjacent tokens are not separated by spaces. It is possible to authenticate and manage annotators, define roles and fine-grained access rights, as well as customize specific settings for different languages. Out of 18 language teams, 13 used FLAT as their main annotation environment. The 5 remaining teams either used other, generic or in-house, annotation tools, or converted existing VMWE-annotated corpora.

3.3 Consistency Checks and Homogenisation

Even though the guidelines heavily evolved during the two-stage pilot annotation, there were still questions from annotators at the beginning of the final annotation phase. We used an issue tracker system (gitlab) in which language leaders could share questions with other language teams.

High-quality annotation standards require independent double annotation of a corpus followed by adjudication, which we could not systematically apply due to time and resource constraints. For most languages each text was handled by one annotator only (except for a small corpus subset used to compute inter-annotator agreement, cf. § 4.2). This practice is known to yield inattention errors and inconsistencies between annotators, and since the number of annotators per language varies from 1 to 10, we used consistency support tools.

Firstly, some languages (BG, FR, HU, IT, PL, and PT) kept a list of VMWEs and their classification, agreed on by the annotators and updated over time. Secondly, some languages (DE, ES, FR, HE, IT, PL, PT, and RO) performed a step of homogenisation once the annotation was complete. An in-house script read the annotated corpus and generated an HTML page where all positive and negative examples of a given VMWE were grouped. Entries were sorted so that similar VMWEs appear nearby – for instance occurrences of **pay** a **visit** would appear next to occurrences of **receive** a **visit**. In this way, noise and silence errors could easily be spotted and manually corrected. The tool was mostly used by language leaders and/or highly committed annotators.

4 Corpora

Tables 4 and 5 provide overall statistics of the training and test corpora created for the shared task. We show the number of sentences and tokens in each language, the overall number of annotated VMWEs and the detailed counts per category. In total, the corpora contain 230,062 sentences for training and 44,314 sentences for testing. These correspond to 4,5M and 900K tokens, with 52,724 and 9,494 annotated VMWEs. The amount and distribution of VMWEs over categories varies considerably among languages.

No category was used in all languages but the two universal categories, ID and LVC, were used in almost all languages. In HU, no ID was annotated due to the genre of the corpus, mainly com-

---

[8] github.com/proycon/flat, flat.science.ru.nl
[9] http://proycon.github.io/folia

posed of legal texts. In FA, no categorisation of the annotated VMWEs was performed, therefore, the OTH category has special semantics there: it does not mean that a VMWE cannot be categorised because of its linguistic characteristics, but rather that the categorisation tests were not applied.

The most frequent category is IReflV, in spite of it being quasi-universal, mainly due to its prevalence in CS. IReflVs were annotated in all Romance and Slavic languages, and in DE and SV. VPCs were annotated in DE, SV, EL, HE, HU, IT, and SL. No language-specific category was defined. However, the high frequency of OTH in some languages is a hint that they might be necessary, especially for non-Indo-European languages like HE, MT and TR.

Table 6 provides statistics about the length and discontinuities of annotated VMWEs in terms of the number of tokens. The average lengths range between 2.1 (PL) and 2.85 (DE) tokens. DE has the greatest dispersion for lengths: the mean absolute deviation (MAD) is 1.44 while it is less than 0.75 for all other languages. DE is also atypical with more than 10% of VMWEs containing one token only (length=1), mainly separable VPCs, e.g. *auf/machen* (lit. *out/make*) 'open'. The right part of Table 6 shows the length of discontinuities. The data sets vary greatly across languages. While for BG, FA and IT, more than 80% of VMWEs are continuous, for DE, 30.5% of VMWEs have discontinuities of 4 or more tokens.

All the corpora are freely available. The VMWE annotations are released under Creative Commons licenses, with constraints on commercial use and sharing for some languages. Some languages use data from other corpora, including additional annotations (§ 5). These are released under the terms of the original corpora.

4.1 Format

The official format of the annotated data is the parseme-tsv format[10], exemplified in Figure 1. It is adapted from the CoNLL format, with one token per line and an empty line indicating the end of a sentence. Each token is represented by 4 tab-separated columns featuring (i) the position of the token in the sentence or a range of positions (e.g., 1-2) in case of multiword tokens such as contractions, (ii) the token surface form, (iii) an optional

nsp flag indicating that the current token is adjacent to the next one, and (iv) an optional VMWE code composed of the VMWE's consecutive number in the sentence and – for the initial token in a VMWE – its category (e.g., 2:ID if a token starts an idiom which is the second VMWE in the current sentence). In case of nested, coordinated or overlapping VMWEs multiple codes are separated with a semicolon.

Formatting of the final corpus required a language-specific tokenisation procedure, which can be particularly tedious in languages presenting contractions. For instance, in FR, *du* is a contraction of the preposition *de* and the article *le*.

Some language teams resorted to previously annotated corpora which have been converted to the parseme-tsv format automatically (or semi-automatically if some tokenisation rules were revisited). Finally, scripts for converting the parseme-tsv format into the FoLiA format and back were developed to ensure corpus compatibility with FLAT.

Note that tokenisation is closely related to MWE identification, and it has been shown that performing both tasks jointly may enhance the quality of their results (Nasr et al., 2015). However, the data we provided consist of pre-tokenised sentences. This implies that we expect typical systems to perform tokenisation prior to VMWE identification, and that we do not allow the tokenisation output to be modified with respect to the ground truth. The latter is necessary since the evaluation measures are token-based (§ 6). This approach may disadvantage systems which expect untokenised raw text on input, and apply their own tokenisation methods, whether jointly with VMWE identification or not. We are aware of this bias, and we did encourage such systems to participate in the shared task, provided that they define re-tokenisation methods so as to adapt their outputs to the tokenisation imposed by us.

4.2 Inter-Annotator Agreement

Inter-annotator agreement (IAA) measures are meant to assess the hardness of the annotation task, as well as the quality of its methodology and of the resulting annotations. Defining such measures is not always straightforward due the challenges listed in Section 3.

To assess unitising, we report the per-VMWE

---

[10] `http://typo.uni-konstanz.`
`de/parseme/index.php/2-general/`
`184-parseme-shared-task-format-of-the-final-annotation`

```
1-2  Wouldn't              |  1  They
  1  Would                 |  2  were
  2  not                   |  3  letting      1:VPC;2:VPC
  3  questioning           |  4  him
  4  colonial              |  5  in           1
  5  boundaries            |  6  and
  6  open           1:ID   |  7  out          2
  7  a                     |  8  .            nsp
  8  dangerous             |
  9  Pandora    nsp 1      |
 10  '         nsp 1       |
 11  s             1       |
 12  box       nsp 1       |
 13  ?                     |
```

Figure 1: Annotation of two sample sentences containing a contraction (*wouldn't*), a verbal idiom, and two coordinated VPCs.

	#S	#T	#A_1	#A_2	F_{unit}	κ_{unit}	κ_{cat}
BG	608	27491	298	261	0.816	0.738	0.925
EL	1383	33964	217	299	0.686	0.632	0.745
ES	524	10059	54	61	0.383	0.319	0.672
FA	200	5076	302	251	0.739	0.479	n/a
FR	1000	24666	220	205	0.819	0.782	0.93
HE	1000	20938	196	206	0.522	0.435	0.587
HU	308	8359	229	248	0.899	0.827	1.0
IT	2000	52639	336	316	0.417	0.331	0.78
PL	1175	19533	336	220	0.529	0.434	0.939
PT	2000	41636	411	448	0.771	0.724	0.964
RO	2500	43728	183	243	0.709	0.685	0.592
TR	6000	107734	3093	3241	0.711	0.578	0.871

Table 1: IAA scores: #S, and #T show the the number of sentences and tokens in the corpora used for measuring the IAA, respectively. #A_1 and #A_2 refer to the number of VMWE instances annotated by each of the annotators.

F-score (F_{unit})[11], as defined in § 6, and an estimated Cohen's κ (κ_{unit}). Measuring IAA, particularly κ, for unitising is not straightforward due to the absence of negative examples, that is, spans for which both annotators agreed that they are not VMWEs. From an extreme perspective, any combination of a verb with other tokens (of any length) in a sentence can be a VMWE.[12] Consequently, one can argue that the probability of chance agreement approaches 0, and IAA can be measured simply using the observed agreement, the F-score. However, in order to provide a lower bound for the reported F-scores, we assume that the total number of stimuli in the annotated corpora is approximately equivalent to the number of verbs, which can roughly be estimated by the number of sentences: κ_{unit} is the IAA for unitising based on this assumption. To assess categorisation, we apply the standard κ (κ_{cat}) to the VMWEs for which annotators agree on the span.

All available IAA results are presented in Table 1. For some languages the IAA in this unitising is rather low. We believe that this results from particular annotation conditions. In ES, the annotated corpus is small (cf. Table 4) so the annotators gathered relatively few experience with the task. A similar effect occurs in PL and FA, where the first annotator performed the whole annotation of the train and test corpora, while the second annotator only worked on the IAA-dedicated corpus. The cases of HE, and especially of IT, should be studied more thoroughly in the future. Note also that in some languages the numbers from Table 1 are

a lower bound for the quality of the final corpus, due to post-annotation homogenisation (§ 3.3).

A novel proposal of the holistic γ measure (Mathet et al., 2015) combines unitising and categorization agreement in one IAA score, because both annotation subtasks are interdependent. In our case, however, separate IAA measures seem preferable both due to the nature of VMWEs and to our annotation methodology. Firstly, VMWEs are know for their variable degree of non-compositionality, i.e. their idiomaticity is a matter of scale. Current corpus annotation standards and identification tools require the MWE-hood, conversely, to be a binary property, which sub-optimally models a large number of grey-zone VMWE candidates. However, once the decision of the status of a VMWE candidate, as valid, has been taken, its categorization appears to be significantly simpler, as shown in the last 2 columns of Table 1 (except for Romanian). Secondly, our annotation guidelines are structured in two main decision trees - an identification and a categorization tree - to be applied mostly sequentially.[13] Therefore, separate evaluation of these two stages may be helpful in enhancing the guidelines.

5 Shared Task Organization

Corpora were annotated for VMWEs by different language teams. Before concluding the annotation of the full corpora, we requested language teams to provide a small annotated sample of 200 sentences. These were released as a trial corpus meant

---

[11]Note that F-score is symmetrical, so none of the two annotators is prioritized.

[12]Also note that annotated segments can overlap.

[13]Identification hypotheses may be questioned in the categorization process in case of LVCs or IReflVs though.

to help participants develop or adapt their systems to the shared task particularities.

The full corpora were split by the organizers into train and test sets. Given the heterogeneous nature and size of the corpora, the splitting method was chosen individually for each language. As a general rule, we tried to create test sets that (a) contained around 500 annotated VMWEs and (b) did not overlap with the released trial data. When the annotated corpus was small (e.g. in SV), we favoured the size of the test data rather than of the training data, so as to lessen the evaluation bias.

For all languages except BG, HE and LT, we also released companion files in a format close to CONLL-U[14]. They contain extra linguistic information which could be used by systems as features. For CS, FA, MT, RO and SL, the companion files contain morphological data only (lemmas, POS-tags and morphological features). For the other languages, they also include syntactic dependencies. Depending on the language, these files were obtained from existing manually annotated corpora and/or treebanks such as UD, or from the output of automatic analysis tools such as UD-Pipe[15]. A brief description of the companion files is provided in the README of each language.

The test corpus was turned into a blind test corpus by removing all VMWE annotations. After its release, participants had 1 week to provide the predictions output by their systems in the parseme-tsv format. Predicting VMWE categories was not required and evaluation measures did not take them into account (§ 6). Participants did not need to submit results for all languages and it was possible to predict only certain MWE categories.

Each participant could submit results in the two tracks of the shared task: closed and open. The *closed* track aims at evaluating systems more strictly, independently of the resources they have access too. Systems in this track, therefore, learn their VMWE identification models using *only* the VMWE-annotated training corpora and the companion files, when available. Cross-lingual systems which predict VMWE annotations for one language using files provided for other languages were still considered in the closed track. Systems

using other knowledge sources such as raw monolingual corpora, lexicons, grammars or language models trained on external resources were considered in the *open* track. This track includes purely symbolic and rule-based systems. Open track systems can use any resource they have access to, as long as it is described in the abstract and/or in the system description paper.

We published participation policies stating that data providers and organizers are allowed to participate in the shared task. Although we acknowledge that this policy is non-standard and introduces biases to system evaluation, we were more interested in cross-language discussions than in a real competition. Moreover, many languages have only a few NLP teams working on them, so adopting an exclusive approach would actually exclude the whole language from participation. Nonetheless, systems were not allowed to be trained on any test corpus (even if authors had access to it in advance) or to use resources (lexicons, MWE lists, etc.) employed or built during the annotation phase.

6 Evaluation Measures

The quality of system predictions is measured with the standard metrics of precision (P), recall (R) and F_1-score (F). VMWE categories are not taken into account in system ranking, and we do not require participant systems to predict them.[16]

Token	Gold	System1	System2	System3
t1	1	1	1	1;4
t2	1	2	3	3
t3	2	2	2	2;4

Table 2: Toy gold corpus with 3 tokens, 2 gold VMWEs, and 3 system predictions. VMWE codes do not include VMWE categories.

Each VMWE annotation or prediction can be represented as a set of token identifiers. Consider Table 2, which presents a toy gold corpus containing 2 VMWEs over 3 tokens[17] and 3 system predictions. If G denotes the set of gold VMWEs and Si the set of VMWEs predicted by system i, then the following holds[18]:

- $G = \{\{t1,t2\}, \{t3\}\}, |G| = 2, ||G|| = 3.$
- $S1 = \{\{t1\}, \{t2,t3\}\}, |S1| = 2, ||S1|| = 3.$
- $S2 = \{\{t1\}, \{t2\}, \{t3\}\}, |S2| = 3, ||S2|| = 3.$
- $S3 = \{\{t1\}, \{t2\}, \{t3\}, \{t1,t3\}\}, |S3| = 4, ||S3|| = 5.$

A simple way to obtain P, R and F is to consider every VMWE as an indivisible instance, and calculate the ratio of the VMWEs that were correctly predicted (precision) and correctly retrieved (recall). We call this the **per-VMWE** scoring. The per-VMWE scoring for the sample in Table 2 is calculated as follows, with TPi being the number of true positive VMWEs predicted by system i:

- $TP1 = |G \cap S1| = |\varnothing| = 0$
  $R = TP1/|G| = 0/2$
  $P = TP1/|S1| = 0/2.$
- $TP2 = |G \cap S2| = |\{\{t3\}\}| = 1$
  $R = TP2/|G| = 1/2.$
  $P = TP2/|S2| = 1/3.$
- $TP3 = |G \cap S3| = |\{\{t3\}\}| = 1$
  $R = TP3/|G| = 1/2$
  $P = TP3/|S3| = 1/4.$

Per-VMWE scores may be too penalising for large VMWEs or VMWEs containing elements whose lexicalisation is uncertain (e.g. definite or indefinite articles: *a*, *the*, etc.). We define, thus, an alternative **per-token** evaluation measure, which allows a VMWE to be partially matched. Such a measure must be applicable to all VMWEs, which is difficult, given the complexity of possible scenarios allowed in the representation of VMWEs, as discussed in Section 3. This complexity hinders the use of evaluation measures found in the literature. For example, Schneider et al. (2014a) use a measure based on pairs of MWE tokens, which is not always possible here given single-token VMWEs. The solution we adopted considers all possible bijections between the VMWEs in the gold and system sets, and takes a matching that maximizes the number of correct token predictions (true positives, denoted below as TPi_{max} for each system i). The application of this metric to the system outcome in Tab. 2 is the following:

- $TP1_{max} = |\{t1,t2\} \cap \{t1\}| + |\{t3\} \cap \{t2,t3\}| = 2$
  $R = TP1_{max}/||G|| = 2/3$
  $P = TP1_{max}/||S1|| = 2/3.$
- $TP2_{max} = |\{t1,t2\} \cap \{t1\}| + |\{t3\} \cap \{t3\}| + |\varnothing \cap \{t2\}| = 2$
  $R = TP2_{max}/||G|| = 2/3$
  $P = TP2_{max}/||S2|| = 2/3.$
- $TP3_{max} = |\{t1,t2\} \cap \{t1\}| + |\{t3\} \cap \{t3\}| + |\varnothing \cap \{t2\}| + |\varnothing \cap \{t1,t3\}| = 2$
  $R = TP3_{max}/||G|| = 2/3$
  $P = TP3_{max}/||S3|| = 2/5.$

---

the sum of sizes of the elements in A.

Formally, let $G = \{g_1, g_2, \ldots, g_{|G|}\}$ and $S = \{s_1, s_2, \ldots, s_{|S|}\}$ be the ordered sets of gold and system VMWEs in a given sentence, respectively[19]. Let B be the set of all bijections $b : \{1, 2, .., N\} \rightarrow \{1, 2, .., N\}$, where $N = max(|G|, |S|)$. We define $g_i = \varnothing$ for $i > |G|$, and $s_i = \varnothing$ for $i > |S|$.

We denote by TP_{max} the maximum number of true positives for any possible bijection (we calculate over a set of pairs, taking the intersection of each pair and then adding up the number of matched tokens over all intersections):

$$TP_{max} = max_{b \in B}|g_1 \cap s_{b(1)}| + |g_2 \cap s_{b(2)}| + \ldots + |g_N \cap s_{b(N)}| \tag{1}$$

The values of TP_{max} are added up for all sentences in the corpus, and precision/recall values are calculated accordingly. Let TP_{max}^j, G^j, S^j and N^j be the values of TP_{max}, G, S and N for the j-th sentence. For a corpus of M sentences, we define:

$$P = \frac{\sum_{j=1}^{M} TP_{max}^j}{\sum_{j=1}^{M} ||S^j||} \quad R = \frac{\sum_{j=1}^{M} TP_{max}^j}{\sum_{j=1}^{M} ||G^j||} \tag{2}$$

In any of the denominators above is equal to 0 (i.e. either the corpus contains no VMWEs or the system found no VMWE occurrence) the corresponding measure is defined as equal to 0.

Note that these measures operate both on a micro scale (the optimal bijections are looked for within a given sentence) and a macro scale (the results are summed up for all sentences in the corpus). Alternatively, micro-only measures, i.e. the average values of precision and recall for individual sentences, could be considered. Given that the density of VMWEs per sentence can vary greatly, and in many languages the majority of sentences do not contain any VMWE, we believe that the macro measures are more appropriate.

Note also that the measures in (2) are comparable to the CEAF-M measures (Luo, 2005) used in the coreference resolution task.[20] There, mentions are grouped into entities (clusters) and the best bijection between gold and system entities is searched for. The main difference with our approach resides in the fact that, while coreference

---

[19] We require an ordering so as to be able to define a bijection where some elements do not match anything.

[20] Notable is also the similarity of CEAF with the holistic γ evoked in section 4.2.

is an equivalence relation, i.e. each mention belongs to exactly one entity, VMWEs can exhibit overlapping and nesting. This specificity (as in other related tasks, e.g. named entity recognition) necessarily leads to counter-intuitive results if recall or precision are considered alone. A system which tags all possibles subsets of the tokens of a given sentence as VMWEs will always achieve recall equal to 1, while its precision will be above 0. Note, however, that precision cannot be artificially increased by repeating the same annotations, since the system results (i.e. S and s_i above) are defined as sets.

Potential overlapping and nesting of VMWEs is also the reason of the theoretical exponential complexity of (2) in function of the length of a sentence. In our shared task, the maximum number of VMWEs in a sentence, whether in a gold corpus or in a system prediction (denoted by $N_{max} = max_{j=1,...,M} N^j$), never exceeds 20. The theoretical time complexity of both measures in (2) is $\mathcal{O}(N_{max}^3 \times M)$.

7 System Results

Seven systems participated in the challenge and submitted a total of 71 runs. One system (LATL) participated in the open track and six in the closed track. Two points of satisfaction are that (i) each one of the 18 languages was covered and (ii) 5 of the 7 systems were multilingual. Systems were ranked based on their per-token and per-VMWE F-scores, within the open and the closed track. Results and rankings are reported, by language groups, in Tables 7–10.

Most systems used techniques originally developed for parsing: LATL employed Fips, a rule-based multilingual parser; the TRANSITION system is a simplified version of a transition-based dependency parsing system; LIF employed a probabilistic transition-based dependency parser and the SZEGED system made use of the POS and dependency modules of the Bohnet parser. The ADAPT and RACAI systems employed sequence labelling with CRFs. Finally, MUMULS exploited neural networks by using the open source library TensorFlow.

In general, scores for precision are much higher than for recall. This can be explained by the fact that most MWEs occur only once or twice in the corpora, which implies that many of the MWEs of the test data were not observed in the training data.

As expected, for most systems their per-VMWE scores are (sometimes substantially) lower than their per-token scores. In some cases, however, the opposite happens, which might be due to frequent errors in long VMWEs.

The most popular language of the shared task was FR, as all systems submitted predictions for French MWEs. Based on the numerical results, FA, RO, CS and PL were the easiest languages, i.e. ones for which the best F-scores were obtained. In contrast, somewhat more modest performance resulted for SV, HE, LT and MT, which is clearly a consequence of the lesser amount of training examples for these languages (see Tab. 4). The results for BG, HE, and LT would probably be higher if companion CONLL-U files with morphological/syntactic data could be provided. This would notably allow systems to neutralize inflection, which is particularly rich in verbs in all of these languages, as well as in nouns and adjectives in the first three of them.

FA is an outstanding case (with F-score of the best system exceeding 0.9) and its results are probably correlated with two factors. Firstly, light verbs are explicitly marked as such in the morphological companion files. Secondly, the density of VMWEs is exceptionally high. If we assume, roughly, one verb per sentence, almost each FA verb is the head of a VMWE, and the system prediction boils down to identifying its lexicalized arguments. Further analysis of this phenomenon should notably include data on the most frequent POS-tags and functions of the lexicalized verbal arguments (e.g. how often is it a nominal direct object) and the average length of VMWEs in this language.

Another interesting case is CS, where the size of the annotated data is considerable. This dataset was obtained by adapting annotations from the Prague Dependency Treebank (PDT) to the annotation guidelines and formats of this shared task (Uresová et al., 2016; Bejček et al., 2017). PDT is a long-standing treebank annotation project with advanced modelling and processing facilities. From our perspective it is as a good representative of a high-quality large-scale MWE modelling effort. In a sense, the results obtained for this language can be considered a benchmark for VMWE identification tools.

The relatively high results for RO, CS and PL might relate to the high ratio of IReflVs in these languages. Since the reflexive marker is most often realised by the same form, (CS) *se*, (PL) *się* and (RO) *se* 'self', the task complexity is reduced to identifying its head verb (often adjacent) and establishing the compositionality status of the bigram. Similar effects would be expected, but are not observed, in SL and BG, maybe due to the smaller sizes of the datasets, and to the missing companion file for BG.

Note also the high precision of the leading systems in RO, PL, PT, FR and HU, which might be related to the high proportion of LVCs in these languages, and with the fact that some very frequent light verbs, such as (RO) *da* 'give', (PL) *prowadzić* 'carry on', (PT) *fazer* 'make', (FR) *effectuer* 'perform' and (HU) *hoz* 'bring', connect with a large number of nominal arguments. A similar correlation would be expected, but is not observed, in EL, and especially in TR, where the size of the dataset is substantial. Typological particularities of these languages might be responsible for this missing correlation.

8 Conclusions and Future Work

We have described a highly multilingual collaborative VMWE-dedicated framework meant to unify terminology and annotation methodology, as well as to boost the development of VMWE identification tools. These efforts resulted in (i) the release of openly available VMWE-annotated corpora of over 5 million words, with generally high quality of annotations, in 18 languages, and (ii) a shared task with 7 participating systems. VMWE identification, both manual and automatic, proved a challenging task, and the performance varies greatly among languages and systems.

Future work includes a fine-grained linguistic analysis of the annotated corpora on phenomena such as VMWE length, discontinuities, variability, etc. This should allow us to discover similarities and peculiarities among languages, language families and VMWE types. We also wish to extend the initiative to new languages, so as to confront the annotation methodology with new phenomena and increase its universality. Moreover, we aim at converging with other universal initiatives such as UD. These advances should further boost the development and enhancement of VMWE identification systems and MWE-aware parsers.

Acknowledgments

The work described in this paper has been supported by the IC1207 PARSEME COST action[21], as well as national funded projects: LD-PARSEME[22] (LD14117) in the Czech Republic, PARSEME-FR[23] (ANR-14-CERA-0001) in France, and PASTOVU[24] in Lithuania.

We are grateful to Maarten van Gompel for his intensive and friendly help with adapting the FLAT annotation platform to the needs of our community. Our thanks go also to all language leaders and annotators for their contributions to preparing the annotation guidelines and the annotated corpora. The full composition of the annotation team is the following.

Balto-Slavic languages:

- (BG) Ivelina Stoyanova (LGL, LL), Tsvetana Dimitrova, Svetla Koeva, Svetlozara Leseva, Valentina Stefanova, Maria Todorova;
- (CS) Eduard Bejček (LL), Zdeňka Urešová, Milena Hnátková;
- (LT) Jolanta Kovalevskaitė (LL), Loic Boizou, Erika Rimkutė, Ieva Bumbulienė;
- (SL) Simon Krek (LL), Polona Gantar, Taja Kuzman;
- (PL) Agata Savary (LL), Monika Czerepowicka.

Germanic languages:

- (DE) Fabienne Cap (LGL, LL), Glorianna Jagfeld, Agata Savary;
- (EN) Ismail El Maarouf (LL), Teresa Lynn, Michael Oakes, Jamie Findlay, John McCrae, Veronika Vincze;
- (SV) Fabienne Cap (LL), Joakim Nivre, Sara Stymne.

Romance languages:

- (ES) Carla Parra Escartín (LL), Cristina Aceta, Itziar Aduriz, Uxoa Iñurrieta, Carlos Herrero, Héctor Martínez Alonso, Belem Priego Sanchez;
- (FR) Marie Candito (LGL, LL), Matthieu Constant, Ismail El Maarouf, Carlos Ramisch (LGL), Caroline Pasquer, Yannick Parmentier, Jean-Yves Antoine;

---

[21]http://www.parseme.eu
[22]https://ufal.mff.cuni.cz/grants/ld-parseme
[23]http://parsemefr.lif.univ-mrs.fr/
[24]http://mwe.lt/en_US/

- (IT) Johanna Monti (LL), Valeria Caruso, Manuela Cherchi, Anna De Santis, Maria Pia di Buono, Annalisa Raffone;
- (RO) Verginica Barbu Mititelu (LL), Monica-Mihaela Rizea, Mihaela Ionescu, Mihaela Onofrei;
- (PT) Silvio Ricardo Cordeiro (LL), Aline Villavicencio, Carlos Ramisch, Leonardo Zilio, Helena de Medeiros Caseli, Renata Ramisch;

Other languages:

- (EL) Voula Giouli (LGL,LL), Vassiliki Foufi, Aggeliki Fotopoulou, Sevi Louisou;
- (FA) Behrang QasemiZadeh (LL);
- (HE) Chaya Liebeskind (LL), Yaakov Ha-Cohen Kerner (LL), Hevi Elyovich, Ruth Malka;
- (HU) Veronika Vincze (LL), Katalin Simkó, Viktória Kovács;
- (MT) Lonneke van der Plas (LL), Luke Galea (LL), Greta Attard, Kirsty Azzopardi, Janice Bonnici, Jael Busuttil, Ray Fabri, Alison Farrugia, Sara Anne Galea, Albert Gatt, Anabelle Gatt, Amanda Muscat, Michael Spagnol, Nicole Tabone, Marc Tanti;
- (TR) Kübra Adalı (LL), Gülşen Eryiğit (LL), Tutkum Dinç, Ayşenur Miral, Mert Boz, Umut Sulubacak.

References

Kübra Adalı, Tutkum Dinç, Memduh Gokirmak, and Gülşen Eryiğit. 2016. Comprehensive Annotation of Multiword Expressions for Turkish. In *TurCLing 2016, The First International Conference on Turkic Computational Linguistics at CICLING 2016*, pages 60–66, Konya, Turkey, April.

Kfir Bar, Mona Diab, and Abdelati Hawwari. 2014. Arabic Multiword Expressions. In Nachum Dershowitz and Ephraim Nissan, editors, *Language, Culture, Computation. Computational Linguistics and Linguistics: Essays Dedicated to Yaacov Choueka on the Occasion of His 75th Birthday, Part III*, pages 64–81, Berlin, Heidelberg. Springer Berlin Heidelberg.

Eduard Bejček, Jan Hajič, Pavel Straňák, and Zdeňka Urešová. 2017. Extracting Verbal Multiword Data from Rich Treebank Annotation. In *Proceedings of the 15th International Workshop on Treebanks and Linguistic Theories (TLT 15)*, pages 13–24. Indiana University, Bloomington, Indiana University, Bloomington.

Stefan Bott, Nana Khvtisavrishvili, Max Kisselew, and Sabine Schulte im Walde. 2016. GhoSt-PV: A Representative Gold Standard of German Particle Verbs. In *CogALex-V: Proceedings of the 5th Workshop on Cognitive Aspects of the Lexicon at COLING 2016*, pages 125–133.

Marie Candito and Matthieu Constant. 2014. Strategies for Contiguous Multiword Expression Analysis and Dependency Parsing. In *Proceedings of the 52nd Annual Meeting of the Association for Computational Linguistics (Volume 1: Long Papers)*, pages 743–753, Baltimore, Maryland, June. Association for Computational Linguistics.

Matthieu Constant and Joakim Nivre. 2016. A Transition-Based System for Joint Lexical and Syntactic Analysis. In *Proceedings of the 54th Annual Meeting of the Association for Computational Linguistics (Volume 1: Long Papers)*, pages 161–171, Berlin, Germany, August. Association for Computational Linguistics.

Paul Cook, Afsaneh Fazly, and Suzanne Stevenson. 2008. The VNC-Tokens Dataset. In *Proceedings of the LREC Workshop Towards a Shared Task for Multiword Expressions (MWE 2008)*, pages 19–22, Marrakech, Morocco.

Jenny Rose Finkel and Christopher D. Manning. 2009. Joint Parsing and Named Entity Recognition. In *HLT-NAACL*, pages 326–334. The Association for Computational Linguistics.

Spence Green, Marie-Catherine de Marneffe, John Bauer, and Christopher D. Manning. 2011. Multiword Expression Identification with Tree Substitution Grammars: A Parsing tour de force with French. In *Proceedings of the 2011 Conference on Empirical Methods in Natural Language Processing*, pages 725–735, Edinburgh, Scotland, UK., July. Association for Computational Linguistics.

Spence Green, Marie-Catherine de Marneffe, and Christopher D. Manning. 2013. Parsing Models for Identifying Multiword Expressions. *Computational Linguistics*, 39(1):195–227.

Heiki-Jaan Kaalep and Kadri Muischnek. 2006. Multi-Word Verbs in a Flective Language: The Case of Estonian. In *Proceedings of the EACL Workshop on Multi-Word Expressions in a Multilingual Contexts*, pages 57–64, Trento, Italy. ACL.

Heiki-Jaan Kaalep and Kadri Muischnek. 2008. Multi-Word Verbs of Estonian: a Database and a Corpus. In *Proceedings of the LREC Workshop Towards a Shared Task for Multiword Expressions (MWE 2008)*, pages 23–26, Marrakech, Morocco.

Joseph Le Roux, Antoine Rozenknop, and Matthieu Constant. 2014. Syntactic Parsing and Compound Recognition via Dual Decomposition: Application to French. In *Proceedings of COLING 2014, the 25th International Conference on Computational*

Lang.	ID	LVC	Quasi-universal / OTH
BG	бълвам змии и гущери (lit. *to spew snakes and lizards*) 'to shower abuse'	държа под контрол 'to keep under control'	усмихвам се (IReflV) (lit. *to smile self*) 'to smile'
CS	**házet klacky pod nohy** (lit. *to throw sticks under feet*) 'to put obstacles in one's way'	**vyslovovat nesouhlas** (lit. *to voice disagreement*) 'to disagree'	**chovat se** (IReflV) (lit. *to keep SELF*) 'to behave'
DE	**schwarz fahren** (lit. *to drive black*) 'to take a ride without a ticket'	*eine* **Rede halten** (lit. *a speech hold*) 'to give a speech'	**sich enthalten** (IReflV) (lit. *himself contain*) 'to abstain'
EL	χάνω τα αυγά και τα καλάθια (lit. *loose-1SG the eggs and the baskets*) 'to be at a complete and utter loss'	κάνω μία πρόταση (lit. *make-1SG a proposal*) 'to propose'	μπαίνω μέσα (VPC) (lit. *get-1SG in*) 'to go bankrupt'
ES	**hacer de tripas corazón** (lit. *make of intestines heart*) 'to pluck up the courage'	**hacer** una **foto** (lit. *to make a picture*) 'to take a picture'	**coser y cantar** (OTH) (lit. *to sew and to sing*) 'easy as pie, a piece of cake'
FA	دسته گل به آب دادن (lit. *give flower bouquet to water*) 'to mess up, to do sth. wrong'	امتحان کردن (lit. *to do exam*) 'to test'	به خود آمدن (lit. *to come to self*) 'to gain focus'
FR	**voir le jour** (lit. *to see the daylight*) 'to be born'	**avoir** du **courage** 'to have courage'	**se suicider** (IReflV) 'to suicide'
HE	אבד עליו כלח **'avad** 'alav **kelax** (lit. *kelax is lost on him*) 'he is outdated'	הגיע למסקנה **hgiʾ lmsqnh** (lit. *to come to a conclusion*) 'to conclude'	לא הבישן למד **la hbišn lmd** 'one who is bashful does not learn'
HU	**kinyír** (lit. *out.cut*) 'to kill'	**szabályozást ad** (lit. *control-ACC give*) 'to regulate'	**feltüntet** (VPC) (lit. *up.strike*) 'to mark'
IT	**entrare in vigore** (lit. *to enter into force*) 'to come into effect'	**fare** un **discorso** (lit. *to give a speech*) 'to give a speech'	**buttare giù** (VPC) (lit. *throw down*) 'to swallow'
LT	**pramušti dugną** (lit. *to break the-bottom*) 'to collapse'	**turéti veiklų** (lit. *to have activities*) 'to be busy, to have side jobs'	
MT	għasfur żgħir qalli (lit. *a bird small told me*) 'to hear something from the grapevine'	ħa deċizjoni 'to take a decision'	iqum u joqgħod (OTH) (lit. *jump and stay*) 'to fidget'
PL	**rzucać grochem o ścianę** (lit. *throw peas against a wall*) 'to try to convince somebody in vain'	**odnieść sukces** (lit. *to carry-away a success*) 'to be successful'	**bać się** (IReflV) (lit. *to fear SELF*) 'to be afraid'
PT	**fazer das tripas coração** (lit. *transform the tripes into heart*) 'to try everything possible'	**fazer** uma **promessa** 'to make a promise'	**se queixar** (IReflV) 'to complain'
RO	a **trage pe sfoară** (lit. *to pull on rope*) 'to fool'	a **face** o **vizită** (lit. *to make a visit*) 'to pay a visit'	a **se gândi** (IReflV) 'to think'
SL	**spati kot ubit** (lit. *sleep like dead*) 'to sleep soundly'	**postaviti vprašanje** (lit. *to put a question*) 'to pose a question'	**bati se** (IReflV) 'to be afraid'
SV	*att* **Plocka russinen ur kakan** (lit. *to pick the raisins out of the cake*) 'to choose only the best things'	**ta** ett **beslut** 'to take a decision'	**det knallar och går** (OTH) (lit. *it trots and walks*) 'it is OK/as usual'
TR	**yüzüstü bırakmak** (lit. *facedown to leave (sb)*) 'to forsake'	**engel olmak** (lit. *obstacle to become*) 'to prevent'	**karar vermek** (OTH) (lit. *decision to give*) 'to decide'

Table 3: Examples of various categories of VMWEs (IDs, LVCs, quasi-universal or other VMWEs) in all 18 languages.

Language	Sentences	Tokens	VMWE	ID	IReflV	LVC	OTH	VPC
BG	6,913	157,647	1,933	417	1,079	435	2	0
CS	43,955	740,530	12,852	1,419	8,851	2,580	2	0
DE	6,261	120,840	2,447	1,005	111	178	10	1,143
EL	5,244	142,322	1,518	515	0	955	16	32
ES	2,502	102,090	748	196	336	214	2	0
FA	2,736	46,530	2,707	0	0	0	2,707	0
FR	17,880	450,221	4,462	1,786	1,313	1,362	1	0
HE	4,673	99,790	1,282	86	0	253	535	408
HU	3,569	87,777	2,999	0	0	584	0	2,415
IT	15,728	387,325	1,954	913	580	395	4	62
LT	12,153	209,636	402	229	0	173	0	0
MT	5,965	141,096	772	261	0	434	77	0
PL	11,578	191,239	3,149	317	1,548	1,284	0	0
PT	19,640	359,345	3,447	820	515	2,110	2	0
RO	45,469	778,674	4,040	524	2,496	1,019	1	0
SL	8,881	183,285	1,787	283	945	186	2	371
SV	200	3,376	56	9	3	13	0	31
TR	16,715	334,880	6,169	2,911	0	2,624	634	0
Total	230,062	4,536,603	52,724	11,691	17,777	14,799	3,995	4,462

Table 4: Overview of the training corpora: number of sentences, tokens, and annotated VMWEs, followed by broken down number of annotations per VMWE category.

Language	Sentences	Tokens	VMWE	ID	IReflV	LVC	OTH	VPC
BG	1,947	42,481	473	100	297	76	0	0
CS	5,476	92,663	1,684	192	1,149	343	0	0
DE	1,239	24,016	500	214	20	40	0	226
EL	3,567	83,943	500	127	0	336	21	16
ES	2,132	57,717	500	166	220	106	8	0
FA	490	8,677	500	0	0	0	500	0
FR	1,667	35,784	500	119	105	271	5	0
HE	2,327	47,571	500	30	0	127	158	185
HU	742	20,398	500	0	0	146	0	354
IT	1,272	40,523	500	250	150	87	2	11
LT	2,710	46,599	100	58	0	42	0	0
MT	4,635	11,1189	500	185	0	259	56	0
PL	2,028	29,695	500	66	265	169	0	0
PT	2,600	54,675	500	90	81	329	0	0
RO	6,031	100,753	500	75	290	135	0	0
SL	2,530	52,579	500	92	253	45	2	108
SV	1,600	26,141	236	51	14	14	2	155
TR	1,321	27,197	501	249	0	199	53	0
Total	44,314	902,601	9,494	2,064	2,844	2,724	807	1,055

Table 5: Overview of the test corpora: number of sentences, tokens, and annotated VMWEs, followed by broken down number of annotations per VMWE category.

	Length of VMWE			Length of discontinuities (excl. VMWEs of length 1)								
Lang.	Avg	MAD	=1	Avg	MAD	0	%0	1	2	3	>3	%>3
BG	2.45	0.63	1	0.64	1.05	1586	82.1	206	33	25	82	(4.2%)
CS	2.3	0.46	0	1.35	1.53	6625	51.5	2357	1465	944	1461	(11.4%)
DE	2.85	1.44	715	2.96	2.94	619	35.7	283	159	142	529	(30.5%)
EL	2.46	0.61	3	0.94	1.08	870	57.4	389	124	50	82	(5.4%)
ES	2.24	0.39	0	0.47	0.66	523	69.9	162	33	14	16	(2.1%)
FA	2.16	0.27	0	0.42	0.7	2243	82.9	202	103	60	99	(3.7%)
FR	2.29	0.44	1	0.65	0.8	2761	61.9	1116	336	125	123	(2.8%)
HE	2.71	0.75	0	0.47	0.74	1011	78.9	129	54	43	45	(3.5%)
HU	4.78	13.27	2205	1.01	1.29	506	63.7	178	34	15	61	(7.7%)
IT	2.59	0.64	2	0.28	0.46	1580	80.9	278	56	22	16	(0.8%)
LT	2.35	0.53	0	0.72	0.94	261	64.9	79	36	9	17	(4.2%)
MT	2.66	0.69	7	0.34	0.53	589	77.0	123	33	12	8	(1.0%)
PL	2.11	0.2	0	0.53	0.77	2307	73.3	470	195	90	87	(2.8%)
PT	2.24	0.41	76	0.67	0.78	1964	58.3	1016	223	82	86	(2.6%)
RO	2.15	0.25	1	0.55	0.72	2612	64.7	689	693	32	13	(0.3%)
SL	2.28	0.44	14	1.47	1.54	787	44.4	445	221	118	202	(11.4%)
SV	2.14	0.25	0	0.38	0.59	44	78.6	7	3	1	1	(1.8%)
TR	2.06	0.11	3	0.57	0.57	3043	49.4	2900	162	33	28	(0.5%)

Table 6: Length in number of tokens of VMWEs and of discontinuities in the training corpora. Columns 1-3: average and mean absolute deviation (MAD) for length, number of VMWEs with length 1 (=1). Columns 4-10: average and MAD for the length of discontinuities, absolute and relative number of continuous VMWEs, number of VMWEs with discontinuities of length 1, 2 and 3. Last 2 columns: absolute and relative number of VMWEs with discontinuities of length > 3.

Lang	System	Track	P-MWE	R-MWE	F-MWE	Rank-MWE	P-token	R-token	F-token	Rank-token
DE	SZEGED	closed	0.5154	0.3340	0.4053	2	0.6592	0.3468	0.4545	1
DE	TRANSITION	closed	0.5503	0.3280	0.4110	1	0.5966	0.3133	0.4109	2
DE	ADAPT	closed	0.3308	0.1740	0.2280	3	0.7059	0.2837	0.4048	3
DE	MUMULS	closed	0.3277	0.1560	0.2114	4	0.6988	0.2286	0.3445	4
DE	RACAI	closed	0.3652	0.1300	0.1917	5	0.6716	0.1793	0.2830	5
SV	ADAPT	closed	0.4860	0.2203	0.3032	2	0.5253	0.2249	0.3149	1
SV	SZEGED	closed	0.2482	0.2966	0.2703	3	0.2961	0.3294	0.3119	2
SV	TRANSITION	closed	0.5100	0.2161	0.3036	1	0.5369	0.2150	0.3070	3
SV	RACAI	closed	0.5758	0.1610	0.2517	4	0.6538	0.1677	0.2669	4

Table 7: Results for Germanic languages.

Lang	System	Track	P-MWE	R-MWE	F-MWE	Rank-MWE	P-token	R-token	F-token	Rank-token
BG	TRANSITION	closed	0.6887	0.5518	0.6127	1	0.7898	0.5691	0.6615	1
BG	MUMULS	closed	0.3581	0.3362	0.3468	2	0.7686	0.4809	0.5916	2
CS	TRANSITION	closed	0.7897	0.6560	0.7167	1	0.8246	0.6655	0.7365	1
CS	ADAPT	closed	0.5931	0.5621	0.5772	3	0.8191	0.6561	0.7286	2
CS	RACAI	closed	0.7009	0.5918	0.6418	2	0.8190	0.6228	0.7076	3
CS	MUMULS	closed	0.4413	0.1028	0.1667	4	0.7747	0.1387	0.2352	4
LT	TRANSITION	closed	0.6667	0.1800	0.2835	1	0.6786	0.1557	0.2533	1
LT	MUMULS	closed	0.0000	0.0000	0.0000	n/a	0.0000	0.0000	0.0000	n/a
PL	ADAPT	closed	0.7798	0.6020	0.6795	2	0.8742	0.6228	0.7274	1
PL	TRANSITION	closed	0.7709	0.6260	0.6909	1	0.8000	0.6312	0.7056	2
PL	MUMULS	closed	0.6562	0.5460	0.5961	3	0.8310	0.6013	0.6977	3
PL	SZEGED	closed	0.0000	0.0000	0.0000	n/a	0.0000	0.0000	0.0000	n/a
SL	TRANSITION	closed	0.4343	0.4300	0.4322	1	0.4796	0.4522	0.4655	1
SL	MUMULS	closed	0.3557	0.2760	0.3108	3	0.6142	0.3628	0.4562	2
SL	ADAPT	closed	0.5142	0.2900	0.3708	2	0.7285	0.3262	0.4506	3
SL	RACAI	closed	0.5503	0.2080	0.3019	4	0.7339	0.2145	0.3320	4

Table 8: Results for Balto-Slavic languages.

Lang	System	Track	P-MWE	R-MWE	F-MWE	Rank-MWE	P-token	R-token	F-token	Rank-token
ES	TRANSITION	closed	0.6122	0.5400	0.5739	1	0.6574	0.5252	0.5839	1
ES	ADAPT	closed	0.6105	0.3480	0.4433	2	0.7448	0.3670	0.4917	2
ES	MUMULS	closed	0.3673	0.3100	0.3362	4	0.6252	0.3995	0.4875	3
ES	SZEGED	closed	0.2575	0.5000	0.3399	3	0.3635	0.5629	0.4418	4
ES	RACAI	closed	0.6447	0.1960	0.3006	5	0.7233	0.1967	0.3093	5
FR	ADAPT	closed	0.6147	0.4340	0.5088	2	0.8088	0.4964	0.6152	1
FR	TRANSITION	closed	0.7484	0.4700	0.5774	1	0.7947	0.4856	0.6028	2
FR	RACAI	closed	0.7415	0.3500	0.4755	3	0.7872	0.3673	0.5009	3
FR	SZEGED	closed	0.0639	0.0520	0.0573	6	0.5218	0.2482	0.3364	4
FR	MUMULS	closed	0.1466	0.0680	0.0929	5	0.5089	0.2067	0.2940	5
FR	LIF	closed	0.8056	0.0580	0.1082	4	0.8194	0.0532	0.1000	6
FR	LATL	open	0.4815	0.4680	0.4746	1	0.5865	0.5108	0.5461	1
IT	TRANSITION	closed	0.5354	0.3180	0.3990	1	0.6134	0.3378	0.4357	1
IT	SZEGED	closed	0.1503	0.1560	0.1531	4	0.4054	0.3064	0.3490	2
IT	ADAPT	closed	0.6174	0.1420	0.2309	2	0.6964	0.1532	0.2511	3
IT	RACAI	closed	0.6125	0.0980	0.1690	3	0.6837	0.1053	0.1824	4
PT	TRANSITION	closed	0.7543	0.6080	0.6733	1	0.8005	0.6370	0.7094	1
PT	ADAPT	closed	0.6410	0.5320	0.5814	2	0.8348	0.6054	0.7018	2
PT	MUMULS	closed	0.5358	0.3740	0.4405	3	0.8247	0.4717	0.6001	3
PT	SZEGED	closed	0.0129	0.0080	0.0099	4	0.6837	0.1987	0.3079	4
RO	MUMULS	closed	0.7683	0.7760	0.7721	2	0.8620	0.8112	0.8358	1
RO	ADAPT	closed	0.7548	0.7140	0.7338	4	0.8832	0.7636	0.8190	2
RO	TRANSITION	closed	0.7097	0.8020	0.7531	3	0.7440	0.8449	0.7912	3
RO	RACAI	closed	0.8652	0.7060	0.7775	1	0.8773	0.7019	0.7799	4

Table 9: Results for Romance languages.

Lang	System	Track	P-MWE	R-MWE	F-MWE	Rank-MWE	P-token	R-token	F-token	Rank-token
EL	TRANSITION	closed	0.3612	0.4500	0.4007	1	0.4635	0.4742	0.4688	1
EL	ADAPT	closed	0.3437	0.2880	0.3134	4	0.5380	0.3601	0.4314	2
EL	MUMULS	closed	0.2087	0.2580	0.2308	5	0.4294	0.4143	0.4217	3
EL	SZEGED	closed	0.3084	0.3300	0.3188	2	0.4451	0.3757	0.4075	4
EL	RACAI	closed	0.4286	0.2520	0.3174	3	0.5616	0.2953	0.3871	5
FA	TRANSITION	closed	0.8770	0.8560	0.8664	1	0.9159	0.8885	0.9020	1
FA	ADAPT	closed	0.7976	0.8040	0.8008	2	0.8660	0.8416	0.8536	2
HE	TRANSITION	closed	0.7397	0.2160	0.3344	1	0.7537	0.1975	0.3130	1
HE	MUMULS	closed	0.0000	0.0000	0.0000	n/a	0.0000	0.0000	0.0000	n/a
HU	SZEGED	closed	0.7936	0.6934	0.7401	1	0.8057	0.6317	0.7081	1
HU	MUMULS	closed	0.6291	0.6152	0.6221	5	0.7132	0.6657	0.6886	2
HU	TRANSITION	closed	0.6484	0.7575	0.6987	2	0.6502	0.7012	0.6747	3
HU	ADAPT	closed	0.7570	0.5992	0.6689	3	0.7846	0.5710	0.6610	4
HU	RACAI	closed	0.8029	0.5471	0.6508	4	0.8208	0.5015	0.6226	5
MT	TRANSITION	closed	0.1565	0.1340	0.1444	1	0.1843	0.1460	0.1629	1
MT	ADAPT	closed	0.2043	0.0380	0.0641	2	0.3084	0.0518	0.0887	2
MT	RACAI	closed	0.2333	0.0280	0.0500	3	0.2481	0.0259	0.0469	3
MT	MUMULS	closed	0.0000	0.0000	0.0000	n/a	0.0000	0.0000	0.0000	n/a
TR	TRANSITION	closed	0.6106	0.5070	0.5540	1	0.6123	0.5039	0.5528	1
TR	ADAPT	closed	0.4541	0.4052	0.4283	3	0.5993	0.4728	0.5285	2
TR	RACAI	closed	0.6304	0.4391	0.5176	2	0.6340	0.4348	0.5159	3
TR	MUMULS	closed	0.4557	0.2774	0.3449	4	0.6452	0.3502	0.4540	4

Table 10: Results for other languages.

Linguistics: Technical Papers, pages 1875–1885, Dublin, Ireland, August. Dublin City University and Association for Computational Linguistics.

Xiaoqiang Luo. 2005. On Coreference Resolution Performance Metrics. In *Proceedings of Human Language Technology Conference and Conference on Empirical Methods in Natural Language Processing*, pages 25–32, Vancouver, British Columbia, Canada, October. Association for Computational Linguistics.

Yann Mathet, Antoine Widlöcher, and Jean-Philippe Métivier. 2015. The unified and holistic method gamma (γ) for inter-annotator agreement measure and alignment. *Computational Linguistics*, 41(3):437–479.

Ryan McDonald, Joakim Nivre, Yvonne Quirmbach-Brundage, Yoav Goldberg, Dipanjan Das, Kuzman Ganchev, Keith Hall, Slav Petrov, Hao Zhang, Oscar Täckström, Claudia Bedini, Núria Bertomeu Castelló, and Jungmee Lee. 2013. Universal Dependency Annotation for Multilingual Parsing. In *Proceedings of the 51st Annual Meeting of the Association for Computational Linguistics (Volume 2: Short Papers)*, pages 92–97, Sofia, Bulgaria, August. Association for Computational Linguistics.

Alexis Nasr, Carlos Ramisch, José Deulofeu, and André Valli. 2015. Joint Dependency Parsing and Multiword Expression Tokenization. In *Proceedings of the 53rd Annual Meeting of the Association for Computational Linguistics and the 7th International Joint Conference on Natural Language Processing (Volume 1: Long Papers)*, pages 1116–1126, Beijing, China, July. Association for Computational Linguistics.

Joakim Nivre and Veronika Vincze. 2015. Light Verb Constructions in Universal Dependencies. In *IC1207 COST PARSEME 5th general meeting*, Iaşi, Romania.

Siva Reddy, Diana McCarthy, and Suresh Manandhar. 2011. An Empirical Study on Compositionality in Compound Nouns. In *Proceedings of 5th International Joint Conference on Natural Language Processing*, pages 210–218, Chiang Mai, Thailand, November. Asian Federation of Natural Language Processing.

Victoria Rosén, Gyri Smørdal Losnegaard, Koenraad De Smedt, Eduard Bejček, Agata Savary, Adam Przepiórkowski, Petya Osenova, and Verginica Barbu Mititelu. 2015. A survey of multiword expressions in treebanks. In *Proceedings of the 14th International Workshop on Treebanks & Linguistic Theories conference*, Warsaw, Poland, December.

Ivan A. Sag, Timothy Baldwin, Francis Bond, Ann Copestake, and Dan Flickinger. 2002. Multiword Expressions: A Pain in the Neck for NLP. In *Proceedings of the 3rd International Conference on Intelligent Text Processing and Computational Linguistics (CICLing-2002)*, pages 1–15, Mexico City, Mexico.

Nathan Schneider, Emily Danchik, Chris Dyer, and Noah A. Smith. 2014a. Discriminative lexical semantic segmentation with gaps: running the MWE gamut. *Transactions of the Association for Computational Linguistics*, 2:193–206, April.

Nathan Schneider, Spencer Onuffer, Nora Kazour, Emily Danchik, Michael T. Mordowanec, Henrietta Conrad, and Noah A. Smith. 2014b. Comprehensive Annotation of Multiword Expressions in a Social Web Corpus. In Nicoletta Calzolari (Conference Chair), Khalid Choukri, Thierry Declerck, Hrafn Loftsson, Bente Maegaard, Joseph Mariani, Asuncion Moreno, Jan Odijk, and Stelios Piperidis, editors, *Proceedings of the Ninth International Conference on Language Resources and Evaluation (LREC'14)*, Reykjavik, Iceland, may. European Language Resources Association (ELRA).

Nathan Schneider, Dirk Hovy, Anders Johannsen, and Marine Carpuat. 2016. SemEval-2016 Task 10: Detecting Minimal Semantic Units and their Meanings (DiMSUM). In *Proceedings of the 10th International Workshop on Semantic Evaluation (SemEval-2016)*, pages 546–559, San Diego, California, June. Association for Computational Linguistics.

Yuancheng Tu and Dan Roth. 2011. Learning English Light Verb Constructions: Contextual or Statistical. In *Proceedings of the Workshop on Multiword Expressions: from Parsing and Generation to the Real World*, pages 31–39, Portland, Oregon, USA, June. Association for Computational Linguistics.

Yuancheng Tu and Dan Roth. 2012. Sorting out the Most Confusing English Phrasal Verbs. In *Proceedings of the First Joint Conference on Lexical and Computational Semantics - Volume 1: Proceedings of the Main Conference and the Shared Task, and Volume 2: Proceedings of the Sixth International Workshop on Semantic Evaluation*, SemEval '12, pages 65–69, Stroudsburg, PA, USA. Association for Computational Linguistics.

Zdenka Uresová, Eduard Bejcek, and Jan Hajic. 2016. Inherently pronominal verbs in czech: Description and conversion based on treebank annotation. In Valia Kordoni, Kostadin Cholakov, Markus Egg, Stella Markantonatou, and Preslav Nakov, editors, *Proceedings of the 12th Workshop on Multiword Expressions, MWE@ACL 2016, Berlin, Germany, August 11, 2016*. The Association for Computer Linguistics.

Maarten van Gompel and Martin Reynaert. 2013. FoLiA: A practical XML format for linguistic annotation - a descriptive and comparative study. *Computational Linguistics in the Netherlands Journal*, 3:63–81, 12/2013.

Veronika Vincze and János Csirik. 2010. Hungarian Corpus of Light Verb Constructions. In *Proceedings of the 23rd International Conference on Computational Linguistics (Coling 2010)*, pages 1110–1118, Beijing, China. Coling 2010 Organizing Committee.

Veronika Vincze, István Nagy T., and Gábor Berend. 2011. Multiword Expressions and Named Entities in the Wiki50 Corpus. In *Proceedings of the International Conference Recent Advances in Natural Language Processing 2011*, pages 289–295, Hissar, Bulgaria, September. RANLP 2011 Organising Committee.

Veronika Vincze, János Zsibrita, and István Nagy T. 2013. Dependency Parsing for Identifying Hungarian Light Verb Constructions. In *Proceedings of the Sixth International Joint Conference on Natural Language Processing*, pages 207–215, Nagoya, Japan, October. Asian Federation of Natural Language Processing.

Jakub Waszczuk, Agata Savary, and Yannick Parmentier. 2016. Promoting multiword expressions in A* TAG parsing. In Nicoletta Calzolari, Yuji Matsumoto, and Rashmi Prasad, editors, *COLING 2016, 26th International Conference on Computational Linguistics, Proceedings of the Conference: Technical Papers, December 11-16, 2016, Osaka, Japan*, pages 429–439. ACL.

Eric Wehrli, Violeta Seretan, and Luka Nerima. 2010. Sentence Analysis and Collocation Identification. In *Proceedings of the Workshop on Multiword Expressions: from Theory to Applications (MWE 2010)*, pages 27–35, Beijing, China, August. Association for Computational Linguistics.

Eric Wehrli. 2014. The Relevance of Collocations for Parsing. In *Proceedings of the 10th Workshop on Multiword Expressions (MWE)*, pages 26–32, Gothenburg, Sweden, April. Association for Computational Linguistics.

USzeged: Identifying Verbal Multiword Expressions with POS Tagging and Parsing Techniques

Katalin Ilona Simkó[1], Viktória Kovács[2] and Veronika Vincze[3]

[1,3]University of Szeged, Institute of Informatics
[1,2]University of Szeged, Department of General Linguistics
[3]MTA-SZTE Research Group on Artificial Intelligence
[1]`simko@hung.u-szeged.hu`
[2]`viktoria.kovacs12@gmail.com`
[3]`vinczev@inf.u-szeged.hu`

Abstract

The paper describes our system submitted for the Workshop on PARSEME's Shared Task on automatic identification of verbal multiword expressions . It uses POS tagging and dependency parsing to identify single- and multi-token verbal MWEs in text. Our system is language-independent and competed on nine of the eighteen languages. Our paper describes how our system works and gives its error analysis for the languages it was submitted for.

1 Introduction

In our paper, we give a description of the USzeged team's system for the shared task on automatic identification of verbal multiword expressions. We used POS tagging and dependency parsing to identify the verbal MWEs in the text. Our system is language-independent, but relies on POS tagged, dependency analyzed training data. We submitted results for nine out of the eighteen languages, but could be extended to any language if provided with POS tagging and dependency analysis of the training database.

In the paper, we first describe how the system works in detail, then show the results achieved in the shared task on the nine languages with both POS tagging and dependency analysis, last we give an error analysis of our output.

2 Shared task

Our system was built for the shared task on automatic identification of verbal multiword expressions[1] organized as part of the 2017 MWE workshop.

The shared task's aim is to identify verbal MWEs in multiple languages. In total, 18 languages are covered that were annotated using guidelines taking universal and language-specific phenomena into account.

The guideline identifies five different types of verbal MWEs: idioms (ID), light verb constructions (LVC), verb-particle constructions (VPC), inherently reflexive verbs (IRefIV) and other. Their identification in NLP is difficult because they are often discontinuous and non-compositional, the categories are heterogeneous and the structures show high syntactic variability.

Our team created the Hungarian shared task database and VMWE annotation. Our system is mostly based on our experiences with the Hungarian data in this annotation phase.

3 System description

Our system works through the connection of MWEs and parsing, an approach described by many sources (Constant and Nivre, 2016; Nasr et al., 2015; Candito and Constant, 2014; Green et al., 2011; Waszczuk et al., 2016; Wehrli et al., 2010; Green et al., 2013) and is one the basic ideas behind the work done by the PARSEME group [2].

The idea for our system is directly based on the work described in Vincze et al. (2013) to use dependency parsing to find MWEs. As a high number of the languages of the shared task are morphologically rich and have free word order, therefore syntactically flexible MWEs might not be adjacent, this approach seems a better fit for the task than sequence labeling or similar strategies.

The system of that paper uses dependency relations specific to syntactic relation and MWE type, for example light verb constructions that are made up of a verb-object relation syntactically, get the

---

[1]`http://multiword.sourceforge.net/`
`PHITE.php?sitesig=CONF&page=CONF_05_MWE_`
`2017___lb__EACL__rb__&subpage=CONF_40_`
`Shared_Task`

[2]`http://typo.uni-konstanz.de/parseme/`

Proceedings of the 13th Workshop on Multiword Expressions (MWE 2017), pages 48–53,
Valencia, Spain, April 4. ©2017 Association for Computational Linguistics

label OBJ-LVC in the merged annotation.

In contrast, our system uses only the MWE type as a merged dependency label and it also applies to single-token MWEs. As multiple languages had single-token MWEs as well as multi-token ones dealt with in dependency parsing, we expanded the approach using POS tagging.

MWEs have specific morphological, syntactic and semantic properties. Our approach treats multi-token MWEs on the level of syntax – similarly to the MWE dependency relation in the Universal Dependency grammar (Nivre, 2015) – and single-token MWEs on the level of morphology.

Our system works in four steps, and the main MWE identification happens within POS tagging and dependency parsing of the text. Our system relies on the POS tagging and dependency annotations provided by the organizers of the shared task in the companion CoNLL files and the verbal MWE annotation of the texts and is completely language-independent given those inputs.

In the first step, we prepared the training file from the above mentioned inputs. We merged the training MWE annotation into its dependency annotation for single and multi-token MWEs separately. The single-token MWEs POS tag got replaced with their MWE type, while for the multi-token MWEs the dependency graphs' label changed: the label of the token lower in the tree was replaced with a label with the MWE type.

Figures 1-3 show the single-token MWE's change in POS tag and multi-token MWE dependency relabeling for VPCs and LVCs in a Hungarian example.

For multi-token MWEs our approach is based on our theory that the lower MWE element will be directly connected to the other MWE element(s). We do not change the structure of the dependency relations in the tree, but change the dependency label of the lower MWE element to the MWE type, therefore making the MWE element retraceable from the dependency annotation of the sentence. For example *lát* and *el* in Example 2 make up a VPC, so the dependency relation label of the lower element, *el* changes from the general syntactic label **PREVERB** to the MWE label **VPC**, with this **VPC** label now connecting the two elements of the MWE.

For MWEs of more than two tokens, the conversion replaces the dependency labels of all MWE elements below the highest one. In example 4, the highest element of the idiom *az első követ veti* ("casts the first stone") is the verb, *vetette* (cast.Sg3.Past). All other elements' dependency labels are changed to **ID**.

The second step is training the parser: we used the Bohnet parser (Bohnet, 2010) for both POS tagging and dependency parsing. For the single-token MWEs, we trained the Bohnet parser's POS tagger module on the MWE-merged corpora and its dependency parser for the multi-token MWEs. The parser would treat the MWE POS tags and dependency labels as any other POS tag and dependency label.

We did the same for each language and created POS tagging and dependency parsing models capable of identifying MWEs for them. In the case of some of the languages in the shared task, we had to omit sentences from the training data that were overly long (spanning over 500 tokens in some cases) and caused errors in training.

Third, we ran the POS tagging and dependency parsing models of each language on their respective test corpora. The output contains the MWE POS tags and dependency labels used in that language as well as the standard POS and syntactic ones.

The fourth and last step is to extract the MWE tags and labels from the output of the POS tagger and the dependency parser. The MWE POS tagged words are annotated as single-token MWEs of the type of their POS tag. From the MWE dependency labels, we annotate the words connected by the MWE label as making up a multi-token MWE of that type.

4 Results

We submitted our system for all languages in the shared task with provided dependency analysis and POS tagging. POS tagging was needed for the single-token MWEs frequent in some languages, while we used dependency analysis in identifying multi-token MWEs. We attempted to use just the POS tagging component of our system on the languages that only had POS tagging available to give partial results (i.e. identifying only single-token MWEs), but we found that these languages incidentally had no or very few single-token MWEs, therefore not providing adequate training data.

Our results on the nine languages are in Table 1. Our system was submitted for German, Greek, Spanish, French, Hungarian, Italian, Polish, Por-

bekezdés	NOUN	SubPOS=c|Num=s|Cas=n|NumP=none|PerP=none|NumPd=none
bekezdés	VPC	SubPOS=c|Num=s|Cas=n|NumP=none|PerP=none|NumPd=none
határozathozatal	NOUN	SubPOS=c|Num=s|Cas=n|NumP=none|PerP=none|NumPd=none
határozathozatal	LVC	SubPOS=c|Num=s|Cas=n|NumP=none|PerP=none|NumPd=none

Figure 1: Adding the VPC and LVC single-token MWE POS tags to *bekezdés* (lit. in+starting, "paragraph") and *határozathozatal* (lit. decision+bringing, "decision-making").

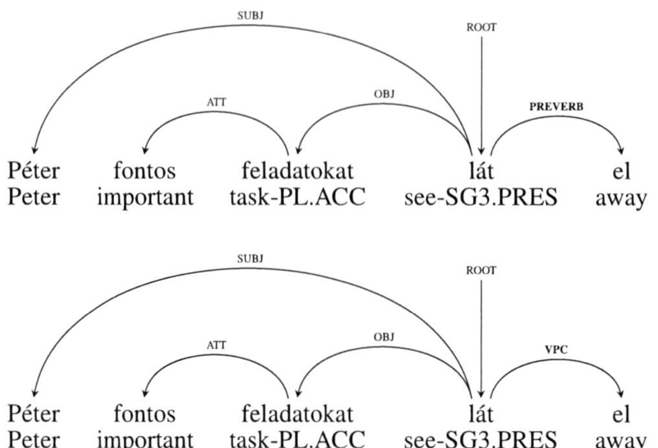

Figure 2: Adding the VPC multi-token MWEs label to the dependency graph in the sentence *Peter takes care of important tasks*.

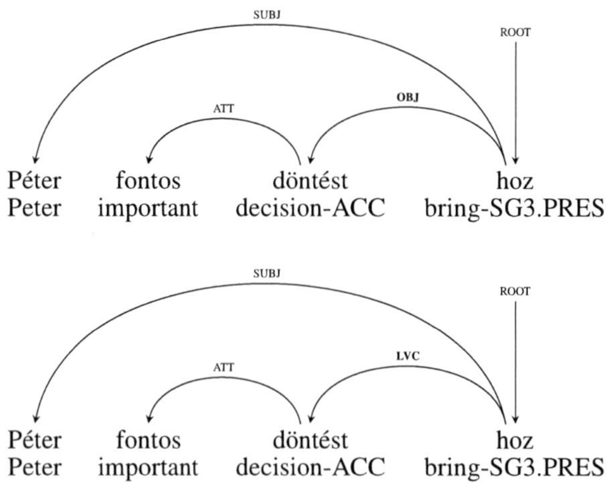

Figure 3: Adding the LVC multi-token MWE label to the dependency graph in the sentence *Peter makes an important decision*.

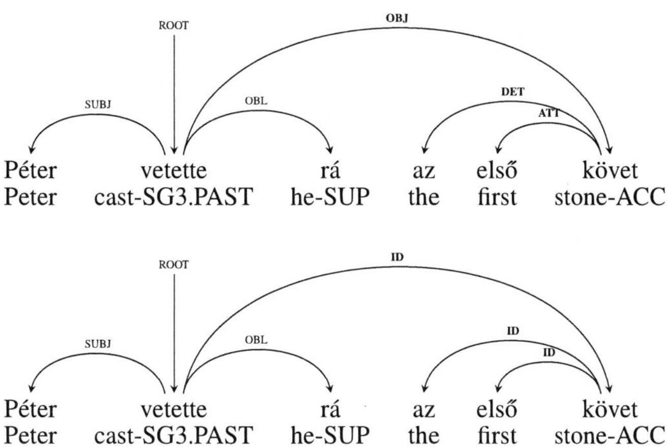

Figure 4: Adding the ID multi-token MWE label to the dependency graph in the sentence *Peter cast the first stone on him.*

tuguese, and Swedish.

The F-scores show great differences between languages, but so did they for the other systems entered. Compared to the other, mostly closed track systems, the USzeged system ranked close to or at the top on German, Hungarian, and Swedish. For the other languages (except for Polish and Portuguese, where ours is the worst performing system), we ranked in the mid-range. These results are related to the way our system works and the verbal MWE types frequent in the languages.

5   Error analysis

After receiving the gold annotation for the test corpora, we investigated the strengths and weaknesses of our system.

The shared task data was annotated for five types of verbal MWEs: light verb constructions, verb-particle constructions, inherently reflexive verbs, idioms, and "other".

Our error analysis showed that our system performs by far best on the verb-particle construction category, correctly identifying around 60% of VPCs, but only about 40% of other types. Verb-particle constructions are most likely to have a syntactic relationship between the MWE elements, which would support why our system is good at identifying them.

German, Hungarian, and Swedish were also the languages with the highest proportions of the VPC type of verbal MWEs in the shared task, which also correlates with why our system performed best on them. Romance languages contain almost no VPCs and the remaining ones have much less also. In this way, our achieved results seem to be dependent on the type of verbal MWEs frequent in that language because of the inherent characteristics of the system.

For French and Italian, our system also performed worse on IRefIVs. Generally, we had some trouble identifying longer IDs and LVCs and MWEs including prepositions. A further source of error was when there was no syntactic edge in between members of a specific MWE, for instance, in German, the copula *sein* "be" was often indirectly connected to the other words of the MWE (e.g. *im Rennen sein* "to compete"), hence our method was not able to recognize it as part of the MWE. We plan to revise our system to not only relabel dependency relations, but also restructure a tree in an attempt to deal with these issues.

6   Conclusions

In our paper, we described the USzeged verbal MWE identifying tool developed for the PARSEME Shared Task. Our system merged the MWE annotation with the POS tagging and dependency annotation of the text and used a standard POS tagger and dependency parser to identify verbal MWEs in texts. The system is language-independent given those inputs, but the overall results it achieves seem to rely on the type of verbal MWEs frequent in the given language.

	System	P-MWE	R-MWE	F-MWE	P-token	R-token	F-token
DE	BEST, USZEGED	0.5154	0.3340	0.4053	0.6592	0.3468	0.4545
	LAST	0.3652	0.1300	0.1917	0.6716	0.1793	0.2830
EL	BEST	0.3612	0.4500	0.4007	0.4635	0.4742	0.4688
	USZEGED	0.3084	0.3300	0.3188	0.4451	0.3757	0.4075
	LAST	0.4286	0.2520	0.3174	0.5616	0.2953	0.3871
ES	BEST	0.6122	0.5400	0.5739	0.6574	0.5252	0.5839
	USZEGED	0.2575	0.5000	0.3399	0.3635	0.5629	0.4418
	LAST	0.6447	0.1960	0.3006	0.7233	0.1967	0.3093
FR	BEST	0.6147	0.4340	0.5088	0.8088	0.4964	0.6152
	USZEGED	0.0639	0.0520	0.0573	0.5218	0.2482	0.3364
	LAST	0.8056	0.0580	0.1082	0.8194	0.0532	0.1000
HU	BEST, USZEGED	0.7936	0.6934	0.7401	0.8057	0.6317	0.7081
	LAST	0.8029	0.5471	0.6508	0.8208	0.5015	0.6226
IT	BEST	0.5354	0.3180	0.3990	0.6134	0.3378	0.4357
	USZEGED	0.1503	0.1560	0.1531	0.4054	0.3064	0.3490
	LAST	0.6125	0.0980	0.1690	0.6837	0.1053	0.1824
PL	BEST	0.7798	0.6020	0.6795	0.8742	0.6228	0.7274
	LAST, USZEGED	0.0000	0.0000	0.0000	0.0000	0.0000	0.0000
PT	BEST	0.7543	0.6080	0.6733	0.8005	0.6370	0.7094
	LAST, USZEGED	0.0129	0.0080	0.0099	0.6837	0.1987	0.3079
SV	BEST	0.4860	0.2203	0.3032	0.5253	0.2249	0.3149
	USZEGED	0.2482	0.2966	0.2703	0.2961	0.3294	0.3119
	LAST	0.5758	0.1610	0.2517	0.6538	0.1677	0.2669

Table 1: Best, last and USzeged systems' results for the languages ranked by per-token F-scores.

References

Bernd Bohnet. 2010. Top accuracy and fast dependency parsing is not a contradiction. In *Proceedings of the 23rd International Conference on Computational Linguistics (Coling 2010)*, pages 89–97.

Marie Candito and Matthieu Constant. 2014. Strategies for contiguous multiword expression analysis and dependency parsing. In *Proceedings of the 52nd Annual Meeting of the Association for Computational Linguistics (Volume 1: Long Papers)*, pages 743–753, Baltimore, Maryland, June. Association for Computational Linguistics.

Matthieu Constant and Joakim Nivre. 2016. A transition-based system for joint lexical and syntactic analysis. In *Proceedings of the 54th Annual Meeting of the Association for Computational Linguistics (Volume 1: Long Papers)*, pages 161–171, Berlin, Germany, August. Association for Computational Linguistics.

Spence Green, Marie-Catherine de Marneffe, John Bauer, and Christopher D. Manning. 2011. Multiword expression identification with tree substitution grammars: A parsing tour de force with french. In *Proceedings of the 2011 Conference on Empirical Methods in Natural Language Processing*, pages 725–735, Edinburgh, Scotland, UK., July. Association for Computational Linguistics.

Spence Green, Marie-Catherine de Marneffe, and Christopher D. Manning. 2013. Parsing Models for Identifying Multiword Expressions. *Computational Linguistics*, 39(1):195–227.

Alexis Nasr, Carlos Ramisch, José Deulofeu, and André Valli. 2015. Joint dependency parsing and multiword expression tokenization. In *Proceedings of the 53rd Annual Meeting of the Association for Computational Linguistics and the 7th International Joint Conference on Natural Language Processing (Volume 1: Long Papers)*, pages 1116–1126, Beijing, China, July. Association for Computational Linguistics.

Joakim Nivre. 2015. Towards a Universal Grammar for Natural Language Processing. In Alexander Gelbukh, editor, *Computational Linguistics and Intelligent Text Processing*, pages 3–16. Springer.

Veronika Vincze, János Zsibrita, and István Nagy T. 2013. Dependency parsing for identifying hungarian light verb constructions. In *Proceedings of the Sixth International Joint Conference on Natural Language Processing*, pages 207–215, Nagoya, Japan, October. Asian Federation of Natural Language Processing.

Jakub Waszczuk, Agata Savary, and Yannick Parmentier. 2016. Promoting multiword expressions in A* TAG parsing. In *COLING 2016, 26th International Conference on Computational Linguistics, Proceedings of the Conference: Technical Papers, December 11-16, 2016, Osaka, Japan*, pages 429–439.

Eric Wehrli, Violeta Seretan, and Luka Nerima. 2010. Sentence analysis and collocation identification. In *Proceedings of the Workshop on Multiword Expressions: from Theory to Applications (MWE 2010)*, pages 27–35, Beijing, China, August. Association for Computational Linguistics.

Parsing and MWE Detection: Fips at the PARSEME Shared Task

Vasiliki Foufi and **Luka Nerima** and **Éric Wehrli**
LATL-CUI, University of Geneva
7 route de Drize
CH-1227 Carouge, Switzerland
{vasiliki.foufi, luka.nerima, eric.wehrli}@unige.ch

Abstract

Identifying multiword expressions (MWEs) in a sentence in order to ensure their proper processing in subsequent applications, like machine translation, and performing the syntactic analysis of the sentence are interrelated processes. In our approach, priority is given to parsing alternatives involving collocations, and hence collocational information helps the parser through the maze of alternatives, with the aim to lead to substantial improvements in the performance of both tasks (collocation identification and parsing), and in that of a subsequent task (machine translation). In this paper, we are going to present our system and the procedure that we have followed in order to participate to the open track of the PARSEME shared task on automatic identification of verbal multiword expressions (VMWEs) in running texts.

1 Introduction

Multiword expressions (MWEs) are lexical units consisting of more than one word (in the intuitive sense of 'word'). There are several types of MWEs, including idioms (*a frog in the throat, break a leg*), fixed phrases (*per se, by and large, rock'n roll*), noun compounds (*traffic light, cable car*), phrasal verbs (*look up, take off*), etc. While easily mastered by native speakers, their detection and/or their interpretation pose a major challenge for computational systems, due in part to their flexible and heterogeneous nature.

In our research, MWEs are categorized in five subclasses: compounds, discontinuous words, named entities, collocations and idioms. While the first three are expressions of lexical category

(N, V, Adj, etc.) and can therefore be listed along with simple words, collocations and idioms are expressions of phrasal category (NPs, VPs, etc.). The identification of compounds and named entities can be achieved during the lexical analysis, but the identification of discontinuous words (e.g. particle verbs or phrasal verbs), collocations and idioms requires grammatical data and should be viewed as part of the parsing process.

In this paper, we will primarily focus on collocations, roughly defined as arbitrary and conventional associations of two words (not counting grammatical words) in a particular grammatical configuration (adjective-noun, noun-noun, verb-object, etc.) and especially on the categories of verbal collocations defined in the framework of the PARSEME shared task.

Section 2 will give a brief review of MWEs and previous work. Section 3 will describe how our system handles MWEs, the way they are represented in its lexical database and will also be concerned with the treatment of collocation types which present a fair amount of syntactic flexibility (e.g. verb-object). For instance, verbal collocations may undergo syntactic processes such as passivization, relativization, interrogation and even pronominalization, which can leave the collocation constituents far away from each other and/or reverse their canonical order. Section 4 will present the modifications made in order to adapt our system to the requirements of the shared task and the section 5 the evaluation and results.

2 Multiword expressions: a brief review of related work

The standard approach in dealing with MWEs in parsing is to apply a 'words-with-spaces' preprocessing step, which marks the MWEs in the input sentence as units which will later be integrated as

54

Proceedings of the 13th Workshop on Multiword Expressions (MWE 2017), pages 54–59,
Valencia, Spain, April 4. ©2017 Association for Computational Linguistics

single blocks in the parse tree built during analysis (Brun, 1998; Zhang and Kordoni, 2006). This method is not really adequate for processing collocations. Unlike other expressions that are fixed or semi-fixed, several collocation types do not allow a 'words-with-spaces' treatment because they have a high morphosyntactic flexibility. On the other hand, Alegria et al. (2004) and Villavicencio et al. (2007) adopted a compositional approach to the encoding of MWEs, able to capture more morphosyntactically flexible MWEs. Alegria et al. (2004) showed that by using a MWE processor in the preprocessing stage, a significant improvement in the POS tagging precision is obtained. However, as argued by many researchers, e.g. (Heid, 1994; Seretan, 2011; Wehrli and Nerima, 2013), collocation identification is best performed on the basis of parsed material. This is due to the fact that collocations are co-occurrences of lexical items in a specific syntactic configuration. Additionally, Nasr et al. (2015) have developed a joint parsing and MWE identification model for the detection and representation of ambiguous complex function words. Constant and Nivre (2016) developed a transition-based parser which combines two factorized substructures: a standard tree representing the syntactic dependencies between the lexical elements of a sentence and a forest of lexical trees including MWE identified in the sentence.

3 The Fips parser

Our system is a multilingual parser, available for several languages, i.e. French, English, German, Italian, Spanish, Modern Greek, Romanian and Portuguese (Wehrli, 2007; Wehrli and Nerima, 2015). It relies on generative grammar concepts and is basically made up of a generic parsing module which can be refined in order to suit the specific needs of a particular language. It is a constituent parser that functions as follows: it scans an input string from left to right, without any backtracking. The parsing algorithm, iteratively, performs the following three steps:

- get the next lexical item and project the relevant phrasal category
  $X \rightarrow XP$, where $X \in \{V, N, Adj, ... \}$

- merge XP with the structure in its left context (the structure already built);

- (syntactically) interpret XP, triggering procedures

  - to build predicate-argument structures
  - to create chains linking preposed elements to their trace
  - to find the antecedent of (3rd person) personal pronouns

The parsing procedure is a one pass (no preprocessing, no post-processing) scan of the input text, using rules to build up constituent structures and (syntactic) interpretation procedures to determine the dependency relations between constituents (grammatical functions, etc.), including cases of long-distance dependencies. One of the key components of the parser is its lexicon which contains detailed morphosyntactic and semantic information, selectional properties, valency information, and syntactico-semantic features that are likely to influence the syntactic analysis.

3.1 The lexicon

The lexicon is built manually and contains fine grained information required by the parser. It is organized as a relational database with four main tables:

- **words**, representing all morphological forms (spellings) of the words of a language, grouped into inflectional paradigms;

- **lexemes**, describing more abstract lexical forms which correspond to the syntactic and semantic readings of a word (a lexeme corresponds roughly to a standard dictionary entry);

- **collocations**, which describe multi-word expressions combining two lexical items, not counting function words;

- **variants**, which list all the alternative written forms for a word, e.g. the written forms of British English vs American English, the spellings introduced by a spelling reform, presence of both literary and modern forms in Greek, etc.

3.2 Representation of MWEs in the lexicon

In the introduction, we mentioned that in our research the MWEs are categorized in five subclasses, i.e. compounds, discontinuous words, named entities, collocations and idioms. Let's see how they are represented in the lexical database.

Compounds and named entities are represented by the same structure as simple words. An entry describes the syntactic and (some) semantic properties of the word: lexical category (POS), type (e.g. common noun, auxiliary verb), subtype, selectional features, argument structure, semantic features, thematic roles, etc. Each entry is associated with the inflectional paradigm of the word, that is all the inflected forms of the word along with the morphological features (number, gender, person, case, etc.). The possible spaces or hyphens of the compounds are processed at the lexical analyzer level in order to distinguish those that are separators from those belonging to the compound.

Discontinuous words, such as particle verbs or phrasal verbs, are represented in the same way as simple words as well, except that the orthographic string contains the bare verb only, the particle being represented separately in a specific field. The benefit of such an approach is that the phrasal verb inherits the inflectional paradigm of the basic verb. For agglutinative languages, a lexical analyzer will detect and separate the particle from the basic verb.

Collocations are defined as associations of two lexical units (not counting function words) in a specific syntactic relation (for instance adjective - noun, verb - noun (object), etc.). A lexical unit can be a word or a collocation. The definition is therefore recursive and enables to encode collocations that have more than two words. For instance, the French collocation *tomber en panne d'essence* ('to run out of gas') is composed of the word *tomber* and the collocation *panne d'essence*. Similarly, the English collocation *guaranteed minimum wage* is composed of the word *guaranteed* and collocation *minimum wage*.

In addition to the two lexical units, a collocation entry encodes the following information: the citation form, the collocation type (i.e. the syntactic relation between its two components), the preposition (if any) and a set of syntactic frozenness constraints.

For the time being, we represent idioms like collocations, with more restriction features (cannot passivize, no modifiers, etc.) and are, therefore, stored in the same database table. Reducing idioms to collocations with specific features, though convenient and appropriate for large classes of id-

ioms, is nevertheless not general enough. In particular, it does not allow for the representation of idioms with fixed phrases, such as *to get a foot in the door*.

3.3 Parsing and collocations

3.3.1 Collocation identification mechanism

The collocation identification mechanism is integrated in the parser. In the present version of the parser, collocations, if present in the lexicon, are identified in the input sentence during the analysis of that sentence, rather than at the end. In this way, priority can be given to parsing alternatives involving collocations. Thus collocational information helps the parser through the maze of alternatives as shown in Wehrli (2014). To fulfil the goal of interconnecting the parsing procedure and the identification of collocations, we have incorporated the collocation identification mechanism within the constituent attachment procedure (see next section). Our parser, like many grammar-based parsers, uses left attachment and right attachment rules to build respectively left subconstituents and right subconstituents. The grammar used for the computational modelling comprises rules and procedures. Attachment rules describe the conditions under which constituents can combine, while procedures compute properties such as long-distance dependencies, agreement, control properties, argument-structure building, and so on.

3.3.2 Treatment of collocations

The identification of a collocation occurs when the second lexical unit of the collocation is attached, either by means of a left attachment rule (e.g. adjective-noun, noun-noun) or by means of a right-attachment rule (e.g. noun-adjective, noun-prep-noun, verb-object). In the example *Paul took up a new challenge*, when the parser reads the noun *challenge* and attaches it (along with the prenominal adjective) as complement of the incomplete direct object of the verb *take up*, the identification procedure considers iteratively all the governing nodes of the attached noun and checks whether the association of the lexical head of the governing node and the attached element constitutes an entry in the collocation database. The process stops at the first governing node of a major category (noun, verb or adjective). In our example, going up from *challenge*, the process stops at the verb *take up*. Since *take up - challenge* is an entry in the collocation database and its type (verb-object) corresponds to the syntactic configuration, the identification process succeeds.

As already pointed out, in several cases the two constituents of a collocation can be very far apart, or do not appear in the expected order. For instance, verb-object collocations may undergo syntactic processes such as passivization, relativization, interrogation and even pronominalization, which can leave the collocation constituents far away from each other and/or reverse their canonical order.

In passive constructions, the direct object is promoted to the subject position leaving a trace, i.e. an empty constituent in the direct object position. The detection of a verb-object collocation in a passive sentence is thus triggered by the insertion of the empty constituent in direct object position. The collocation identification procedure checks whether the antecedent of the (empty) direct object and the verb constitute a (verb-object) collocation. In the example *The decision was made*, the noun *decision* of the collocation *to make a decision* precedes the verb.

Another transformation that can affect some collocation types is pronominalization. In such cases, it is important to identify the antecedent of the pronoun which can be found either in the same sentence or in the context. The example cited below illustrates a sentence where the pronoun *it* refers to the noun *money*. Since the pronoun is the subject of the passive form *would be well spent*, it is interpreted as direct object of the verb and therefore stands for an occurrence of the collocation *to spend money*:

...though where the money would come from, and how to ensure that it would be well spent, is unclear.

To handle them, the identification procedure sketched above must be slightly modified so that not only the attachment of a lexical item triggers the identification process, but also the attachment of the trace of a preposed lexical item. In such a case, the search will consider the antecedent of the trace. This shows, again, that the main advantage provided by a syntactic parser in such a task is its ability to identify collocations even when complex grammatical processes disturb the canonical order of constituents.

4 Setup for the shared task

In this section, we are going to present the experiment that was performed for French in the framework of the open track of the shared task on automatic identification of VMWEs and the modifications that were made to our parser in order to fulfill this task. Verbal MWEs include idioms (*let the cat out of the bag*), light verb constructions (*make a decision*), verb-particle constructions (*give up*)[1], and inherently reflexive verbs (*se taire, s'appuyer* 'to shut up', 'to rely on' in French).

4.1 Implementation

As the Fips parser already includes a collocation identification module and produces full syntactic trees for the constituents of the sentence, including the verbal constructions, our participation to the Shared Task consisted essentially in developing a transformation code between the PARSEME and Fips input - output formats. There were three kinds of transformation needed: (i) the reconstitution of the raw text from the tokenized one that was already provided (ii) the alignement of the provided tokens with the tokens generated by Fips and (iii) the copy of the Fips detected VMWE to the tokenized parsemetsv file, i.e. the annotation of the identified VMWEs.

4.1.1 Raw text

The Fips parser requires raw text input. This led us to develop a pre-processor that reconstructs the original text from the tokenized data provided for the shared task. This development was rather easy for French as the file included as a comment the original text for each given sentence. For the other languages, the pre-processor consisted in concatenating the tokens, taking into account the *ns* field indicating the presence or absence of a space character.

4.1.2 Tokens alignment

The shared task evaluation measures being token-based, for understandable evaluation reasons, the systems were asked to produce the results using strictly the same tokenization as those given in the data sets. In general, the parsemetsv and the Fips tokenization of words are identical but in numerous cases they differ. The trend in parsemetsv tokenization is to consider two words separated

---

[1]Verb-particle constructions don't exist in French, but they exist in German and English, languages for which we originally intended to participate.

by a space as two different tokens. On the other hand, the Fips tokenization procedure is based on linguistic criteria, i.e. a token is a significant lexical unit. Thus, Fips groups together two or more words if they form a complex lexical unit, for instance the French compound nouns *pomme de terre* ("potato"), the German preposition *je nach* ("according to") or complex fixed adverbial phrases such as *by and large*. On the other hand, Fips may treat single words as multiple tokens. For instance, the German compounds are decomposed, so that *Medaillengewinner* ("medal winner") will be presented as two tokens (*Medaillen* and *Gewinner*). The parsemetsv format exhibits some special treatment for some tokens, e.g. the contracted determiner *du* ("of the") in French that generates three lines of data or for the treatment of the hyphen.

What appeared at first glance like a first year Computer Science student assignment turn out to be a little bit more complicated.

4.1.3 VMWEs annotation

The Fips parser can produce several output formats: syntactic tree, tagger, XML/TEI, etc[2]. We chose the Fips tagger output developed for the SwissAdmin project (Scherrer et al., 2014) because it gives all the necessary information for the VMWE annotation and, like in pasemetsv, it outputs one token per line. In short, each (Fips) token is displayed on one line, divided in six columns: the token, the Universal POS tag, the richer Fips tag, the lemma, the grammatical function / valency (if any), the collocation (if any)[3]. The annotation of VMWEs is processed sentence by sentence and takes place as follows: the Fips output (aligned with the parsemetsv data file) is sequentially traversed line by line. For each verb token, the following tests are performed (in the following priority order). Note that in every case the annotations take place in the parsemetsv (aligned) data file:

- if the verb is reflexive, it is flagged; the Fips output is then traversed backward and the first encountered reflexive pronoun is flagged;

- if the verb is a light verb and the grammatical function displays a direct object, it is flagged; the Fips output is then traversed forward until the direct object is encountered; if the direct object is not encountered, a backward traversal is performed (in

order to deal with the passive forms);

- if the verb is impersonal, the verb is flagged; the algorithm looks for the subject in order to annotate it;

- if the verb is part of a verbal collocation, it is flagged as OTH (OTHER) and a treatment similar to the one for the light verb is performed in order to annotate the complement(s).

5 Evaluation and results

Evaluation metrics are precision, recall and F1, both strict (per VMWE) and fuzzy (per token, i.e. taking partial matches into account). The token-based F1 takes into account:

- discontinuities (*take something into account*);

- overlapping (*take a walk and then a long shower*);

- embeddings both at the syntactic level (*take the fact that I didn't give up into account*) and at the level of lexicalized components (*let the cat out of the bag*).

However, VMWE categories (e.g., LVC, ID, IReflV, VPC) were ignored by the evaluation metrics.

We measured the best F1 score from all possible matches between the set of MWE token ranks in the gold and system sentences by looking at all possible ways of matching MWEs in both sets. In the evaluation per MWE, our system achieved 0.4815 precision with a recall of 0.4680 and F-measure of 0.4746. In the evaluation per token, our system achieved 0.5865 precision with a recall of 0.5108 and F-measure of 0.5461.

6 Conclusion

The good performance achieved by the Fips system confirms that deep syntactic information helps to identify MWEs and especially VMWEs. Although the VMWE annotation would be more accurate if it was based on the syntactic tree, the "flat" rich tagger output chosen for the alignment ease with the required parsemetsv tokenization was a good solution. An enhancement to this output would be to implement a token identification scheme so as to establish explicit links between the verbs and their arguments (instead of sequentially traverse the sentence and rely on the orthographic form of the word).

---

[2]The Fips parsing service is available at http://latlapps.unige.ch/Parser

[3]See Scherrer et al. (2014) for more details and examples.

References

Iñaki Alegria, Olatz Ansa, Xabier Artola, Nerea Ezeiza, Koldo Gojenola, and Ruben Urizar. 2004. Representation and treatment of multiword expressions in basque. In Tanaka Takaaki, Aline Villavicencio, Francis Bond, and Anna Korhonen, editors, *Second acl workshop on multiword expressions: integrating processing*. Association for Computational Linguistics.

Caroline Brun. 1998. Terminology finite-state preprocessing for computational lfg. In *Proceedings of COLING 1998*, page 196–200.

Matthieu Constant and Joakim Nivre. 2016. A transition-based system for joint lexical and syntactic analysis. In *Proceedings of the 54th Annual Meeting of the Association for Computational Linguistics (Volume 1: Long Papers)*, pages 161–171, Berlin, Germany.

Ulrich Heid. 1994. On ways words work together – topics in lexical combinatorics. In *Proceedings of the 2007 Joint Conference on Empirical Methods in Natural Language Processing and Computational Natural Language Learning (EMNLP-CoNLL)*, Prague, Czech Republic.

Alexis Nasr, Carlos Ramisch, José Deulofeu, and André Valli. 2015. Joint dependency parsing and multiword expression tokenization. In *Proceedings of the 53rd Annual Meeting of the Association for Computational Linguistics and the 7th International Joint Conference on Natural Language Processing (Volume 1: Long Papers)*, pages 1116–1126, Beijing, China.

Yves Scherrer, Luka Nerima, Lorenza Russo, Maria Ivanova, and Eric Wehrli. 2014. Swissadmin: A multilingual tagged parallel corpus of press releases. In *Proceedings of the Ninth International Conference on Language Resources and Evaluation (LREC'14)*, Reykjavik, Iceland.

Violeta Seretan. 2011. *Syntax-Based Collocation Extraction*. Springer.

Aline Villavicencio, Valia Kordoni, Yi Zhang, Marco Idiart, and Carlos Ramisch. 2007. Validation and evaluation of automatically acquired multiword expressions for grammar engineering. In *Proceedings of the 2007 Joint Conference on Empirical Methods in Natural Language Processing and Computational Natural Language Learning (EMNLP-CoNLL)*, Prague, Czech Republic.

Eric Wehrli and Luka Nerima. 2013. Sentence analysis and collocation identification. In *Proceedings of the Workshop on Multiword Units in Machine Translation and Translation Technology, MT Summit XIV*, pages 12–17, Nice, France.

Eric Wehrli and Luka Nerima. 2015. The fips multilingual parser. In Nuria Gala, Reinhard Rapp, and G. Bel, editors, *Festschrift in honour of Michael Zock*. Springer.

Eric Wehrli. 2007. Fips, a deep linguistic multilingual parser. In *Proceedings of the ACL 2007 Workshop on Deep Linguistic Parsing*, pages 120–127, Prague, Czech Republic.

Eric Wehrli. 2014. The relevance of collocations for parsing. In *Proceedings of the 10th Workshop on Multiword Expressions, MWE@EACL 2014*, pages 26–32, Gothenburg, Sweden.

Yi Zhang and Valia Kordoni. 2006. Automated deep lexical acquisition for robust open texts processing. In *Proceedings of LREC-2006*, Genoa, Italy.

Neural Networks for Multi-Word Expression Detection

Natalia Klyueva[1], Antoine Doucet[2] and Milan Straka[1]

[1]Charles University, Prague, Czech Republic
[2]University of La Rochelle, France
{klyueva,straka}@ufal.mff.cuni.cz
{antoine.doucet}@univ-lr.fr

Abstract

In this paper we describe the MUMULS system that participated to the 2017 shared task on automatic identification of verbal multiword expressions (VMWEs). The MUMULS system was implemented using a supervised approach based on recurrent neural networks using the open source library TensorFlow. The model was trained on a data set containing annotated VMWEs as well as morphological and syntactic information. The MU-MULS system performed the identification of VMWEs in 15 languages, it was one of few systems that could categorize VMWEs type in nearly all languages.

1 Introduction

Multiword expressions (MWEs) present groups of words in which the meaning of the whole is not derived from the meaning of its parts. The task of processing multiword expressions is crucial in many NLP areas, such as machine translation, terminology extraction etc.

This paper describes the MUMULS system[1] which was evaluated through its participation to the PARSEME shared task on automatic identification of verbal MWEs[2] (VMWEs).

The experimental data set of the shared task is the result of a massive collaborative effort that produced training and evaluation data sets, available in 18 languages. The subsequent corpus was built by experts of each of the languages who manually annotated all VMWEs. The training and test sets respectively consist of a total of about 4.5 and 0.9

million tokens, containing 52,724 and 9,494 annotated VMWEs.

For most languages, a `.conllu` file provided morphological and syntactic information for each token. In addition, the training data set was indicating for each token, whether it belonged to an MWE, which one, and the type of that MWE. The MWE types are IReflV(inherently reflexive verb), LVC (light verb construction), VPC (Verb-particle construction), ID (idiomatic expression) and OTH - other types.

The goal of systems is to identify the VMWEs from text and to recognize to what type they belong. The data set and full evaluation procedure is more extensively described in the overview paper of the PARSEME shared task(Savary et al., 2017).

Since MUMULS did not make use of any other resources than those provided by the shared task organisers, the system participated in the "closed track" (as opposed to the open track, in which participants could make use of any external resources).

The rest of the paper is organised as follows. Section 2 describes the MUMULS system. We then present the results (Section 3) which are analysed in Section 4, before we conclude and suggest future works.

2 System description

For the task of automatic detection of multiword expression researchers use language-independent approaches that combine association measures like mutual information or dice coefficient with machine learning approaches (Tsvetkov and Wintner, 2011), (Pecina, 2008). Neural networks were exploited in a number of papers for the task very related to ours, e.g. (Martínez-Santiago et al., 2002). Our system does not directly use the techniques presented in the mentioned papers, but

---

[1]MUltilingual MULtiword Sequences
[2]http://multiword.sourceforge.net/
sharedtask2017

Proceedings of the 13th Workshop on Multiword Expressions (MWE 2017), pages 60–65,
Valencia, Spain, April 4. ©2017 Association for Computational Linguistics

some ideas behind are very similar to ours. Now that the annotated data described above are available for multiple languages, the natural thing is to exploit is a supervised approach, for which we have chosen deep artificial neural networks.

Deep learning algorithms have recently been applied to a vast majority of NLP tasks. Several frameworks to train deep models were introduced that simplify a lot the deploying process, like Theano, Torch, CNTK and recently an open source framework from Google Tensor-Flow,[3] which we used for training our MWE tagger, called *mwe_tagger*.[4]

Generally the task at hand resembles POS tagging, with inputs as various columns from them the CoNLL-U files, and outputs as the respective mwe tags from parsemetsv files.

Our model is based on a bi-directional recurrent neural network (Graves and Schmidhuber, 2005) with gated-recurrent units – GRUs (Cho et al., 2014). In (Chung et al., 2014) the GRUs performance is empirically evaluated and demonstrates sufficient results for long distance dependencies, which is especially important for processing discontinuous MWEs.

The linguistic attributes (features) used to predict the output tag and the output tag itself is extracted from the training data files `train.conllu` and `train.parsemetsv` combined and transformed into the following form (example for French):

```
Steffi    Steffi    PROPN    _
rend      rendre    VERB     LVC
visite    visite    NOUN     CONT
à         à         ADP      _
Monica    Monica    PROPN    _
```

Our model cannot take into account the numbering of MWEs in case more of them are present in one sentence, and we delete the numbers leaving only the name of MWE tags and substituting the continuation of the MWE with the symbol CONT.[5] For Romanian, the extended POS tag with more morphological features was used instead of UPOS tag. If the CoNLL-U file was not provided for a language, the lemma/POS attributes were substituted by underscores.

In the neural network, every input word is represented as a concatenation of embeddings of its form, lemma and POS tag. We use randomly initialized embeddings with dimension 100 for those three attributes.

We then process the words using a bi-directional recurrent neural network with single-layer GRUs of 100 cells. Finally we map the results for each word to an output layer with soft-max activation function returning the distribution of possible output tags.

The network is trained using Adam optimizer (Kingma and Ba, 2014) to minimize the cross-entropy loss, using fixed learning rate of 0.001 and default hyperparameters.

The model was trained using batches of 64 sentences, for 14 epochs. Increasing the number of epochs or batch size did not lead to any improvement in the accuracy.

We trained the model on a cluster with multi-core CPU machines with 8 parallel threads.

The converted data were split into training, development and test sets to set the initial model, taking the first 10 % of the corpus as a development set, consequent 80 % as a training set and the last 10 % as a test set. We did not perform any cross-validation using different parts for train, test and dev while training which may result in poor score for some languages when the blind test data might be very different from the training. The final model that was used to tag the blind test data was trained on the joined train and test sets from the initial experiments, with the development set staying the same.

The final evaluation of the system was made by the script provided by the organizers which measures precision, recall and F-score for token-based and MWE-based predictions.

3 Experiment Results

Table 1 presents the results of the MUMULS system for all the languages for which it produced non-zero results. Out of 18 available languages, MUMULS was experimented over 17. We found the bug that was introduced during data pre-processing for Czech language that caused recall issues, the re-trained model with very same setup as for other languages had higher score, which we additionally included in the result table. We did not include the languages for which we were not able to produce any predictions.

---

[3] `www.tensorflow.org`

[4] The scripts are available at `https://github.com/natalink/mwe_sharedtask`

[5] Our architecture unfortunately does not allow to handle properly neither embedding nor overlapping of MWEs.

Lang	P-MWE	R-MWE	F-MWE	P-token	R-token	F-token	Rank-MWE	Rank-token
DE	0.3277	0.1560	0.2114	0.6988	0.2286	0.3445	3	3
BG	0.3581	0.3362	0.3468	0.7686	0.4809	0.5916	2	2
CS	0.4413	0.1028	0.1667	0.7747	0.1387	0.2352	4	4
CS-fixed	0.6241	0.6875	0.6548	0.7629	0.7784	0.7705	2	1
PL	0.6562	0.5460	0.5961	0.8310	0.6013	0.6977	3	3
SL	0.3557	0.2760	0.3108	0.6142	0.3628	0.4562	3	2
ES	0.3673	0.3100	0.3362	0.6252	0.3995	0.4875	3	3
FR	0.1466	0.0680	0.0929	0.5089	0.2067	0.2940	5	4
PT	0.5358	0.3740	0.4405	0.8247	0.4717	0.6001	3	3
RO	0.7683	0.7760	0.7721	0.8620	0.8112	0.8358	2	1
EL	0.2087	0.2580	0.2308	0.4294	0.4143	0.4217	4	3
HU	0.6291	0.6152	0.6221	0.7132	0.6657	0.6886	4	1
TR	0.4557	0.2774	0.3449	0.6452	0.3502	0.4540	4	4

Table 1: Results of MUMULS, organized by language groups, separated by horizontal lines (Germanic, Slavic, Romance, others).

Table 2 provides the accuracy in terms of f-measure for the individual types of VMWEs. It can be seen that the system scored better in more 'syntactic' MWEs like IREflV, LVC or VPC, and generally (with the exception of French) the score for those categories is higher than for idioms.

4 Linguistic evaluation

We provide a short errors analysis for a couple of languages looking for possible reasons for the errors in tagging. Just to note, we do not do any statistical analysis, rather just observations on the test data.

Those observations should be taken with caution because slightly changing parameters of the algorithm may lead to different annotations (tags), making the provided observations inappropriate.

4.1 MWEs not seen in the training data

We did not use cross-validation, and one of the natural questions is how much the model overfit the training data and fail to generalize. Next are the examples of MWEs which are not present in the training data, but a construction was tagged in the test:

- Czech LVC: *přicházet s náměty* – 'come with proposals'. In training data a very similar construction with a synonymous predicative noun *přicházet s návrhy* – 'come with suggestions' is annotated, whereas in gold test the first one is not

- Bulgarian IReflV: The verb *se konsultira* – 'consulting' is not in train.parsemetsv, but yet marked by the mwe_tagger.

Thus, we can say that the mwe_tagger can make generalizations to some extent.

4.2 Analysis of distinct types of MWEs

We observe the following errors for several MWE types and for several languages:

- not all the tokens of an MWE are marked. This entails the difference between MWE-based and token-based scores from the Table 2. Examples:

  – In Czech the verb is marked as reflexive, but the particle is not tagged as the continuation of the MWE

  – Some of the LVC part is not tagged, generally it is a predicative noun. E.g. in Polish *mieć problem* – 'have problem' the word *problem* was not tagged.

  – The particular case is analytical tense formation, like e.g. future tense in Czech. In the MWE *se bude hodit* – 'will be useful' mwe_tagger marked only the reflexive particle and the verb, but not the auxiliary verb *bude* – 'will be' which has to be annotated according to the annotation guidelines, so it was also penalized by the evaluation script.

- a token is marked as MWE, while it should not.

  – Often the reason is that some similar construction is tagged in the training data, e.g. in French *Comment Angiox agit -il* – 'How does Angiox work' learned from numerous examples of an idiom *il s'agit* – 'it's about'.

  – Sometimes more tokens around LVC are marked without any logical explanation. In Polish, *po zgaszeniu-LVC zadawał-LVC pytanie-LVC* – 'after switching_off (he) put question' the word totally unrelated to LVC was marked, while it did not occur at all in the training data.

	LVC		IReflV		VPC		ID		OTH	
Lang	mwe	token	mwe	token	mwe	token	mwe	token	mwe	token
DE	0.00	0.06	0.01	0.02	0.14	0.24	0.04	0.22	0.00	0.00
BG	0.00	0.08	0.41	0.64	0.00	0.00	0.00	0.08	0.00	0.00
CS	0.12	0.19	0.65	**0.73**	0.00	0.00	0.05	0.11	0.00	0.00
PL	0.18	0.28	0.53	0.61	0.00	0.00	0.00	0.09	0.00	0.00
SL	0.00	0.01	0.33	0.47	0.10	0.20	0.02	0.09	0.00	0.00
ES	0.10	0.18	0.31	0.42	0.00	0.00	0.06	0.18	0.00	0.00
FR	0.02	0.09	0.02	0.11	0.00	0.00	0.12	**0.33**	0.00	0.00
PT	0.37	**0.49**	0.12	0.18	0.00	0.00	0.06	0.18	0.00	0.00
RO	0.26	0.35	0.55	0.62	0.00	0.00	0.03	0.13	0.00	0.00
EL	0.16	0.30	0.00	0.00	0.03	0.04	0.03	0.15	0.00	0.03
HE	0.07	0.16	0.00	0.00	0.06	0.13	0.00	0.03	0.03	0.12
HU	0.12	0.29	0.00	0.00	0.37	**0.51**	0.00	0.00	0.00	0.00
TR	0.30	0.38	0.00	0.00	0.00	0.00	0.17	0.24	0.09	0.14

Table 2: F-score for the distinct MWE categories

In addition to the above, we present observations on individual MWE types and the issues our tagger had with them.

4.2.1 IReflV

IReflV is the most frequent MWE tag, and it is relatively easy to identify reflexives in the text with the help of some rules. However, the mwe_tagger encountered several problems that we will demonstrate for a few languages:

- it is hard for an algorithm to distinguish between inherently reflexive verbs and other very structurally similar "deagentive", passive or reciprocal constructions, more see (Kettnerová and Lopatková, 2014), (Bejček et al., 2017) or the guidelines manual[6]. E.g. in Bulgarian, *se ubedjat* – '(they will) be convinced' was tagged by the mwe_tagger, but it was just passivisation from *ubedjat* – 'convince', not the true reflexive verb. In Polish *oblizując się* – 'licking (lips)' was also tagged, whereas it should not according to the guidelines definition.

- For French, there are two forms that clitic takes - full and contracted (in case it comes before a vowel). This might lead to some bias and thus influence the prediction results.

- For Portuguese, the system was supposedly confused by the clitic being either 1) separated by a hyphen within one token or 2) with a hyphen ending the verb and clitic on the next line: e.g. MWEs *refiro-me* – 'refer', *corresponder- se(next token)* – 'correspond' were not marked as such by mwe-tagger. The verb-clitic IReflV as two separate tokens without a hyphen were generally tagged by the system properly.

Overall, it seems like inherently reflexive verbs are more probable to be detected correctly for Slavic languages with the exception of Romanian. We can suggest that for Slavic languages the role of clitics is different than that in Romance languages, but that claim will need more thorough analysis of the annotated data.

4.2.2 LVC

The second most frequent MWE tag was LVC - light verb construction - an MWE generally formed by a verb and a noun where the verb looses its initial meaning and the whole construction takes the semantics of the noun. There are no consistent criteria on which expressions should be considered as LVC, and for this shared task the special tests were created on how to distinguish LVC from non-LVC.

Below are some examples of how the tagger tackled LVCs for different languages.

- Some LVC tokens might be marked as idioms (ID). In Czech,e.g. *dali pokoj* – 'lit. give piece – let alone' was predicted as LVC, whereas it is marked as idiom in the gold test file.

- In some cases the LVC are not marked, even though they are present in the training data, like LVC in Romanian *face referire* – 'referred to' was not tagged, though was quite frequent in the training data

[6]http://parsemefr.lif.univ-mrs.fr/
guidelines-hypertext/?page=060_Specific_
tests_-_categorize_VMWEs/040_Inherently_
reflexive_verbs

- Discontinuous LVCs where the components are separated by a number of other tokens, are often not detected. E.g. in Romanian *pune astfel accent* – 'put such emphasis' only one word in between the LVC components led to the predicative noun not to be tagged

In general, the score for LVC predictions is lower than that for IReflV.

4.2.3 Idioms

ID - idiom - was a tag which was very hard to detect. The F-measure for this tag never got more than 0.3 (for French), it was 0.1 in average. We have studied a Czech output file and all the idioms were coming from the training data.

The generalizations like in the case of IReflV or LVC constructions will not work and are not desirable in this case as this can lead to improper tagging, like in the following example in Czech. *nestál na vrcholu* – '(did not) stand on the top' was detected as an idiom(ID), though the meaning was literal in this case (*stand on the mountain top*). probably from one single example from the training data: *dosahnout vrcholu* – 'reach the top'.

For French language, the detection of idioms worked better than that for other categories. This may be, above all, attributed to the fact that idioms annotated in French were quite frequent in the training data, e.g. *il faut* – 'it is necessary' or *pris en compte* – 'take into account'.

For proper handling of the idioms, using special lexical resources will be the most efficient measure.

5 Conclusion

We have presented the system MUMULS that participated in the shared task of identification of MWEs. MUMULS was a neural network deployed within the framework TensorFlow that learned to detect MWEs based on manually annotated corpora. Overall, the systems participating in the closed track for some languages have approximately the same F-score while for others it may vary. The results of the shared task might as well depend on the consistency and quality of the annotations of the training data.

We are waiting for further details on other approaches so as to be able to better understand why our system outperformed other systems for some languages, and why it underperformed for some others.

Acknowledgments

The research was held during the PARSEME Short Term Scientific Mission funded by the grant IC1207-070117-081755. This work has been using language resources and tools developed, stored and distributed by the LINDAT/CLARIN project of the Ministry of Education, Youth and Sports of the Czech Republic (project LM2015071)

References

Eduard Bejček, Jan Hajič, Pavel Straňák, and Zdeňka Urešová. 2017. Extracting verbal multiword data from rich treebank annotation. In *Proceedings of the 15th International Workshop on Treebanks and Linguistic Theories (TLT 15)*, pages 13–24. Indiana University, Bloomington, Indiana University, Bloomington.

Kyunghyun Cho, Bart van Merrienboer, Dzmitry Bahdanau, and Yoshua Bengio, 2014. *Proceedings of SSST-8, Eighth Workshop on Syntax, Semantics and Structure in Statistical Translation*, chapter On the Properties of Neural Machine Translation: Encoder–Decoder Approaches, pages 103–111. Association for Computational Linguistics.

Junyoung Chung, Caglar Gulcehre, Kyunghyun Cho, and Yoshua Bengio. 2014. Empirical evaluation of gated recurrent neural networks on sequence modeling.

Alex Graves and Jürgen Schmidhuber. 2005. Framewise phoneme classification with bidirectional lstm and other neural network architectures. *Neural Networks*, 18(5):602–610.

Václava Kettnerová and Markéta Lopatková. 2014. Reflexive verbs in a valency lexicon: The case of czech reflexive morphemes. In Andrea Abel, Chiara Vettori, and Natascia Ralli, editors, *Proceedings of the XVI EURALEX International Congress: The User in Focus*, pages 1007–1023, Bolzano/Bozen, Italy. EURAC research, EURAC research.

Diederik P. Kingma and Jimmy Ba. 2014. Adam: A method for stochastic optimization. *CoRR*, abs/1412.6980.

Fernando Martínez-Santiago, Manuel Carlos Díaz-Galiano, Maite Teresa Martín-Valdivia, Víctor Manuel Rivas-Santos, and Luis Alfonso Ureña-López. 2002. Using neural networks for multiword recognition in ir. In *Proceedings of Conference of International Society of Knowledge Organization (ISKO-02), Granada, Spain*, pages 559–564.

Pavel Pecina. 2008. A machine learning approach to multiword expression extraction. In *Proceedings of the LREC 2008 Workshop Towards a Shared Task for Multiword Expressions*, pages 54–57, Marrakech, Morocco. ELRA.

Agata Savary, Carlos Ramisch, Silvio Cordeiro, Federico Sangati, Veronika Vincze, Behrang Qasem-iZadeh, Marie Candito, Fabienne Cap, Voula Giouli, Ivelina Stoyanova, and Antoine Doucet. 2017. The PARSEME Shared Task on Automatic Identification of Verbal Multi-word Expressions. In *Proceedings of the 13th Workshop on Multiword Expressions (MWE 2017)*, Valencia, Spain.

Yulia Tsvetkov and Shuly Wintner. 2011. Identification of multi-word expressions by combining multiple linguistic information sources. In *Proceedings of the 2011 Conference on Empirical Methods in Natural Language Processing*, pages 836–845. Association for Computational Linguistics.

Factoring Ambiguity out of the Prediction of Compositionality
for German Multi-Word Expressions

Stefan Bott and **Sabine Schulte im Walde**
Institut für Maschinelle Sprachverabeitung
Universität Stuttgart
Pfaffenwaldring 5b, 70569 Stuttgart, Germany
{stefan.bott,schulte}@ims.uni-stuttgart.de

Abstract

Ambiguity represents an obstacle for distributional semantic models (DSMs), which typically subsume the contexts of all word senses within one vector. While individual vector space approaches have been concerned with sense discrimination (e.g., Schütze (1998), Erk (2009), Erk and Pado (2010)), such discrimination has rarely been integrated into DSMs across semantic tasks. This paper presents a soft-clustering approach to sense discrimination that filters sense-irrelevant features when predicting the degrees of compositionality for German noun-noun compounds and German particle verbs.

1 Introduction

Addressing the compositionality of complex words is a crucial ingredient for lexicography and NLP applications, to know whether the expression should be treated as a whole, or through its constituents, and what the expression means. For example, studies such as Cholakov and Kordoni (2014), Weller et al. (2014), Cap et al. (2015), and Salehi et al. (2015b) have integrated the prediction of multi-word compositionality into statistical machine translation.

We are interested in predicting the degrees of compositionality of two types of German multi-word expressions: (i) German noun-noun compounds (NCs) represent nominal multi-word expressions (MWEs), e.g., *Feuer|werk* 'fire works' is composed of the constituents *Feuer* 'fire' and *Werk* 'opus'. (ii) German particle verbs (PVs) are complex verbs such as *an|strahlen* ('beam/smile at') which are composed of a separable prefix particle (*an*) and a base verb (*strahlen* 'beam'/'smile'). Both types of German MWEs are

highly frequent and highly productive in the lexicon. Table 1 presents some example MWEs and their constituents with human ratings on compositionality.[1]

Automatic approaches to predict compositionality degrees typically exploit distributional semantic models (DSMs), i.e. vector representations relying on the *distributional hypothesis* (Harris, 1954; Firth, 1957), that words with similar distributions have related meanings. Regarding the compositionality prediction, DSMs represent the meanings of the MWEs and their constituents by distributional vectors, and the similarity of a compound–constituent vector pair is taken as the predicted degree of compound-constituent compositionality. Existing approaches addressed the compositionality of NCs (Reddy et al., 2011; Salehi and Cook, 2013; Schulte im Walde et al., 2013; Salehi et al., 2014) and complex verbs (Baldwin, 2005; Bannard, 2005; Bott and Schulte im Walde, 2015), mainly dfor English and for German.

A major obstacle for DSMs is their conflation of contexts across individual word senses. DSMs typically subsume evidence of cooccurring items within one vector for the target word type, rather than discriminating contextual evidence for the specific target word senses. Taking the German noun-noun compound *Blatt|salat* 'leaf salad' as an example, its modifier constituent *Blatt* has at least four senses: 'leaf', 'sheet of paper', 'newspaper' and 'hand of cards'. If we had individual sense vectors for each sense of *Blatt*, a DSM might successfully predict a strong compositionality for the compound *Blatt|salat* regarding this constituent, when comparing the compound vector with the 'leaf' sense vector, because the vectors agree on

---

[1]The scales for mean ratings were 1–7 for noun-noun compounds, and 1–6 for particle verbs. Examples were taken from the two gold standards described in section 2.

66

Proceedings of the 13th Workshop on Multiword Expressions (MWE 2017), pages 66–72,
Valencia, Spain, April 4. ©2017 Association for Computational Linguistics

Multi-Word Expressions				Mean Ratings	
				Modifier	Head
Ahorn|blatt	'maple leaf'	maple	leaf	5.64	5.71
Blatt|salat	'green salad'	leaf	salad	3.56	5.68
See|zunge	'sole'	sea	tongue	3.57	3.27
Löwen|zahn	'dandelion'	lion	tooth	2.10	2.23
Fliegen|pilz	'toadstool'	fly/bow tie	mushroom	1.93	6.55
Fleisch|wolf	'meat chopper'	meat	wolf	6.00	1.90
an|leuchten	'illuminate'	an_{PRT}	illuminate	–	5.95
auf|horchen	'listen attentively'	auf_{PRT}	listen	–	4.55
aus|reizen	'exhaust'	aus_{PRT}	provoke	–	3.62
ein|fallen	'remember/invade'	ein_{PRT}	fall	–	2.54
an|stiften	'instigate'	an_{PRT}	create	–	1.80

Table 1: Examples of German noun-noun compounds and German particle verbs, accompanied by translations and human mean ratings on the degrees of compound-constituent compositionality.

salient features such as *green* and *fresh*. But traditionally, the constituent vector contains distributional information across all *Blatt* senses, and the similarity between the conflated word type vector and the compound vector is most probably determined by the predominant sense of the word type (which does not necessarily coincide with the relevant sense).

While individual vector space approaches have been concerned with sense discrimination (e.g., Schütze (1998), Erk (2009), Erk and Pado (2010)), the approaches have rarely been integrated into DSMs across semantic tasks. Alternatively, sense disambiguation/discrimination approaches have been developed for *SemEval* tasks on Word Sense Disambiguation/Discrimination and (Cross-lingual) Lexical Substitution (McCarthy and Navigli, 2007; Mihalcea et al., 2010; Jurgens and Klapaftis, 2013). As to our knowledge, few systems have attempted to distinguish between word senses and then address various semantic relatedness tasks, such as Li and Jurafsky (2015) and Iacobacci et al. (2015). Computational compositionality assessment has been studied for NCs (Reddy et al., 2011; Schulte im Walde et al., 2013; Salehi and Cook, 2013; Schulte im Walde et al., 2016a) and PVs (McCarthy et al., 2003; Baldwin et al., 2003; Bannard, 2005; Kühner and Schulte im Walde, 2010). Most similar to our current work is Salehi et al. (2015a), who addressed the problem of semantic ambiguity in MWEs by using a multi-sense skip gram model with two to five embeddings per word. They expected multiple embeddings to capture different word senses. They could, however, not find an improvement over the use of single-word embeddings.

In this paper, we suggest soft clustering as an approximation to separate the different senses of a word type. We expect that the assignments of compound and constituent words to clusters reflect the differences between word senses, and that the underlying features refer to the features of the respective word sense. We assume further that if we find a pair $<\mu, \kappa>$ of an MWE μ and one of its constituents κ with high distributional similarity in the same cluster, this indicates closeness in meaning and therefore strong compositionality. We exploit the soft clusters by (a) identifying the relevant senses of the MWE and constituents based on overlap in cluster assignment, and by (b) comparing reduced vectors of MWEs and constituents when taking into account only a subset of cluster-based salient sense features, in order to optimize the prediction of compositionality.

2 Experiment Setup

Distributional Semantics Models Our DSM is a word space model that uses lemmatized words as dimensions in the high-dimensional vectors space (Sahlgren, 2006; Turney and Pantel, 2010). The associative strength between target and context words is measured as Local Mutual Information (LMI) (Evert, 2004), based on context word frequency. The context of the targets is defined as a window of n words to the left and the right of the target. We use the cosine value of the angle between two vectors as a measure for semantic similarity and compositionality. For technical reasons we ignore context words with a count of 5 or less or an LMI value below 0.

We use the word vectors in three ways here: (a) we use them directly as *window models* in order to measure the distance between vector pairs for an MWE and each of its components (e.g. *Blatt\|salat* vs. *Blatt*). We also use them (b) as an input matrix for soft clustering and (c) we build word vector models for each cluster.

LSC for Soft Clustering We use Latent Semantic Classes (LSC) as a soft clustering algorithm (Rooth, 1998; Rooth et al., 1999). LSC is a two-dimensional soft-clustering algorithm which learns three probability distributions: (a) across the clusters, (b) for the output probabilities of each element within a cluster and (c) for each feature type with regard to a cluster. The access to all three probability distributions is crucial for our approach, since it allows to determine which features are salient for individual clusters.

The Pipeline We create two types of models: The *window models* are simple word space models which use LMI values based on counts of context words. The *clustering models* apply soft clustering as a previous step to the determination of distributional similarity. For their construction, we use the window-based models as an input to the LSC algorithm. The clusters produced by LSC are used to create individual models for each cluster C in a way that each of these cluster-specific models only contain vectors for the target words which are contained in C and represent only those features as dimensions which are predicted to be salient features for C. The models vary with respect to the number of clusters created.

With this, we expect that in our example of *Blatt|salat* some clusters will capture the *leaf*-sense and others the *sheet-* or other senses. The comparison between the vectors for *Blatt* and *Blatt|salat* is then done separately for each cluster, where the context dimensions of the vectors are reduced to only those context words which are also salient features of each cluster. We expect that the pair of our example only occur in clusters which can be attributed to the *leaf*-sense.

Comparison across Clusters In cases like the NC *Blatt|salat* it appears that the word sense which should be considered for compositionality assessment is the one which is distributionally closest to the target MWE. But this is not necessarily the case for all MWEs. The PV *zu|schlagen* is one example: it can mean both *to hit hard and quickly* or *to take advantage of a good offer/bargain*; in this case the MWE itself is ambiguous. The base verb *schlagen* means *to hit*, so one sense of the PV is highly compositional

and the other sense is less so; nevertheless none of the senses is predominant. We use three methods to compare the distributional similarity across clusters: *highest*, *lowest* and *average*. In the first two methods (*highest/lowest*) we select the cluster with the highest/lowest distributional similarity between μ and κ and use its similarity value. In the last method (*average*) the average similarity is computed among those clusters which contain both the MWE μ and the target component κ, while clusters which do not contain the pair $<\mu, \kappa>$ are ignored.

Thresholds The fact that LSC outputs probabilities for both targets and features allows to set two different thresholds on these probabilities. The threshold on the target output probability (t-threshold) controls the number of clusters to which a target element will be assigned. The lower the threshold is set, the more elements each cluster will contain. Lower threshold values also lead to higher average numbers of clusters to which each element is assigned. The t-threshold influences the predictions of our models in that low values also increase the likelihood for each Cluster C and for each pair $<\alpha, \beta>$ of a MWE and a constituent word that both α and β are included in C. The threshold on the feature output probability (f-threshold) allows to filter the vectors for both elements of $<\alpha, \beta>$ according to each cluster C so that only the dimensions representing the salient features for C are included in the vectors.

Corpus For the extraction of features we use the SdeWaC (v.3, 880 million words) corpus (Faaß and Eckart, 2013), in a tokenized (Schmid, 2000), POS-tagged and lemmatized (Schmid, 1994) version.

Gold Standards For NCs and PVs we use the following gold standards:

- GS-NN: 868 German NCs (Schulte im Walde et al., 2016b) randomly selected from different frequency ranges, different ambiguity levels of the heads and different levels of modifier and head productivity. NCs were annotated by eight native speakers on a scale from 1 to 6 for compositionality with respect to both head and modifier constituents.
- GS-PV: 354 PVs, for 11 verb particles. PVs were randomly selected, balanced over 3 frequency bands. The PVs were automatically

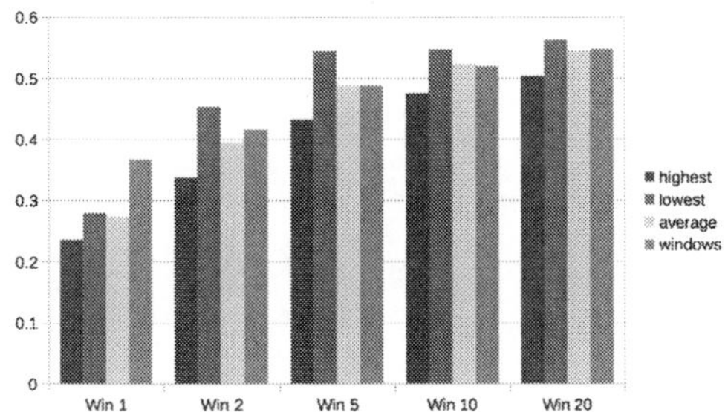

Figure 1: Results (in ρ values) for different window sizes for the NC-head gold standard

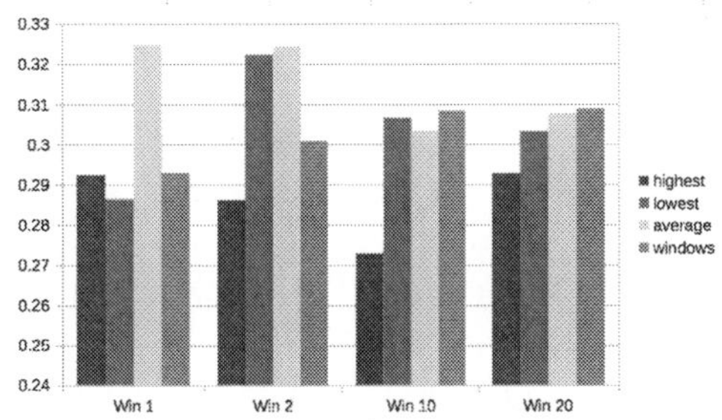

Figure 2: Results (in ρ values) for different window sizes for the PV gold standard

harvested from various corpora, assigned to 3 different frequency ranges per particle and then automatically selected. Some manual revision was done to filter out non-existing PVs resulting from lemmatization errors. Ratings were obtained with Amazon Mechanical Turk.[2]

Feature Sets We were interested in which parts of speech provide the best predictive features for compositionality. We use only content-word categories: adjectives, nouns and verbs. We use four different combinations: all content words and categories in isolation.

Measures Distributional similarity is measured with the cosine between vectors. The cosine similarity values are used to rank the compared pairs from lowest to highest. For the evaluation, system rankings and human judgment rankings of MWEs are compared to each other with Spearman's rank order correlation ρ (Siegel and Castellan, 1988). Spearman's ρ is a non-parametric measure which assesses monotonic relationships of ranks that range between -1 (inverse correlation) and 1 (perfect correlation); a ρ value of 0 indicates a lack of correlation. Significance is determined with the use of the Fisher transformation.

Soft clustering does not guarantee that each of the pairs of NCs and a constituent word is placed together in at least one of the clusters. This may potentially lead to problems of coverage. In practice, however, we experience coverage problems only for very restrictive threshold settings.

---

[2]This gold standard is a preliminary, but not identical, version of the one presented in Bott et al. (2016). It was also used in Bott and Schulte im Walde (2014).

3 Results and Discussion

Figure 1 and 2 show the results for different window sizes for NCs and PVs. The two figures have different scales and higher ρ scores are obtained for NCs. The values are compared to the results of the window-based models. The predictions of compositionality levels become more accurate with increasing window sizes. For NC compositionality apparently more general information about the larger context plays an important role. Interestingly, no negative effect from larger contexts can be observed, even if smaller contexts tend to concentrate on closely related words such as complements, modifiers and the complementary parts of collocations in which the target word takes part. All ρ values above 0.108 are statistically highly significant (p<0.001 for n=868), which applies to nearly all of the observed values.

Regarding PV compositionality, window models increase their performance with larger context sizes, but this is not true for clustering models. The latter tend to perform better with small to medium window sizes and in this range clustering models clearly outperform window models. Also NC compositionality tends to be better predicted with the clustering-based models, but to a degree. It is also interesting to note that the successful combination cluster methods are different for NC (where *highest* performs best) and PVs (for which the *average* method yields the best results). This suggests a more fundamental difference in the two types of MWEs. One of the possible differences lies in the average degree of ambiguity of the MWEs and their constituents. NCs have a strong tendency to be less ambiguous than their constituent nouns. PVs, on the other hand, are often highly ambiguous themselves.

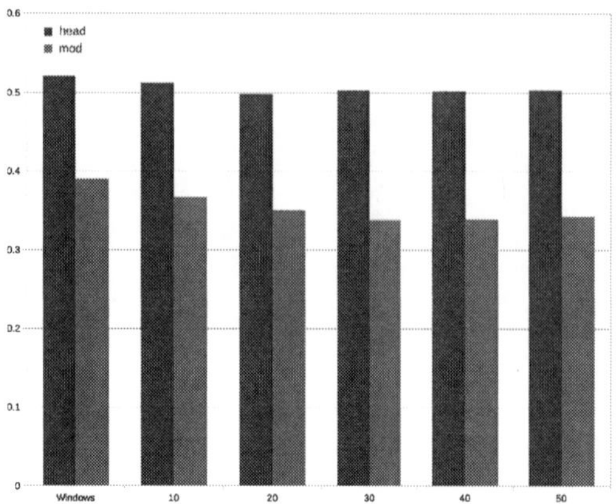

Figure 3: Results for different numbers of clusters for the NC gold standard (heads vs. modifiers)

Figure 3 shows the effect of the number of clusters which are used in the clustering stage. The graphic shows that the number of clusters has not a strong influence on performance, but slightly better results can be observed with smaller numbers of clusters. This might be due to the fact that larger numbers of clusters split up the feature space into smaller segments and the feature vectors tend to suffer from sparseness. Figure 3 also shows that the predictions for the noun compound compositionality with respect to the heads are generally better than with respect to the modifiers. This is probably a consequence of the fact that meaning of NCs is in most cases more strongly determined by the meanings of their heads than their modifiers. This might explain the observed asymmetry. This finding is in line with earlier studies (Hätty, 2016; Schulte im Walde et al., 2016a) which investigated the asymmetry between the properties of heads and modifiers in noun-noun compounds. They showed that head constituent properties, such as their ambiguity or frequency, influence the predictability of NC compositionality to a much larger degree than modifier constituent properties.

As for feature selection, we found that adjectives represented the least reliable predictive features for compositionality assessment, while nouns were the most reliable ones. The use of the latter even leads to a slightly better performance than the use of the full feature set that contains all content word categories.

Figure 4 shows the influence of the target and the feature thresholds on compositionality predic-

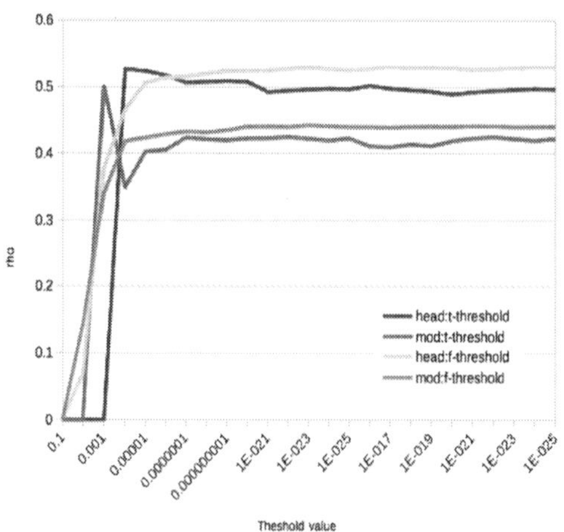

Figure 4: ρ values for variations over thresholds (NC gold standard)

tion. As expected, very high threshold values lead to poor performance since they cause very sparse vector representations. Lowering the threshold the performance curve raises steeply and reaches a stable plateau which is observable in this figure.

4 Conclusions

We started this paper with a theoretical justification to factor out the influence of ambiguity from the prediction of compositionality across multi-word expressions. We applied soft clustering to extract word-sense vectors from word-type vectors, in order to strengthen salient sense features and improve the prediction of compound–constituent compositionality. Both NCs and PVs benefit from the use of clustering in distributional modeling, but in different ways. First, PVs benefit much more than NCs. Second, the optimal type of the combination method which calculates a global similarity score per compound–constituent pair from the cluster-specific DSMs differs between the two types of MWEs. This suggests an underlying difference between them.

In future work we will explore alternative ways to treat the ambiguity of constituent words more adequately. We further plan to examine why different types of MWEs tend to benefit from the clustering approach but with different cluster combination methods. We will also extend our investigation to other semantic relatedness tasks, such as the distinction between semantic relations, which potentially suffer from the same ambiguity issue.

References

Timothy Baldwin, Colin Bannard, Takaaki Tanaka, and Dominic Widdows. 2003. An empirical model of multiword expression decomposability. In *Proceedings of the ACL 2003 Workshop on Multiword Expressions*, pages 89–96, Sapporo, Japan. Association for Computational Linguistics.

Timothy Baldwin. 2005. Deep lexical acquisition of verb–particle constructions. *Computer Speech and Language*, 19:398–414.

Collin Bannard. 2005. Learning about the meaning of verb–particle constructions from corpora. *Computer Speech and Language*, 19:467–478.

Stefan Bott and Sabine Schulte im Walde. 2014. Syntactic transfer patterns of German particle verbs and their impact on lexical semantics. In *Proceedings of the Third Joint Conference on Lexical and Computational Semantics (*SEM 2014)*, pages 182–192, Dublin, Ireland. Association for Computational Linguistics and Dublin City University.

Stefan Bott and Sabine Schulte im Walde. 2015. Exploiting fine-grained syntactic transfer features to predict the compositionality of German particle verbs. In *Proceedings of the 11th International Conference on Computational Semantics*, pages 34–39, London, UK. Association for Computational Linguistics.

Stefan Bott, Nana Khvtisavrishvili, Max Kisselew, and Sabine Schulte im Walde. 2016. G$_h$ost-pv: A representative gold standard of German particle verbs. In *Proceedings of the 5th Workshop on Cognitive Aspects of the Lexicon (CogALex - V)*, pages 125–133, Osaka, Japan. The COLING 2016 Organizing Committee.

Fabienne Cap, Manju Nirmal, Marion Weller, and Sabine Schulte im Walde. 2015. How to account for idiomatic German support verb constructions in statistical machine translation. In *Proceedings of the 11th Workshop on Multiword Expressions*, pages 19–28, Denver, Colorado. Association for Computational Linguistics.

Kostadin Cholakov and Valia Kordoni. 2014. Better statistical machine translation through linguistic treatment of phrasal verbs. In *Proceedings of the 2014 Conference on Empirical Methods in Natural Language Processing (EMNLP)*, pages 196–201, Doha, Qatar. Association for Computational Linguistics.

Katrin Erk and Sebastian Pado. 2010. Exemplar-based models for word meaning in context. In *Proceedings of the ACL 2010 Conference Short Papers*, pages 92–97, Uppsala, Sweden. Association for Computational Linguistics.

Katrin Erk. 2009. Representing words in regions in vector space. In *Proceedings of the 13th Conference on Computational Natural Language Learning*, pages 57–65, Boulder, CO.

Stefan Evert. 2004. The statistical analysis of morphosyntactic distributions. In *Proceedings of the Fourth International Conference on Language Resources and Evaluation (LREC-2004)*, pages 1539–1542, Lisbon, Portugal. European Language Resources Association (ELRA). ACL Anthology Identifier: L04-1509.

Gertrud Faaß and Kerstin Eckart. 2013. SdeWaC – a corpus of parsable sentences from the web. In *Proceedings of the International Conference of the German Society for Computational Linguistics and Language Technology*, pages 61–68, Darmstadt, Germany.

John R. Firth. 1957. *Papers in Linguistics 1934-51*. Longmans, London, UK.

Zellig Harris. 1954. Distributional structure. *Word*, 10(23):146–162.

Anna Hätty. 2016. Vector space models of compositionality for German and English noun-noun compounds. Master Thesis. Institut für Maschinelle Sprachverarbeitung, Universität Stuttgart.

Ignacio Iacobacci, Mohammad Taher Pilehvar, and Roberto Navigli. 2015. SensEmbed: Learning sense embeddings for word and relational similarity. In *Proceedings of the 53rd Annual Meeting of the Association for Computational Linguistics and the 7th International Joint Conference on Natural Language Processing*, pages 95–105, Beijing, China. Association for Computational Linguistics.

David Jurgens and Ioannis Klapaftis. 2013. SemEval-2013 Task 13: Word sense induction for graded and non-graded senses. In *Second Joint Conference on Lexical and Computational Semantics (*SEM), Proceedings of the Seventh International Workshop on Semantic Evaluation (SemEval 2013)*, pages 290–299, Atlanta, Georgia, USA. Association for Computational Linguistics.

Natalie Kühner and Sabine Schulte im Walde. 2010. Determining the degree of compositionality of German particle verbs by clustering approaches. In *Proceedings of the 10th Conference on Natural Language Processing*, pages 47–56, Saarbrücken, Germany.

Jiwei Li and Dan Jurafsky. 2015. Do multi-sense embeddings improve natural language understanding? In *Proceedings of the 2015 Conference on Empirical Methods in Natural Language Processing*, pages 1722–1732, Lisbon, Portugal. Association for Computational Linguistics.

Diana McCarthy and Roberto Navigli. 2007. SemEval-2007 Task 10: English lexical substitution task. In *Proceedings of the Fourth International Workshop on Semantic Evaluations (SemEval-2007)*, pages 48–53, Prague, Czech Republic. Association for Computational Linguistics.

Diana McCarthy, Bill Keller, and John Carroll. 2003. Detecting a continuum of compositionality in phrasal verbs. In *Proceedings of the ACL-SIGLEX Workshop on Multiword Expressions: Analysis, Acquisition and Treatment*, Sapporo, Japan.

Rada Mihalcea, Ravi Sinha, and Diana McCarthy. 2010. SemEval-2010 Task 2: Cross-lingual lexical substitution. In *Proceedings of the 5th International Workshop on Semantic Evaluation*, pages 9–14, Uppsala, Sweden. Association for Computational Linguistics.

Siva Reddy, Diana McCarthy, and Suresh Manandhar. 2011. An empirical study on compositionality in compound nouns. In *Proceedings of 5th International Joint Conference on Natural Language Processing*, pages 210–218, Chiang Mai, Thailand. Asian Federation of Natural Language Processing.

Mats Rooth, Stefan Riezler, Detlef Prescher, Glenn Carroll, and Franz Beil. 1999. Inducing a semantically annotated lexicon via EM-based clustering. In *Proceedings of the 37th Annual Meeting of the Association for Computational Linguistics*, pages 104–111, College Park, Maryland, USA. Association for Computational Linguistics.

Mats Rooth. 1998. Two-dimensional clusters in grammatical relations. In *Inducing Lexicons with the EM Algorithm*, AIMS Report 4(3). Institut für Maschinelle Sprachverarbeitung, Universität Stuttgart.

Magnus Sahlgren. 2006. *The Word-Space Model: Using Distributional Analysis to Represent Syntagmatic and Paradigmatic Relations between Words in High-Dimensional Vector Spaces*. Ph.D. thesis, Stockholm University.

Bahar Salehi and Paul Cook. 2013. Predicting the compositionality of multiword expressions using translations in multiple languages. In *Second Joint Conference on Lexical and Computational Semantics (*SEM)*, pages 266–275, Atlanta, Georgia, USA. Association for Computational Linguistics.

Bahar Salehi, Paul Cook, and Timothy Baldwin. 2014. Using distributional similarity of multi-way translations to predict multiword expression compositionality. In *Proceedings of the 14th Conference of the European Chapter of the Association for Computational Linguistics*, pages 472–481, Gothenburg, Sweden. Association for Computational Linguistics.

Bahar Salehi, Paul Cook, and Timothy Baldwin. 2015a. A word embedding approach to predicting the compositionality of multiword expressions. In *Proceedings of the 2015 Conference of the North American Chapter of the Association for Computational Linguistics: Human Language Technologies*, pages 977–983, Denver, Colorado. Association for Computational Linguistics.

Bahar Salehi, Nitika Mathur, Paul Cook, and Timothy Baldwin. 2015b. The impact of multiword expression compositionality on machine translation evaluation. In *Proceedings of the 11th Workshop on Multiword Expressions*, pages 54–59, Denver, Colorado. Association for Computational Linguistics.

Helmut Schmid. 1994. Probabilistic part-of-speech tagging using decision trees. In *Proceedings of the International Conference on New Methods in Language Processing*, pages 44–49. Manchester, UK.

Helmut Schmid. 2000. Unsupervised learning of period disambiguation for tokenisation. Technical report, Universität Stuttgart.

Sabine Schulte im Walde, Stefan Müller, and Stefan Roller. 2013. Exploring vector space models to predict the compositionality of German noun-noun compounds. In *Second Joint Conference on Lexical and Computational Semantics (*SEM)*, pages 255–265, Atlanta, Georgia, USA. Association for Computational Linguistics.

Sabine Schulte im Walde, Anna Hätty, and Stefan Bott. 2016a. The role of modifier and head properties in predicting the compositionality of English and German noun-noun compounds: A vector-space perspective. In *Proceedings of the Fifth Joint Conference on Lexical and Computational Semantics*, pages 148–158, Berlin, Germany. Association for Computational Linguistics.

Sabine Schulte im Walde, Anna Hätty, Stefan Bott, and Nana Khvtisavrishvili. 2016b. $G_h$ost-NN: A representative gold standard of German noun-noun compounds. In *Proceedings of the Tenth International Conference on Language Resources and Evaluation (LREC'16)*, pages 2285–2292, Portoroz, Slovenia. European Language Resources Association (ELRA).

Hinrich Schütze. 1998. Automatic word sense discrimination. *Computational Linguistics*, 24(1):97–123. Special Issue on Word Sense Disambiguation.

Sidney Siegel and N. John Castellan. 1988. *Nonparametric Statistics for the Behavioral Sciences*. McGraw-Hill, Boston, MA.

Peter D. Turney and Patrick Pantel. 2010. From frequency to meaning: Vector space models of semantics. *Journal of Artificial Intelligence Research*, 37:141–188.

Marion Weller, Fabienne Cap, Stefan Müller, Sabine Schulte im Walde, and Alexander Fraser. 2014. Distinguishing degrees of compositionality in compound splitting for statistical machine translation. In *Proceedings of the First Workshop on Computational Approaches to Compound Analysis (ComAComA 2014)*, pages 81–90, Dublin, Ireland. Association for Computational Linguistics and Dublin City University.

Multiword expressions and lexicalism: the view from LFG

Jamie Y. Findlay

University of Oxford / Oxford, UK

`jamie.findlay@ling-phil.ox.ac.uk`

Abstract

Multiword expressions (MWEs) pose a problem for lexicalist theories like Lexical Functional Grammar (LFG), since they are *prima facie* counterexamples to a strong form of the lexical integrity principle, which entails that a lexical item can only be realised as a single, syntactically atomic word. In this paper, I demonstrate some of the problems facing any strongly lexicalist account of MWEs, and argue that the lexical integrity principle must be weakened. I conclude by sketching a formalism which integrates a Tree Adjoining Grammar into the LFG architecture, taking advantage of this relaxation.

1 Multiword expressions

Baldwin & Kim (2010, 269) define multiword expressions (MWEs), as

> lexical items that: (a) can be decomposed into multiple lexemes; and (b) display lexical, syntactic, semantic, pragmatic and/or statistical idiomaticity.

This is a very broad definition, covering everything from full-fledged idioms like *cut the mustard* to mere hackneyed expressions like *never tell me the odds*. In this paper, my focus is on semantic idiomaticity, this being the prototypical feature of MWEs, but what I say has implications for, and is not incompatible with, the other kinds as well.

2 LFG

Lexical Functional Grammar (LFG: Kaplan and Bresnan, 1982; Dalrymple, 2001; Bresnan et al., 2015) is a constraint-based, lexicalist approach to the architecture of the grammar. Its primary focus has always been syntax, but with a special interest

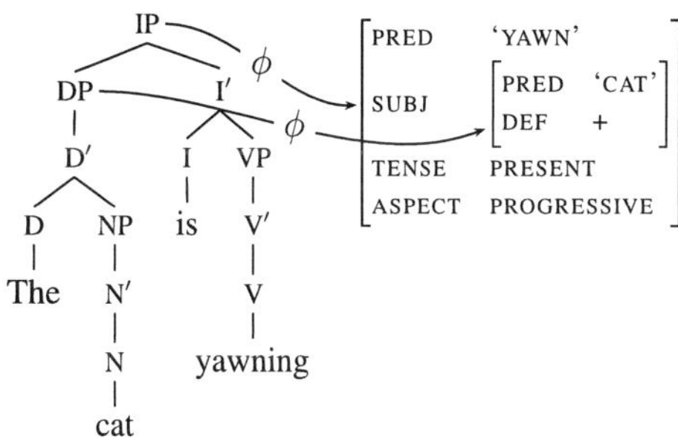

Figure 1: C-structure and f-structure for *The cat is yawning*.

in the interfaces between this and other components of the grammar, including argument structure (e.g. Kibort, 2007), morphology (e.g. Butt et al., 1996), semantics (e.g. Dalrymple, 1999), information structure (e.g. Dalrymple and Nikolaeva, 2011), and prosody (e.g. Mycock and Lowe, 2013).

A syntactic analysis in LFG involves two formally distinct kinds of object: c(onstituent)-structure, which is a phrase-structure tree that represents linear order as well as hierarchical relationships like constituency; and f(unctional)-structure, which is an attribute-value matrix that represents more abstract, functional relations like 'subject-of'. The two are connected via the function ϕ. An example is given in Figure 1.

The correspondence between c-structure and f-structure is controlled via annotations on the tree, provided either by phrase structure rules or the lexical entries themselves. The convention in writing such annotations is to use $\uparrow$ and $\downarrow$ as metavariables, representing $\phi(\hat{*})$ and $\phi(*)$ respectively, where $*$ is a variable representing the c-structure node where an annotation appears, and $\hat{*}$ represents the mother of that node. Thus, for example, the canonical English subject and object

Proceedings of the 13th Workshop on Multiword Expressions (MWE 2017), pages 73–79,
Valencia, Spain, April 4. ©2017 Association for Computational Linguistics

rules can be written as follows:

(1)   IP $\rightarrow$ DP   I$'$
                    $(\uparrow \text{SUBJ}) = \downarrow$ $\uparrow = \downarrow$

(2)   V$'$ $\rightarrow$ V   DP
                    $\uparrow = \downarrow$ $(\uparrow \text{OBJ}) = \downarrow$

These say, essentially, that an IP can be made up of a DP which is the subject of the clause, and an I$'$, while a V$'$ can be made up of a V, and a DP which is the object of the clause.

I omit the annotations on the tree in Figure 1 for reasons of space, but in principle all nodes are annotated. Finding the f-structure is then a matter of finding the minimal f-structure which satisfies all of the equations. In this way, the f-structure constrains the over-generation of the context-free c-structure, expanding the grammar's expressive power.

LFG subscribes to a strong version of the *lexical integrity principle* (LIP), namely that

> [m]orphologically complete words are leaves of the c-structure tree and each leaf corresponds to one and only one c-structure node.
> (Bresnan, 2001, 93)

This means that c-structure leaves are words, and that words are c-structure leaves. The original motivation for LIP was to ensure that syntactic rules should be 'blind' to morphology. But, in its strong version, it works in the other direction too. This facet of LIP is what Ackerman et al. (2011) call the *principle of unary expression* (PUE):

> In syntax, a lexeme is uniformly expressed as a single morphophonologically integrated and syntactically atomic word form.

If we think of MWEs as lexemes, then they are clearly a challenge to this principle. But even if we instead claim they are some kind of 'listeme' (Di Sciullo and Williams, 1987), there remains the question of how a single object, be it in 'the list' or the lexicon, can be realised as multiple potentially disjoint word forms in the syntax. MWEs thus remain at least a *prima facie* challenge to a strongly lexicalist theory.

3   Lexical ambiguity approaches

For any strongly lexicalist theory which adheres to (at least the spirit of) PUE, the most obvious way to deal with MWEs is via what we might call the lexical ambiguity approach (LA). In such an approach, MWEs are treated as made up of special words which combine to give the appropriate meaning for the whole expression. Words like *pull* and *strings* become ambiguous, meaning either **pull$'$** and **strings$'$** or **exploit$'$** and **connections$'$**, and so the semantic idiomaticity is encoded directly in the lexical entries. This sidesteps the PUE issue, since MWEs are not single lexical items, but rather collections of separate lexical items which conspire to create the overall meaning. For this reason, versions of LA have been popular in various lexicalist theories: see, for instance, Sailer (2000) for HPSG, Arnold (2015) for LFG, Kay et al. (2015) for SBCG, and Lichte and Kallmeyer (2016) for LTAG. However, LA has a large number of shortcomings which mean that it is untenable as a general position.

Although LA seems to naturally explain so-called decomposable idioms, where the meaning of the whole can be distributed across the parts (since this is exactly what the approach does), it is not so clear how it should handle non-decomposable idioms, like *kick the bucket*, *blow off steam*, *shoot the breeze*, etc., where there is no obvious way of breaking down the meaning of the idiom such that its parts correspond to the words that make up the expression. Solutions have been proposed: for instance, Lichte and Kallmeyer (2016) argue for what they call 'idiomatic mirroring', whereby each of the parts of the idiom contributes the meaning of the whole expression, so that *kick* means **die$'$**, *bucket* means **die$'$**, and, presumably, *the* means **die$'$** as well. A similar approach is pursued in work by Sascha Bargmann and Manfred Sailer (Bargmann and Sailer, 2005, in prep.). Both proposals, however, assume a semantics which allows for redundancy, a decision which is crucial for idiomatic mirroring to work. In a strictly resource-sensitive conception of the syntax-semantics interface like LFG+Glue (Dalrymple, 1999; Asudeh, 2012), each contribution to the semantics must contribute something to the meaning, with the result that multiple items cannot contribute the same semantics without a concomitant change in meaning (*big, big man* means something different from *big man*, for example).

Without idiomatic mirroring, we are forced to assume that only one of the words in the expression bears the meaning, and that the rest are semantically inert. For example, perhaps there is a *kick$_{id}$* which means **die$'$**, and selects for special semantically inert forms *the$_{id}$* and *bucket$_{id}$*. Notice, however, that the choice of where to locate the meaning is ultimately arbitrary. We may as well have *bucket$_{id}$* meaning **die$'$**, or even *the$_{id}$*, provided they select for the other inert forms and then pass their meaning up to the whole VP. Such arbitrariness seems undesirable.

It also leads to another formal issue: we now face an explosive proliferation of semantically inert forms throughout the lexicon. What is more, each of these must be restricted so that it does not appear outside of the appropriate expression. But this means that the *the* in *kick the bucket* can't be the same *the* as in *shoot the breeze*. We need as many *the*s as there are expressions which include it. Instead of having to expand the lexicon by as many entries as there are MWEs, we have to expand it by as many entries as there are *words in MWEs*, which is much less appealing, and smacks of redundancy.

One empirical issue facing LA relates to the psycholinguistic findings on processing. Swinney and Cutler (1979) showed that idioms are processed in the same way as regular compositional expressions; i.e. there is no special 'idiom mode' of comprehension. At the same time, others have found that idiomatic meanings are processed faster and in preference to literal ones (Estill and Kemper, 1982; Gibbs, 1986; Cronk, 1992). If both these things are true, then LA is in trouble: in this approach, there is no reason to think idioms or other MWEs should be processed any faster; if anything, we might expect them to be slower, since they involve ambiguity by definition.

Rather, the psycholinguistic findings plead for what seems intuitively appealing anyway: that MWEs are inserted *en bloc*, being stored in the lexicon as units. But this requires there to be objects in the lexicon which are larger than single words, defined as terminal nodes in a tree, which necessitates abandoning PUE.

4 TAG-LFG

Really, we want to be able to extend the domain of the lexical entry so that it can naturally include MWEs. This can be readily achieved in Lexicalised Tree Adjoining Grammar (LTAG: Joshi et al., 1975), which has successfully been used to analyse MWEs in the past (e.g. Abeillé, 1995).

One of the key strengths of any TAG-based approach is its *extended domain of locality*. Since the operation of adjunction allows trees to grow 'from the inside out', as it were, relationships can be

encoded locally even when the elements involved may end up arbitrarily far apart. This is precisely the situation which obtains with idioms and other MWEs which allow for syntactic flexibility.

What is more, a TAG-based approach where MWEs are multiply-anchored trees (that is, trees with more than one terminal node specified in the lexicon, so that they contain more than one word) aligns with the psycholinguistic findings. A parse involving a MWE will involve fewer elementary trees: for example, in a parse of *John kicked the bucket*, instead of the four trees for *John*, *kicked*, *the*, and *bucket*, it will just involve the two for *John* and *kicked the bucket*, explaining the increased processing speed (Abeillé, 1995).

However, I am not advocating that LFG practitioners should abandon LFG in favour of LTAG. Space precludes a full defence of the virtues of LFG here, but I believe it possesses a number of advantageous features we should like to retain. Firstly, there is the separation of abstract grammatical information from the constituency-based syntactic tree. A detailed and dedicated level of representation for functional information is motivated by the fact that it is important in grammatical description and not necessarily determined by phrase structure. For example, functional information is relevant in terms of describing binding domains (Dalrymple, 1993), or for phenomena related to the functional/accessibility hierarchy (Keenan and Comrie, 1977), or in describing argument alternation (Bresnan, 1982).

Secondly, LFG has grown beyond just c- and f-structure, and now has a well-developed grammatical architecture encompassing many different levels of representation, from phonological, to morphological, to semantic and information structure, and the relations and constraints that exist between them. This *correspondence architecture* (on which see Asudeh, 2012, 49–54) is a powerful tool for describing the multi-modal phenomenon that is natural language, and something we would like to preserve.

With this in mind, then, what we should like to do is to incorporate the advantages of the TAG-style extended domain of locality into the pre-existing LFG architecture. The most obvious way to do this is to replace the context-free grammar of LFG's c-structure with a TAG instead.[1] Let us call

---

[1] This has been proposed before, though never developed: e.g. Kameyama (1986), Burheim (1996), Rambow (1996) (sadly these manuscripts have proved impossible to track

this variant TAG-LFG. In the rest of this section I will sketch its key features.

The first thing to note is that such a move does not increase the expressive power of LFG. Of course, a TAG is mildly context sensitive, which is more powerful than the context-free grammar of LFG's c-structure. However, LFG is not just c-structure, and the presence of f-structure already pushes LFGs beyond the mildly context-sensitive space (Berwick, 1982). Thus, although we are empowering a part of the formalism, we are not increasing the power of the formalism as a whole.

Since c-structure nodes in LFG can be 'decorated' with functional information, another concern is how to handle these during substitution and adjunction. Substitution is straightforward: since no elementary tree will be annotated on its root node, we simply retain the annotation on the substitution target. For adjunction, feature-based TAG standardly makes use of top and bottom features (Vijay-Shanker, 1987). Since in TAG-LFG we are unifying features from the whole tree in one place, the f-structure, rather than locally on each node, we do not need to separate annotations in the same way. Instead, at the top of the adjunction structure, annotations are retained from the target, while at the bottom, they are retained from the foot of the auxiliary tree. This is equivalent to seeing adjunction as two instances of substitution following a dividing up of the tree; in each case the target retains its annotations.

Let us now turn to the question of representation. In standard LFG, a lexical entry is a triple (W, C, F), where W is a word form, i.e. the terminal node in the phrase-structure tree, C is a c-structure category, i.e. the pre-terminal node, and F is a functional description, i.e. a set of expressions spelling out additional linguistic information via the correspondence architecture. In TAG-LFG, a lexical entry is instead a triple $(\langle W \rangle, T, F)$, consisting of a list of word forms, a tree, provided by some metagrammar (Crabbé et al., 2013), and a functional description. A simple example for a non-decomposable idiom is given in

down). See also Clément and Kinyon (2003) for a proposal to generate both LFG and TAG grammars from the same set of linguistic descriptions (encoded in a metagrammar).

A reviewer points out potential similarities with LFG-DOP (Bod and Kaplan, 1998; see also references in Arnold and Linardaki, 2007), which combines LFG with Data-Oriented Parsing (Bod, 1992). This also makes use of tree fragments, but it still relies on a lexicon stated in terms of context-free rules to generate these fragments, and thus is still reliant on a version of LA to encode MWEs in the lexicon.

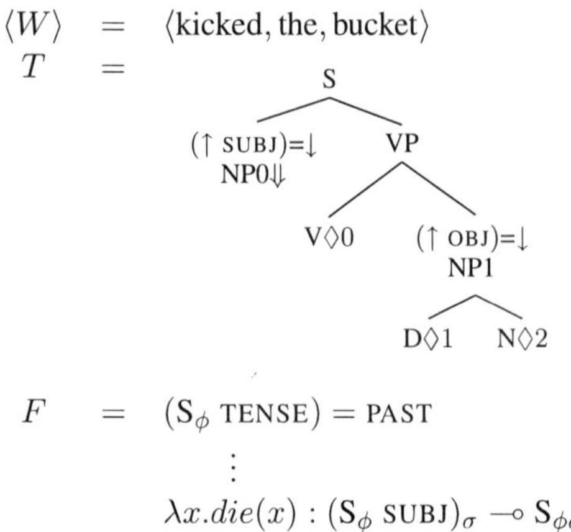

Figure 2: TAG-LFG lexical entry for *kicked the bucket*

Figure 2.[2] The word forms occur as a list because the trees for MWEs will be multiply anchored. For regular lexical entries, this list will be a singleton. The lexical anchors, marked with $\Diamond$s, are numbered according to the list index of the word form that is to be inserted there. The functional description remains the same, although it now allows reference to more remote nodes, and so instead of $\uparrow$ or $\downarrow$ I use node labels as a shorthand for the nodes in question.[3,4]

In Figure 2, I have given the semantics in the form of a *meaning constructor*. This is an object used in Glue Semantics, the theory of the syntax-semantics interface most often coupled with LFG (Dalrymple, 1999; Asudeh, 2012). It consists, on the left-hand side, of a formula in some 'meaning language', in this case a lambda expression, and, on the right-hand side, of an expression in linear logic (Girard, 1987) over s(emantic)-structures (projected from f-structures via the σ function), which controls composition. In this case, it says that the meaning of the whole sentence is obtained by applying $\lambda x.die(x)$ to the meaning of the sentence's subject.

By associating the meaning constructor not with any particular node in the tree, but with the tree as a whole, via the lexical entry, we avoid the arbitrariness of having to choose one word to host the

[2]To avoid confusion with the LFG metavariable $\downarrow$, I use the symbol $\Downarrow$ to represent a TAG substitution site.

[3]In reality, the node labels are not the nodes: they are the output of a node labelling function λ applied to each node (Kaplan, 1995).

[4]S_ϕ is shorthand for $\phi(S)$, and $S_{\phi\sigma}$ for $\sigma(\phi(S))$, i.e. the f-structure and s(emantic)-structure corresponding to S, respectively.

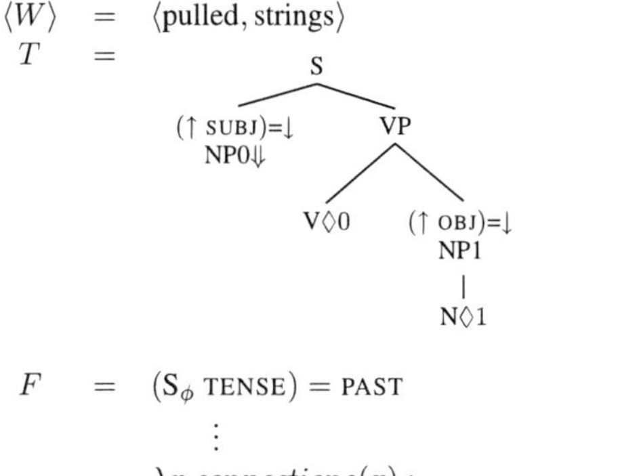

$$F = (S_\phi \text{ TENSE}) = \text{PAST}$$

$$\vdots$$

$$\lambda x.connections(x) :$$
$$(\text{NP1}_{\phi\sigma} \text{ VAR}) \multimap (\text{NP1}_{\phi\sigma} \text{ RESTR})$$
$$\lambda x\lambda y.exploit(x,y) :$$
$$(S_\phi \text{ SUBJ})_\sigma \multimap (S_\phi \text{ OBJ})_\sigma \multimap S_{\phi\sigma}$$

Figure 3: TAG-LFG lexical entry for *pulled strings*

meaning. It remains possible to represent decomposable idioms, too, since we can simply include multiple meaning constructors in the f-description, separating out the meaning and referring to the relevant parts as required. Figure 3 gives an example for *pull strings*. In this case, two meaning constructors are present, one for each of the decomposable 'parts' of the idiomatic meaning.[5] This allows for internal modification of *strings*, for example (e.g. *pull family strings*).

The varying syntactic flexibility of MWEs can be accounted for by the standard TAG approach of associating each lexeme with different families of elementary trees. For example, assuming a more abstract level of *lexemic entry*, which is used to generate the set of lexical entries associated with each lexeme (or listeme) (Dalrymple, 2015), we can simply say that the lexemic entry for *kick the bucket* is associated with only the active voice tree, while that for *pull strings* is associated with many others, including trees for *wh*-questions, passive, and relative clauses. This results in different sets of potential lexical entries for each expression, and thus different potential syntactic configurations.

One other notable property of idioms is that the words they contain are morphologically related to independently existing words: for example, *kick* in *kick the bucket* inflects like a regular English verb (such as literal *kick*), while *come* in *come a cropper* inflects irregularly in just the same way as literal *come* (e.g. *he came a cropper*). Space

---

[5]For simplicity, I ignore questions about the semantics of plurality on the object.

precludes a full treatment of this here, but it is straightforward enough to implement, for example by having the idiomatic lexemic entry select its word forms from the 'form' paradigms of existing lexemes (Stump, 2001, 2002). Note that such a relationship, whereby parts of a lexical entry draw from the morphological paradigm of independent words, is not unique to MWEs: for example, the lexeme UNDERSTAND is, in terms of inflection, made up of UNDER+STAND, where the second part is identical in inflectional terms to the independent verb STAND, e.g. it shares the irregular past tense form, as in *understood*. Thus, such a mechanism is needed independently of the present proposal, and its extension to TAG-LFG should not pose any undue problems.

5 Conclusion

Strongly lexicalist theories which subscribe to the principle of unary expression cannot deal with MWEs. They are forced to adopt some version of the lexical ambiguity approach, which ultimately fails both formally and empirically. Once we abandon PUE, the question then open to us is how to represent MWEs at the interface between the lexicon and syntax. A formalism like (L)TAG offers an elegant and well-tested means of doing just this. And with minimal modifications, and no increase in generative power, it can be integrated into the LFG architecture.

Acknowledgements

I would like to thank many people for their helpful comments and discussions on this topic, including Ash Asudeh, Alex Biswas, Mary Dalrymple, Timm Lichte, John Lowe, Stephen Pulman, and Andrew Spencer. Special thanks also to the anonymous reviewers, whose advice greatly improved this paper. Of course, any mistakes which remain are mine alone. This work was completed while I was the recipient of a UK Arts and Humanities Research Council studentship (grant reference AH/L503885/1), which I gratefully acknowledge.

References

Anne Abeillé. 1995. The flexibility of French idioms: A representation with Lexicalized Tree Adjoining Grammar. In Martin Everaert, Erik-Jan van der Linden, André Schenk, and Rob Schreuder, editors, *Idioms: Structural and psychological perspectives*. Lawrence Erlbaum, Hove, UK.

Farrell Ackerman, Gregory T. Stump, and Gert Webelhuth. 2011. Lexicalism, periphrasis, and implicative morphology. In Robert D. Borsley and Kersti Börjars, editors, *Non-transformational syntax: Formal and explicit models of grammar*, pages 325–358. Wiley-Blackwell, Oxford, UK.

Doug Arnold and Evita Linardaki. 2007. Linguistic constraints in LFG-DOP. In Miriam Butt and Tracy Holloway King, editors, *Proceedings of the LFG07 Conference*, pages 66–86. CSLI Publications, Stanford, CA.

Doug Arnold. 2015. A Glue Semantics for structurally regular MWEs. Poster presented at the PARSEME 5th general meeting, 23–24th September 2015, Iaşi, Romania.

Ash Asudeh. 2012. *The logic of pronominal resumption*. Oxford University Press, Oxford, UK.

Timothy Baldwin and Su Nam Kim. 2010. Multiword Expressions. In Nitin Indurkhya and Fred J. Damerau, editors, *Handbook of Natural Language Processing* (2nd edn.), pages 267–292. CRC Press, Boca Raton, FL.

Sascha Bargmann and Manfred Sailer. 2015. The syntactic flexibility of non-decomposable idioms. Poster presented at the PARSEME 4th general meeting, 19–20 March 2015, Valletta, Malta.

Sascha Bargmann and Manfred Sailer. In prep. The syntactic flexibility of semantically non-decomposable idioms. In Manfred Sailer and Stella Markantonatou, editors, *Multiword expressions: Insights from a multi-lingual perspective*. Language Science Press, Berlin, DE.

Robert C. Berwick. 1982. Computational complexity and Lexical-Functional Grammar. *American Journal of Computational Linguistics*, 8:97–109.

Rens Bod and Ronald Kaplan. 1998. A probabilistic corpus-driven model for Lexical-Functional analysis. In *Proceedings of the 36th Annual Meeting of the Association for Computational Linguistics and 17th International Conference on Computational Linguistics, Volume 1*, pages 145–151, Montreal, Quebec, Canada, August. Association for Computational Linguistics.

Rens Bod. 1992. A computational model of language performance: Data Oriented Parsing. In *Proceedings of the 15th International Conference on Computational Linguistics (Volume 3: Project notes with demonstrations)*, pages 855–859, Nantes, France, August. International Committee on Computational Linguistics, Association for Computational Linguistics.

Joan Bresnan, Ash Asudeh, Ida Toivonen, and Stephen Wechsler. 2015. *Lexical-functional syntax* (2nd edn.). Wiley-Blackwell, Oxford, UK.

Joan Bresnan. 1982. The passive in lexical theory. In Joan Bresnan, editor, *The mental representation of grammatical relations*, pages 3–86. MIT Press, Cambridge, MA.

Joan Bresnan. 2001. *Lexical-functional syntax*. Blackwell, Oxford, UK.

Tore Burheim. 1996. Aspects of merging Lexical-Functional Grammar with Lexicalized Tree-Adjoining Grammar. Unpublished ms., University of Bergen.

Miriam Butt, María-Eugenia Niño, and Frédérique Segond. 1996. Multilingual processing of auxiliaries within LFG. In Dafydd Gibbon, editor, *Natural language processing and speech technology: Results of the 3rd KONVENS Conference, Universität Bielefeld, October 1996*, pages 111–122. Mouton de Gruyter, Berlin.

Lionel Clément and Alexandra Kinyon. 2003. Generating parallel multilingual LFG-TAG grammars from a MetaGrammar. In *Proceedings of the 41st Annual Meeting of the Association for Computational Linguistics*, pages 184–191, Sapporo, Japan, July. Association for Computational Linguistics.

Benoît Crabbé, Denys Duchier, Claire Gardent, Joseph Le Roux, and Yannick Parmentier. 2013. XMG: eXtensible MetaGrammar. *Computational Linguistics*, 39(3):591–629.

Brian C. Cronk. 1992. The comprehension of idioms: The effects of familiarity, literalness, and usage. *Applied Psycholinguistics*, 13:131–146.

Mary Dalrymple and Irina Nikolaeva. 2011. *Objects and information structure*. Cambridge University Press, Cambridge, UK.

Mary Dalrymple. 1993. *The syntax of anaphoric binding*. Number 36 in CSLI Lecture Notes. CSLI Publications, Stanford, CA.

Mary Dalrymple, editor. 1999. *Semantics and syntax in Lexical Functional Grammar: The resource logic approach*. MIT Press, Cambridge, MA.

Mary Dalrymple. 2001. *Lexical Functional Grammar*. Number 34 in Syntax and Semantics. Academic Press, Stanford, CA.

Mary Dalrymple. 2015. Morphology in the LFG architecture. In Miriam Butt and Tracy Holloway King, editors, *Proceedings of the LFG15 Conference*, pages 64–83. CSLI Publications, Stanford, CA.

Anna Maria Di Sciullo and Edwin Williams. 1987. *On the definition of word*. Number 14 in Linguistic Inquiry monographs. MIT Press, Cambridge, MA.

Robert B. Estill and Susan Kemper. 1982. Interpreting idioms. *Journal of Psycholinguistic Research*, 11(6):559–568.

Raymond W. Gibbs, Jr. 1986. Skating on thin ice: Literal meaning and understanding idioms in context. *Discourse Processes*, 9:17–30.

Jean-Yves Girard. 1987. Linear logic. *Theoretical Computer Science*, 50(1):1–102.

Aravind K. Joshi, Leon S. Levy, and Masako Takahashi. 1975. Tree adjunct grammars. *Journal of Computer and System Sciences*, 10(1):136–163.

Megumi Kameyama. 1986. Characterising Lexical Functional Grammar (LFG) in terms of Tree Adjoining Grammar (TAG). Unpublished ms., Department of Computer and Information Science, University of Pennsylvania.

Ronald M. Kaplan and Joan Bresnan. 1982. Lexical-Functional Grammar: A formal system for grammatical representation. In Joan Bresnan, editor, *The mental representation of grammatical relations*, pages 173–281. MIT Press, Cambridge, MA.

Ronald M. Kaplan. 1995. The formal architecture of Lexical-Functional Grammar. In Mary Dalrymple, Ronald M. Kaplan, John T. Maxwell, III,, and Annie Zaenen, editors, *Formal issues in Lexical-Functional Grammar*, pages 7–28. CSLI Publications, Stanford, CA.

Paul Kay, Ivan A. Sag, and Daniel P. Flickinger. 2015. A lexical theory of phrasal idioms. Unpublished ms., CSLI, Stanford.

Edward L. Keenan and Bernard Comrie. 1977. Noun phrase accessibility and Universal Grammar. *Linguistic Inquiry*, 8:63–99.

Anna Kibort. 2007. Extending the applicability of Lexical Mapping Theory. In Miriam Butt and Tracy Holloway King, editors, *Proceedings of the LFG07 Conference*, pages 250–270. CSLI Publications, Stanford, CA.

Timm Lichte and Laura Kallmeyer. 2016. Same syntax, different semantics: A compositional approach to idiomaticity in multi-word expressions. In Christopher Piñón, editor, *Empirical Issues in Syntax and Semantics 11*. Colloque de Syntaxe et Sémantique à Paris (CSSP), Paris.

Louise Mycock and John Lowe. 2013. The prosodic marking of discourse functions. In Miriam Butt and Tracy Holloway King, editors, *Proceedings of the LFG13 Conference*, pages 440–460. CSLI Publications, Stanford, CA.

Owen Rambow. 1996. Word order, clause union, and the formal machinery of syntax. In Miriam Butt and Tracy Holloway King, editors, *Proceedings of the LFG96 Conference*. CSLI Publications, Stanford, CA.

Manfred Sailer. 2000. Combinatorial semantics and idiomatic expressions in Head-Driven Phrase Structure Grammar. Doctoral dissertation, Eberhard-Karls-Universität Tübingen.

Gregory T. Stump. 2001. *Inflectional morphology: A theory of paradigm structure*. Cambridge University Press, Cambridge, UK.

Gregory T. Stump. 2002. Morphological and syntactic paradigms: Arguments for a theory of paradigm linkage. In Geert Booij and Jaap van Marle, editors, *Yearbook of morphology 2001*, pages 147–180. Kluwer, Dordrecht, NL.

David A. Swinney and Anne Cutler. 1979. The access and processing of idiomatic expressions. *Journal of Verbal Learning and Verbal Behavior*, 18:523–534.

K. Vijay-Shanker. 1987. A study of Tree Adjoining Grammars. Doctoral dissertation, University of Pennsylvania.

Understanding Idiomatic Variation

Kristina Geeraert[1], R. Harald Baayen[2,3] and John Newman[3,4]

[1]Department of Linguistics, KU Leuven, Belgium
[2]Department of Linguistics, University of Tübingen, Germany
[3]Department of Linguistics, University of Alberta, Canada
[4]School of Languages, Literatures, Cultures & Linguistics, Monash University, Australia
`kristina.geeraert@kuleuven.be, harald.baayen@uni-tuebingen.de,`
`john.newman@ualberta.ca`

Abstract

This study investigates the processing of idiomatic variants through an eye-tracking experiment. Four types of idiom variants were included, in addition to the canonical form and the literal meaning. Results suggest that modifications to idioms, modulo obvious effects of length differences, are not more difficult to process than the canonical forms themselves. This fits with recent corpus findings.

1 Introduction

Idioms have traditionally been regarded as multiword units whose meaning can not be derived from the meaning of its parts (Bobrow and Bell, 1973). This has led some researchers to claim that idioms are semantically opaque, that their structure is syntactically fixed, and they are stored whole as a 'large word'. Thus, research investigating how idioms are understood has focused predominantly on the canonical form and how it differed from a literal paraphrase (Swinney and Cutler, 1979; Gibbs, 1980; Cacciari and Tabossi, 1988; Titone and Connine, 1999).

Recent corpus-based research however has shown that idioms can in fact occur with a range of variation (Moon, 1998; Barlow, 2000; Langlotz, 2006; Schröder, 2013). Idioms can undergo syntactic variation (e.g. *they have really bitten the bullet this time* and *her new-found reputation was a bubble that would burst*), be lexically varied (e.g. *throw/toss in the towel, miss the boat/bus*), truncated (e.g. *[he who pays the piper] calls the tune*), and even modified with adverbials or adjectives (e.g. *spill royal beans, pulling political strings, make rapid headway*). This variation can even occur with nondecomposable idioms (Duffley, 2013), such as *kick the bucket* (e.g. *no buckets have been kicked, when his parents kick their*

gold-plated bucket, and *my phone kicked the pail last week*). These studies have illustrated that idioms are not nearly as fixed or rigid in form as previously assumed.

Few studies have investigated idiomatic variation from an experimental perspective. Gibbs and colleagues (Gibbs et al., 1989; Gibbs and Nayak, 1989) explored lexical and syntactic variation of decomposable and nondecomposable idioms using a semantic similarity rating task. They found that decomposable idioms (i.e. idioms whose constituents contribute to the meaning of the whole, as in *pop the question*) were rated as more similar in meaning to a literal paraphrase than were nondecomposable idioms, or idioms whose constituents do not contribute meaning to the whole (e.g. *kick the bucket*). However, nondecomposable idioms can be modified in context while retaining their idiomatic meaning, as was demonstrated by Duffley (2013). Moreover, replication studies do not return consistent results. The role of decomposability has not proven to be a reliable measure, with participants performing at chance when classifying idioms into decomposability categories (Titone and Connine, 1994b; Tabossi et al., 2008). In addition, decomposable and nondecomposable idioms are not always found to be significantly different (Tabossi et al., 2008). Finally, semantic similarity has been shown to be largely predicted by the same local contexts as observed in corpora (Miller and Charles, 1991), suggesting that the semantic similarity measure collected in these studies simply reflected how interchangeable the variant is with its paraphrase and did not accurately reflect the comprehension of these variants.

Meanwhile, McGlone et al. (1994) explored the semantic productivity of idiom variation. Variants in this study produced a new idiomatic meaning based on the original (e.g. *shatter the ice*, from *break the ice*, meaning 'to break an uncomfortable or stiff social situation in one fell swoop').

80

Proceedings of the 13th Workshop on Multiword Expressions (MWE 2017), pages 80–90,
Valencia, Spain, April 4. ©2017 Association for Computational Linguistics

Using self-paced reading, they measured the reaction time for participants to read the final sentence of a story, which contained idioms, variants, or literal paraphrases. They found that participants were significantly faster at reading the canonical form of the idiom, but that the variants were read as fast as the literal paraphrases. They suggest that canonical forms of idioms are accessed whole, but that variants are processed like literal language and are therefore processed slower. While the results show that modified idioms can be understood in context, they did not control for the type of variation. They used instances of lexical variation (e.g. *shatter the ice*), quantification (e.g. *not spill a single bean*), and even hyperboles (e.g. *it's raining the whole kennel*). Based on their findings, it is uncertain whether some types of variation are easier to comprehend than others.

The current study explores the processing of several types of variation, as well as the literal meaning of the idiom, through an eye-tracking experiment. Two research questions are explored: (1) are variants processed differently from the canonical form; and (2) are variants processed differently from each other. The first question plans to determine whether variants are still processed differently from the canonical form when the type of variation is controlled for (e.g. is lexical variation more difficult to comprehend than the original idiom?). Second, by including several types of variation and controlling for them, a comparison can be made between the different types of variants (e.g. Are there processing differences between, say, lexical variation and partial forms of an expression?).

While this experiment was largely exploratory, we did have some predictions about the results. For example, formal idiom blends are typically regarded in the literature as 'errors' or 'slips of the tongue' (Fay, 1982; Cutting and Bock, 1997). We therefore hypothesized that idiom blends would be more difficult to process due to this 'error-like' nature. Meanwhile, some idioms can occur in "idiom sets" or "clusters", such as *shake/quake/quiver in one's boots* or *down the drain/chute/tube/toilet* (Moon, 1998). We hypothesized that lexical variation would not be more difficult to understand than the canonical form. Lastly, partial or truncated forms of an expression have words omitted and should be faster to read, whereas additional adjectives inserted into the expression should take addi-

tional time due to the presence of an extra word.

The remainder of the paper proceeds as follows: We first describe the design of the experiment and the materials used. Next, we present the results, focusing on two areas of interest: the idiom as a whole and the altered word within the idiom. Finally, we discuss our findings and how they fit into the larger discussion on idioms.

2   Methodology

2.1   Materials

Sixty idioms were extracted from the Oxford Dictionary of English Idioms (Ayto, 2009) and the Collins COBUILD Idioms Dictionary (Sinclair, 2011). The form listed in the dictionary was regarded as the canonical form. If more than one form was listed then the form most familiar to the first author was used, as she spoke the same variety as the participants in the study. These idioms varied in length and syntactic structure: 20 three-word idioms consisting of a verb and a noun phrase (i.e. V-NP, e.g. *rock the boat*); 20 four-word idioms consisting of a verb and a prepositional phrase (i.e. V-PP, e.g. *jump on the bandwagon*); and 20 five- or six-word idioms (10 each) consisting of a verb, noun phrase, and a prepositional phrase (i.e. V-NP-PP, e.g. *hear something through the grapevine*). Two contexts were created for each idiom: one literal and one figurative (e.g. *I used to pretend I could talk to plants, and I would hear things through the grapevine* = literal; and *I used to be a socialite, and I would hear things through the grapevine* = figurative). Both contexts had identical final clauses, with the idiom in sentence-final position. As syntactic variation is possible with idioms (Moon, 1998; Schröder, 2013), the contexts in this study were not restricted to the present tense.

These idioms were manipulated for four types of variation within the figurative context (i.e. the context was identical for all variants), in addition to the canonical form. First, lexical variation, where one of the lexical items within the expression was altered to a synonymous or near-synonymous word (e.g. *discover something through the grapevine*). Synonyms were selected based on their naturalness in the context to convey a similar meaning.[1] Second, partial form of the idiom, where only a portion of the idiom was

---

[1]An online thesaurus (http://www.thesaurus.com/) was often utilized for synonymous words.

presented, usually a key word or words (e.g. *use the grapevine*). In order for the sentence to still be grammatically correct, pronouns or lexically-vague words replaced the missing elements of the expression, such as *it, them, things* for nouns, or *have, be, do, use* for verbs. Third, integrated concept, where an additional concept was integrated into the idiom (e.g. *hear something through the judgemental grapevine*). These additional concepts expanded or emphasized the figurative contexts in which the idiom occurred. Finally, formal idiom blend, where two idioms were blended together (e.g. *get wind through the grapevine –* blending *hear something through the grapevine* with *get wind of something*). Each experimental idiom (i.e. the 60 idioms selected) was paired with a non-experimental idiom for use in the idiom blend condition. These "blending" idioms were chosen for their intuitive plausibility, but controlled for their syntax and semantics (Cutting and Bock, 1997).

Half of the idioms had the beginning portion of the expression altered (verb), while the other half had alternations made to the final portion of the expression (noun). In total, there are six conditions: one in a literal context and five in a figurative context (i.e. one canonical form and four variants). The experiment utilized a Latin-square design, where every participant saw each idiom once in one of the six conditions. Six versions of the experiment were created, each one containing 10 idioms in each of the six conditions.

CONDITIONS:

1. **Literal Meaning** of the idiom in its canonical form
   (e.g. *While the guys were reshingling, they suddenly went through the roof.*)

2. **Canonical Form** of the idiom in a figurative context
   (e.g. *Although these were new stocks, they suddenly went through the roof.*)

3. **Lexical Variation** of the idiom in a figurative context
   (e.g. *Although these were new stocks, they suddenly went through the ceiling.*)

4. **Partial Form** of the idiom in a figurative context
   (e.g. *Although these were new stocks, they suddenly went through it.*)

5. **Integrated Concept** within the idiom in a figurative context
   (e.g. *Although these were new stocks, they suddenly went through the investment roof.*)

6. **Idiom Blend** of two idioms in a figurative context
   (e.g. *Although these were new stocks, they suddenly went through the charts.*)

Since the "blending idioms" only occurred in one condition (i.e. Idiom Blend), they were used as fillers in their canonical form in the other five versions of the experiment, occurring in either a figurative or literal context. Each blending idiom was excluded as a control in the version of the experiment where it occurred in the idiom blend condition in order to avoid a bias in the materials. Therefore, in each version of the experiment, 10 of the blending idioms occurred in the idiom blend condition, while the remaining 50 appeared in their canonical form as fillers. Of these fillers, 20 occurred in a figurative context and 30 occurred in a literal context. This was done to increase the number of literal contexts in the experiment so that they were not so underrepresented. In sum, each participant saw 110 items: 60 experimental idioms (10 in each of the six conditions) and 50 blending idioms as fillers.

Finally, six practice sentences were created using six "practice" idioms. These idioms all occurred in their canonical form. Three were in a figurative context and three in a literal context. These were the same for all participants.

2.2 Procedure

This experiment used the Eye-Link 1000, desk-top mounted video-based eye-tracking device, manufactured by SR Research. The eye-tracker sampled the pupil location and size at a rate of 1000Hz, and was calibrated using a 9-point calibration grid. Calibration occurred at the beginning of the experiment, after the practice, and again after every 22 sentences, for a total of five blocks. The computer screen resolution was set to 1920 x 1080 pixels.

The stimuli were presented in two parts. Participants first saw the "context clause" (e.g. *Although these were new stocks,*), followed by the "idiom clause" (e.g. *they suddenly went through the roof.*) on a separate screen. Each trial began with a fixation cross presented for 1,000 msec on the left side of a light-grey screen. Next, they saw the context clause, also on a light-grey background, in a bold, black, Courier New 30-point font. Every clause was displayed in full and fit on one line. To exit this screen, participants had to trigger an invisible boundary in the bottom right corner. A blank, light-grey screen was presented for 1,000 msec before the fixation cross preceding the idiom clause appeared. The sequence of screens for the idiom clause was identical to the context clause.

Ten percent of the stimuli were followed by a true/false comprehension question, which pertained to the immediately preceding sentence, and were presented randomly throughout the experiment. Participants pushed one of two buttons on a game controller to answer these questions, which were clearly labelled on the question screen. The experiment began with a practice session, which consisted of six practice sentences and three questions. These were the same for all participants, although their order varied.

All participants had normal or corrected-to-normal vision. The right eye of each participant was tracked. Participants sat approximately 85cm from the computer screen, with the camera placed on the desk about 35cm in front of the computer screen. The participants sat in a soundproof booth, while the experimenter sat outside the booth, running the experiment. The lights were kept on. The experiment was self-paced and took about 45 minutes to complete. Each participant was given an opportunity for a short break halfway through the experiment.

After the participants had completed the eye-tracking portion, they were asked to indicate their knowledge of each expression in a separate task. Each idiom appeared on the computer screen, in its canonical form, in a black, bold, 22-point Courier New font, centered on a white background. Above the idiom was the question "Do you know this expression?"; below were two boxes, one labelled 'yes' and the other labelled 'no'. Using the mouse, participants clicked on the appropriate box to respond. The mouse repositioned itself to the center of the screen on each trial.

At the end of this second task, participants were presented with a few additional questions, pertaining to their idiom usage (e.g. How often do you use these expressions?; Do you like using these expressions?). Below each question was a Visual Analogue Scale (VAS), which is a continuous graphical rating scale (Hayes and Patterson, 1921; Freyd, 1923; Funke and Reips, 2012). Participants responded by clicking the mouse anywhere along the VAS scale. The scale was labelled with a 'thumbs-up' image on the right for a positive response and a 'thumbs-down' image on the left for a negative one. Lastly, participants were asked to rate the acceptability of seven prescriptively 'incorrect' sentences, shown below, using the same VAS scale. These sentences attempted to elicit a measure of the participant's flexibility with language and non-standard usage.

Language Questions (LQs):

1. The only option the school board has is to lay off a large *amount* of people.

2. Slot machines are thought to be more *addicting* than table games.

3. The document had to be signed by both Susan and *I*.

4. While cleaning the kitchen, Sally looked up and saw a spider on the *roof.*

5. I thought it could*'ve went* either way.

6. She *could care* less what he had to say about it.

7. You have to balance your life, *irregardless* of what anybody thinks.

2.3 Participants

Sixty University of Alberta linguistics undergraduate students participated in this experiment. All were native speakers of Canadian English. There were 43 female and 17 male participants, ranging from 17–29 years of age. Four participants were left-handed. All participants were reimbursed for their time with course credit.

3 Results

The results were analyzed using mixed-effects linear regression, using the `lme4` package (Bates et al., 2014) in R (R Core Team, 2014). Only the results for the Total Fixation Duration (i.e. the total amount of time spent fixating on the Area Of Interest, or AOI) will be discussed. We focus on two AOIs: the idiom as a whole (i.e. the summed fixations on all words within the idiom) and the altered word within the idiom (i.e. the synonymous word in lexical variation, the additional word in the integrated concept, the semantically vague 'replacement' word in partial forms, and the word from another idiom in the idiom blend). The analyses focus on the 60 experimental idioms. Further information about this study and the results can be found in Geeraert (2016).

Ten predictor variables appeared significant in the models. `Condition` is a factor indicating the type of variation with which the idiom occurred (e.g. lexical variation, partial form). `Length` specifies the number of words within the idiom's canonical form. `PortionAltered` is a factor specifying which part of the idiom (i.e. beginning/verb or ending/noun) was manipulated in the variant. `Trial` is the standardized order of presentation of the stimuli in the experiment. As the stimuli was presented randomly, this order will be different for each participant.

`MeanVariationRating` is a standardized mean measure of acceptability for the particular idiom with a specific type of variation. This measure was collected in a separate experiment, where participants were asked to rate the acceptability of the variants in the same contexts. These ratings were included to determine if participants' preferences influence their ease of comprehension.

As the decomposability classification is unreliable (Titone and Connine, 1994b; Tabossi et al., 2008), two measures reflecting the semantic contribution of the constituents were utilized instead. `meanTransparencyRating` is a standardized average measure of transparency for the idiom's meaning as a whole. These ratings were collected in a separate experiment, where participants saw each idiom, along with its definition and an example, and were asked to rate how obvious was the meaning of the expression. The average rating for each idiom was included as a predictor to determine whether the overall transparency of the idiom influences speakers' processing of variants. `LSA.Score.Paraphrase` is a measure of similarity using Latent Semantic Analysis (LSA), between the words in the idiom and its paraphrase (e.g. *spill the beans* 'reveal a secret'). This score was obtained from a pairwise comparison of two texts (i.e. an idiom and its paraphrase), which compares the local contexts in order to obtain a value of similarity (Landauer et al., 1998).[2] This measure allows us to control for the idiom's compositionality. If the exact words in the idiom have little to do with the expression's meaning, then the LSA score will be small (e.g. *cut the mustard –* 'be acceptable' = 0.07). But if the words used share meaning or contribute to the idiom's meaning, then the LSA score will be larger (e.g. *stop something in its tracks –* 'stop something' = 0.87).

As idioms are multi-word expressions, multiple frequency measures were obtained: the frequency of the idiom, frequencies of the individual words, and all possible combinations of adjacent words (e.g. word1 and word2; word2 and word3; word1 and word2 and word3). To avoid collinearity, a Principal Components Analysis (PCA) was conducted on these frequency measures. Only the first Principal Component (henceforth `PC1.logFrequency`) is significant.

Several participant-related variables are also significant. `KnowIdiom` is a factor indicating the participant's knowledge of each idiom (i.e. 'yes' or 'no'). `Gender` is a factor specifying whether the participant is male or female. Finally, a second PCA was conducted on the rating responses for the seven Language Questions (LQs) above. Only PC2 (henceforth `PC2.LQ`) was significant. This variable is used to reflect the participant's flexibility with language usage.

3.1 Idiom as Area of Interest

The first model examines the summed fixation durations on the idiom as a whole. The fixed effects for this model are shown in Table 1. `Condition` occurs in two significant interactions; the first, between `Condition` and `KnowIdiom`, is shown in the left panel of Figure 1. The canonical form, and the majority of variants, show the same general pattern: shorter fixation durations on known idioms. These variants (except integrated concepts) are therefore shown in grey, as they do not significantly differ from the canonical form. Partial forms however show a different pattern. Fixation durations on this variant are relatively similar regardless of whether the participant is familiar with the expression or not; thus a facilitation effect for knowing the idiom is not observed as it is with the other variants. This particular variant is fixated upon less than the canonical form, likely due to it being shorter in length (i.e. fewer number of words). This is in line with longer fixations observed on integrated concepts – an additional word is integrated into the idiom, making it longer in length and requiring additional fixations.

The second interaction, shown in the second panel of Figure 1, is between `Condition` and `Length`. The general pattern observed here is that longer idioms show longer summed fixation durations, as expected, due to the increased number of words in the idiom. Lexical variation, formal idiom blends, and the literal meaning of the idiom are not significantly different from the canonical form (shown in grey). The other two variants show a pattern that is significantly different from the canonical form. Idioms with integrated concepts show a slight inhibitory effect of length, where an additional concept is more

---

[2]The LSA scores were obtained from the English Lexicon Project (Balota et al., 2007), available at http://lsa.colorado.edu/.

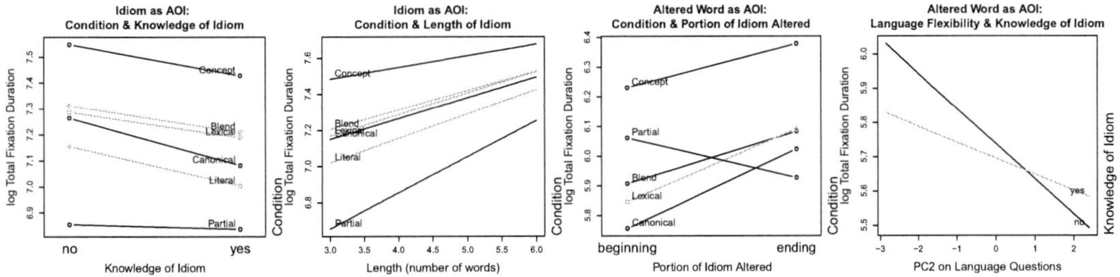

Figure 1: Interactions in the Mixed-Effects Linear Regression Models for the Summed Total Fixation Duration on the Whole Idiom and the Altered Word as an Area of Interest. Lines in grey represent factors levels which are not significantly different or slopes which are not significant.

difficult to integrate into shorter idioms (i.e. extra time is needed). However, partial forms of shorter idioms have even fewer words to fixate upon and therefore show considerably shorter fixation durations. In sum, durations on integrated concepts and partial forms are more comparable to the canonical form when the idiom is longer.[3]

Interestingly, the literal meaning of the idiom shows shorter fixation durations than the canonical form. These fixations are not significantly shorter ($t = -1.94$), but certainly trending towards significance. The literality of the expressions (Titone and Connine, 1994a) may be contributing to this result. Nevertheless, a general pattern is evident based on these two above interactions with `Condition`: variants of the same length as the canonical form are not processed significantly different from this canonical form.

The model presented in Table 1 also shows six main effects. Longer fixation durations are observed on the whole idiom if the beginning of the idiom (i.e. the verb) was altered. This is not dependent on the type of variation, but rather all variants are easier to process if the change comes later in the expression (see `PortionAltered`). This is a different result than that of Gibbs and colleagues (Gibbs et al., 1989; Gibbs and Nayak, 1989) who found no difference with ratings in whether the noun or verb was altered.

A significant main effect is also observed for `meanVariationRating`. Variants which re-

	Estimate	Std. Error	t-value
Intercept	6.71	0.09	75.97
Condition=Concept	0.49	0.10	5.04
Condition=Blend	0.08	0.10	0.75
Condition=Lexical	0.01	0.10	0.05
Condition=Literal	-0.19	0.10	-1.94
Condition=Partial	-0.75	0.16	-4.80
KnowIdiom=Yes	-0.18	0.04	-4.32
Length	0.11	0.02	6.76
PortionAltered=Ending	-0.06	0.02	-2.52
PC2.LQ	-0.07	0.03	-2.42
LSA.Score.Paraphrase	0.24	0.07	3.49
meanVariationRating	-0.06	0.01	-7.23
Gender=Male	-0.17	0.08	-2.17
Trial	-0.04	0.01	-3.78
I(KnowIdiom=Yes|Condition=Concept)	0.06	0.05	1.16
I(KnowIdiom=Yes|Condition=Blend)	0.08	0.06	1.42
I(KnowIdiom=Yes|Condition=Lexical)	0.08	0.06	1.52
I(KnowIdiom=Yes|Condition=Literal)	0.03	0.06	0.55
I(KnowIdiom=Yes|Condition=Partial)	0.17	0.06	2.75
I(Length|Condition=Concept)	-0.05	0.02	-2.62
I(Length|Condition=Blend)	-0.01	0.02	-0.36
I(Length|Condition=Lexical)	0.00	0.02	0.20
I(Length|Condition=Literal)	0.02	0.02	1.04
I(Length|Condition=Partial)	0.08	0.03	2.48

Table 1: Fixed Effects for the Idiom as AOI

ceived higher acceptability ratings are fixated on less long, suggesting preferred variants are easier to understand and interpret (or perhaps variants easier to interpret are preferred). Additionally, longer fixation durations appear on idioms which have higher LSA scores for the idiom's paraphrase (i.e. `LSA.Score.Paraphrase`). This finding seems initially surprising, as previous analyses on the comprehension of idioms suggest that idioms are easier to understand when the individual components contribute meaning to the whole (Gibbs et al., 1989). However, the LSA scores indicate how similar the local contexts are between the idiom and its paraphrase (i.e. how interchangable is the expression with its paraphrase). When the LSA score is high (i.e. the paraphrase is easily interchangable) then looking time increases as the contexts are not distinctive for the idiom. But if the LSA score is low, then the idiom and its paraphrase are less interchangable, making the context more distinctive and the idiom more predictable. Interestingly, `meanTransparencyRating` is

---

[3] `PC1.logFrequency` was also significant in the Idiom as AOI model. However, this variable is strongly correlated with `Length` ($r = -0.9$). This correlation is unsurprising given that `PC1.logFrequency` was created using adjacent co-occurrence frequencies. Model comparison shows that `Length` is the more significant predictor in this model, producing a considerably lower AIC value, and therefore was retained at the expense of `PC1.logFrequency`.

not significant. The degree to which the idiom is considered 'obvious in meaning' does not seem to influence the comprehension of idioms or variants.

A main effect was also observed for `PC2.LQ`, a latent variable representing the participants' flexibility with language (i.e. the more they find nonstandard or erroneous forms acceptable). Shorter fixations are observed on the idioms, both the canonical form and variants, if speakers are more flexible with language. It is interesting to note that this finding is not restricted to variants. `Gender` also shows a significant main effect – males tend to fixate less long on the idiom than females, although we are not quite sure why. Finally, a main effect of `Trial` is also significant; participants fixate less long on the idiom the further into the experiment they get. But the degree to which each participant is affected by the order of presentation varies, as evidenced by significant by-Subject random slopes for `Trial`. By-Item random slopes for `Condition` with correlation parameters are also significant in this model. These slopes indicate that participants' fixation durations vary depending on which idiom occurred in which condition – participants found certain idioms easier or more difficult to understand depending on the condition in which they occurred.[4]

3.2 Altered Word as Area of Interest

We also investigated the fixation duration on the Altered Word (i.e. the word in the idiom that was manipulated). The fixed effects for this model are shown in Table 2. Since there is no altered word in the literal condition, this section focuses on the four idiom variants (i.e. lexical variation, partial forms, idiom blends, and integrated concepts) and how they compare to the canonical form.

The interaction between `Condition` and `PortionAltered` is seen in the third panel of Figure 1. The overall pattern is that longer fixation durations occur at the end of the idiom, which is also true for the canonical form. Since the idiom occurs at the end of a sentence, these longer fixations on the canonical form and variants may reflect a sentence wrap-up effect (Rayner et al., 2000; Hirotani et al., 2006). Nevertheless, the altered word for most variants shows significantly longer fixations than the canonical form. This is not true of lexical variation, which is the only variant that does not have significantly longer fixations

than the canonical form (t = 1.54). In other words, a lexically altered variant is just as easy to process as the canonical form. Partial forms however appear considerably different from the canonical form. Longer fixations are observed on the altered word when the beginning has been altered, such as *use the grapevine*. But when the ending is altered (e.g. *spilled it*), fixations on the altered word are not significantly different from the canonical form (t = -1.44). Since altering the verb does not always result in significantly longer fixations (cf. the non-significantly different lexical variant when the beginning is altered), this finding suggests that altering the verb to a semantically vague verb, in order to make the sentence grammatical, significantly inhibits processing.

The second interaction, shown in the last panel of Figure 1, is between between knowledge of the idiom (i.e. `KnowIdiom`) and the participant's flexibility with language (i.e. `PC2.LQ`). Flexibility with language only appears to be facilitative for those who do not know the idiom, illustrated by the non-significant slope for those who know the expression (t = -1.29). Other strategies are apparently relied upon to interpret the alternation when knowledge of the expression is not available.

Additional main effects are also observed on the altered word. Fixation durations are longer on the altered word when the co-occurrence frequencies of the idiom are higher. Thus, altering part of a more frequent sequence causes greater processing costs. In addition, participants have shorter fixation durations when the variant is rated as more acceptable (i.e. `meanVariationRating`). The more the variation strategy is preferred for a particular idiom, the easier it is to interpret. Finally, the further the participants get into the experiment (i.e. `Trial`), the shorter their fixation durations on the altered words.

	Estimate	Std. Error	t-value
Intercept	5.70	0.06	98.48
Condition=Concept	0.47	0.06	8.28
Condition=Blend	0.15	0.06	2.67
Condition=Lexical	0.09	0.06	1.54
Condition=Partial	0.30	0.07	4.61
PortionAltered=Ending	0.27	0.06	4.49
KnowIdiom=Yes	-0.04	0.03	-1.29
PC2.LQ	-0.10	0.03	-3.12
PC1.logFrequency	0.03	0.01	4.70
meanVariationRating	-0.07	0.02	-4.27
Trial	-0.04	0.01	-2.79
I(PortionAltered=Ending|Condition=Concept)	-0.12	0.08	-1.46
I(PortionAltered=Ending|Condition=Blend)	-0.09	0.08	-1.17
I(PortionAltered=Ending|Condition=Lexical)	-0.02	0.08	-0.26
I(PortionAltered=Ending|Condition=Partial)	-0.40	0.09	-4.42
I(PC2.LQ|KnowIdiom=Yes)	0.06	0.02	2.27

Table 2: Fixed Effects for the Altered Word as AOI

---

[4]Both models have the same random effects structure.

3.3 Spillover from the Altered Word

As the idiom occurred in sentence-final position, spillover effects from an altered noun (i.e. the end of the idiom) are not able to be determined. However, for variants in which the beginning portion of the idiom was altered (the verb), it may appear to the participant reading the text as though the ending was manipulated (e.g. as if the 'blending idiom' was the intended idiom in *call the strings*, or part of an idiom was inserted into an otherwise non-idiomatic text, such as *use the grapevine*); therefore, we examined the fixation duration on the first content word after the verb when the verb was manipulated (i.e. the alternation occurred at the beginning of the idiom).

Only main effects are observed in the model, shown in Table 3. Spillover effects are observed for all variant types (i.e. `Condition`), but the longest durations are for integrated concepts and partial forms. Incorporating an additional word into an idiom results in a processing cost likely due to the surprisal of this extra word. Integrating this additional information into the idiom and idiomatic context requires extra time. The largest spillover effect is with partial forms. It appears that the semantically vague words used in these sentences (to make them grammatical) make these partial forms more difficult to comprehend and cause considerable spillover effects. It remains to be determined whether partial forms from more naturalistic language produce this same effect.

The last two effects are `PC1.Frequency` and `KnowIdiom`. The higher the co-occurrences frequencies of the idiom, the longer the fixation duration on the first content word after the alternation. Modifying a frequent multi-word sequence inhibits processing. However, these spillover effects are reduced if the idiom is familiar (i.e. `KnowIdiom`).

	Estimate	Std. Error	t-value
Intercept	5.95	0.08	73.41
Condition=Concept	0.27	0.07	3.76
Condition=Blend	0.17	0.06	2.75
Condition=Lexical	0.14	0.05	2.92
Condition=Partial	0.30	0.06	4.62
PC1.logFrequency	0.04	0.01	3.54
KnowIdiom=Yes	-0.11	0.05	-2.32

Table 3: Fixed Effects for the First Content Word After the Verb

4 Discussion

This study further confirms that idioms are not nearly as fixed or frozen as previously assumed, but can actually be modified in a variety of ways while still retaining their idiomatic meaning. Furthermore, this modification does not always end in a processing disadvantage, answering our first research question. Some variants, in fact, do not show any 'variant' processing costs. Lexical variation, formal idiom blends, and a literal meaning of the idiom are not processed significantly longer than the canonical form. Longer fixations are observed on the altered word (at least for idiom blends) and some spillover effects are observed if the verb was altered, but this does not result in longer processing times for the idiom as a whole. These results are partly in line with our predictions. Only formal idiom blends were predicted to be processed slower than the canonical form, due to the potential surprisal at this 'erroneous' form. But that is not what is observed. Intentional or not, altering a word within an idiom to a synonymous or non-synonymous word does not result in a processing cost.

Some variants, on the other hand, are processed differently from the canonical form. The variant showing the greatest difference from the canonical form is the partial form of the idiom (e.g. *use the grapevine*). This idiom variant is fixated on less than the canonical form, as predicted, largely due to the omission of a word (or words) from the expression. Yet despite this overall shorter fixation, participants fixated significantly longer on the 'replacement' verbs (i.e. the semantically vague verbs used to connect the idiom to the sentence) and significant spillover effects were observed on the first content word after these verbs. A similar inhibitory effect was not observed if the ending of the expression was modified (e.g. *spilled it*). These results are likely due to the design of the experiment. Using tightly controlled stimuli made these partial forms unnatural and difficult to interpret. A study investigating partial forms in naturally occurring language may shed more light on the degree of difficulty for processing this variant.

Idioms with additional integrated concepts are also processed significantly different from the canonical form, but this longer fixation time observed on the whole idiom is largely attributable to the extra word in the expression. This extra word makes the reading time longer, as expected. This longer duration on the whole idiom is very similar to the Altered Word AOI, suggesting that this variant experiences very little processing costs over and above having to read an extra word.

Meanwhile, not all variant types are processed differently from each other, answering our second research question. Lexical variation and formal idiom blends are actually processed quite similarly, showing comparable durations to each other in addition to the canonical form. These variants maintain the same length as the original expression, and perhaps better maintain the idiom's original metaphorical meaning, leading to comparable fixation durations between these two variants. However, other variants are processed quite differently. Adding an additional element (integrated concept) or omitting part of the expression (partial form) results in processing differences – requiring longer or shorter reading times, respectively.

These findings of course do not imply that all idioms can be altered using all variation strategies. Variability with the different strategies is also evident in the results. The random effects structure in both models had significant by-Item random slopes with correlation parameters for `Condition`. This indicates that specific idioms can be easier or more difficult to process depending with which condition (i.e. variation strategy) they occurred. Furthermore, idiom variants which are preferred (i.e. rated as more acceptable) show shorter reading times, or are easier to process. These results reveal that the way in which each idiom is modified can greatly affect how easy it is to understand.

This study also incorporated additional, and sometimes novel, predictor variables to shed new light on idioms and idiomatic variation. An objective measure of compositionality (i.e. LSA scores), was used in this study, and interestingly, these scores are only predictive for the idiom as a whole, and not at the word level, suggestive of the analytical nature of idiom interpretation and not necessarily reflective of a bottom-up (i.e. decomposable) process (Gibbs et al., 1989). Meanwhile, length is surprisingly seldom investigated in the literature (Fanari et al., 2010), yet appears to play a role in idiomatic comprehension. The same can be said for speaker-specific variables. Every speaker's independent knowledge of each idiom (not just an average measure of familiarity), as well as their general flexibility with nonstandard or erroneous usage, proves facilitative in understanding idioms and idiom variants.

In sum, this study found that some variant types are processed similarly to (i.e. not significantly different from) the canonical form. Not all alternations to the canonical form resulted in a processing disadvantage. These findings suggest then that idioms are not processed differently from literal language, as some scholars have claimed (Swinney and Cutler, 1979; Sprenger et al., 2006). Proposing that idioms are stored as 'large words' and understood, say upon activation of an 'idiom key' (Cacciari and Tabossi, 1988), runs into difficulty when the idiom is varied but does not take any longer to process than the canonical form (or a literal meaning of this form). All variant forms would therefore also have to be stored, burdening the Mental Lexicon with a plethora of (infrequent) forms.

More recent approaches to language challenge the traditional view of the Mental Lexicon (i.e. as a list of dictionary entries) and instead suggest that words themselves do not possess meaning but rather are cues to meaning, modulated by experience and context (Elman, 2004; Ramscar and Baayen, 2013). Under this view, idioms would not need to be regarded any differently, but would simply be a sequence of words which are cues to the intended meaning. Geeraert et al. (2017) investigated this approach with idioms using the Naive Discriminative Learner (NDL), which utilizes wide learning networks to approximate error implicit learning. They found that the idiomatic meaning receives initial support upon encountering the first word, and continues to receive support for the duration of the idiom. Alternations to the idiom affect the activation of the idiomatic meaning. If a word is changed or omitted, there is an abrupt decline in activation. However, the idiomatic meaning can also be repaired after such a decline, as with integrated concepts. Those findings are in line with the results from this study. We can manipulate idioms in various ways and still understand them, and in some instances, without any processing costs.

Acknowledgments

This study was supported by an Izaak Walton Killam memorial scholarship awarded to the first author. In addition, we would like to thank Lauren Rudat for her suggestions on improving the stimuli, and to the anonymous reviewers for their suggestions on improving the paper.

References

John Ayto, editor. 2009. *From the horse's mouth: Oxford dictionary of English idioms*. Oxford University Press, Oxford.

David A. Balota, Melvin J. Yap, Michael J. Cortese, Keith A. Hutchison, Brett Kessler, Bjorn Loftis, James H. Neely, Douglas L. Nelson, Greg B. Simpson, and Rebecca Treiman. 2007. English lexicon project. *Behavior Research Methods*, 39(3):445–459.

Michael Barlow. 2000. Usage, blends and grammar. In Michael Barlow and Suzanne Kemmer, editors, *Usage-based models of language*, pages 315–345. CSLI Publications, Stanford, CA.

Douglas Bates, Martin Maechler, Ben Bolker, and Steven Walker. 2014. lme4: Linear mixed-effects models using eigen and S4.

Samuel A. Bobrow and Susan M. Bell. 1973. On catching on to idiomatic expressions. *Memory and Cognition*, 1:343–346.

Cristina Cacciari and Patrizia Tabossi. 1988. The comprehension of idioms. *Journal of Memory and Language*, 27:668–683.

J. Cooper Cutting and Kathryn Bock. 1997. That's the way the cookie bounces: Syntactic and semantic components of experimentally elicited idiom blends. *Memory & Cognition*, 25(1):57–71.

Patrick J. Duffley. 2013. How creativity strains conventionality in the use of idiomatic expressions. In Mike Borkent, Barbara Dancygier, and Jennifer Hinnell, editors, *Language and the creative mind*, pages 49–61. CSLI Publications, Stanford, CA.

Jeffrey L. Elman. 2004. An alternative view of the mental lexicon. *Trends in Cognitive Sciences*, 8(7):301–306.

Rachele Fanari, Cristina Cacciari, and Patrizia Tabossi. 2010. The role of idiom length and context in spoken idiom comprehension. *European Journal of Cognitive Psychology*, 22(3):321–334.

David Fay. 1982. Substitutions and splices: A study of sentence blends. In Anne Cutler, editor, *Slips of the tongue and language production*, pages 163–195. Mouton de Gruyter, Amsterdam.

Max Freyd. 1923. The graphic rating scale. *The Journal of Educational Psychology*, 14:83–102.

Frederik Funke and Ulf-Dietrich Reips. 2012. Why semantic differentials in web-based research should be made from visual analogue scales and not from 5-point scales. *Field Methods*, 24(3):310–327.

Kristina Geeraert, John Newman, and R. Harald Baayen. 2017. Idiom variation: Experimental data and a blueprint of a computational model. In Morten Christiansen and Inbal Arnon, editors, *More than words: The role of multiword sequences in language learning and use*, Topics in Cognitive Science. Wiley, doi:10.1111/tops.12263.

Kristina Geeraert. 2016. *Climbing on the bandwagon of idiomatic variation: A multi-methodological approach*. Ph.D. thesis, University of Alberta.

Raymond W. Gibbs and Nandini P. Nayak. 1989. Psycholinguistic studies on the syntactic behavior of idioms. *Cognitive Psychology*, 21:100–138.

Raymond W. Gibbs, Nandini P. Nayak, John L. Bolton, and Melissa E. Keppel. 1989. Speakers' assumptions about the lexical flexibility of idioms. *Memory & Cognition*, 17(1):58–68.

Raymond W. Gibbs. 1980. Spilling the beans on understanding and memory for idioms in conversation. *Memory & Cognition*, 8(2):149–156.

M. H. S. Hayes and D. G. Patterson. 1921. Experimental development of the graphic rating scale. *Psychology Bulletin*, 18:98–99.

Masako Hirotani, Lyn Frazier, and Keith Rayner. 2006. Punctuation and intonation effects on clause and sentence wrap-up: Evidence from eye movements. *Journal of Memory and Language*, 54:425–443.

Thomas K. Landauer, Peter W. Foltz, and Darrell Laham. 1998. Introduction to latent semantic analysis. *Discourse Processes*, 25:259–184.

Andreas Langlotz. 2006. *Idiomatic creativity: A cognitive-linguistic model of idiom-representation and idiom-variation in English*. John Benjamins.

Matthew S. McGlone, Sam Glucksberg, and Cristina Cacciari. 1994. Semantic productivity and idiom comprehension. *Discourse Processes*, 17:167–190.

George A. Miller and Walter G. Charles. 1991. Contextual correlates of semantic similarity. *Language and Cognitive Processes*, 6(1):1–28.

Rosamund Moon. 1998. *Fixed expressions and idioms in English*. Oxford University Press, Oxford.

R Core Team. 2014. R: A language and environment for statistical computing.

Michael Ramscar and R. Harald Baayen. 2013. Production, comprehension, and synthesis: A communicative perspective on language. *Frontiers in Psychology*, May 02.

Keith Rayner, Gretchen Kambe, and Susan A. Duffy. 2000. The effect of clause wrap-up on eye movements during reading. *The Quarterly Journal of Experimental Psychology*, 53A(4):1061–1080.

Daniela Schröder. 2013. *The syntactic flexibility of idioms: A corpus-based approach*. AVM, Munich.

John Sinclair, editor. 2011. *Collins COBUILD idioms dictionary*. Harper Collins.

Simone A. Sprenger, Willem J. M. Levelt, and Gerard Kempen. 2006. Lexical access during the production of idiomatic phrases. *Journal of Memory and Language*, 54:161–184.

David A. Swinney and Anne Cutler. 1979. The access and processing of idiomatic expressions. *Journal of Verbal Learning and Verbal Behaviour*, 18:523–534.

Patrizia Tabossi, Rachele Fanari, and Kinou Wolf. 2008. Processing idiomatic expressions: Effects of semantic compositionality. *Journal of Experimental Psychology: Learning, Memory, and Cognition*, 34(2):313–327.

Debra A. Titone and Cynthia M. Connine. 1994a. Comprehension of idiomatic expressions: Effects of predictability and literality. *Journal of Experimental Psychology: Learning, Memory, and Cognition*, 20(5):1126–1138.

Debra A. Titone and Cynthia M. Connine. 1994b. Descriptive norms for 171 idiomatic expressions: Familiarity, compositionality, predictability, and literality. *Metaphor and Symbolic Activity*, 9(4):247–270.

Debra A. Titone and Cynthia M. Connine. 1999. On the compositional and noncompositional nature of idiomatic expressions. *Journal of Pragmatics*, 31:1655–1674.

Discovering Light Verb Constructions and their Translations from Parallel Corpora without Word Alignment

Natalie Vargas [1]**, Carlos Ramisch** [2] **and Helena de M. Caseli** [1]

[1] Federal University of São Carlos, São Carlos, Brazil
`{helenacaseli, natalie.vargas}@dc.ufscar.br`

[2] Aix Marseille Univ, CNRS, LIF, Marseille, France
`carlos.ramisch@lif.univ-mrs.fr`

Abstract

We propose a method for joint unsupervised discovery of multiword expressions (MWEs) and their translations from parallel corpora. First, we apply independent monolingual MWE extraction in source and target languages simultaneously. Then, we calculate translation probability, association score and distributional similarity of co-occurring pairs. Finally, we rank all translations of a given MWE using a linear combination of these features. Preliminary experiments on light verb constructions show promising results.

1 Introduction

The automatic discovery of multiword expressions (MWEs) has been a topic of interest in the computational linguistics community for a while (Choueka, 1988; Church and Hanks, 1990). In the last 20 years, *multilingual* discovery of MWEs has gained some popularity thanks to the widespread use of statistical machine translation (MT), automatic word alignment tools and freely available parallel corpora (Zarrieß and Kuhn, 2009; Attia et al., 2010; Caseli et al., 2010). MWEs tend to be non compositional or show some kind of lexico-syntactic inflexibility, which is often reflected in translation asymmetries (Manning and Schütze, 1999). Therefore, parallel corpora are rich resources to mine for MWEs. Techniques adapted from machine translation can help to exploit translation information for the specific needs of MWE discovery.

Parallel corpora can be useful for MWE discovery in many ways. First, a second (target) language can be used to model features, which in turn help in the discovery of new MWEs in a single (source) language (Salehi and Cook, 2013; Caseli et al., 2010; Tsvetkov and Wintner, 2014). Second, one can also use parallel data to discover the translations of known multiword lexical units (Morin and Daille, 2010). Finally, it is possible to perform both simultaneously, generating a bilingual lexicon of MWEs and their potential translations from the parallel corpus, as proposed in this paper.

The goal of our paper is to propose a new method for unsupervised joint discovery of MWEs and their translations. It consists in discovering potential MWEs on source and target texts independently, and then trying to match them without using automatic word alignment. It is important to emphasize that we are not against the use of word alignment for this task, but we are interested in seeing how the automatic discovery of MWEs can be performed without relying on this information. Moreover, our experiments focus on light verb constructions such as *to make a presentation* and *to take a walk*, which generally contain non-adjacent tokens and thus would probably not be captured by standard word alignment methods. We study several features to rank automatically extracted candidates that could be translations of each other. We show preliminary results that indicate this approach is promising and point towards future improvements.

2 Related Work

Multilingual resources in general can be used for MWE discovery. Attia et al. (2010), for instance, do not rely on parallel texts but on short Wikipedia page titles, cross-linked across multiple languages. They consider that, if a page whose title contains a cross-lingual link to a page whose title is a single word (in any available language), then the original page title is probably a MWE. Similarly, translation links in Wiktionary can be exploited, among

Proceedings of the 13th Workshop on Multiword Expressions (MWE 2017), pages 91–96,
Valencia, Spain, April 4. ©2017 Association for Computational Linguistics

other features, for predicting the compositionality of MWEs (Salehi et al., 2014a).

Another possibility to model non-translatability without recurring to parallel corpora consists in building up artificial word-for-word MWE translations using bilingual single-word dictionaries. Afterwards, the existence of these automatically generated potential translations can be assessed in large monolingual corpora (Morin and Daille, 2010). This can be used as a feature, among other sources of information, in supervised or semi-supervised monolingual MWE discovery (Tsvetkov and Wintner, 2011; Rondon et al., 2015). Bilingual dictionaries can also be used to predict the compositionality of MWEs by estimating the string similarity (Salehi and Cook, 2013) or distributional similarity (Salehi et al., 2014b) between translations of an MWE and of the single words it contains.

Melamed (1997) describes one of the earliest attempts to extract MWEs from parallel corpora. The method is based on lexical alignment and mutual information. Statistical lexical alignment can provide straightforward MWE candidates, which can be further filtered using POS patterns and association scores. If two or more words in a source language are aligned to the same word on the target side, the source is likely an MWE (Caseli et al., 2010). Conversely, one can assume that some types of MWEs such as verb-noun combinations tend to be translated as MWEs with the same syntactic structure, using aligned dependency-parsed corpora for discovery (Zarrieß and Kuhn, 2009). Instead of focusing on 1-to-many alignments, Tsvetkov and Wintner (2010) propose a method which incrementally removes from parallel sentences word pairs that are surely not MWEs. Therefore, they use bilingual dictionaries and alignment reliability scores. The remaining units are considered candidate MWEs.

Bilingual lexicons containing MWEs are important resources for MT systems. It has been shown that the presence of MWEs can harm the quality of both statistical (Ramisch et al., 2013) and rule-based (Barreiro et al., 2014) MT systems. Simple techniques for taking MWEs into account such as binary features (Carpuat and Diab, 2010) and special token markers (Cap et al., 2015) can help improving translation quality. However, this may not suffice if the expressions are not correctly identified with the help of bilingual MWE lexicons.

3 Bilingual MWE Lexicon Creation

Most existing methods exploit parallel corpora to discover MWEs in a single language. They use translation information, among other sources, to confirm the idiosyncratic behaviour of the MWE in the source language, but do not output possible translations as a result of the discovery algorithm. In this section, we propose a method to create probabilistic bilingual MWE dictionaries using minimal supervision.

First, we extract MWE candidates from pre-processed (POS-tagged and lemmatized) source and target texts separately. In our experiments, the texts were pre-processed by TreeTagger (Schmid, 1994). We explicitly configured it not to segment sentences, since we need to preserve the alignment between source and target sentences in our input parallel corpus.

To allow the extraction of these monolingual MWE candidates, it is necessary to manually define POS patterns in both languages. This step requires some knowledge about the languages and about the syntactic patterns of the MWEs that we want to extract. These patterns were defined using the mwetoolkit corpus query language and candidate extraction tools (Ramisch, 2015).[1] In this first moment, we focused on MWEs translated into MWEs, but we believe that the technique could be adapted to MWEs translated into single words. For instance, one could extract verbal MWEs from the source corpus and try to match them with single-word verbs in the target language. In theory, any monolingual MWE discovery approach could be used to obtain candidates on each side of the parallel corpus independently.

The process described above outputs two sets of candidates. The first set $S = \{s_1, s_2, \ldots, s_{|S|}\}$ contains MWE candidates s_i extracted from the source corpus. The second set $T = \{t_1, t_2, \ldots, t_{|T|}\}$ contains MWE candidates t_j extracted from the target corpus. Then, we try to map source MWEs s_i to their target correspondences t_j. To do so, we calculate the **conditional probability** of each potential translation (t_j) in T given a source (s_i):

$$P(t_j|s_i) = \frac{c(s_i, t_j)}{c(s_i)}$$

Here, $c(s_i, t_j)$ is the number of times a source candidate s_i was found in a sentence whose transla-

---

tion contained t_j and $c(s_i)$ is simply the number of occurrences of the candidate in the source corpus. Since candidates s_i and t_j can be discontinuous, their numbers of occurrences are not necessarily n-gram counts, but must be obtained during monolingual candidate discovery as output by the mwetoolkit.

Another measure that we use to rank translations is the **t-score**. This association score estimates to what extent the co-occurrence of a group of words is outstanding compared to random chance co-occurrence. For each target candidate $t_j = w_1^{t_j} w_2^{t_j} \ldots w_n^{t_j}$, formed by n words $w_k^{t_j}$, we compute the expected number of occurrences by multiplying all individual word probabilities $\frac{c(w_k^{t_j})}{N}$ and then scaling this joint probability by the total number of tokens in the target corpus N:

$$E(t_j) = \frac{c(w_1^{t_j}) \times c(w_2^{t_j}) \times \ldots \times c(w_n^{t_j})}{N^{n-1}}$$

The t-score, also obtained using the mwetoolkit, is the difference between observed and expected counts normalized by an estimate of the standard deviation of the distribution:

$$tscore(t_j) = \frac{c(t_j) - E(t_j)}{\sqrt{c(t_j)}}$$

Finally, we calculate the multilingual distributional **similarity** between pairs s_i and t_j. This score is based on a pre-trained vector space model which uses sentence alignment information to ensure that words that are translations of each other end up being close in the resulting semantic space. Since each unit s_i and t_j is composed of m and n words, respectively, we use the average cosine similarity between all possible $m \times n$ source-target pairs present in the semantic space:[2]

$$Sim(s_i, t_j) = \frac{1}{m \times n} \sum_{\substack{k = 1..m \\ l = 1..n}} cos(w_k^{s_i}, w_l^{t_j})$$

The bilingual semantic space is obtained using MultiVec (Bérard et al., 2016).[3] Distributional similarity between source and target candidate words is obtained using the *bag of words* mode.

The three scores are normalized so that their values fall between 0 and 1. The final score F is simply a log-linear combination of these scores:

$$F(t_j|s_i) = \sum_{f \in \{P, tscore, Sim\}} -\log norm(f(t_j, s_i))$$

The lower its value, the more likely a given pair of source and target MWEs is.

4   Experimental Setup

For this work, the pre-processed texts (POS-tagged source and target texts) were obtained from the FAPESP parallel corpus containing 166,719 aligned sentences of Brazilian Portuguese texts translated into English (Aziz and Specia, 2011). The source corpus contains 4,191,942 tokens and the target corpus contains 4,499,064 tokens.[4]

Our experiments employ manually defined patterns for the monolingual step. These patterns target light-verb constructions in Portuguese and some possible translations into English:

GET+ADJ   The first pattern consists of the Portuguese verb *ficar* (*to become*) immediately followed by an adjective. This frequent construction often indicates a change of state (inchoative). On the target language (English), we build a similar pattern consisting of verbs *to be/become/get* + an adjective, which we assume as being frequent translations for the source construction.

MAKE+N   This pattern is formed by the verb *realizar* (*to make*) followed by a noun. Between the verb and the noun there can be any number of adjectives, adverbs or determinants, which are ignored in the extracted candidate. For the translation, we build an equivalent pattern with verbs *to make/carry* due to the high occurrence of *carry out* in the target corpus.

TAKE+N   This pattern is formed by verbs *fazer/tomar/dar* (*to make/take/give*) followed by a noun. We allow intervening elements as for MAKE+N. In English, we use verbs *to make/do/take*. Notice that verb *to give* was considered as an unlikely translation and disregarded.

5   Preliminary Results

As mentioned in Section 3, we used the mwetoolkit to apply the patterns and calculate t-scores

---

[2]The normalization factor may be less than $m \times n$ when some pairs $w_k^{s_i}, w_l^{t_j}$ do not occur in the semantic space.

[3]https://github.com/eske/multivec

[4]http://www.nilc.icmc.usp.br/nilc/
tools/Fapesp\%20Corpora

	MWE source	MWE target	# T	ts T	Sim	F
1	**ficar doente**	**get sick**	2	0.51	0.53	1.44
2	**ficar doente**	**become ill**	2	0.50	0.46	1.51
3	ficar doente	be normal	1	0.52	0.41	1.84
4	**ficar doente**	**become sick**	1	0.49	0.41	1.86
5	ficar doente	be tolerant	1	0.50	0.33	1.95
1	**ficar pronto**	**be ready**	46	0.72	0.67	0.41
2	**ficar pronto**	**become ready**	5	0.50	0.60	1.58
3	**ficar pronto**	**get ready**	1	0.58	0.69	2.15
4	ficar pronto	be capable	2	0.74	0.25	2.18
5	ficar pronto	be necessary	1	0.87	0.40	2.22
6	ficar pronto	be fundamental	1	0.74	0.26	2.47

Table 1: Pattern GET+ADJ: *ficar doente/pronto* (*get sick/ready*). Correct pairs are in bold.

	MWE source	MWE target	# T	ts T	Sim	F
1	**realizar teste**	**carry test**	20	0.50	0.73	0.71
2	**realizar teste**	**carry trial**	3	0.29	0.63	1.85
3	realizar teste	carry field	4	0.26	0.47	1.89
4	realizar teste	make assessment	4	0.22	0.28	2.18
5	realizar teste	make use	1	1.00	0.24	2.19
6	**realizar teste**	**make test**	1	0.23	0.62	2.43
7	realizar teste	make comparison	1	0.38	0.30	2.51
8	**realizar teste**	**carry test**	1	0.17	0.65	2.54
9	realizar teste	carry safety	1	0.17	0.53	2.64
10	realizar teste	make prototype	1	0.23	0.37	2.64
11	realizar teste	make search	1	0.15	0.24	3.02
1	realizar substituição	carry identification	1	0.19	0.45	1.67

Table 2: Pattern MAKE+N: *realizar teste/substituição* (*make test/replacement*). Correct pairs are in bold.

and MultiVec for bilingual similarity. Unfortunately, quantitative evaluation was not yet performed. Nonetheless, in this section, we present some examples of discovered MWEs along with their translations. We point out positive and negative results in this small sample that give us an idea of our approach's potential.

Table 1 shows ranked examples extracted from the source and target corpus for the first pattern. The entries are ranked by final score, more likely translations appear on the top of the table and the correct ones are in bold. According to these examples, the MWE pairs with lowest scores are correctly aligned to a valid translation. In addition to the final score (F), target t-score (ts T) and similarity (Sim), the table also shows how many times the source MWE co-occurred with the target MWE (# T). This information allows us to calculate the conditional probability.

It is important to point out that our approach does not work for all cases, as some spurious pairs also occur. For example, in the first half of table 1, *become sick* is indeed a possible translation for *ficar doente* but it appears in a worst position compared to *be normal*, which is not a possible translation. Beyond the conditional probability, distributional similarity and t-score seem to help in some cases. For instance, *get ready* appears only once as a translation of *ficar pronto*, but still it gets a better score than *be capable*, a wrong translation with higher conditional probability. In general, we have observed that the pattern GET+ADJ is quite "easy" to translate as these constructions show a high degree of regularity.

Table 2 shows the results of the extraction for MAKE+N. The results for *realizar teste* show that the best ranked MWEs are the corrected translations. The last row of this table shows a drawback of our approach: that it is not possible to obtain reliable probability scores when the pattern just appears once.

The results in table 3 show the extraction for the last pattern, TAKE+N. Despite the first half of this table presenting good results for *do comparison* and *make comparison*, the second half shows that some patterns do not work for the target side. The verb *dar* in Portuguese is a productive light verb, specially when combined with participles (*dar uma caminhada/corrida/passeada* lit. *to give a walk/run/stroll*). On the other hand, the translations usually involve a single verb and not a light-verb construction. This indicates that further error analysis is required, studying the three verbs in this pattern separately.

	MWE source	MWE target	# T	ts T	Sim	F
1	**fazer comparação**	**make comparison**	4	0.37	0.64	1.16
2	**fazer comparação**	**do comparison**	1	0.23	0.56	2.04
3	fazer comparação	make method	1	0.21	0.44	2.18
4	fazer comparação	make drug	1	0.23	0.33	2.27
1	dar início	do thing	4	0.44	0.15	1.76
2	dar início	do Sul	1	1.00	0.13	2.06
3	dar início	make vaccine	1	0.31	0.24	2.30
4	dar início	make list	1	0.26	0.24	2.37
5	dar início	make roster	1	0.24	0.21	2.47

Table 3: Pattern TAKE+N: *fazer comparação* (*make comparison*) and *dar início* (lit. *give beginning* 'to start'). Correct pairs are in bold.

6 Conclusions and Future Work

This paper constitutes our first proposal towards automatic discovery of bilingual MWE lexicons. While preliminary results are promising, the obvious next step is to design an evaluation protocol and apply it. Having this goal set, the idea is testing the approach first with other patterns and, then, making a robust evaluation.

We would also like to extrapolate this method to other language pairs and MWE categories, specially those MWE translated as single words. In this case, we are still investigating solutions but one of them consists in using monolingual word embeddings and similarity measures in order to define if the translation should be an MWE or a single word.

We believe that the method itself can be improved in many ways. For instance, we would like to design a distributional similarity measure able to focus on valid alignments. We would also like to experiment with different weights for the scores (e.g. similarity seems more important than t-score). Optimizing, that is, learning these weights from small amounts of supervised data, sounds appealing as well.

At the moment, the extraction patterns represent a bottleneck and bias the obtained results towards more plausible translations. We would like to find a way to get rid of them, specially when it comes to the target side. Another point that must be underlined is the fact that, as we are not discarding the use of word alignment in the future, we would like to perform a systematic quantitative comparison with related work and methods based on word alignment.

Acknowledgments

We would like to thank the São Paulo Research Foundation (FAPESP) for the grants #2013/50757-0 (AIM-WEST project) and #2016/13002-0 (MMeaning project). This work has been partly funded by projects PARSEME (Cost Action IC1207), PARSEME-FR (ANR-14-CERA-0001), and AIM-WEST (FAPERGS-INRIA 1706-2551/13-7).

References

Mohammed Attia, Antonio Toral, Lamia Tounsi, Pavel Pecina, and Josef van Genabith. 2010. Automatic extraction of Arabic multiword expressions. In Éric Laporte, Preslav Nakov, Carlos Ramisch, and Aline Villavicencio, editors, *Proc. of the COLING Workshop on MWEs: from Theory to Applications (MWE 2010)*, pages 18–26, Beijing, China, Aug. ACL.

Wilker Aziz and Lucia Specia. 2011. Fully automatic compilation of a Portuguese-English parallel corpus for statistical machine translation. In *STIL 2011*, Cuiabá, MT, Obtober.

Anabela Barreiro, Johanna Monti, Brigitte Orliac, Susanne Preuß, Kutz Arrieta, Wang Ling, Fernando Batista, and Isabel Trancoso. 2014. Linguistic evaluation of support verb constructions by openlogos and google translate. In *Proc. of the Ninth LREC (LREC 2014)*, Reykjavik, Iceland, May. ELRA.

Alexandre Bérard, Christophe Servan, Olivier Pietquin, and Laurent Besacier. 2016. MultiVec: a Multilingual and Multilevel Representation Learning Toolkit for NLP. In *The 10th edition of the Language Resources and Evaluation Conference (LREC 2016)*, May.

Fabienne Cap, Manju Nirmal, Marion Weller, and Sabine Schulte im Walde. 2015. How to account for idiomatic German support verb constructions in statistical machine translation. In *Proc. of the 11th Workshop on MWEs (MWE 2015)* (con, 2015), pages 19–28.

Marine Carpuat and Mona Diab. 2010. Task-based evaluation of multiword expressions: a pilot study in statistical machine translation. In *Proc. of HLT: The 2010 Annual Conf. of the NAACL (NAACL 2003)*, pages 242–245, Los Angeles, California, Jun. ACL.

Helena de Medeiros Caseli, Carlos Ramisch, Maria das Graças Volpe Nunes, and Aline Villavicencio. 2010. Alignment-based extraction of multiword expressions. In *Lang. Res. & Eval. Special Issue on Multiword expression: hard going or plain sailing* (jou, 2010), pages 59–77.

Yaacov Choueka. 1988. Looking for needles in a haystack or locating interesting collocational expressions in large textual databases. In Christian Fluhr and Donald E. Walker, editors, *Proceedings of the 2nd International Conference on Computer-Assisted Information Retrieval (Recherche d'Information et ses Applications - RIA 1988)*, pages 609–624, Cambridge, MA, USA, Mar. CID.

Kenneth Church and Patrick Hanks. 1990. Word association norms mutual information, and lexicography. *Comp. Ling.*, 16(1):22–29.

2015. *Proc. of the 11th Workshop on MWEs (MWE 2015)*, Denver, Colorado, USA. ACL.

2010. *Lang. Res. & Eval. Special Issue on Multiword expression: hard going or plain sailing*, 44(1-2), Apr.

Christopher D. Manning and Hinrich Schütze. 1999. *Foundations of statistical natural language processing*. MIT Press, Cambridge, USA. 620 p.

I. Dan Melamed. 1997. Automatic discovery of non-compositional compounds in parallel data. In *Proc. of the 2nd EMNLP (EMNLP-2)*, pages 97–108, Brown University, RI, USA, Aug. ACL.

Emmanuel Morin and Béatrice Daille. 2010. Compositionality and lexical alignment of multi-word terms. In *Lang. Res. & Eval. Special Issue on Multiword expression: hard going or plain sailing* (jou, 2010), pages 79–95.

Carlos Ramisch, Laurent Besacier, and Oleksandr Kobzar. 2013. How hard is it to automatically translate phrasal verbs from English to French? In Ruslan Mitkov, Johanna Monti, Gloria Corpas Pastor, and Violeta Seretan, editors, *Proc. of the MT Summit 2013 MUMTTT workshop (MUMTTT 2013)*, pages 53–61, Nice, France, Sep.

Carlos Ramisch. 2015. *Multiword Expressions Acquisition: A Generic and Open Framework*, volume XIV of *Theory and Applications of Natural Language Processing*. Springer.

Alexandre Rondon, Helena de Medeiros Caseli, and Carlos Ramisch. 2015. Never-ending multiword expressions learning. In *Proc. of the 11th Workshop on MWEs (MWE 2015)* (con, 2015), pages 45–53.

Bahar Salehi and Paul Cook. 2013. Predicting the compositionality of multiword expressions using translations in multiple languages. In *Second Joint Conference on Lexical and Computational Semantics (*SEM), Volume 1: Proceedings of the Main Conference and the Shared Task: Semantic Textual Similarity*, pages 266–275, Atlanta, Georgia, USA, June. Association for Computational Linguistics.

Bahar Salehi, Paul Cook, and Timothy Baldwin. 2014a. Detecting non-compositional mwe components using wiktionary. In *Proceedings of the 2014 Conference on Empirical Methods in Natural Language Processing (EMNLP)*, pages 1792–1797, Doha, Qatar, October. Association for Computational Linguistics.

Bahar Salehi, Paul Cook, and Timothy Baldwin. 2014b. Using distributional similarity of multi-way translations to predict multiword expression compositionality. In *Proceedings of the 14th Conference of the European Chapter of the Association for Computational Linguistics*, pages 472–481, Gothenburg, Sweden, April. Association for Computational Linguistics.

Helmut Schmid. 1994. Probabilistic part-of-speech tagging using decision trees. In *Proceedings of the International Conference on New Methods in Language Processing*, pages 44–49.

Yulia Tsvetkov and Shuly Wintner. 2010. Extraction of multi-word expressions from small parallel corpora. In Chu-Ren Huang and Dan Jurafsky, editors, *Proc. of the 23rd COLING (COLING 2010) — Posters*, pages 1256–1264, Beijing, China, Aug. The Coling 2010 Organizing Committee.

Yulia Tsvetkov and Shuly Wintner. 2011. Identification of multi-word expressions by combining multiple linguistic information sources. In Regina Barzilay and Mark Johnson, editors, *Proc. of the 2011 EMNLP (EMNLP 2011)*, pages 836–845, Edinburgh, Scotland, UK, Jul. ACL.

Yulia Tsvetkov and Shuly Wintner. 2014. Identification of multiword expressions by combining multiple linguistic information sources. *Comp. Ling.*, 40(2):449–468.

Sina Zarrieß and Jonas Kuhn. 2009. Exploiting translational correspondences for pattern-independent MWE identification. In Dimitra Anastasiou, Chikara Hashimoto, Preslav Nakov, and Su Nam Kim, editors, *Proc. of the ACL Workshop on MWEs: Identification, Interpretation, Disambiguation, Applications (MWE 2009)*, pages 23–30, Suntec, Singapore, Aug. ACL.

Identification of Multiword Expressions for Latvian and Lithuanian: Hybrid Approach

Justina Mandravickaitė
Vilnius University, Lithuania
Baltic Institute of Advanced
Technology, Lithuania
`justina@bpti.lt`

Tomas Krilavičius
Vytautas Magnus University, Lithuania
Baltic Institute of Advanced
Technology, Lithuania
`t.krilavicius@bpti.lt`

Abstract

We discuss an experiment on automatic identification of bi-gram multiword expressions in parallel Latvian and Lithuanian corpora. Raw corpora, lexical association measures (LAMs) and supervised machine learning (ML) are used due to deficit and quality of lexical resources (e.g., POS-tagger, parser) and tools. While combining LAMs with ML is rather effective for other languages, it has shown some nice results for Lithuanian and Latvian as well. Combining LAMs with ML we have achieved 92,4% precision and 52,2% recall for Latvian and 95,1% precision and 77,8% recall for Lithuanian.

1 Introduction

We explore applicability of the automatic detection of multi-word expressions (MWEs) in Latvian (LV) and Lithuanian (LT). Both languages belong to Baltic language group and are synthetic (favor morphologically complex words), thus simple statistical approaches for identification of MWEs do not provide satisfactory results, as the morphological richness leads to lexical sparseness. Representations, such as bag of words ignore variation of MWEs components (Sharoff, 2004). The relatively free word order in both languages does not improve the situation. Lexical resources for complementing or replacing statistical approaches are limited. However, exploration of MWEs flexibility and morpho-syntactic rules could improve detection of MWEs in Lithuanian easier. But even most of the hybrid methods cannot be implemented in a straightforward manner due to limited availability of lexical resources and tools, e.g. POS tagger, parser, etc.

Thus possibility of detecting Latvian and Lithuanian MWEs by combining lexical association measures and machine learning could be a right approach in this situation. Machine learning allows various properties of text to be encoded in feature vectors (lexical, morphological, syntactic, semantic, contextual, etc.) associated with output classes, as well as identifying complex non-linear relations. It permits capturing elaborate features in languages with complex morphology.

2 Combining LAMs and Supervised Machine Learning

Combination of *lexical association measures* (LAMs) and supervised machine learning algorithms is already under scrutiny, (Zilio et al., 2011) use it for the extraction and evaluation of MWEs from the English part of *Europarl Parallel Corpus*, extracted from the proceedings of the European Parliament; (Dubremetz and Nivre, 2014) explores extraction of nominal MWEs from the French part of the Europarl corpus using application of the same method. Performance of different combinations of LAMs is discussed in (Pecina and Schlesinger, 2006; Pecina, 2008a; Pecina, 2008b; Pecina, 2010).

LAMs compute an association score for each collocation candidate assessing the degree of connection between its components. Scores can be used for the extraction of collocation candidates, ranking and classification (rejecting collocations below (above) threshold).

Different groups of collocations differ in sensitivity to certain association measures depending on their types, e.g., collocations where components statistically occur more often than incidentally, *Log-likelihood ratio*, x^2 *test*, *Odds ratio*, *Jaccard*, *Pointwise mutual information* perform better, while for collocations occurring in the different contexts than their components (non-

Proceedings of the 13th Workshop on Multiword Expressions (MWE 2017), pages 97–101,
Valencia, Spain, April 4. ©2017 Association for Computational Linguistics

compositionality principle) *J-S divergence, K-L divergence, Skew divergence, Cosine similarity* in vector space are preferred suggested (Pecina, 2008b). For discontinuous MWE (with other words in amidst the components of MWE), *Left context entropy* and *Right context entropy* perform better (Pecina, 2008b).

Combining association measures, even a relatively small number, helps in the collocation extraction task (Pecina, 2008a), (Pecina and Schlesinger, 2006), (Pecina, 2010), however there is no the best universal combination of association measures, since the task of collocation extraction depends on the corpora, language and type/notion of MWEs.

3 Experimental Setup

We use LAMs combined with supervised machine learning. LAMs are calculated using *mwetoolkit*[1] (Ramisch, 2015), and WEKA[2] (Hall et al., 2009) is used to train selected classifiers LAMs.

In this paper we disccuss experiments with bi-gram MWEs only, but we plan to extended definitions of LAMs to tri- and tetra-grams, which is not always straighforward, and explore LAMs+ML approach for longer MWE in future research.

Candidate MWE bi-grams were extracted from the raw text with *mwetoolkit*: frequencies of separate words and bi-grams are counted, hapaxes are removed, and values of 5 association measures (*Maximum Likelihood Estimation, Dice's coefficient, Pointwise Mutual Information, Student's t score* and *Log-likelihood score*) (Ramisch, 2015) are calculated. For each language, the results were evaluated against the reference lists, based on EuroVoc - Multilingual Thesaurus of the European Union[3].

The results were evaluated against the reference list of bi-gram MWE (converted to ARFF file with the values of **true** (MWE) and **false** (not MWE)) using WEKA. Selected algorithms (*Naïve Bayes* (John and Langley, 1995), *OneR* (rule-based classifier; (Holte, 1993)), *Bayesian Network* (Su et al., 2008) and *Random Forest* (Breiman, 2001)) were applied for automatic identification of MWEs. Feature vectors were constructed from LAMs values for each MWE candidate and its appearance in reference list (**true/false**).

SMOTE (it re-samples a dataset by applying the *Synthetic Minority Oversampling TEchnique*) (Chawla et al., 2002) and Resample (it produces a random subsample of a dataset using either sampling with or without replacement) (Hall et al., 2009) filters were used to deal with data sparseness.

To **evaluate** performance we employ (i) *precision* $P = \frac{tp}{tp+fp}$, (ii) *recall* $R = \frac{tp}{tp+fn}$ and (iii) *F-score* $F_1 = 2 \cdot \frac{P \cdot R}{P+R}$, where tp, fp and fn are *true positives* (correctly identified MWEs), *false positives* (expressions incorrectly identified as MWEs) and false negatives (incorrectly identified as non-MWEs), correspondingly (Powers, 2011; Perry et al., 1955).

Association measures and supervised machine learning algorithms were combined in 3 ways: (i) without any filter, (ii) with the SMOTE filter and (iii) with the Resample filter. All the models were tested using standard 10-fold cross-validation.

4 Corpus and Reference Source

4.1 Corpus

1/3 of Latvian and Lithuanian parts of *JRC-Acquis Multilingual Parallel Corpus* (Steinberger et al., 2006)[4], containing the total body of European Union law applicable to its member states (selected texts written since 1950s), i.e., $\sim$ 9 mil. words for each language, were used. Preprocessing consisted of tokenizing (one sentence per line) and lowercasing only, because the goal is to get the best possible results without relying on special linguistic tools, e.g., POS tagger, parser.

4.2 Reference Source for Evaluation of MWE Candidates

As there was known *gold standard* MWE evaluation resources for Latvian and Lithuanian, we use bi-grams from EuroVoc (a Multilingual Thesaurus of the European Union). We use separate lists for each language to evaluate MWE candidates with calculated LAMs values, resulting in `.arff` file with numerical values of LAMs and logical values showing, whether record is **true** (MWE) and **false** (not MWE). Latvian reference list consists of 3608 bi-gram terms, while Lithuanian list has 3783 bi-gram items. Number of bigrams was different, because MWEs in Lithuanian/Latvian not

---

[1]`http://mwetoolkit.sourceforge.net`
[2]`http://www.cs.waikato.ac.nz/ml/weka/`
[3]EuroVoc, the EU's multi-lingual thesaurus, `http://eurovoc.europa.eu/drupal/`
[4]`https://ec.europa.eu/jrc/en/language-technologies/jrc-acquis`

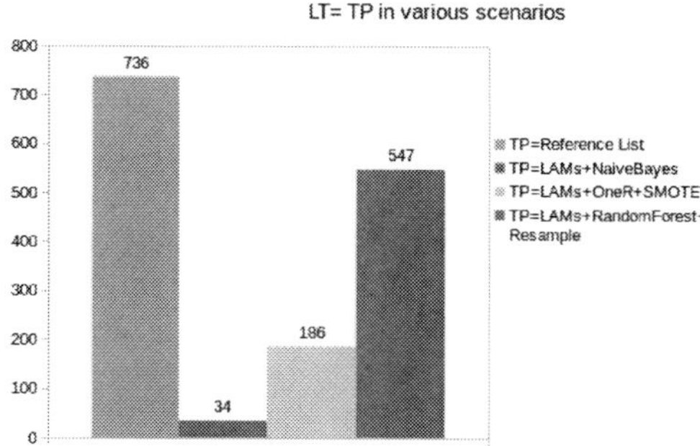

Figure 1: Lithuanian TP in various scenarios

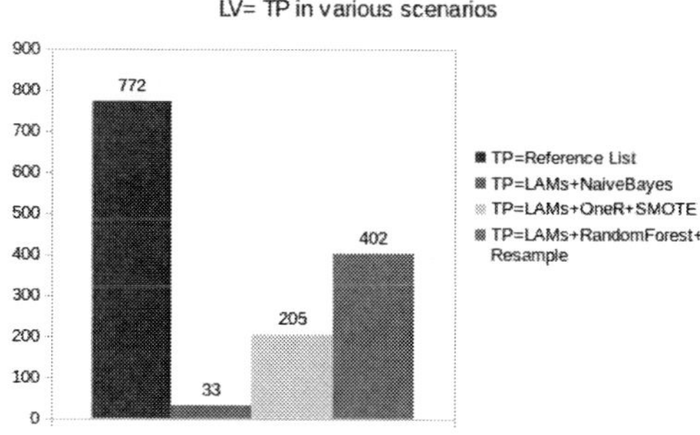

Figure 2: Latvian TP in various scenarios

always had their equivalents as bi-grams in other language and vice versa, e.g. coal - *akmens anglys* (Lithuanian), *akmeņogles* (Latvian); pasture fattening - *ganomasis gyvulių penėjimas* (Lithuanian), *nobarošana ganībās* (Latvian)

5 Results

We experimented with 736 (LT) and 772 (LV) MWEs present in the corresponding corpus from the reference. See Figures 1 and 2 for results, Table 1 for summary of experimental results (LAMs only, LAMs combined with a supervised machine learning, LAMs combined with a supervised machine learning and filters).

Referece list was based on EuroVoc which mostly contained the EU institutions related terms, hence MWEs mostly fitted into 3 categories: Noun + Noun, Adjective + Noun and Abbreviation or Acronym + Noun. However, as we did not use either POS tagger or parser (see the beginning of the paper), detailed morpho-syntactic analysis is in our future plans.

Using only the lexical association measures implemented in the *mwetoolkit* against the reference, performance was low: $R = 21.4\%$ and 19.4%, and $P = 0.1\%$ and 0.2%, and $F_1 = 0.3\%$ and 0.2%, for LV and LT, respectively. Almost any candidate MWE out of the 558 772 (LV) and 587 406 (LT) was identified as an MWE. Thus, association measures did not suffice for the successful extraction of MWEs for Latvian and Lithuanian.

The best results for Latvian without any filter were achieved with the Naïve Bayes classifier (33/772 correct MWEs), reaching P=0.6%, R=4.3% and F1=1.1%.

Using SMOTE the best results were achieved with the OneR classifier (205/772 correct MWEs; $P = 100\%, R = 13.3\%$ and $F_1 = 23.4\%$) and using the Resample filter – with the Random Forest classifier (402/772 correct MWEs with $P = 92.4\%, R = 52.2\%$ and $F_1 = 66.7\%$).

The best results for Lithuanian without any filter were achieved with the Naïve Bayes classifier (34/736 correct MWEs with $P = 0.6\%, R = 4.6\%$ and $F_1 = 1.1\%$). Using SMOTE the best results were achieved with the OneR classifier (186/736 correct MWEs, having $P = 100\%, R = 12.6\%$ and $F_1 = 22.4\%$) and using the Resample filter – with the Random Forest classifier (547/736 correct MWEs; we reached $P = 95.1\%, R = 77.8\%$ and $F_1 = 85.6\%$).

Results show, that combining LAMs with supervised ML improves extraction of MWEs for both languages.

6 Analysis of Misclassified MWE Candidates

Configuration LAMs + Random Forest + Resample performed best for both languages. However, there were misclassified MWE candidates and below there is a more detailed analysis of errors made by Random Forest classifier.

6.1 False Positives

For Lithuanian 22 unique items were misclassified as MWEs and for Latvian - 31 (sampling was done with replacement, thus some items were repeated). False positives belong to one of 3 groups of errors (see Table 2):

(i) good candidates for MWE, but not present in the EuroVoc, and thus not included in the reference list (e.g., LT: *augimo stimuliatorius* (growth stimulator), *traktorių konstrukcijos* (tractor constructions); LV: *valsts slieksnis* (national threshold), *valsts tiesības* (state law)); (ii) error, occurred due to low frequency (2-3); (iii) real False Positive

Scenario	Precision	Recall	F-meas.
Latvian			
LAMs	0.1%	21.4%	0.3%
LAMs+NaiveBayes	0.6%	4.3%	1.1%
LAMs+OneR+SMOTE	**100%**	13.3%	23.4%
LAMs+Random Forest+Resample	92.4%	**52.2%**	**66.7%**
Lithuanian			
LAMs	0.2%	19.4%	0.2%
LAMs+NaiveBayes	0.6%	4.6%	1.1%
LAMs+OneR+SMOTE	**100%**	12.6%	22.4%
LAMs+RandomForest+Resample	95.1%	**77.8%**	**85.6%**

Table 1: Summary of the results for Latvian and Lithuanian

Latvian	
MWE, not in EuroVoc	6
Low frequency	18
Debatable MWE candidates	7
Lithuanian	
MWE, not in EuroVoc	6
Low frequency	8
Real false positives	7

Table 2: Summary of False Positives for Latvian and Lithuanian

Latvian	
Very low frequency (2-3)	109
Low frequency (3-10)	227
Lithuanian	
Very low frequency (2-3)	47
Low frequency (3-10)	85

Table 3: Summary of False Negatives for Latvian and Lithuanian

or debatable MWE candidate that needs confirmation.

6.2 False Negatives

For Lithuanian 132 unique items were misclassified as non-MWEs and for Latvian - 336 (sampling was done with replacement, thus some items were repeated). False negatives belong to one of 2 groups of errors (see Table 3):

(i) error, occurred due to extremely low frequency (2-3); (ii) error, occured due to relatively low frequency (3-10). For most misclassified items in the group of extremely low frequency there were pairs of MWE candidates with the same LAMs values (e.g., LT: *vertikalusis susitarimas* & *valdybų susitarimas* (vertical agreement & board agreement); LV: *vispārējais budžets* & *vispārējais labums* (general budget & overall benefit)). Low frequency group mostly had unique combinations of LAMs values.

Results show that heavier filtering according to frequencies should be considered, e.g., filtering out candidates with < 20 occurrences (Evert, 2008). Beside frequency, other LAMs have to be taken into consideration as there is a possibility

that *Maximum Likelihood Estimation, Dice's coefficient, Pointwise Mutual Information, Student's t score* and *Log-likelihood score* were not capable to capture all the properties of MWE candidates correctly.

7 Conclusions

We report our experiment for extraction bi-gram MWEs for Latvian and Lithuanian by combining lexical association measures and supervised machine learning. This method appears to be more effective for Lithuanian than Latvian. All in all, using ML together with LAMs improved results: the best configuration LAMs + Random Forest + Resample filter achieved $F_1 = 66.7\%$ for Latvian and $F_1 = 85.6\%$ for Lithuanian. However, an exception was the second-best configuration LAMs + OneR + SMOTE, where results for Latvian were slightly better ($F_1 = 23.4\%$) than for Lithuanian ($F_1 = 22.4\%$).

Future plans include further analysis of low frequency MWEs, because it was a reason for a significant number of errors. Exploration of other LAMs could help to deal with it, and correctly capture complexities of Latvian and Lithuanian. Using EuroVoc is a poor man's solution, using it resulted in getting a high number of False Positives, which seem to be good candidates for MWEs. Of course, it would be interesting to move from bi-grams, to tri- and tetra-grams as well.

Acknowledgments

This research was funded by a grant (No. LIP-027/2016) from the Research Council of Lithuania.

References

Leo Breiman. 2001. Random forests. *Machine learning*, 45(1):5–32.

Nitesh V. Chawla, Kevin W. Bowyer, Lawrence O. Hall, and W. Philip Kegelmeyer. 2002. Smote: synthetic minority over-sampling technique. *Journal of artificial intelligence research*, pages 321–357.

Marie Dubremetz and Joakim Nivre. 2014. Extraction of nominal multiword expressions in french. *EACL 2014*, page 72.

Stefan Evert. 2008. A lexicographic evaluation of german adjective-noun collocations. *Towards a Shared Task for Multiword Expressions (MWE 2008)*, page 3.

Mark Hall, Eibe Frank, Geoffrey Holmes, Bernhard Pfahringer, Peter Reutemann, and Ian H Witten. 2009. The weka data mining software: an update. *ACM SIGKDD explorations newsletter*, 11(1):10–18.

Robert C Holte. 1993. Very simple classification rules perform well on most commonly used datasets. *Machine learning*, 11(1):63–90.

George H John and Pat Langley. 1995. Estimating continuous distributions in bayesian classifiers. In *Proceedings of the Eleventh conference on Uncertainty in artificial intelligence*, pages 338–345. Morgan Kaufmann Publishers Inc.

Pavel Pecina and Pavel Schlesinger. 2006. Combining association measures for collocation extraction. In *Proceedings of the COLING/ACL on Main conference poster sessions*, pages 651–658. Association for Computational Linguistics.

Pavel Pecina. 2008a. *Lexical Association Measures: Collocation ExtractionLexical Association Measures: Collocation Extraction*. Ph.D. thesis, Faculty of Mathematics and Physics, Charles University in Prague, Prague, Czech Republic.

Pavel Pecina. 2008b. A machine learning approach to multiword expression extraction. In *Proceedings of the LREC Workshop Towards a Shared Task for Multiword Expressions (MWE 2008)*, pages 54–61. Citeseer.

Pavel Pecina. 2010. Lexical association measures and collocation extraction. *Language resources and evaluation*, 44(1-2):137–158.

James W Perry, Allen Kent, and Madeline M Berry. 1955. Machine literature searching x. machine language; factors underlying its design and development. *American Documentation*, 6(4):242–254.

David Martin Powers. 2011. Evaluation: from precision, recall and f-measure to roc, informedness, markedness and correlation.

Carlos Ramisch. 2015. *Multiword expressions acquisition: A generic and open framework*. Theory and Applications of Natural Language Processing series XIV, Springer.

Serge Sharoff. 2004. What is at stake: a case study of russian expressions starting with a preposition. In *Proceedings of the Workshop on Multiword Expressions: Integrating Processing*, pages 17–23. Association for Computational Linguistics.

Ralf Steinberger, Bruno Pouliquen, Anna Widiger, Camelia Ignat, Tomaz Erjavec, Dan Tufis, and Dániel Varga. 2006. The jrc-acquis: A multilingual aligned parallel corpus with 20+ languages. *arXiv preprint cs/0609058*.

Jiang Su, Harry Zhang, Charles X Ling, and Stan Matwin. 2008. Discriminative parameter learning for bayesian networks. In *Proceedings of the 25th international conference on Machine learning*, pages 1016–1023. ACM.

Leonardo Zilio, Luiz Svoboda, Luiz Henrique Longhi Rossi, and Rafael Martins Feitosa. 2011. Automatic extraction and evaluation of mwe. In *8th Brazilian Symposium in Information and Human Language Technology*, pages 214–218.

Show Me Your Variance and I Tell You Who You Are –
Deriving Compound Compositionality from Word Alignments

Fabienne Cap

Department of Linguistics and Philology
Uppsala University
`fabienne.cap@lingfil.uu.se`

Abstract

We use word alignment variance as an indicator for the non-compositionality of German and English noun compounds. Our work-in-progress results are on their own not competitive with state-of-the art approaches, but they show that alignment variance is correlated with compositionality and thus worth a closer look in the future.

1 Introduction

A compound is a combination of two or more words to build a new word. Many languages (e.g. German) allow for the productive creation of new compounds from scratch. While most of such newly created compounds are compositional, i.e. the meaning of the whole can be predicted based on the meaning of its parts, there also exist lexicalised compounds which have partly or completely lost their compositional meaning (or never had one in the first place).

For many NLP applications, it is crucial to distinguish compositional from non-compositional compounds, e.g. in order to decide whether or not to split a German closed compound into its parts in order to reduce data sparsity.

This paper presents some first results on calculating compositionality scores for German and English noun compounds based on the variance of translations they exhibit when word-aligned to another language. We assume that non-compositional compounds exhibit a greater alignment variance than compositional constructions, because many non-compositional compounds...

i) are lexicalised and lexicalised counterparts are sometimes missing in the other language. The translators will instead describe the semantic content of the compound and these descriptions are very likely to differ for each occurrence. In contrast, if a compositional compound does not exist in the other language, it can most probably be created ad hoc by the translator. E.g: *Herzblut* (non-comp.: "passion/commit-ment/dedication", lit.: "heart blood") vs. *Herzbus*[1] (lit: "heart bus").

ii) may occur in contexts where they are used literally. The found translations cover occurences in both kinds of contexts and thus exhibit a larger variance than purely compositional contructions. E.g.: *Blütezeit* (non-comp.: "heyday", comp.: "blossom", lit.: "bloom time") vs. *Blütenhonig* (lit.: "blossom honey").

iii) may occur mostly (sometimes only) within larger idiomatic expressions, which in turn, similar to i), often lack an exact counterpart in the other language and are thus translated with more variance. E.g.: *auf gleicher Augenhöhe sein* (non-comp.: "to be on equal terms" lit.: "to be on the same eye level")

In our experiments, we find that translational variance in fact is a possible indicator for the compositionality of both German and English compounds and worth further improvement and investigation in the future.

2 Related Work

There has been a tremendous interest and a wide range of proposed solutions to the automatic extraction of multiword expressions (MWEs)

---

[1]This example has been made up from scratch. It could denote a bus providing healthcare for people suffering from heart diseases, following the pattern of "Blutbus" - a bus in which blood can be donated or alternatively a bus with a heart on it.

Proceedings of the 13th Workshop on Multiword Expressions (MWE 2017), pages 102–107,
Valencia, Spain, April 4. ©2017 Association for Computational Linguistics

and/or the prediction of their semantic non-compositionality, which is one of their most prominent features. We restrict our review to a selection of word-alignment or translation-based approaches.

Villada Moirón and Tiedemann (2006) used word alignments to predict the idiomaticity of Dutch MWEs (preposition+NP). They calculated the variance of the alignments for each component word, and we follow their approach in the present work. Moreover, they compared the alignments of the words when occurring within an MWE vs. when occurring independently. Medeiros de Caseli et al. (2010) used alignment assymetries to identify MWEs of Brazilian Portuguese.

More recently, Salehi and Cook (2013) used string similarity to compare the translations of English MWEs with the translations of their parts. Translations were obtained lexicon-based. Salehi et al. (2014) use distributional similarity measures to identify MWE candidates in the source language. In order to determine the compositionality of the constructions they then translate the components (using a lexicon) and calculate distributional similarity for their translations. This approach was evaluated for English and German MWEs.

3 Methodology

3.1 Compound Splitting

In German, noun compounds are written as one word without spaces, e.g. *Schriftgröße* ("font size"). In order to access the word alignments of its component parts (*Schrift* ("font") and *Größe* ("size")) they have to be split prior to the word alignment process. We do so using a rule-based morphological analyser for German (Schmid et al., 2004) whose analyses are disambiguated using corpus heuristics in a two-step approach (Fritzinger and Fraser, 2010). In order to improve word alignment accuracy between German and English, we lemmatise all German nouns using the same rule-based morphological analyser.

For our experiments on English noun compounds, no preprocessing on the English data is performed.

3.2 Measuring Translational Variance

German We run word alignment on the English and the modified German parallel corpus. After the alignment, we mark the German compounds which have previously been split in the

(a) Schriftgröße (102 occurrences, TE: 1.451)

Word		Alignments
Schrift	=	font (65), text (7), fonts (3), size (3), type (2), character (2), sizes (2), font text (1), record (1) (... 16 more singletons ...)
Größe	=	size (74), sizes (13), relative size (1), (... 14 more singletons ...)

(b) Schriftzug (89 occurrences, TE: 3.827)

Word		Alignments
Schrift	=	lettering (10), logo (6), label (5), logotype (4), text (3), writing (3), texts (3), inscription (2), sticker (2), etched (2), word (1) , imprints (1), (... 47 more singletons ...)
Zug	=	lettering (10), label (5), logo (5), logotype (4), of (4), inscription (3), sticker (2), letters (2), writings (1), nameplate (1), handwriting (1), (... 51 more singletons ...)

Table 1: Local alignments for the compositional *Schrifgröße* ("font size") and the non-compositional *Schriftzug* ("lettering").

German section of the parallel corpus, e.g. *Schrift* → *Schrift_MOD*, *Größe* → *Größe_HEAD*. Then, alignments for all occurrences of e.g. *Schrift* ("font") are collected in which *Schrift* occurs in the modifier position of the word *Schriftgröße* ("font size"). The same procedure applies to all occurrences of the head *Größe* ("size"). Table 1 (a) illustrates to which words *Schrift* and *Größe* have been aligned to, we call these alignments **local alignments**.

From these local alignments we then calculate the *translational entropy* (TE) scores as described in (Villada Moirón and Tiedemann, 2006). Details are given in Equation (1), where T_s is the compound with its two parts, $P(t|s)$ is the proportion of alignment t among all alignments of the word s in the context of the given compound.

$$H(T_s|s) = -\sum_{t \in T_s} P(t|s) \log P(t|s) \qquad (1)$$

High translational variance results in high TE scores. Recall from our hypothesis that the higher the translational variance, the more likely the present compound is non-compositional. We thus rank all compounds in descending order of their TE score. The example given in Table 1 illustrates the greater variance of local alignments for the non-compositional compound *Schriftzug* ("lettering") as opposed to the compositional compound *Schriftgröße*. It can be seen that there are dominant alignments for both parts of *Schriftgröße*, namely *Schrift* → font (65 times) and *Größe* →

size (74) times. In total the modifier is aligned to 25 different words and the head to 17 different words. Comparing these numbers to the non-compositional example *Schriftzug*, we find that the most frequent alignments are less dominant and there is an overall higher variance. The modifier *Schrift* (lit. "writing, font") is aligned to 59 different words, most of which occurred only once and the head *Zug* (lit. "characteristic") is aligned to 62 different words. This results in a TE score of 1.451 for *Schriftgröße* and a score of 3.827 for *Schriftzug*.

English For our experiments on English noun compounds, we apply the same procedure as described above for German. We use exactly the same word alignment file: the English section is left in its original shape, but German compounds are split and lemmatised for better word alignment quality. After alignment we mark English compounds. In the German experiment we split the compounds and thus knew where they occurred, but for English we do not have information about the presence of compounds. We thus rely on our evaluation data set consisting of English compounds and mark only those compounds in the English section of the parallel text which have occurred there. The remaining steps are the same as for German.

4 Experimental Settings

4.1 Data

Word Alignment We perform statistical word alignment using MGIZA++ (Gao and Vogel, 2008) based on parallel data provided for the annual shared tasks on machine translation[2]. The parallel corpus for German-English is mainly composed of Europarl and web-crawled texts, but also contains some translated newspaper texts. In total it consists of ca. 4.5 million sentences.

German Evaluation We evaluate our compositionality ranking of German noun-noun compounds against two available gold standard annotations, which are both part of the Ghost-NN dataset (Schulte im Walde et al., 2016b). The first one (VDHB) consists of 244 noun-noun compounds, originally annotated by von der Heide and Borgwaldt (2009) for both modifier and head compositionality on a 7-point scale (with 1 being

opaque and 7 being compositional). It has been enriched by Schulte im Walde et al. (2016b) with more annotations (in part using Amazon's Mechanical Turk) in order to produce more and thus more reliable ratings. The second one (GHOST-NN) is the full Ghost-NN dataset consisting of 868 German noun-noun compounds annotated in the same manner as VDHB. Note that GHOST-NN includes VDHB.

English Evaluation For English, we base our evaluation on a dataset of 1048 English noun-noun compounds (Farahmand et al., 2015), annotated by 4 trained experts for a binary decision on compositionality. In the present study, we rely on these binary annotations and ignore the conventionalisation scores that come with the dataset.

4.2 Parameters

Frequency Ranges Due to the fact that we base our scores on statistical word alignment, we exclude all compounds that have occurred less than 5 times in the parallel corpus from our ranking. As word alignment becomes more reliable with more occurrences, we investigate 5 different frequency spans throughout all experiments with minimal occurrences of 5, 10, 25, 50 and 100 times.

Compositionality Ranges This parameter applies only to the English experiments, where 4 annotators assigned a binary compositionaly scores to the evaluation data set. We investigate two different compositionality ranges $\geq 50\%$ (at least two of the 4 annotators assigned non-compositional to the compound) and $\geq 75\%$, respectively.

Translational Entropy Scores We use up to three translational entropy scores: one based on the local alignments of the modifier (*mod.te*), one based on the alignments of the head (*head.te*) and finally, one for both (*te*), which is simply the average of the two.

4.3 Evaluation

We evaluate our rankings with respect to the German and English gold standards. Due to their different characteristics, we chose different evaluation metrics for the German and the English ranking, respectively.

German The VDHB and the GHOST data sets are both annotated with a compositionality score ranging from 1 to 7. As a consequence, the values

---

[2]http://www.statmt.org/wmt15

GHOST	minimal frequency				
	5	10	25	50	100
#compounds	640	504	343	209	116
mod.freq	-0.0200	-0.0453	-0.0209	-0.0572	-0.0447
mod.lmi	-0.0233	-0.414	-0.0213	-0.0462	0.0358
mod.te	0.1010	0.1355	0.1509	0.1407	0.1534
head.freq	0.0200	0.0198	-0.0697	-0.0290	-0.0227
head.lmi	-0.0094	-0.0088	-0.0565	-0.0127	0.0249
head.te	0.1602	0.1885	0.2213	0.2620	0.1845

Table 2: ρ-value results for the GHOST dataset.

VDHB	minimal frequency				
	5	10	25	50	100
#compounds	143	110	76	43	18
mod.vector	0.5839	0.5478	0.5237	0.4713	0.2301
mod.te	-0.0175	-0.043	-0.0524	-0.0663	-0.0877
head.vector	0.5942	0.5871	0.5946	0.4804	0.4634
head.te	0.1268	0.1205	0.1643	0.3392	0.4407

Table 3: ρ-value results for the VDHB data set.

of these data sets present a continuum of compositionality scores. This is in line with how our lists are ranked according to the TE scores. Following previous works (e.g. Schulte im Walde et al. (2016a)), we use the Spearman Rank-Order Correlation Coefficient ρ (Siegel and Castellan, 1988) to evaluate how well our ranking is correlated with the ranking of the gold annotations.

English Due to the binary nature of the English data set we use, there are only 5 possible compositionality values (0, 0.25, 0.5, 0.75 and 1.0) and thus only 5 possible ranking positions. We thus use the uninterpolated average precision (*uap*, Manning and Schütze (1999)) to indicate the quality of the ranking.

5 Results

5.1 German

GHOST data set The results for the GHOST data set are given in Table 2. We compare the rank correlations of our rankings for modifiers (*mod.te*) and heads (*head.te*) to two simple baselines: *(mod|head).freq* = ranked in decreasing frequency of the compound and *(mod|head).lmi* = ranked in decreasing local mutual information (LMI) score (Evert, 2005). Not all compounds of the GHOST data set occurred in all frequency ranges. We thus give the number of compounds for each range in Table 2. The baselines perform poorly and rarely achieve positive ρ-values. The TE rankings improve with the frequencies of the compounds. An optimal value seems to be located between 25 and 50. For the highest frequency range of 100 we get mixed results. It can be seen that the correlations are higher overall when the lists have been ranked according to the TE score of their heads.

VDHB data set The results for the VDHB data set are given in Table 3. Again, not all compounds of the original set have occurred in all frequency ranges[3]. Only 18 of the 244 compounds occurred $\geq$100 times, which makes the results less conclusive. For this data set, we had access to the ranking of (Schulte im Walde et al., 2016a) and thus compare our results to theirs (*(mod|head).vector* in Table 3). Note that the numbers given here differ from those given in (Schulte im Walde et al., 2016a) because they are not calculated on the whole VDHB dataset but only on subsets of it. We can see from the results that the TE rankings most of the time do not even come near the performance of the vector-based ranking. It comes close only for *head.te* and a minimal frequency of 100, which apply only to 18 compounds, thus this result may not be very reliable. However, these results are nevertheless useful for further attempts of using TE scores for compositionality calculations. First, we can see that the head.te values significantly outperforms the mod.te values. This shows that the alignment variance of the compound head is more important when predicting the compounds' compositionality than the alignment variance of its modifier. Second, we see again, that the TE ranking correlation improves with increased minimal frequency constraints of the compounds to be ranked.

5.2 English

Our results for the compositionality ranking of English noun-noun compounds are given in Table 4. Note that not all of the 1042 compounds of the gold standard occurred in all frequency ranges in our corpus. We give the total number of compounds together with the number of noncompositional compounds thereof, depending on the compositionality range in the first two rows of Tables 4(a)+(b). As for the German GHOST data set above, we compare our rankings here to a simple frequency-based ranking (*freq* in Table 4) using the uninterpolated average precision (*uap*). We can see from Table 4 that all TE rank-

---

[3]We attribute this to the fact that half of the parallel corpus is based on the Europarl corpus, where words like *Kaffeepad* ("coffee pad") do not occur.

(a) Compositionality ≥ 0.50

	minimal frequency				
	5	**10**	**25**	**50**	**100**
#compounds	610	478	332	236	155
#opaque	138	116	84	61	35
freq	0.259	0.264	0.272	0.277	0.302
mod.te	0.295	0.308	0.299	0.296	0.258
head.te	0.279	0.291	0.293	0.297	0.262
te	0.295	0.306	0.299	0.299	0.256

(b) Compositionality ≥ 0.75

	minimal frequency				
	5	**10**	**25**	**50**	**100**
#compounds	610	478	332	236	155
#opaque	91	75	55	41	23
freq	0.176	0.180	0.188	0.194	0.218
mod.te	0.216	0.225	0.228	0.234	0.192
head.te	0.211	0.221	0.233	0.243	0.220
te	0.220	0.229	0.233	0.240	0.198

Table 4: Uap scores for the English dataset.

ings outperform the frequency-based baseline for both compositionality ranges and for minimal frequencies up to 50. In the high-frequent range, the frequency-based ranking slightly outperforms our TE ranking, but note that in this range only 35 non-compositional compounds occur in the compositionality ≥ 50 range occur (and only 23 for ≥ 75). The quality of the rankings improves with a higher minimal frequency of up to 50 and the head scores again seem to be more informative for compositionality.

6   Conclusion and Future Work

We have shown that translational entropy scores calculated from word alignments show a small correlation with compound compositionality. Our results showed that translational entropy scores are most reliable when calculated for compounds which occurred at least 25 times in the parallel corpus. Moreover, for German, we found that the alignment variance of the compound head is a better indicator for non-compositionality than variance observed for compound modifiers. For English the diffference is less clear and should be subject to further investigation in the future.

The major drawback of this approach is its dependence on parallel resources. We found that many compounds of the gold standards do not (or not sufficiently often) occur in the parallel corpus to produce reliable results. Nevertheless we are convinced that translational entropy scores can be used as an informative feature combined with previous (e.g. vector-based) approaches to compositionality identification.

For the future, we plan to compare and combine the translational entropy scores other scoring metrics based on word alignments. One example is to compare the alignments of the components when they occur in the context of the compound vs. when they occur independently similar to (Villada Moirón and Tiedemann, 2006) and (Salehi and Cook, 2013). Moreover, we will take the symmetry of word alignments into account and add a feature that indicates how many alignments were 1:1 vs. 1:n. Finally, we want to experiment with a wider range of languages on which the alignment is calculated, preferably including more contrastive languages.

Acknowledgements

This project has been funded by a VINNMER Marie Curie Incoming Grant within VINNOVAs Mobility for Growth programme. Thanks to the anonymous reviewers for their constructive comments and to Schulte im Walde et al. (2016a) for sharing their results to enable a direct comparison.

References

Stefan Evert. 2005. *The Statistics of Word Cooccurrences: Word Pairs and Collocations*. University of Stuttgart, PhD dissertation.

Meghdad Farahmand, Aaron Smith, and Joakim Nivre. 2015. A multiword expression dataset: Annotating non-compositionality and conventionalization for english noun compounds. In *MWE-NAACl'15: Proceedings of the 11th Workshop on Multiword Expressions*.

Fabienne Fritzinger and Alexander Fraser. 2010. How to avoid Burning Ducks: Combining Linguistic Analysis and Corpus Statistics for German Compound Processing. In *ACL'10: Proceedings of the 5th Workshop on Statistical Machine Translation and Metrics MATR of the 48th Annual Meeting of the Association for Computational Linguistics*, pages 224–234.

Qin Gao and Stephan Vogel. 2008. Parallel Implementations of Word Alignment Tool. In *ACL'08: Proceedings of the Workshop on Software Engineering, Testing, and Quality Assurance for Natural Language Processing of the 46th Annual Meeting of the Association for Computational Linguistics*, pages 49–57. Association for Computational Linguistics.

Christopher D. Manning and Hinrich Schütze. 1999. *Foundations of Statistical Natural Language Processing*. The MIT Press, Cambridge, Massachusetts.

Helena Medeiros de Caseli, Carlos Ramisch, Maria das Graças Volpe Nunes, and Aline Villavicencio. 2010. Alignment-based extraction of multiword expressions. *Language resources and evaluation*, 44(1-2):59–77.

Bahar Salehi and Paul Cook. 2013. Predicting the compositionality of multiword expressions using translations in multiple languages. In **SEM'13: Proceedings of the Second Joint Conference on Lexical and Computational Semantics*, pages 266–275.

Bahar Salehi, Paul Cook, and Timothy Baldwin. 2014. Using distributional similarity of multi-way translations to predict multiword expression compositionality. In *EACL'14: Proceedings of the Annual Meeting of the European Chapter of the Association for Computational Linguistics*, pages 472–481.

Helmut Schmid, Arne Fitschen, and Ulrich Heid. 2004. SMOR: A German Computational Morphology Covering Derivation, Composition and Inflection. In *LREC '04: Proceedings of the 4th Conference on Language Resources and Evaluation*, pages 1263–1266.

Sabine Schulte im Walde, Anna Hätty, and Stefan Bott. 2016a. The role of modifier and head properties in predicting the compositionality of english and german noun-noun compounds: A vector-space perspective. In **SEM'16: Proceedings of the Fifth Joint Conference on Lexical and Computational Semantics*, pages 148–158, Berlin, Germany. Association for Computational Linguistics.

Sabine Schulte im Walde, Anna Hätty, Stefan Bott, and Nana Khvtisavrishvili. 2016b. GhoSt-NN: A Representative Gold Standard of German Noun-Noun Compounds. In *LREC'16: Proceedings of the 10th International Conference on Language Resources and Evaluation*, pages 2285–2292.

Sidney Siegel and N. John Castellan. 1988. *Nonparametric Statistics for the Behavioral Sciences*.

Begoña Villada Moirón and Jörg Tiedemann. 2006. Identifying idiomatic expressions using automatic word-alignment. In *Proceedings of the EACL 2006 Workshop on multi-word-expressions in a multilingual context*, pages 33–40.

Claudia von der Heide and Susanne Borgwaldt. 2009. Assoziationen zu Unter-, Basis- und Oberbegriffen. Eine explorative Studie. In *Proceedings of the 9th Norddeutsches Linguistisches Kolloquium*, pages 51–74.

Semantic annotation to characterize contextual variation in terminological noun compounds: a pilot study

Melania Cabezas-García
LexiCon Research Group
University of Granada
Granada, Spain
melaniacabezas@ugr.es

Antonio San Martín
LexiCon Research Group
Maynooth University
Maynooth, Ireland
antonio.sanmartin@nuim.ie

Abstract

Noun compounds (NCs) are semantically complex and not fully compositional, as is often assumed. This paper presents a pilot study regarding the semantic annotation of environmental NCs with a view to accessing their semantics and exploring their domain-based contextual variation. Our results showed that the semantic annotation of NCs afforded important insights into how context impacts their conceptualization.

1 Introduction

In English, noun compounds (NCs) are the lexical units that are most often used to convey expert knowledge (Daille et al., 2004; Nakov, 2013; Hendrickx et al., 2013). Terminological NCs can be considered a type of multi-word term (MWT) because they are non-idiomatic multi-word units that belong to a specialized domain and lie in the intersection between terms and multi-word expressions (MWEs) (SanJuan et al., 2005; Frantzi et al., 2000; Ramisch, 2015). They are characterized by their semantic complexity since two or more concepts are juxtaposed without any explicit indication of the relation linking them (Ó Séaghdha and Copestake, 2013). This relation is determined largely by the context and the frame (i.e. system of concepts related in such a way that one concept evokes the entire system (Fillmore, 1982)) to which the NC belongs. In other words, they are not fully compositional and their conceptualization can differ depending on the context and the semantic frame in which it is embedded.

This paper describes the use of semantic annotation to explore how domain-based context modulates the meaning of NCs. To this end, the annotated concordance lines were used to identify and analyze the argument structure of the propositions underlying this kind of MWT. The micro-contexts (i.e. the relation of a predicate with its arguments and adjuncts) are directly related to the semantic load of the compound term, because they specify the hidden relation between its components (Cabezas-García and Faber, 2016).

In the following section, a short account of the particularities of NCs and the phenomenon of contextual variation is provided. Then, section 3 describes the materials and methods used in this pilot study. Section 4 expounds the results of the study and discusses their significance. Finally, section 5 presents the conclusions derived from this research and mentions the issues that will be addressed in future work.

2 Contextual Variation in Noun Compounds

2.1 Noun Compounds

NCs are very frequent in specialized texts written in English (Daille et al., 2004; Nakov, 2013; Hendrickx et al., 2013). They are a sequence of nouns that function as a single noun (Downing, 1977), e.g., *water loss* or *population growth*. In endocentric NCs, one term is the head and the other is its modifier (Nakov, 2013) (e.g., *power generation*). Alternatively, in exocentric NCs, the MWT is not a hyponym of one of its elements, and thus appears to lack a head (Bauer, 2008) (e.g. *saber tooth*). Endocentric NCs (the focus of this study) are characterized by their (i) headedness; (ii) transparency, (iii) syntactic ambiguity; and (iv) language-dependency (Nakov, 2013).

NCs have underlying propositions, which can be inferred by the term formation processes highlighted in Levi (1978), involving predicate deletion (e.g. *power system*, instead of a *system produces power*) and predicate nominalization (e.g.

Proceedings of the 13th Workshop on Multiword Expressions (MWE 2017), pages 108–113,
Valencia, Spain, April 4. ©2017 Association for Computational Linguistics

heat transfer, instead of *heat is transferred*). These propositions underlying the NCs take the form of a predicate with its arguments, which are necessary for the meaning of the verb, and its adjuncts (optional complements) (Tesnière, 1976). The relation of a predicate to its argument structure is known as micro-context. This is a key factor that provides access to the conceptual load of terms, since the predicate, which is the syntactic-semantic core of the sentence, can only be successfully addressed through its complement structure (Cabezas-García and Faber, 2016).

2.2 Contextual Variation

The notion of context plays a crucial role in various disciplines that employ it in different ways. In this paper, context refers to any factor that affects the interpretation of a sign or an expression (Kecskes, 2014). This sense includes linguistic factors (different types of co-text), discursive factors (channel, communicative purpose, degree of formality, topic, and level of specialization), sociocultural factors (social activity in which communication is embedded, and the relation between participants) as well as spatiotemporal factors (San Martín, 2016).

Lexical units do not carry meaning in themselves, but rather trigger the mental representation of meaning in context (Fauconnier, 1994). Meaning is construed in every usage event. Depending on the context, certain segments of the knowledge conventionally associated with a lexical unit are activated and give rise to meaning. Therefore, meaning does not exist outside of context. Without contextual restrictions, lexical units can be said to have semantic potential, which is all the conceptual content that a lexical unit is capable of invoking (Evans, 2009). The semantic potential of a lexical unit constitutes a considerable amount of information, all of which is never fully activated in a single use event. It includes one or more concepts and their underlying conceptual frames.

Given that context is never identical, the meaning of a lexical unit is variable. This phenomenon by which the semantic potential of a lexical unit produces different meanings depending on the context is called contextual variation. Although in practice, it is sometimes difficult to distinguish between a high degree of contextual variation and polysemy, these two phenomena are theoretically different. Polysemy occurs when the semantic potential of a lexical unit refers to more than one concept. For example, *organism* is a polysemic term because it designates two different concepts: ORGANISM (living being) and ORGANISM (system or organization). In contrast, *ozone* is an example of contextual variation because it designates a single concept (OZONE). When *ozone* appears in the context of Atmospheric Science, it is conceptualized as an important allotropic form of oxygen that is present in the atmosphere. However, in the context of Water Treatment and Supply, it is conceived as a powerful virucidal agent used to disinfect water.

In this paper, we focus on domain-based contextual variation because discourse topic is the contextual factor that best predicts how the semantic potential of a term is restricted in actual usage events (San Martín, 2016). In our analysis, *domain* is synonymous to *knowledge field*.

3 Materials and Methods

A corpus of English texts on environmental science was manually compiled. The corpus consisted of 4,743,025 tokens, and was composed of 16 subcorpora of specialized and semi-specialized texts. Each subcorpus had approximately 300,000 tokens and focused on a specific environmental domain (e.g. Agronomy, Hydrology, etc.).

Each subcorpus was uploaded separately to the term extractor TermoStat (Drouin, 2003) (http://termostat.ling.umontreal.ca/). The search was set to complex terms. The 16 resulting lists of terms were automatically compared. In order to ensure representativeness and significant contextual variation, we only retained the two-term NCs designating processes that had a minimum of 10 occurrences in at least three subdomains (i.e. 10 NCs in total). The MWTs chosen were those designating processes because these units have underlying propositions with a clear argument structure, thus enabling the analysis of micro-contexts (i.e. the relation between a predicate and its arguments and adjuncts), which are key factors in the conceptualization of this kind of MWT (Cabezas-García and Faber, 2016). This pilot study focuses solely on the analysis of *water loss*, with a view to developing an annotation protocol for the rest of MWTs.

We also uploaded the corpus to Sketch Engine (Kilgarriff et al., 2014) (https://www.sketchengine.co.uk/), an online corpus analysis application that allowed us to generate concordance lines, which were subsequently processed with an annotation tool. As previously mentioned, NCs designating processes all have underlying propositions. Nakov and Hearst (2006) confirmed that verb paraphrases are useful for disambiguating these compound terms and eliciting their meaning. Thus, in order to access the concordances that allude to the semantics of the MWT in question, we not only downloaded the concordance lines where the NC appeared but also the concordances where paraphrases had been used (see Figure 1).

ws you to record how much water is lost through evaporation over a
f the unavoidable irrigation water losses percolating down into the ι
ion. This is a combination of water lost by evaporation from the soil
ption loss. In general, more water is lost from a forested catchment
)f a stone mulch is to reduce water loss from the soil and to elimina

Figure 1: Concordance lines of *water loss* and its verb paraphrases in the domain of Hydrology.

For example, in the case of *water loss*, concordance lines such as "...combination of *water lost* by evaporation from..." were analyzed, as well as those where the NC occurred. This made it possible to access a larger number of examples of the process conveyed by *water loss* (i.e. "a SOURCE ceases to have [LOSE] a PATIENT [WATER]"). The loss process is encoded by verbs conveying a similar meaning though from different perspectives (e.g. *lose*, *evaporate*, *extract*, *release*, etc.).

The next step was the annotation of the concordance lines, following the semantic annotation methodology in L'Homme (2012), which is based on FrameNet (Ruppenhofer et al., 2010). Two human annotators, who established a common tagset and guidelines, annotated the concordance lines with the help of the UAM CorpusTool (O'Donnell, 2008) (http://www.corpustool.com/), an open-source environment for the annotation of text corpora. This tool also allows users to search the corpus, perform statistical studies, analyze file information, etc. The semantic labels [1]used were: (i) PREDICATIVE_TERM, (ii) ARGUMENT, and (iii) ADJUNCT. The predicative term was further specified as VERB or NOUN, and the arguments and adjuncts as AGENT, PATIENT, SOURCE, TIME, LOCATION, RESULT, CAUSE, MANNER, QUANTITY, MEDIUM, DESTINATION, INSTRUMENT, or AIM. The annotation was performed on all the concordance lines given the limited size of the study, but larger annotation tasks would benefit from a selection of contexts, as proposed in L'Homme and Pimentel (2012). Once the texts were annotated, the UAM Corpus Tool software generated summaries of the linguistic designations that filled the arguments and adjuncts slots depending on the contextual domain, and their frequency of occurrence, which were subsequently compared.

4 Results and Discussion

The analysis of the NCs by means of semantic annotation afforded insights into their specific conceptualization for each given contextual domain. Thanks to the annotated concordances, it was possible to compare the conceptualization of the micro-contexts of the NCs in each contextual domain. Particularly, we made use of the automatic generation of lists of the linguistic instantiations that filled each argument and adjunct slots, depending on the contextual domain. This allowed the characterization and analysis of the argument structure of the predicate (see Figure 2).

In a hypertonic environment[AD:LOCATION], most prokaryotes[AR:SOURCE] lose[PT:VERB] water[AR:PATIENT] and shrink away from their wall (plasmolyze).

For example, marine fishes[AR:SOURCE], such as the cod in Figure 44.4a, constantly[AD:MANNER] lose[PT:VERB] water[AR:PATIENT] by osmosis[AD:CAUSE].

Despite these and other adaptations, most terrestrial animals[AR:SOURCE] lose[PT:VERB] water[AR:PATIENT] through many routes: in urine[AD:MEDIUM] and feces[AD:MEDIUM], across their skin[AD:MEDIUM], and from the surfaces of gas exchange organs[AD:MEDIUM].

Figure 2: Annotation of propositions underlying *water loss* in the domain of Biology.

Since the linguistic realizations of the arguments and adjuncts were summarized in the annotation tool, it was possible to compare the conceptualization of the NC, thus allowing the characterization of contextual variation.

Therefore, the semantic annotation of the concordance lines confirmed that contextual variation

[1]It is well-known that the distinction between arguments and adjuncts and the choice of the number and types of semantic labels is problematic. Although this did not cause problems in this work (due to the limited coverage of this pilot study), it is an issue that will be carefully considered in further research.

in NCs is reflected in their argument structure. In other words, the arguments and adjuncts of the predicate underlying a NC, such as *water loss*, were filled by different conceptual categories, depending on the contextual domain.

In regard to *water loss*, the contextual variation was found to manifest itself in the SOURCE of water loss, an argument that is not explicit in the compound. This means that the SOURCE (as reflected in its linguistic designations and those of the adjuncts) varies, depending on the specialized domain. When used in Agronomy, the water loss SOURCE was usually a plant entity (e.g. *plant*, *leaf*, etc.). In contrast, in Hydrology, this SOURCE was generally a waterbody (e.g. *river*, *aquifer*, *lake*, etc.). Finally, in Biology, the preference was for animals (e.g. *animal*, *animal cell*, *blood*, etc.) or some type of living organism. Table 1 shows the linguistic instantiations of the water loss SOURCE in Biology, which highlight the frequency of animal entities in this argument slot.

Category	Designations
ANIMAL	*animal* (7), *animal cell* (5), *blood* (3), *filtrate* (3), *egg* (1), *waste* (1), *body* (1), *tissue* (1)
PLANT	*plant* (3), *leaf* (1), *plant cell* (1)
BACTERIA	*prokaryote* (2), *endospore* (1), *Halobacterium cell* (1)
AIR	*air* (2)
SOIL	*soil* (1)

Table 1: Linguistic designations (with frequency of occurrence) filling the SOURCE argument in Biology for *water loss*.

As previously noted, depending on the domain context (Biology, Agronomy or Hydrology), the argument slot (i.e. SOURCE of *water loss*) is designated by a different set of semantically related units. Furthermore, this preference for a specific semantic category in the argument determining the variation (i.e. SOURCE of *water loss*) is reflected in the linguistic realizations of the adjuncts. For example, in Agronomy, the SOURCE argument is filled by plant entities, and the most frequent adjuncts were MEDIUM or CAUSE with linguistic realizations that also belong to the vegetable kingdom: *stoma* and *leaf*, and *transpiration* and *evaporation*, respectively.

Moreover, even though the same NC (*water loss*) sometimes involved the same SOURCE (*wa-loss*) sometimes involved the same SOURCE (*wa-*

terbody), its conceptualization was found to have different nuances in each context. For instance, when comparing *water loss from a waterbody* in the domains of Agronomy and Hydrology, it was found that their conceptualizations differed. Whereas in Agronomy texts, *water loss* generally referred to the natural loss of water, in Hydrology texts, *water loss* referred to an artificial process with specific purposes.

This was reflected in the adjuncts and their linguistic realizations. For example, the INSTRUMENT adjunct in Hydrology texts was mainly designated by manmade structures, such as *canal*, *well*, *aqueduct*, *floodgate*, etc. Contextual differences were also evident in the verbs used in the paraphrases. More specifically in Agronomy, the most frequent predicates were *lose*, *evaporate*, *remove*, *transpire*, *absorb*, *draw*, *leave*, and *move*, whereas in Hydrology, there was a preference for predicates with a human/instrument AGENT (e.g. *extract*, *release*, *transmit*, *transfer*, *draw*, *divert*, and *abstract*).

The analysis of micro-contexts and of the linguistic realizations of the arguments and adjuncts was also found to be a useful method for frame-based terminological management (Faber, 2015; L'Homme, 2016). When the argument structure of *water loss* and its linguistic realizations are analyzed, a general picture of the conceptualization of the MWT in each subdomain can be obtained. For instance, this analysis reveals the type of entities that can lose water, the medium in which water is lost, the causes and results of the water loss, etc. For this reason, the identification and annotation of the arguments and adjuncts of the verbs provide insights into the conceptualization of terms and their relations with concepts in larger frames.

5   Conclusions

This research focused on the use of semantic annotation to characterize the micro-contexts that underlie a NC. The results confirmed that contextual variation in NCs designating processes is manifested in their underlying argument structure. Access to the domain-specific conceptualization was accomplished by annotating the NCs as well as the paraphrases that made the hidden verb explicit. This made it possible to identify the conceptual relations between the terms in the compound, which is one of the difficulties of MWTs. Moreover, in regard to the methodology, our results confirmed that the semantic annotation of micro-contexts is an effective technique to study the conceptualization of NCs, namely those representing specialized processes.

In future work, a more in-depth research on the advantages of semantic annotation will be carried out with a view to identifying the role of micro-contexts in NC formation. For the characterization of the different phenomena arising from domain-based contextual variation in MWTs, we also plan to further refine our semantic annotation methodology using WordNet synsets and combine them with the extraction of semantic relations by means of knowledge patterns.

We will also implement the semantic annotation of MWTs for the modeling of this kind of term in the environmental terminological knowledge base EcoLexicon (http://ecolexicon.ugr.es/). Since both endeavors will be multilingual, the results will ultimately be applied to the development of translation rules for MWTs.

Acknowledgements

This research was carried out as part of project FF2014-52740-P, Cognitive and Neurological Bases for Terminology-enhanced Translation (CONTENT), funded by the Spanish Ministry of Economy and Competitiveness. Funding was also provided by an FPU grant given by the Spanish Ministry of Education to the first author. Finally, we would like to thank the anonymous reviewers for their useful comments.

References

Laurie Bauer. 2008. Les composés exocentriques de l'anglais. In D. Amiot, editor, *La composition dans une perspective typologique*, pages 35–47. Artois Presses Université, Arras.

Melania Cabezas-García and Pamela Faber. 2016. Exploring the Semantics of Multi-word Terms by Means of Paraphrases. In *EnTRetextos International Conference on Specialized Translation*, Valencia.

Béatrice Daille, Samuel Dufour-Kowalski, and Emmanuel Morin. 2004. French-English multi-word term alignment based on lexical context analysis. In *Proceedings of the Fourth International Conference on Language Resources and Evaluation (LREC'04)*, pages 919–922.

Pamela Downing. 1977. On the creation and use of English compound nouns. *Language*, (53):810–842.

Patrick Drouin. 2003. Term extraction using non-technical corpora as a point of leverage. *Terminology*, 9(1):99–115.

Vyvyan Evans. 2009. *How Words Mean: Lexical Concepts, Cognitive Models, and Meaning Construction*. Oxford University Press, Oxford.

Pamela Faber. 2015. Frames as a framework for terminology. In Hendrik Kockaert and Frieda Steurs, editors, *Handbook of Terminology*, pages 14–33. John Benjamins, Amsterdam / Philadelphia.

Gilles Fauconnier. 1994. *Mental spaces: aspects of meaning construction in natural language*. Cambridge University Press, Cambridge, New York.

Charles Fillmore. 1982. Frame Semantics. In The Linguistic Society of Korea, editor, *Linguistics in the morning calm. Selected papers from SICOL-1981*, pages 111–137. Hanshin Publishing Company, Seoul.

Katerina Frantzi, Sophia Ananiadou, and Hideki Mima. 2000. Automatic recognition of multi-word terms: The C-value/NC-value method. *International Journal on Digital Libraries*, 3(2):115–130.

Iris Hendrickx, Zornitsa Kozareva, Preslav Nakov, Diarmuid Ó Séaghdha, Stan Szpakowicz, and Tony Veale. 2013. SemEval-2013 Task 4: Free Paraphrases of Noun Compounds. In *Second Joint Conference on Lexical and Computational Semantics (*SEM), Volume 2: Proceedings of the Seventh International Workshop on Semantic Evaluation (SemEval 2013)*, volume 2, pages 138–143.

Istvan Kecskes. 2014. *Intercultural Pragmatics*. Oxford University Press, Oxford, New York.

Adam Kilgarriff, Vít Baisa, Jan Bušta, Miloš Jakubíček, Vojtěch Ková, Jan Michelfeit, Pavel Rychlý, and Vít Suchomel. 2014. The Sketch Engine: ten years on. *Lexicography*, 1(1):7–36.

Judith Levi. 1978. *The Syntax and Semantics of Complex Nominals*. Academic Press, New York.

Marie-Claude L'Homme and Janine Pimentel. 2012. Capturing Syntactico-semantic Regularities among Terms : An Application of the FrameNet Methodology to Terminology. In *Proceedings of LREC 2012*, pages 262–268, Istanbul.

Marie-Claude L'Homme. 2012. Adding syntactico-semantic information to specialized dictionaries: an application of the FrameNet methodology. *Lexicographica*, 28(1):233–252.

Marie-Claude L'Homme. 2016. Terminologie de l'environnement et Sémantique des cadres. In *Congrès mondial de linguistique française (CMLF 2016)*, Tours, France.

Preslav Nakov and Marti A. Hearst. 2006. Using Verbs to Characterize Noun-Noun Relations. *Artificial Intelligence Methodology Systems and Applications*, 4183:233–244.

Preslav Nakov. 2013. On the interpretation of noun compounds: Syntax, semantics, and entailment. *Natural Language Engineering*, 19(03):291–330.

Diarmuid Ó Séaghdha and Ann Copestake. 2013. Interpreting compound nouns with kernel methods. *Natural Language Engineering*, 19(3):331–356.

Mick O'Donnell. 2008. Demonstration of the UAM CorpusTool for text and image annotation. In *Proceedings of the ACL-08:HLT Demo Session*, number June, pages 13–16, Columbus, Ohio.

Carlos Ramisch. 2015. *Multiword Expressions Acquisition: A Generic and Open Framework*. Springer, Cham.

Josef Ruppenhofer, Michael Ellsworth, Miriam R. L. Petruck, and Jan Johnson, Christopher R. Scheffczyk. 2010. *Framenet II: Extended theory and practice*.

Antonio San Martín. 2016. *La representación de la variación contextual mediante definiciones terminológicas flexibles*. Ph.D. thesis, University of Granada.

Eric SanJuan, James Dowdall, Fidelia Ibekwe-SanJuan, and Fabio Rinaldi. 2005. A symbolic approach to automatic multiword term structuring. *Computer Speech and Language*, 19(4):524–542.

Lucien Tesnière. 1976. *Eléments de syntaxe structurale*. Klincksieck, Paris.

Detection of Verbal Multi-Word Expressions via Conditional Random Fields with Syntactic Dependency Features and Semantic Re-Ranking

Alfredo Maldonado[1], Lifeng Han[2], Erwan Moreau[1],
Ashjan Alsulaimani[1], Koel Dutta Chowdhury[2], Carl Vogel[1] and Qun Liu[2]

ADAPT Centre
[1]Trinity College Dublin, Ireland
[2]Dublin City University, Ireland
{firstname.lastname}@adaptcentre.ie

Abstract

A description of a system for identifying Verbal Multi-Word Expressions (VMWEs) in running text is presented. The system mainly exploits universal syntactic dependency features through a Conditional Random Fields (CRF) sequence model. The system competed in the Closed Track at the PARSEME VMWE Shared Task 2017, ranking 2nd place in most languages on full VMWE-based evaluation and 1st in three languages on token-based evaluation. In addition, this paper presents an option to re-rank the 10 best CRF-predicted sequences via semantic vectors, boosting its scores above other systems in the competition. We also show that all systems in the competition would struggle to beat a simple lookup baseline system and argue for a more purpose-specific evaluation scheme.

1 Introduction

The automatic identification of Multi-Word Expressions (MWEs) or collocations has long been recognised as an important but challenging task in Natural Language Processing (NLP) (Sinclair, 1991; Sag et al., 2001). An effort in response to this challenge is the Shared Task on detecting multi-word, verbal constructions (Savary et al., 2017) organised by the PARSing and Multiword Expressions (PARSEME) European COST Action[1]. The Shared Task consisted of two tracks: a closed one, restricted to the data provided by the organisers, and an open track that permitted participants to employ additional external data.

The ADAPT team participated in the Closed Track with a system[2] that exploits syntactic dependency features in a Conditional Random Fields (CRF) sequence model (Lafferty et al., 2001), ranking 2nd place in the detection of full MWEs in most languages[3]. To the best of our knowledge, this is the first time that a CRF model is applied to the identification of verbal MWEs (VMWEs) in a large collection of distant languages.

In addition to our CRF-based solution officially submitted to the closed track, our team also explored an option to re-rank the top 10 sequences predicted by the CRF decoder using a regression model trained on word co-occurrence semantic vectors computed from Europarl. This semantic re-ranking step would qualify for the open track, however its results were not submitted to the official competition as we were unable to obtain its results in time for it.

This paper describes our official CRF-based solution (Sec. 3), as well as our unofficial Semantic Re-Ranker (Sec. 4). Since the Shared Task's main goal is to enable a discussion of the challenges of identifying VMWEs across languages, this paper also offers some observations (Sec. 5). In particular, we found that test files contain VMWEs that also occur in the training files, helping all systems in the competition, but also implying that a simple lookup system that only predicts MWEs it encountered in the training set will fare very well in the competition, and will in fact beat most systems. We also argue for a more purpose-based evaluation scheme. And we offer our conclusions and ideas for future work (Sec. 6).

2 Related Work

MWEs have long been discussed in NLP research and a myriad of identification techniques

---

[1]http://www.parseme.eu

[2]System details, feature templates, code and experiment instructions: https://github.com/alfredomg/ADAPT-MWE17

[3]Official results: http://bit.ly/2krOu05

Proceedings of the 13th Workshop on Multiword Expressions (MWE 2017), pages 114–120,
Valencia, Spain, April 4. ©2017 Association for Computational Linguistics

have been developed, such as combining statistical and symbolic methods (Sag et al., 2001), single and multi-prototype word embeddings (Salehi et al., 2015), integrating MWE identification within larger NLP tasks such as parsing (Green et al., 2011; Green et al., 2013; Constant et al., 2012) and machine translation (Tsvetkov and Wintner, 2010; Salehi et al., 2014a; Salehi et al., 2014b).

More directly related to our closed-track approach are works such as that of Venkatapathy and Joshi (2006), who showed that information about the degree of compositionality of MWEs helps the word alignment of verbs, and of Boukobza and Rappoport (2009) who used sentence surface features based on the canonical form of VMWEs. In addition, Sun et al. (2013) applied a Hidden Semi-CRF model to capture latent semantics from Chinese microblogging posts; Hosseini et al. (2016) used double-chained CRF for minimal semantic units detection in SemEval task. And Bar et al. (2014) discussed that syntactic construction classes are helpful for verb-noun and verb-particle MWE identification. Schneider et al. (2014) also used a sequence tagger to annotate MWEs, including VMWEs, while Blunsom and Baldwin (2006) and Vincze et al. (2011) have used CRF taggers for identifying contiguous MWEs.

In relation to our open-track approach, Attia et al. (2010) exploited large corpora to identify Arabic MWEs, and Legrand and Collobert (2016) applied fixed-size continuous vector representations for various length of phrases and chunks in the MWE identification task. Constant et al. (2012) used a re-ranker for MWEs in an n-best parser.

3 Official Closed Track: CRF Labelling

We decided to model the problem of VMWE identification as a sequence labelling and classification problem. We operationalise our solution through CRFs (Lafferty et al., 2001), which encode relationships between observations in a sequence. We implemented our solution using the CRF++[4] system. CRFs have been successfully applied to such sequence-sensitive NLP tasks as segmentation, named-entity recognition (Han et al., 2013; Han et al., 2015) and part-of-speech tagging. Our team attempted 15 out of the 18 languages involved in the Shared Task. The data for the languages we did not attempt (Bulgarian, Hebrew and Lithuanian) lacked morpho-syntactic information,

so we felt that we were unlikely to obtain good results with them. It should be noted that of these 15 languages, four (Czech, Farsi, Maltese and Romanian) were provided without syntactic dependency information, although morphological information (i.e. tokens' lemmas and parts of speech (POS)) was indeed supplied.

3.1 Features

We assume that features based on the relationships between the different types of morpho-syntactic information provided by the organisers will help identify VMWEs. Ideally, one feature set (or *feature template* in the terminology of CRF++) per language should be developed. Due to time constraints, we instead developed a feature set for a single language per broad language family (German, French and Polish), assuming that, for our purposes, morpho-syntactic relationships will behave similarly among closely related languages, but not among distant languages.

For each token in the corpora, the direct linguistic features available are its word surface (W), word lemma (L) and POS (P). In the languages where syntactic dependency information is provided, each token also has its head's word surface (HW), its head's word lemma (HL), its head's POS (HP) and the dependency relation between the token and its head (DR). It is possible to create CRF++ feature templates that combine these features in unigrams, bigrams, etc. In addition, it is also possible to combine the predicted output label of the previous token with the output label of the current token (B). We conducted preliminary 5-fold cross validation experiments on German, French and Polish training data independently, using feature templates based on different combinations of these features in unigram, bigram and trigram fashions. Templates exploiting token word surface features (W) performed unsurprisingly worse than those based on token lemmas and POS (L, P). Templates using head features (HL, HP, DR) in addition to token features (L, P) fared better than those relying on token features only. The three final templates developed can be summarised[5] as follows:

- FS3: B, L-2, L-1, L, L+1, L+2, L-2/L-1, L-1/L, L/L+1, L+1/L2, P, HL/DR, P/DR, HP/DR.
- FS4: FS3, P-2, P-1, P, P+1, P+2, P-1/P, P/P+1.
- FS5: FS4, L/HP.

Each template summary above consists of a name (FS3, FS4 or FS5) and a list of feature

---

[4] https://taku910.github.io/crfpp/

[5] Actual templates are on GitHub. See footnote 2.

abbreviations indicating a position relative to the current token and feature conditioning is indicated by a slash. After developing these templates through preliminary experimentation, a further 5-fold cross validation experiment on training data was conducted using each template against each of the 15 languages. For each language, the best performing template (regardless of the language family for which it was developed) was chosen for the final challenge, in which the CRF++ system was trained using that selected template on the full training data for the language, and the prediction output was generated from the blind test set provided. FS3 was chosen for Greek, Spanish, French, Slovenian and Turkish, whilst FS4 was chosen for Swedish and FS5 for the rest of the languages.

3.2 Offical Evaluation

Table 1 shows, under "crf", the F1 scores for each of the VMWE categories in the competition: ID (low-compositional verbal idiomatic expressions), IReflV (reflexive verbs), LVC (light verb constructions), VPC (verb-particle constructions) and OTH (a miscellaneous category for any other language-specific VMWE). The Overall score is also included. The column n shows the count of MWEs in the test set for each category. Scores for which $n = 0$ are omitted as they are undefined. Sections 4 and 5 explain the "sem" and "PS" columns, respectively. On token-based evaluation, our system was ranked in first place in Polish, French and Swedish, second place in eight languages and third in three. For MWE-based scores, our system ranked second place on nine languages.

4 Unofficial Open Track: Semantic Re-Ranking

We implemented an optional post-processing stage intended to improve the performance of our CRF-based method using a distributional semantics approach (Schütze, 1998; Maldonado and Emms, 2011). Intuitively, the goal is to assess the likeliness of a given candidate MWE, and then, based on such features for all the candidate MWEs in a sentence, to select the most likely predicted sequence among a set of 10 potential sequences.

This part of the system receives the output produced by CRF++ in the form of the 10 most likely predictions for every sentence. For every such set of 10 predicted sequences, context vectors are computed for each candidate MWE, using a large third-party corpus. A set of features based on these context vectors is computed for each predicted sequence. These features are then fed to a supervised regression algorithm, which predicts a score for every predicted sequence; the one with the highest score among the set of 10 is the final answer.

4.1 Third-Party Corpus: Europarl

We use Europarl (Koehn, 2005) as third-party corpus, because it is large and contains most languages addressed in this Shared Task. It does not contain Farsi, Maltese and Turkish, which are therefore excluded from this part of the process. For each of the 12 remaining languages, we use only the monolingual Europarl corpus, and we tokenise it using the generic tokeniser provided by the organisers.[6]

4.2 Features

An instance is generated for every predicted sequence. For every candidate MWE in the sequence, we calculate context vectors (i.e. we count the words co-occurring with the MWE[7] in Europarl), and we compute three kinds of features: (1) Features comparing each pseudo-MWE consisting of a single word of the MWE against the full MWE; (2) Features comparing each pseudo-MWE consisting of the MWE minus one word against the full MWE; (3) Features comparing one of the other MWEs found in the 10 predicted sequences against the current MWE. For each category of features, the relative frequency and the similarity score obtained between the context vectors of the pseudo-MWEs and the full MWE are added as features, as well as the number of words (we implemented four kinds of similiarity measures: Jaccard index, Min/Max similarity, Cosine similarity with or without IDF weights).

The main difficulty in representing a predicted sequence as a fixed set of features is that each sentence can contain any number of MWEs, and each MWE can contain any number of words. We opted for "summarising" any non-fixed number of features with three statistics: minimum, mean and maximum. For instance, the similarity scores

---

[6]Discrepancies are to be expected between the tokenisation of the Shared Task corpus (language-specific) and the one performed on Europarl (generic).

[7]There are multiple ways to define the context window for a possibly discontinuous MWE. Here we simply aggregate the 4-words contexts (two words on the left, two on the right) of the words inside the MWE.

Table 1: F1 scores (per category and overall) on the test set for our official CRF-based ("crf") and our unofficial Semantic Re-Ranking ("sem") systems, with per category and overall MWE counts ("n") in the test set. PS refers to the MWEs in the test set that were *Previously Seen* in the training set: the % of Previously Seen MWEs and the F1 Score obtained by interpreting % as a Recall score and assuming a 100% Precision score.

Lang	Eval	ID			IReflV			LVC			OTH			VPC			Overall			PS	
		n	crf	sem	n	crf	sem	n	crf	sem	n	crf	sem	n	crf	sem	n	crf	sem	%	F1
CS	MWE	192	5.48	5.65	1149	59.48	67.36	343	8.36	10.17	0			0			1683	57.72	65.20	92.26	95.97
	Token		10.72	10.85		74.49	75.76		14.52	15.13								72.86	74.55		
DE	MWE	214	14.68	15.95	20	0.71	0.74	40	3.30	4.14	0			226	18.81	23.95	500	22.80	26.93	39.96	57.10
	Token		28.92	26.61		4.81	4.50		8.48	8.73					33.61	35.37		40.48	40.41		
EL	MWE	127	12.45	13.62	0			336	27.28	32.86	21	0.91	0.88	16	2.30	2.24	500	31.34	36.73	34.20	50.97
	Token		19.11	19.57					38.18	40.15		3.97	3.67		3.30	2.82		43.14	45.33		
ES	MWE	166	13.75	14.60	223	42.13	45.09	109	18.27	17.89	11	0.00	1.18	3	0.00	0.00	500	44.33	48.61	52.20	68.59
	Token		21.99	22.45		43.44	46.06		24.04	22.20		0.00	1.16		0.00	0.00		49.17	52.64		
FA	MWE	0			0			0			500	80.08		0			500	80.08		98.80	99.40
	Token											85.36						85.36			
FR	MWE	119	35.59	35.39	105	37.12	40.00	271	15.38	20.93	5	0.00	0.00	0			500	50.88	56.24	28.00	43.75
	Token	316	44.78	42.79	210	40.90	40.56	577	23.07	25.19	5	0.00	0.00	0			1108	61.52	62.68		
HU	MWE	0			0			146	15.16	15.88	0			354	68.89	69.29	499	66.89	67.92	79.76	88.74
	Token								24.84	26.23					65.69	66.45		66.10	67.85		
IT	MWE	250	19.18	19.77	150	17.36	13.11	87	9.90	8.84	2	0.00	0.00	11	4.76	3.81	500	23.09	20.20	37.00	54.01
	Token		22.33	22.40		16.12	12.34		11.39	9.39		0.00	0.00		3.97	3.15		25.11	21.93		
MT	MWE	185	8.63		0			259	3.98		56	0.00		0			500	6.41		47.20	64.13
	Token		10.76						5.57			1.57						8.87			
PL	MWE	66	8.41	8.24	265	64.21	67.88	169	26.31	28.72	0			0			500	67.95	72.40	66.80	80.10
	Token		13.17	12.73		67.90	68.63		30.27	30.80								72.74	74.34		
PT	MWE	90	19.41	20.04	81	18.15	19.60	329	46.24	52.67	0			0			500	58.14	64.64	59.40	74.53
	Token		28.52	27.80		19.68	19.76		57.08	56.83								70.18	71.01		
RO	MWE	75	17.15	18.05	290	51.11	57.74	135	37.83	37.79	0			0			500	73.38	79.26	87.80	93.50
	Token		23.51	23.57		57.96	59.90		41.02	39.46								81.90	83.41		
SL	MWE	92	2.67	3.65	253	40.00	44.77	45	1.22	1.19	2	0.00	0.00	108	15.90	16.50	500	37.08	41.41	41.60	58.76
	Token		5.94	7.77		49.90	49.62		4.30	3.97		0.39	0.36		21.31	20.20		45.06	46.35		
SV	MWE	51	6.33	6.33	14	1.65	1.65	14	6.61	6.61	2	0.00	0.00	155	32.06	32.82	236	30.32	30.90	5.51	10.44
	Token		8.00	8.00		3.27	3.27		6.48	6.48		0.00	0.00		33.40	34.16		31.49	32.04		
TR	MWE	249	25.86		0			199	27.55		53	9.60		0			501	42.83		58.88	74.12
	Token		33.18						35.31			12.00						52.85			

between each individual word and the MWE (n scores) are represented with these three statistics computed over this set of scores. Finally, the probability of the predicted sequence (given by CRF++) is included as a feature. In training mode, the instance is assigned score 1 if it corresponds exactly to the sequence in the gold standard, or 0 otherwise. It might happen that none of the 10 sequences corresponds to the gold sequence: in such cases all the instances are left as negative cases.

4.3 Regression and Sequence Selection

We use the Weka (Hall et al., 2009) implementation of Decision Trees regression (Quinlan, 1992) to train a model which assigns a score in $[0, 1]$ to every instance. Among each group of 10, the predicted sequence with the highest score is selected. We use regression rather than classification because a categorical answer would cause problems in cases where there is either no positive or multiple positive answers for a set of predicted sequences.

4.4 Evaluation

F1 scores on the test set for the Semantic Re-Ranking of CRF outputs can be seen in Table 1 under the "sem" heading. As can be seen, in nearly every language the Semantic Re-Ranking improves the CRF best prediction considerably. These promising results are obtained with the first "proof of concept" version of the Semantic Re-Ranking component, that we plan to develop further in future work.

5 Discussion

The "%" column under "PS" (henceforth PS%), in Table 1, shows the proportion of MWE instances found in the test set that occurred at least once in the training set, i.e. they are "Previously Seen" MWEs. It is reasonable to expect that most systems would benefit from having a large number of previously seen MWEs in the test set. Our systems tend to perform well when PS% is high (e.g. Farsi, Romanian) and poorly when PS% is low (e.g. Swedish), although not in all cases. In fact, this is a trend observed in the other competing systems: the Pearson correlation coefficient be-

Table 2: Number of languages each system ranked at. Systems in grey italics are open systems, the rest are closed. PS and sem are unofficial systems.

Rnk	PS	TRA	sem	MUM	SZE	crf	RAC	LAT	LIF
1	13	1	1						
2		11	3		1				
3		2	5		1	5	2		
4			3	1	2	5	3		
5		1		5	1	3	3	1	
6	2			3	3	2	2		
7				2			2		1

tween PS% and all official systems' scores is 0.63. It would indeed be interesting to re-run the competition using a test set that featured MWEs not present in the training set.

PS could be potentially regarded as a baseline system that simply attempts to find matches of training MWEs in the test set. Such a simple lookup system, which could compete in the Closed Track, would achieve very high scores in several languages. In fact, it would beat all other systems in the competition in most languages. PS% can be interpreted as its Recall score. Since such a lookup system is incapable of "predicting" MWEs it has not seen, we assume it would always achieve a 100% Precision score, allowing us to compute an F1 score, presented in the "F1" column in Table 1, for the baseline PS system. Table 2 shows the number of languages in which each system would rank at each position if we include PS and our unofficial Semantic Re-Ranker scores. Only the 15 languages we attempted are counted. PS would always rank first except only in French and Swedish, the two languages with the lowest proportion of previously seen MWEs. One might contest PS's 100% Precision assumption as it depends on the accuracy of the actual VMWE matching method used. However, under this assumption PSF1 measures the best performing lookup method possible. This reasoning feeds into the simple matching method used: VMWEs are extracted from training and test set files according to their gold standard. PS% is their intersection divided by the total number of test set VMWEs. A VMWE is deemed to be present in both portions if its extracted dependency structure (if provided), lemmas and POS tags are identical in both files. For languages without dependencies, MWEs are matched based on lemmas and POS linear sequences only.

Interesting questions about the Shared Task's F1-based evaluation can also be raised. F1 considers Precision and Recall to be equally important, when in reality their relative importance depends on the purpose of an actual VMWE identification exercise. In a human-mediated lexicographic exercise, for example, where coverage is more important than avoiding false positives, Recall will take precedence. Conversely, in a computer-assisted language learning application concerned with obtaining a small but illustrative list of VMWE examples, Precision will take priority. We suggest that for future iterations of the Shared Task, a few candidate applications be identified and subtasks be organised around them. The identification task's purpose will also inform on the appropriateness of including previously seen MWEs in the test set. In a lexicographic or terminological task, there is usually an interest in identifying *new, unseen* MWEs as opposed to *known* ones, whereas in Machine Translation, the impact of known MWEs in new, unseen sentences is of interest.

6 Conclusions and Future Work

In this paper, we described our VMWE identification systems based on CRF and Semantic Re-Ranking, achieving competitive results. We analysed the role of previously seen MWEs and showed that they help all systems in the competition, including a hypothetical, simple lookup system that would beat all systems in most languages. We also argued for a more purpose-based evaluation scheme. Our future work will focus on language-specific features, rather than on language families. We also intend to explore tree-based CRF methods to better exploit syntactic dependency tree structures. The promising first results obtained with the Semantic Re-Ranker deserve to be explored further. Aspects such as parameter tuning, feature selection and other semantic vector types, like word embeddings (Legrand and Collobert, 2016), might help improve the performance. Finally, we want to explore alternative evaluation methods based on lexicographic and terminological tasks (Maldonado and Lewis, 2016) on the one hand and Machine Translation tasks (Xiong et al., 2016) on the other.

Acknowledgements

The ADAPT Centre for Digital Content Technology is funded under the SFI Research Centres Programme (Grant 13/RC/2106) and is co-funded under the European Regional Development Fund.

References

Mohammed Attia, Lamia Tounsi, Pavel Pecina, Josef van Genabith, and Antonio Toral. 2010. Automatic extraction of Arabic multiword expressions. In *Proceedings of the COLING workshop on multiword expressions: from theory to applications (MWE 2010)*, Beijing.

Kfir Bar, Mona Diab, and Abdelati Hawwari, 2014. *Arabic Multiword Expressions*, pages 64–81. Springer, Berlin.

Phil Blunsom and Timothy Baldwin. 2006. Multilingual deep lexical acquisition for HPSGs via supertagging. In *Proceedings of the 2006 Conference on Empirical Methods in Natural Language Processing*, pages 164–171, Sydney.

Ram Boukobza and Ari Rappoport. 2009. Multi-word expression identification using sentence surface features. In *Proceedings of the 2009 Conference on Empirical Methods in Natural Language Processing*, pages 468–477, Singapore.

Matthieu Constant, Anthony Sigogne, and Patrick Watrin. 2012. Discriminative Strategies to Integrate Multiword Expression Recognition and Parsing. In *Proceedings of the 50th Annual Meeting of the Association for Computational Linguistics*, pages 204–212, Jeju.

Spence Green, Marie-Catherine de Marneffe, John Bauer, and Christopher D. Manning. 2011. Multiword Expression Identification with Tree Substitution Grammars: A Parsing tour de force with French. In *Proceedings of the 2011 Conference on Empirical Methods in Natural Language Processing*, pages 725–735, Edinburgh.

Spence Green, Marie-Catherine de Marneffe, and Christopher D. Manning. 2013. Parsing models for identifying multiword expressions. *Computational Linguistics*, 39(1):195–227.

Mark Hall, Eibe Frank, Geoffrey Holmes, Bernhard Pfahringer, Peter Reutemann, and Ian H. Witten. 2009. The WEKA data mining software: an update. *ACM SIGKDD Explorations*, 11(1):10–18.

Aaron L-F Han, Derek F Wong, and Lidia S Chao. 2013. Chinese Named Entity Recognition with Conditional Random Fields in the Light of Chinese Characteristics. In *Language Processing and Intelligent Information Systems*, pages 57–68. Springer.

Aaron Li-Feng Han, Xiaodong Zeng, Derek F Wong, and Lidia S Chao. 2015. Chinese named entity recognition with graph-based semi-supervised learning model. *Eighth SIGHAN Workshop on Chinese Language Processing*, page 15.

Mohammad Javad Hosseini, Noah A. Smith, and Su-In Lee. 2016. UW-CSE at semeval-2016 task 10: Detecting multiword expressions and supersenses using double-chained conditional random fields. In *Proceedings of the 10th International Workshop on Semantic Evaluation, SemEval@NAACL-HLT 2016, San Diego, CA, USA, June 16-17, 2016*, pages 931–936.

P. Koehn. 2005. Europarl: A parallel corpus for statistical machine translation. In *Proceedings of the 10th Machine Translation Summit*, pages 79–86, Phuket.

John Lafferty, Andrew McCallum, and Fernando C. N. Pereira. 2001. Conditional random fields: Probabilistic models for segmenting and labeling sequence data. In *Proceedings of the Eighteenth International Conference on Machine Learning*, pages 282–289.

Joël Legrand and Ronan Collobert. 2016. Phrase representations for multiword expressions. In *Proceedings of the 12th Workshop on Multiword Expressions*, Berlin.

Alfredo Maldonado and Martin Emms. 2011. Measuring the compositionality of collocations via word co-occurrence vectors: Shared task system description. In *Proceedings of the Workshop on Distributional Semantics and Compositionality*, pages 48–53, Portland, OR.

Alfredo Maldonado and David Lewis. 2016. Self-tuning ongoing terminology extraction retrained on terminology validation decisions. In *Proceedings of The 12th International Conference on Terminology and Knowledge Engineering*, pages 91–100, Copenhagen.

J.R. Quinlan. 1992. Learning with continuous classes. In *Proceedings of the 5th Australian Joint Conference on Artificial Intelligence*, pages 343–348.

Ivan A. Sag, Timothy Baldwin, Francis Bond, Ann Copestake, and Dan Flickinger. 2001. Multiword Expressions: A Pain in the Neck for NLP. In *Proceedings of the 3rd International Conference on Intelligent Text Processing and Computational Linguistics*, pages 1–15.

Bahar Salehi, Paul Cook, and Timothy Baldwin. 2014a. Detecting Non-compositional MWE Components using Wiktionary. In *Proceedings of the 2014 Conference on Empirical Methods in Natural Language Processing*, pages 1792–1797, Doha.

Bahar Salehi, Paul Cook, and Timothy Baldwin. 2014b. Using distributional similarity of multi-way translations to predict multiword expression compositionality. In *Proceedings of the 14th Conference of the European Chapter of the Association for Computational Linguistics*, pages 472–481, Gothenburg.

Bahar Salehi, Paul Cook, and Timothy Baldwin. 2015. A word embedding approach to predicting the compositionality of multiword expressions. In *Proceedings of the 2015 Conference of the North American Chapter of the Association for Computational Linguistics Human Language Technologies*, pages 977–983.

Agata Savary, Carlos Ramisch, Silvio Cordeiro, Federico Sangati, Veronika Vincze, Behrang Qasem-iZadeh, Marie Candito, Fabienne Cap, Voula Giouli, Ivelina Stoyanova, and Antoine Doucet. 2017. The PARSEME Shared Task on Automatic Identification of Verbal Multiword Expressions. In *Proceedings of the 13th Workshop on Multiword Expressions*, Valencia.

Nathan Schneider, Emily Danchik, Chris Dyer, and Noah A. Smith. 2014. Discriminative Lexical Semantic Segmentation with Gaps: Running the MWE Gamut. *Transactions of the Association for Computational Linguistics*, 2:193–206.

Hinrich Schütze. 1998. Automatic Word Sense Discrimination. *Computational Linguistics*, 24(1):97–123.

John Sinclair. 1991. *Corpus, Concordance, Collocation*. Oxford University Press, Oxford.

Xiao Sun, Chengcheng Li, Chenyi Tang, and Fuji Ren. 2013. Mining Semantic Orientation of Multiword Expression from Chinese Microblogging with Discriminative Latent Model. In *Proceedings of 2013 International Conference on Asian Language Processing*, pages 117–120, Urumqi.

Yulia Tsvetkov and Shuly Wintner. 2010. Extraction of multi-word expressions from small parallel corpora. In *Proceedings of the 23rd International Conference on Computational Linguistics*, pages 1256–1264, Beijing.

Sriram Venkatapathy and Aravind K. Joshi. 2006. Using information about multi-word expressions for the word-alignment task. In *Proceedings of the Workshop on Multiword Expressions: Identifying and Exploiting Underlying Properties*, pages 20–27, Sydney.

Veronika Vincze, István Nagy, and Gábor Berend. 2011. Multiword expressions and named entities in the Wiki50 corpus. In *Proceedings of the International Conference on Recent Advances in Natural Language Processing*, pages 289–295, Hissar.

Deyi Xiong, Fandong Meng, and Qun Liu. 2016. Topic-based term translation models for statistical machine translation. *Artificial Intelligence*, 232:54–75.

A data-driven approach to verbal multiword expression detection.
PARSEME Shared Task system description paper

Tiberiu Boroș, Sonia Pipa, Verginica Barbu Mititelu, Dan Tufiș
Research Institute for Artificial Intelligence "Mihai Drăgănescu",
Romanian Academy,
Bucharest, Romania
{tibi,sonia,vergi,tufis}@racai.ro

Abstract

Multiword expressions are groups of words acting as a morphologic, syntactic and semantic unit in linguistic analysis. Verbal multiword expressions represent a subgroup of multiword expressions, namely that in which a verb is the syntactic head of the group considered in its canonical (or dictionary) form. All multiword expressions are a great challenge for natural language processing, but the verbal ones are particularly interesting for tasks such as parsing, as the verb is the central element in the syntactic organization of a sentence. In this paper we introduce our data-driven approach to verbal multiword expressions, which was objectively validated during the PARSEME shared task on verbal multiword expressions identification. We tested our approach on 12 languages, and we provide detailed information about corpora composition, feature selection process, validation procedure and performance on all languages.

1 Introduction

The term "multiword expressions" (MWEs) denotes a group of words that act as a morphologic, syntactic and semantic unit in linguistic analysis: their linguistic behavior (inflection, combination with other words, meaning) cannot be inferred from the characteristics of their components. As the name suggests, verbal MWEs (VMWEs) require the presence of a verb head in the prototypical form of the MWE. The importance of identifying MWEs in natural language processing, as well as the appropriate techniques to deal with this linguistic phenomenon were discussed by (Sag et al., 2002), among others. VMWEs are particularly important for parsing, mainly because the verb is the central element in the syntactic organization of a sentence.

For the present task we focused on both detection and type-labeling of VMWEs. Though similar in nature, detection and type-labeling require different training strategies, at least in the fine-tunning stage of the system. In our case, this meant that the two tasks might require different context windows and feature sets (see Section 3 for more details). Moreover, though we applied our system on twelve languages, we performed fine-tunning of the parameter set only for the Romanian corpus (due to time constraints) and we used the same parameter set for all languages. However, the proposed fine-tunning strategy can be applied on any dataset and, in the future, we plan to make language-dependent optimization and re-run the MWE detection and labeling process for each language with its own parameters.

2 Corpora composition

During the system preparation for the PARSEME shared task on VMWEs identification (Savary et al., 2017) we were granted access to training data in the form of annotated text for 18 languages. The annotation was provided using a custom designed format called parsemetsv[1] (one-token per line with tokenization and VMWEs information, stored as tab-separated values). For some languages, lemmatization and tagging information was provided in CONLL format[2].

From the 18 languages we focused on a subset of 12 languages, because both parsemetsv information and morphosyntactic analysis were pro-

---

[1] http://typo.uni-konstanz.de/parseme/index.php/2-general/184-parseme-shared-task-format-of-the-final-annotation (last accessed 2017-01-29)

[2] http://universaldependencies.org/format.html (last accessed 2017-01-29)

Proceedings of the 13th Workshop on Multiword Expressions (MWE 2017), pages 121–126,
Valencia, Spain, April 4. ©2017 Association for Computational Linguistics

vided for them: RO, FR, CS, DE, EL, ES, HU, IT, MT, SL, SV and TR. The Farsi and and Polish corpora were also provided with all the necessary information, but due to technical difficulties, we were unable to cope with the file encodings before the submission deadline and we were unable to provide an accurate evaluation on these languages.

Regarding granularity, 5 VMWE classes are used in the annotation process:

- **Ligth Verb Constructions (LVC)**: they are made up of a verb and a noun: the former has little if any semantic content, while the latter contributes the semantics of the VMWE;

- **Idioms (ID)**: these are expressions in which the verb can combine with various other words and their key-characteristic is the lack of compositional meaning;

- **Inherently reflexive verbs (IReflV)**: they are made up of a verb and a reflexive clitic and their meaning is different from those occurrences of the verb without the clitic (in case this is possible); the passive, reciprocal, possessive and impersonal constructions are excluded from annotation;

- **Verb-Particle Constructions (VPC)**: they contain a verb and a particle and have a non-compositional meaning;

- **Other (OTH)**: any VMWE that does not fit any of the above mentioned classes.

The LVC and ID categories are considered universal, in the sense that they apply to all languages involved in the shared task[3], whereas IReflV applies to all Romance languages, to all Germanic languages in the shared task and almost all Balto-Slavic ones (the exception is Lithuanian). VPC applies to all Germanic languages, to Italian, Slovene, Greek, Hebrew and Hungarian. Except for Lithuanian, OTH can occur in any language in the task, although not necessarily present in the data.

The distribution of these categories over the training sets for the languages considered here is given in Table 1 below.

---

[3] Although considered applicable, the LVC category did not occur in the Farsi data, while ID did not occur in the Farsi or Hungarian data.

3 Sequence labeling for verbal multiword expression detection

When it comes to automatic identification of VMWEs, aside from rule-based approaches such as tree substitution grammars (Green et al., 2011) and dependency lexicons (Bejcek et al., 2013), several research have addressed statistical methods. These statistical methods refer to n-gram based approaches (Pedersen et al., 2011), Latent Semantic Analysis (LSA) (Katz and Giesbrecht, 2006), word association measures (Pecina, 2008) and many classification-based approaches.

In our approach, which is also a statistical method, we treat VMWEs identification as a sequence labeling approach, in which we employ a Conditional Random Fields (CRF) classifier (Lafferty et al., 2001) trained to predict transitions between labels rather than the labels themselves. For every word inside a sentence we trained the classifier to predict a label using lemma and part-of-speech based features for a window of words centered on the current position. A naive method would use the VMWE type as labels and employ a dummy label for words that do not belong to any unit. However, a more principled approach is to perform VMWE identification in two steps:

- **Head labeling**: in this step we identify words that introduce VMWEs, a good choice for these words being the verb, in head-initial languages.

- **Tail labeling**: in this step we identify the words that link to the head word and contribute to the unit.

Our experiments showed that when the head of a MWE is correctly identified, the linking of the other constituents of the MWE is easier. This reflected also in the fine tuning of the two distinct phases: the head of a MWE was identified using two-word windows and the L+P set of parameters (see section 3) while the linking phase relied on 4-word windows with the same parameters. This two-step approach increased of precision by 9%. Thus we considered that that the two-step approach works significantly better than the one-shot detection and labeling of VMWEs. As mentioned, the two-step approach uses different feature windows for head and tail identification. The larger window (used in tail identification) pro-

VMWE type	CS	DE	EL	ES	FR	HU	IT	MT	RO	SL	SV	TR
IReflV	8851	111	0	336	1313	0	580	0	2496	945	3	0
LVC	2580	178	955	214	1362	584	395	434	1019	186	13	2624
ID	1419	1005	515	196	1786	0	913	261	524	283	9	2911
VPC	0	1143	32	0	0	2415	62	0	0	371	31	0
OTH	2	10	16	2	1	0	4	77	15	2	0	634

Table 1: VMWE distribution in the training corpora for the 12 languages

ved to be inefficient for head labeling, but provided better results in the second step [4].

The training data contained several overlapped VMWEs. In theory, our proposed labeling scheme should be able to handle such cases (i.e., if a head token is also linked as a tail, then that token and its tail should be embedded in the higher VMWE). However, because of their sparseness in the training data, our system did not spot such cases.

4 Validation and feature selection procedure

All our results are reported for a 10-fold validation procedure, which takes into account the distribution of VMWE types in the training corpora. This means that when we split our data into 90% training and 10% validation we strived to preserve the relative distribution of labels in order to report results as close as possible to real-life data.

4.1 Head labeling

After a shallow investigation of different feature sets we established that lemma, part-of-speech (POS) (with attributes) and a combined feature from lemma+POS are the best candidates for fine-tuning. This first feature set is denoted as L+P. We tried to extend this setup by adding 4 new features (whenever possible): gender, person, number and a special flag for reflexive pronouns (L+P+E). In Table 2 we show the detailed results obtained on the Romanian training corpus using the two feature sets (L+P and L+P+E) and varying the feature window size, in the 10-fold validation procedure.

As can easily be seen, the overall F-score of the system decreases for feature windows higher than 2, which indicates over-fitting of the training data. Also, for the window size of 2 the extended feature

W	Feat-set	P	R	F
2	L+P	0.8957	0.8952	**0.8914**
	L+P+E	**0.9012**	0.8769	0.8889
3	L+P	0.8912	0.8842	0.8877
	L+P+E	0.8778	0.8868	0.8823
4	L+P	0.8656	0.8869	0.8761
	L+P+E	0.8378	0.8845	0.8605

Table 2: Results on the training set

set provides a better precision but decreases the recall, yielding in a lower F-score. Thus, our final choice was a window size of two with the L+P feature set.

4.2 Tail labeling

Tail labeling is carried out on an extended feature set in which we added additional information about labels previously assigned during head labeling. Our experiments showed that varying the feature window has little impact on the system's performance and we decided to use a feature window of 4 (totally, 9 words).

In Table 6, for head labeling, the first column represents the words lemmas, the second column contains the part-of-speech with its associated attributes and the third column is used for the label itself. Note that during head labeling we ignore any linked words. Next, for tail labeling we extend the feature-set and we add one column, which is used for head labels. In the training phase we use the head-labels extracted from the training corpus and at runtime we use the classifier to predict these labels in the first phase of the two-step approach.

In the template file[5] (Table 8), each line starts with a string that uniquely identifies the feature (i.e., "U01", "U02", etc.). Next to the identifier we can add any feature (%x) and any combination of features ('/' is used for combining multiple features). Features in the training data are ex-

---

[4]In the feature selection process, described in the next section, we found that the best results are obtained using a feature-window of two (totally, 5 words included) for head labeling and a window of 4 (totally, 9 words included) for tail labeling

[5]standard CRF++ (https://taku910.github.io/crfpp/) template file

Label	P	Stdev	R	Stdev	F-score	Stdev
ID	0.8760	0.0434	0.6421	0.0727	0.7398	0.0612
IReflV	0.8830	0.0207	0.9611	0.0129	0.9202	0.0113
LVC	0.9363	0.0219	0.8590	0.0322	0.8955	0.0202
PREV	0.9837	0.0087	0.9655	0.0105	0.9745	0.0068

Table 3: Detailed results for Romanian reported for every VMWE type using 10- fold validation. The 'PREV' label is used for tail linking

CM	_	IReflV	ID	LVC
_	-	8	13	15
IReflV	38	239	0	0
ID	2	0	37	3
LVC	3	1	0	84

Table 4: Confusion matrix computed for the first fold of the RO corpus. Symbol '_' is used to denote dummy tokens - token does not belong to any VMWE

Head labeling			
Portugalia	Np	_	
s	Ncmprn	IReflV	
—	DASH	_	
avea	Vaip3s	_	
confrunta	Vmp	_	
cu	Sp	_	
acelaşi	Dd3fsr	_	
situaţie	Ncfsrn	_	
:	COLON	_	

Tail labeling			
Portugalia	Np	_	_
s	Ncmprn	IReflv	_
—	DASH	_	_
avea	Vaip3s	_	_
confrunta	Vmp	_	PREV
cu	Sp	_	_
acelaşi	Dd3fsr	_	_
situaţie	Ncfsrn	_	_
:	COLON	_	_

Table 6: Excerpt from the training data - Romanian version of the training corpus

tracted using a "relative coordinate systems". The first coordinate is the relative row index, and the second one is the 0-indexed absolute column position of the feature. For instance, x[-1,1] signifies the lemma (1 - second column) of the previous token (-1 - the above row).

	Strict			
Lang	P	R	F	Rank
CS	0.7009	0.5918	0.6418	2/4
DE	0.3652	0.13	0.1917	4/4
EL	0.4286	0.252	0.3174	2/4
ES	0.6447	0.196	0.3006	4/4
FR	0.7415	0.35	0.4755	3/5
HU	0.8029	0.5471	0.6508	3/4
IT	0.6125	0.098	0.169	3/3
MT	0.2333	0.028	0.05	3/3
RO	0.8652	0.706	0.7775	1/4
SL	0.5503	0.208	0.3019	4/4
SV	0.5758	0.161	0.2517	3/3
TR	0.6304	0.4391	0.5176	2/4

	Fuzzy			
Lang	P	R	F	
CS	0.819	0.6228	0.7076	3/4
DE	0.6716	0.1793	0.283	4/4
EL	0.5616	0.2953	0.3871	4/4
ES	0.7233	0.1967	0.3093	4/4
FR	0.7872	0.3673	0.5009	3/4
HU	0.8208	0.5015	0.6226	4/4
IT	0.6837	0.1053	0.1824	3/3
MT	0.2481	0.0259	0.0469	3/3
RO	0.8773	0.7019	0.7799	4/4
SL	0.7339	0.2145	0.332	4/4
SV	0.6538	0.1677	0.2669	3/3
TR	0.634	0.4348	0.5159	3/4

Table 5: Evaluation campaign results

```
Head labeling template file
U01:%x[0,0]
U02:%x[0,1]
U03:%x[0,0]/%x[0,1]

U04:%x[-1,0]
U05:%x[-1,1]
U06:%x[-1,0]/%x[0,1]
...
3 more similar feature sets
```
```
Tail labeling template file
U01:%x[0,0]
U02:%x[0,1]
U03:%x[0,2]
U04:%x[0,0]/%x[0,1]
...
8 more similar feature sets
```

Table 8: The template file used with the CRF++ classifier

Language	Type	P	R	F	Language	P	R	F
CS	LVC	**0.7460**	**0.2741**	**0.4009**	DE	0.0000	0.0000	0.0000
	IReflV	**0.7109**	**0.7554**	**0.7325**		**0.4000**	**0.1000**	**0.1600**
	VPC	N/A	N/A	N/A		**0.6667**	0.1593	0.2571
	ID	0.5909	0.1354	0.2203		0.3433	**0.1075**	**0.1637**
EL	LVC	**0.4096**	**0.2798**	**0.3316**	ES	**0.6111**	0.2018	**0.3034**
	IReflV	N/A	N/A	N/A		**0.6559**	0.2735	0.3861
	VPC	**0.6667**	**0.2500**	**0.3636**		N/A	N/A	N/A
	ID	**0.2321**	0.1024	0.1421		0.0000	0.0000	0.0000
FR	LVC	**0.7255**	0.1365	0.2298	HU	**0.6383**	0.2055	0.3109
	IReflV	**0.7000**	0.6667	**0.6829**		N/A	N/A	N/A
	VPC	N/A	N/A	N/A		**0.8294**	0.6864	0.7512
	ID	**0.7294**	**0.5210**	**0.6078**		N/A	N/A	N/A
IT	LVC	**0.7000**	0.0805	**0.1443**	MT	0.1837	0.0347	0.0584
	IReflV	0.3636	0.0533	0.0930		N/A	N/A	N/A
	VPC	0.3333	0.0909	0.1429		N/A	N/A	N/A
	ID	**0.6667**	**0.1200**	**0.2034**		**0.2000**	**0.0108**	**0.0205**
RO	LVC	**0.9167**	**0.8148**	**0.8627**	SL	**0.6667**	**0.0444**	**0.0833**
	IReflV	**0.8197**	0.6897	0.7491		**0.5390**	0.3004	0.3858
	VPC	N/A	N/A	N/A		**0.6757**	**0.2315**	**0.3448**
	ID	**0.8864**	**0.5200**	**0.6555**		**0.5000**	0.0109	0.0213
SV	LVC	**0.4000**	0.1429	**0.2105**	TR	**0.6797**	**0.5226**	**0.5909**
	IReflV	0.0000	0.0000	0.0000		N/A	N/A	N/A
	VPC	**0.5614**	**0.2065**	**0.3019**		N/A	N/A	N/A
	ID	**0.5000**	**0.0196**	**0.0377**		**0.5921**	**0.3614**	**0.4489**

Table 7: Strict evaluation results for VMWE type identification. Best results in the challenge are BOLD

4.3 Further discussion of the results

The values reported in Table 2 refer to the overall performance of the system, regardless of the VMWE class. In order to offer a better view on the system performance we provide accuracy figures for every VMWE class (Table 3), as well as the confusion matrix for head labeling computed on the first training fold of the validation (Table 4).

As shown in the confusion matrix, the system rarely confuses one VMWE for another, most errors being omissions - head VMWE tokens being labeled with "_" (dummy) labels. While IReflVs are both numerous and easy to spot, IDs are rare and extremely difficult to label because their identification involves semantics as well as syntactic knowledge. The IDs correctly spotted by the system in this fold may have been "over-fitted" during the training. However, it is highly possible that, with another corpus, ID identification fail mainly because of the ambiguities that arise when trying to determine if the "sum" of the words senses is different from the VMWE sense (a task which is barely handled by the CRF and feature set combination).

5 Results and conclusions

The final evaluation results that we report in this paper are the results obtained during the PAR-SEME shared task on VMWE identification. As previously mentioned, we trained and submitted runs for 12 languages (table 5 summarizes the results)[6]. We must mention that for the shared task, VMWE type identification was not mandatory. However, we as well as three other teams included this information in their submissions. As such, we show detailed results for each VMWE class in Table 7, where we give the results for the strict evaluation.

For Romanian, there is a notable difference in the F-score reported during 10-fold validation and PARSEME evaluation, which is caused mainly by the skewed distribution of VMWE types in the test data. However, the F-score reported for individual VMWE classes are well within the standard deviation computed in table 3. Similar conditions may apply to the other languages. Also, as previously stated, our fine-tunning process was only performed on the Romanian dataset, where we obtained the highest score in the strict evaluation of the system. An identical process can be carried out on any dataset and for best results, one would have to perform this tunning in order to obtain language-dependent optimizations.

The system is freely available and can be obtained by contacting the authors.

[6]http://typo.uni-konstanz.de/parseme/index.php/2-general/142-parseme-shared-task-on-automatic-detection-of-verbal-mwes - accessed 2017-02-15

References

Eduard Bejcek, Pavel Stranák, and Pavel Pecina. 2013. Syntactic identification of occurrences of multiword expressions in text using a lexicon with dependency structures. In *Proc. of the 9th Workshop on Multiword Expressions*, pages 106–115.

Spence Green, Marie-Catherine De Marneffe, John Bauer, and Christopher D Manning. 2011. Multiword expression identification with tree substitution grammars: A parsing tour de force with french. In *Proceedings of the Conference on Empirical Methods in Natural Language Processing*, pages 725–735. Association for Computational Linguistics.

Graham Katz and Eugenie Giesbrecht. 2006. Automatic identification of non-compositional multi-word expressions using latent semantic analysis. In *Proceedings of the Workshop on Multiword Expressions: Identifying and Exploiting Underlying Properties*, pages 12–19. Association for Computational Linguistics.

John Lafferty, Andrew McCallum, Fernando Pereira, et al. 2001. Conditional random fields: Probabilistic models for segmenting and labeling sequence data. In *Proceedings of the eighteenth international conference on machine learning, ICML*, volume 1, pages 282–289.

Pavel Pecina. 2008. A machine learning approach to multiword expression extraction. In *Proceedings of the LREC Workshop Towards a Shared Task for Multiword Expressions (MWE 2008)*, volume 2008, pages 54–61. Citeseer.

Ted Pedersen, Satanjeev Banerjee, Bridget T McInnes, Saiyam Kohli, Mahesh Joshi, and Ying Liu. 2011. The ngram statistics package (text:: nsp): A flexible tool for identifying ngrams, collocations, and word associations. In *Proceedings of the Workshop on Multiword Expressions: from Parsing and Generation to the Real World*, pages 131–133. Association for Computational Linguistics.

Ivan A. Sag, Timothy Baldwin, Francis Bond, Ann Copestake, and Dan Flickinger, 2002. *Multiword Expressions: A Pain in the Neck for NLP*, pages 1–15. Springer Berlin Heidelberg, Berlin, Heidelberg.

Agata Savary, Carlos Ramisch, Silvio Cordeiro, Federico Sangati, Veronika Vincze, Behrang QasemiZadeh, Marie Candito, Fabienne Cap, Voula Giouli, Ivelina Stoyanova, and Antoine Doucet. 2017. The PARSEME Shared Task on Automatic Identification of Verbal Multiword Expressions. In *Proceedings of the 13th Workshop on Multiword Expressions*, Valencia, Spain, April. Association for Computational Linguistics.

The ATILF-LLF System for Parseme Shared Task: a Transition-based Verbal Multiword Expression Tagger

Hazem Al Saied
Université de Lorraine, ATILF, CNRS
Nancy, France
halsaied@atilf.fr

Marie Candito
Université Paris Diderot, LLF
Paris, France
marie.candito@linguist.univ-paris-diderot.fr

Matthieu Constant
Université de Lorraine, ATILF, CNRS
Nancy, France
Mathieu.Constant@univ-lorraine.fr

Abstract

We describe the ATILF-LLF system built for the MWE 2017 Shared Task on automatic identification of verbal multiword expressions. We participated in the closed track only, for all the 18 available languages. Our system is a robust greedy transition-based system, in which MWE are identified through a MERGE transition. The system was meant to accommodate the variety of linguistic resources provided for each language, in terms of accompanying morphological and syntactic information. Using per-MWE Fscore, the system was ranked first[1] for all but two languages (Hungarian and Romanian).

1 Introduction

Verbal multi-word expressions (hereafter VMMEs) tend to exhibit more morphological and syntactic variation than other MWEs, if only because in general the verb is inflected, and it can receive adverbial modifiers. Furthermore some VMWEs, in particular light verb constructions (one of the VMWE categories provided in the shared task), allow for the full range of syntactic variation (extraction, coordination etc...). This renders the VMWE identification task even more challenging than general MWE identification, in which fully frozen and contiguous expressions help increasing the overall performance.

The data sets are quite heterogeneous, both in terms of the number of annotated VMWEs and of accompanying resources (for the closed track).[2]

So our first priority when setting up the architecture was to build a generic system applicable to all the 18 languages, with limited language-specific tuning. We thus chose to participate in the closed track only, relying exclusively on training data, accompanying CoNLL-U file when available, and basic feature engineering. We developed a one-pass greedy transition-based system, which we believe can handle discontinuities elegantly. We integrated more or less informed feature templates, depending on their availability in the data.

We describe our system in section 2, the experimental setup in section 3, the results in section 4 and the related works in section 5. We conclude in section 6 and give perspectives for future work.

2 System description

The identification system we used is a simplified and partial implementation of the system proposed in Constant and Nivre (2016), which is in itself a mild extension of an arc-standard dependency parser (Nivre, 2004). Constant and Nivre (2016) proposed a parsing algorithm that jointly predicts a syntactic dependency tree and a forest of lexical units including MWEs. In particular, in line with Nivre (2014), this system integrates special parsing mechanisms to deal with lexical analysis. Given that the shared task focuses on the lexical task only and that datasets do not always provide syntactic annotations, we have modified the structure of the original system by removing syntax prediction, in order to use the same system for all 18 languages.

A transition-based system consists in applying a sequence of actions (namely *transitions*) to incrementally build the expected output structure in a bottom-up manner. Each transition is

---

[1] 2 systems participated for one language only (French), and 5 systems participated for more than one language.

[2] Some of the data sets contain the tokenized sentences plus VMWEs only (BG, ES, HE, LT), some are accompanied with morphological information such as lemmas and POS (CS, MT, RO, SL), and for the third group (the 10 remaining languages) full dependency parses are provided. See (Savary et al., 2017) for more information on the data sets.

Proceedings of the 13th Workshop on Multiword Expressions (MWE 2017), pages 127–132,
Valencia, Spain, April 4. ©2017 Association for Computational Linguistics

Transition		Configuration
		$([\,], [1,2,3,4,5,6], [\,])$
Shift	$\Rightarrow$	$([1], [2,3,4,5,6], [\,])$
Complete	$\Rightarrow$	$([\,], [2,3,4,5,6], [1])$
Shift	$\Rightarrow$	$([2], [3,4,5,6], [1])$
Shift	$\Rightarrow$	$([2,3], [4,5,6], [1])$
Complete	$\Rightarrow$	$([2], [4,5,6], [1,3])$
Shift	$\Rightarrow$	$([2,4], [5,6], [1,3])$
Complete	$\Rightarrow$	$([2], [5,6], [1,3,4])$
Shift	$\Rightarrow$	$([2,5], [6], [1,3,4])$
Shift	$\Rightarrow$	$([2,5,6], [\,], [1,3,4])$
Merge	$\Rightarrow$	$([2,(5,6)], [\,], [1,3,4])$
Merge	$\Rightarrow$	$([[(2,(5,6))], [\,], [1,3,4])$
Complete	$\Rightarrow$	$([\,], [\,], [1,3,4,(2,(5,6))])$

Figure 1: Transition sequence for tagging *He*$_1$ ***took***$_2$ *this*$_3$ *argument*$_4$ ***into***$_5$ ***account***$_6$.

usually predicted by a classifier given the current state of the parser (namely *configuration*). A configuration in our system consists of a triplet $c = (\sigma, \beta, L)$, where σ is a stack containing units under processing, β is a buffer containing the remaining input tokens, and L is a set of processed lexical units. The processed units correspond either to tokens or to VMWEs. When corresponding to a single token, a lexical unit is composed of one node only, whereas a unit representing a (multi-token) VMWE is represented as a binary lexical tree over the input tokens. Every unit is associated with a set of linguistic attributes (when available in the working dataset): its actual form, lemma, part-of-speech (POS) tag, syntactic head and label. The initial configuration for a sentence $x = x_1, ..., x_n$, *i.e.* a sequence of n tokens, is represented by c_s as: $c_s(x) = ([], [x_1, \ldots, x_n], \emptyset)$ and the set of terminal configurations C_t contains any configuration of the form $c = ([], [], L)$. At the end of the analysis, the identified VMWEs are simply extracted from L.

The transitions of this system are limited to the following: (a) the **Shift** transition takes the first element in the buffer and pushes it onto the stack; (b) the **Merge** transition removes the two top elements of the stack, combines them as a single element, and adds it to the stack;[3] (c) the **Complete** transition moves the upper element of the stack to L, whether the element is a single token or an identified VMWE and finally (d) the **Complete-MWT** transition, only valid for multiword tokens

(MWT), acts as Complete, but also marks the element moved to L as VMWE.[4]

Training such a system means enabling it to classify a configuration into the next transition to apply. This requires an oracle that determines what is an optimal transition sequence given an input sentence and the gold VMWEs. We created a static oracle using a greedy algorithm that performs Complete as soon as possible (i.e. when a non VMWE token or a gold VMWE is on top of the stack) and Merge as late as possible (i.e. when the right-most component of the VMWE is on top of the stack) (see Figure 1). Note that an oracle sequence is exactly composed of $2n$ transitions: every single token requires one Shift and one Complete, and each multi-token VMWE of length m requires m Shifts, $m-1$ Merges and a single Complete.

The proposed system has some limitations with respect to the shared task annotation scheme. First, for now, our system does not handle embedded VMWEs (only the longest VMWE is considered in the oracle, and the transition system cannot predict embeddings). This feature could be straightforwardly activated as VMWEs are represented with lexical trees. Note also that the system cannot handle overlapping MWEs like ***take***$_{1,2}$ *a **bath***$_1$ *then a **shower***$_2$, since it requires a graph representation (not a tree).

3 Experimental setup

For replication purposes, we now describe how the system has been implemented (Subsection 3.1), which feature templates have been used (Subsection 3.2) and how they have been tuned (Subsection 3.3). Simple descriptions of the system settings are provided in Table 1. We thereafter use symbol B_i to indicate the ith element in the buffer. S_0 and S_1 stand for the top and the second top elements of the stack. For every unit X in the stack or the buffer, we denote Xw its word form, Xl its lemma and Xp its POS tag. The concatenation of two elements X and Y is noted XY.

3.1 Implementation

For a given language, and a given train/dev split, we train three SVM classifiers (one vs all, one vs

---

[3] The newly created element is assigned linguistic attributes using basic concatenation rules that would deserve to be improved in future experiments: e.g., the lemma is the concatenation of the lemmas of the two initial elements.

[4] We had to add this transition to cope with MWTs, which are present in some data sets (esp. German). Currently this transition is not predicted by a classifier like the other ones. It is activated under certain hard conditions (cf. Subsection 3.1)

one and error-correcting output codes) and we select the majority vote one.[5]

Note that some configurations only allow for a unique transition type, and thus do not require transition prediction. A configuration with a one token stack and empty buffer requires the application of a Complete, as last transition of the transition sequence. Similarly, a configuration with empty stack and non-empty buffer must lead to a Shift transition.

During the feature tuning phase, for a few languages we added a number of hard-coded procedures aiming at enforcing specific transitions in given contexts. These procedures all use a VMWE dictionary extracted from the training set (hereafter the VMWE dictionary). For German and Hungarian, we noticed a high percentage of VMWEs with one token only.[6] We added the Complete-MWT transition for these languages, which we systematically apply when the head of the stack S_0 is a token appearing as MWT in the VMWE dictionary (cf. setting Q in Table 1). For other languages with long and discontinuous expressions, we used other hard-coded procedures that experimentally proved to be beneficial (setting P in Table 1). We systematically apply a Complete transition when $S_1 l B_0 l$ or $S_1 l B_1 l$ forms a VMWE existing in the VMWE dictionary. Moreover, an obligatory Shift is applied when the concatenation of successive elements in the stack and the buffer belongs to the VMWE dictionary. In particular, we test $S_1 l S_0 l B_0 l$, $S_0 l B_0 l$, $S_0 l B_0 l B_1 l$ and $S_0 l B_0 l B_1 l B_2 l$.

3.2 Feature Templates

A key point in a classical transition-based system is feature engineering, where feature template design and tuning could play a very important role in increasing the accuracy of system results.

Basic Linguistic Features

First of all, depending on their availability in the working dataset and on the activation of related settings (cf. G and J in Table 1), we extracted linguistic attributes in order to generate features such as $S_0 l$, $S_0 p$ and $S_0 w$ where p, l and

Code	F	Setting description
B	+	use of transition history (length 1)
C	+	use of transition history (length 2)
D	+	use of transition history (length 3)
E	+	use of B_1
F	+	use of bigrams ($S_1 S_0$, $S_0 B_0$, $S_1 B_0$, $S_0 B_1$)
G	+	use of lemma
H	+	use of syntax dependencies
I	+	use of trigrams $S_1 S_0 B_0$
J	+	use of POS tag
K	+	use of distance between S_0 and S_1
L	+	use of training corpus VMWE lexicon
M	+	use of distance between S_0 and B_0
N	+	use of ($S_0 B_2$) bigram
O	+	use of stack length
P	-	enabling dictionary-based forced transitions
Q	-	enabling Complete-MWT transition

Table 1: System setting code descriptions. The 'F' column indicates whether the setting is a feature-related setting ('+') used by the classifiers or whether ('-') it is a hard-coded implementation enhancement.

w stand for the lemma, the part of speech, and the word form respectively. The same features are extracted for unigrams S_1, B_0 and B_1 (when used) (cf. E in Table 1).

When enabled, the bigrams features for the pair XY of elements are $XpYp$, $XlYl$, $XwYw$, $XpYl$ and $XlYp$. The trigram-based features are extracted in the same way.
Basically, the involved bigrams are $S_1 S_0$, $S_0 B_0$, $S_1 B_0$ and $S_0 B_1$ (cf. setting F in Table 1), but we also added the $S_0 B_2$ bigram for a few languages (cf. N in Table 1). For trigrams, we only used the features of the $S_1 S_0 B_0$ triple (cf. I in Table 1).

Finally, because the datasets for some languages do not provide the basic linguistic attributes such as lemmas and POS tags, we tried to bridge the gap by extracting unigram "morphological" attributes when POS tag and lemma extraction settings were disabled (cf. G and J in Table 1). The features of S_0 for such languages would be $S_0 w$, $S_0 r$, $S_0 s$ where r and s stand for the last two and three letters of $S_0 w$ respectively.

Syntax-based Features

After integrating classical linguistic attributes, we investigated using more linguistically sophisticated features. First of all, syntactic structure is known to help MWE identification (Fazly et al., 2009; Seretan, 2011; Nagy T. and Vincze, 2014). We therefore inform the system with the

---

[5] The whole system was developed using Python 2.7, with 2,200 lines of code, using the open-source Scikit-learn 0.19 libraries for the SVMs. The code is available on Github: `https://goo.gl/EDFyiM`

[6] These correspond mainly to cases of verb-particle (tagged VPC in the data sets) in which the particle is not separated from the verb.

provided syntactic dependencies when available: for each token B_n that both appears in the buffer and is a syntactic dependent of S_0 with label l, we capture the existence of the dependency using the features $RightDep(S_0, B_n) = True$ and $RightDepLabel(S_0, B_n) = l$. We also use the opposite features $IsGovernedBy(S_0, B_n) = True$ and $IsGovernedByLabel(S_0, G) = l$ when S_0's syntactic governor G appears in the buffer. Other syntax-based features aim at modeling the direction and label of a syntactic relation between the two top elements of the stack (feature $syntacticRelation(S_0, S_1) = \pm l$ is used for S_0 governing/governed by S_1).[7] All these syntactic features (cf. H in Table1) try to capture syntactic regularities between the tokens composing a VMWE.

History-based Features

We found that other traditional transition-based system features were sometimes useful like (local) transition history of the system. We thus added features to represent the sequence of previous transitions (of length one, two or three, cf. settings B, C and D in Table 1).

Distance-based Features

Distance between sentence components is also known to help transition-based dependency parsing (Zhang and Nivre, 2011). We thus added the distance between S_0 and B_0 and the distance between S_0 and S_1 (cf. settings K and M in Table 1).

Dictionary-based Features

We also added features based on the VMWE dictionary automatically extracted from the training set. Such features inform the system when one of the focused elements (S_i, B_j) is a component of a VMWE present in the dictionary (cf. L in Table 1).

Stack-length Features

Using the length of the stack as an additional feature (cf. O in Table 1) has also proven beneficial during our feature tuning.

---

[7]For the shared task, we used gold syntactic features for the languages accompanied with gold dependency companion files, as authorized in the closed track. Performance when using predicted syntax will be evaluated in future work.

Finally, it is worthwhile to note that system settings (cf. Table 1) interact when used to generate the precise set of features. For instance if lemma extraction is disabled (code G) while bigram extraction is enabled (code F), the produced features for e.g. the S_1S_0 bigram would not include the following features: S_1lS_0l, S_1pS_0l and S_1lS_0p.

3.3 Feature Tuning

We first divided the data sets into 3 groups, based on the availability of CoNLL-U files: (a) for **BG, HE and LT** only the VMWEs on tokenized sentences are available; (b) **CS, ES, FA, MT and RO** are accompanied by CoNLL-U files but without syntactic dependency annotations, and (c) **the other languages** are accompanied by a fully annotated CoNLL-U file. In the first tuning period, we tested the various configurations using three pilot languages (BG, CS, FR) representing one group each. In the latest days of the experiments, the set of languages tested was enlarged to all of them and systematic tuning was performed for every language.

4   Results

Table 2 summarizes the results of the system performance over all the languages proposed by the shared task. Each row of the table displays its per-MWE and per-token F-scores for a given language (identified by its ISO 639-1 code) for test dataset, on top of a 5-fold cross-validation (CV) per-MWE F-score on training dataset. The system settings are represented as a sequence of codes described in Table 1.

We can observe that results are very heterogeneous. For instance, five languages (CS, FA, FR, PL, RO) are above 0.70 per-MWE F-score in the case of cross-validation, while seven languages (DE, HE, HU, IT, LT, MT, SV) are below 0.30. In general, we can see an approximative linear correlation between the number of training VMWEs and the performance. This suggests that the size of training datasets is not large enough as systems' performance does not converge. We note though that some languages like CS and TR reach relatively low scores given the size of training data, which shows the high complexity of this task for these languages.

When comparing to the other shared task systems, we can observe that our system is the only one that handled all 18 languages, showing the

| | Corpus | | Shared Task | | | | | | CV | |
| | #VMWE | | MWE-based | | | token-based | | | MWE | |
	Train	Test	F	Rank	delta	F	Rank	delta	F	System setting
BG	1933	473	0,613	1/2	26,59	0,662	1/2	6,99	0,57	B C F I L M
CS	12852	1684	0,717	1/4	7,49	0,736	1/4	0,79	0,71	B C D E F G J K L M O
DE	2447	500	0,411	1/5	0,57	0,411	2/5	-4,36	0,28	F H I K L N P Q
EL	1518	500	0,401	1/5	8,19	0,469	1/5	3,74	0,56	E F G H J K L N
ES	748	500	0,574	1/5	13,06	0,584	1/5	9,22	0,63	B C D E F G H I J K L M
FA	2707	500	0,867	1/2	6,56	0,902	1/2	4,84	0,88	E F G J K M
FR	4462	500	0,577	1/6	6,86	0,603	2/6	-1,24	0,71	E F G H J K L M N
HE	1282	500	0,334	1/2		0,313	1/2		0,17	B C D E F L N P
HU	2999	500	0,699	2/5	-4,14	0,675	3/5	-3,34	0,24	B C D E F G H I J L Q
IT	1954	500	0,399	1/4	16,81	0,436	1/4	8,67	0,27	C F G H J K P
LT	402	100	0,284	1/2		0,253	1/2		0,086	B C D E F I K L M N O P
MT	772	500	0,144	1/4	8,03	0,163	1/4	7,42	0,081	B C D F G J K L O P
PL	3149	500	0,691	1/4	1,14	0,706	2/4	-2,18	0,7	D F G H J L
PT	3447	500	0,673	1/4	9,19	0,71	1/4	0,76	0,65	B C D E F G H I J K L M N O Q
RO	4040	500	0,753	3/4	-2,44	0,791	3/4	-4,46	0,86	B C D E F G I J K M N
SL	1787	500	0,432	1/4	6,14	0,466	1/4	0,93	0,48	D F G J L P
SV	56	236	0,304	1/4	0,04	0,307	2/4	-0,79	0,25	B C D E F G H I J K L M N O
TR	6169	501	0,554	1/4	3,64	0,553	1/4	2,43	0,58	B C D E F G H J M
AVG			*0,524*			*0.541*			*0,484*	

Table 2: Detailed results of all experiments over all the languages. F columns provide F-score results and delta columns display the difference in F-score (times 10^{-2}) between our system and the best other system of the shared task for the current evaluation/language configuration.

robustness of our approach. Moreover, evaluation using per-MWE F-score (i.e. exact VMWE matching) ranks our system first on all languages but two (HU:2nd:, RO:3rd), displaying an average difference of 6.73 points with the best other system in the current evaluation/language pair. Concerning per-token scores (which allow partial matchings), results are relatively lower: our system is ranked first for 12 languages (out of 18), with a positive average difference of 1.84 points as compared with the best other system. Such very enthusiastic results for per-MWE evaluations seem to show that our system succeeds more in considering a MWE as a whole. Further error analysis is needed to explain this trait, and in particular to check the impact of the Merge transition, which transforms sequences of elements into one.

5 Related Work

Previous approaches for VMWE identification include the two-pass method of candidate extraction followed by binary classification (Fazly et al., 2009; Nagy T. and Vincze, 2014).

VMWE identification has also been performed using sequence labeling approaches, with IOB-scheme. For instance, Diab and Bhutada (2009) apply a sequential SVM to identify verb-noun idiomatic combinations in English. Such approaches were used for MWE identification in general (including verbal expressions) ranging from contiguous expressions (Blunsom and Baldwin, 2006) to gappy ones (Schneider et al., 2014).

A joint syntactic analysis and VMWE identification approach using off-the-shelf parsers is another interesting alternative that has shown to help VMWE identification such as light verb constructions (Eryiğit et al., 2011; Vincze et al., 2013).

6 Conclusion and future work

This article presents a simple transition-based system devoted to VMWE identification. In particular, it offers a simple mechanism to handle discontinuity since foreign elements are iteratively discarded from the stack, which is a crucial point for VMWEs. It also has the advantage of being robust, accurate and efficient (linear time complexity). As future work, we would like to apply more sophisticated syntax-based features, as well as more advanced machine-learning techniques like neural networks and word embeddings. We also believe that a dynamic oracle could help increase results to better deal with cases where the system is unsure.

Acknowledgements

This work was partially funded by the French National Research Agency (PARSEME-FR ANR-14-CERA-0001).

References

Phil Blunsom and Timothy Baldwin. 2006. Multilingual deep lexical acquisition for hpsgs via supertagging. In *Proceedings of the 2006 Conference on Empirical Methods in Natural Language Processing*, pages 164–171, Sydney, Australia, July. Association for Computational Linguistics.

Matthieu Constant and Joakim Nivre. 2016. A transition-based system for joint lexical and syntactic analysis. In *Proceedings of the 54th Annual Meeting of the Association for Computational Linguistics (Volume 1: Long Papers)*, pages 161–171, Berlin, Germany, August. Association for Computational Linguistics.

Mona Diab and Pravin Bhutada. 2009. Verb noun construction mwe token classification. In *Proceedings of the Workshop on Multiword Expressions: Identification, Interpretation, Disambiguation and Applications*, pages 17–22, Singapore, August. Association for Computational Linguistics.

Gülşen Eryiğit, Tugay İlbay, and Ozan Arkan Can. 2011. Multiword expressions in statistical dependency parsing. In *Proc. of IWPT Workshop on Statistical Parsing of Morphologically-Rich Languages (SPMRL 2011)*, pages 45–55, Dublin.

Afsaneh Fazly, Paul Cook, and Suzanne Stevenson. 2009. Unsupervised type and token identification of idiomatic expressions. *Computational Linguistics*, 35(1):61–103.

István Nagy T. and Veronika Vincze. 2014. Vpctagger: Detecting verb-particle constructions with syntax-based methods. In *Proceedings of the 10th Workshop on Multiword Expressions (MWE)*, pages 17–25, Gothenburg, Sweden, April. Association for Computational Linguistics.

Joakim Nivre. 2004. Incrementality in deterministic dependency parsing. In Frank Keller, Stephen Clark, Matthew Crocker, and Mark Steedman, editors, *Proceedings of the ACL Workshop Incremental Parsing: Bringing Engineering and Cognition Together*, pages 50–57, Barcelona, Spain, July. Association for Computational Linguistics.

Joakim Nivre. 2014. Transition-Based Parsing with Multiword Expressions. In 2nd *PARSEME General Meeting, Athens, Greece*.

Agata Savary, Carlos Ramisch, Silvio Cordeiro, Federico Sangati, Veronika Vincze, Behrang Qasem-iZadeh, Marie Candito, Fabienne Cap, Voula Giouli, Ivelina Stoyanova, and Antoine Doucet. 2017. The PARSEME Shared Task on Automatic Identification of Verbal Multi-word Expressions. In *Proceedings of the 13th Workshop on Multiword Expressions (MWE 2017)*, Valencia, Spain.

Nathan Schneider, Emily Danchik, Chris Dyer, and Noah A. Smith. 2014. Discriminative lexical semantic segmentation with gaps: running the MWE gamut. *TACL*, 2:193–206.

Violeta Seretan. 2011. *Syntax-based collocation extraction*. Text, Speech and Language Technology. Springer.

Veronika Vincze, János Zsibrita, and István Nagy T. 2013. Dependency parsing for identifying hungarian light verb constructions. In *Proceedings of the Sixth International Joint Conference on Natural Language Processing*, pages 207–215, Nagoya, Japan, October. Asian Federation of Natural Language Processing.

Yue Zhang and Joakim Nivre. 2011. Transition-based dependency parsing with rich non-local features. In *Proceedings of the 49th Annual Meeting of the Association for Computational Linguistics: Human Language Technologies*, pages 188–193, Portland, Oregon, USA, June. Association for Computational Linguistics.

Investigating the Opacity of Verb-Noun Multiword Expression Usages in Context

Shiva Taslimipoor[†], Omid Rohanian[†], Ruslan Mitkov[†] and Afsaneh Fazly[‡]

[†]Research Group in Computational Linguistics, University of Wolverhampton, UK
[‡]VerticalScope Inc., Toronto, Canada
{shiva.taslimi, m.rohanian, r.mitkov}@wlv.ac.uk
afsaneh.fazly@gmail.com

Abstract

This study investigates the supervised token-based identification of Multiword Expressions (MWEs). This is an ongoing research to exploit the information contained in the contexts in which different instances of an expression could occur. This information is used to investigate the question of whether an expression is literal or MWE. Lexical and syntactic context features derived from vector representations are shown to be more effective over traditional statistical measures to identify tokens of MWEs.

1 Introduction

Multiword expressions (MWEs) belong to a class of phraseological phenomena that is ubiquitous in the study of language (Baldwin and Kim, 2010). Scholarly research in MWEs immensely benefit both NLP applications and end users (Granger and Meunier, 2008). Context of an expression has been shown to be discriminative in determining whether a particular token is idiomatic or literal (Fazly et al., 2009; Tu and Roth, 2011). However, in-context investigation of MWEs is an underexplored area.

The most common approach to treat MWEs computationally in any language is by examining corpora using statistical measures (Evert and Krenn, 2005; Ramisch et al., 2010; Villavicencio, 2005). These measures are broadly applied to identifying the types [1] of MWEs. While there is ongoing research to improve the type-based investigation of MWEs (Rondon et al., 2015; Farahmand and Martins, 2014; Salehi and Cook,

---

[1]Type refers to the canonical form of an expression, while token refers to each instance (usage) of the expression in any morphological form in text.

2013), the challenge of token-based identification of MWEs (as in tagging corpora for these expressions) requires more attention (Schneider et al., 2014; Brooke et al., 2014; Monti et al., 2015).

In this study, we focus on a specific variety of MWEs, namely Verb + Noun combinations. This type of MWEs doesn't always correspond to fixed expressions and this leads to computational challenges that make identification difficult (e.g. while *take place* is a fixed expression, *makes sense* is not and can be altered to *makes perfect sense*). The word components in such cases may or may not be inflected and the meaning of the components may or may not be exposed to the meaning of the whole expression. This paper outlines investigation of MWEs of the class Verb + Noun in Italian. Examples of these cases in Italian are *fare uso* 'to make use', *dare vita* 'to create' or *fare paura* 'to frighten'.

We propose a supervised approach that utilises the context of the occurrences of expressions in order to determine whether they are MWEs. Having the whole corpus tagged for our purpose of training a classifier would be a labour-intensive task. A more feasible approach would be to use a special-purpose data, labeled with concordances containing Verb + Noun combinations. We report the preliminary results on the effectiveness of context features extracted from this special-purpose language resource for identification of MWEs.

We differentiate between expressions whose instances occur with a single fixed idiomatic or literal behaviour and the ones that show degrees of ambiguity with regards to potential usages. We partition the dataset in a way to account for both of these groups and the experiments are run separately for each.

To extract context features, we use a word embedding approach (word2vec) (Mikolov et al., 2013) as the state of the art in the study of dis-

Proceedings of the 13th Workshop on Multiword Expressions (MWE 2017), pages 133–138,
Valencia, Spain, April 4. ©2017 Association for Computational Linguistics

tributional similarity. We extract features from the raw corpus without any pre-processing. While we report the results for Italian, the approach is language-independent and can be used for any resource-poor language.

2 Motivation

It is important to consider expressions at the token level when deciding if they are MWEs. The reason being, there are expressions that in some cases occur with an idiomatic sense whereas with a literal sense in others. This could be determined by the context in which they appear. For example take the expression *play games*. It is opaque with regards to its status as an MWE and depending on context could mean different things. For example in *He went to play games online* it has a literal sense but is idiomatic in *Don't play games with me as I want an honest answer*. A traditional classification model that is blind to linguistic context proves to be insufficient in such cases. The following is an example of the same phenomenon in Italian which is the language of interest in this study:

1) Per migliorare il sistema dei trasporti, si dovrebbero **creare ponti** anche verso e da le isole minori.

   'In order to improve the transportation system, the government should **build bridges** both to and from the smaller islands.'

2) Affinch possiamo migliorare la convivenza fra popoli diversi, bisognerebbe **creare ponti**, non sollevare nuovi muri!

   'In order to improve coexistence among different people, we should **build bridges** not raise new walls!'

3 Related Work

With regards to context-based identification of idiomatic expressions, Birke and Sakar (2006) use a slightly modified version of an existing word sense disambiguation algorithm for supervised token-based identification of MWEs. Katz and Giesbrecht (2006) rely primarily on the local context of a token without considering linguistic properties of expressions. Fazly et al. (2009) take into account both linguistic properties and local context in their analysis of MWE tokens. They have employed and evaluated an unsupervised approach on a small sample of human annotated expressions. Their method uses grammatical knowledge about the canonical form of expressions.

There is some recent interest in segmenting texts (Brooke et al., 2014; Schneider et al., 2014) based on MWEs. Brook et al. (2014) propose an unsupervised approach for identifying the types of MWEs and tagging all the token occurrences of identified expressions as MWEs. This methodology might be more useful in the case of longer idiomatic expressions that is the focus of that study. Nevertheless for expressions with fewer words, the aforementioned challenges regarding opacity of tokens limit the efficacy of such techniques. The supervised approach posited by Schneider et al. (2014) results in a corpus of automatically annotated MWEs. However, the literal/idiomatic usages of expressions have not been dealt with in particular in their work.

The idea behind our work is to use concordances of all the occurrences of a Verb + Noun expression in order to decide the degree of idiomaticity of a specific Verb + Noun expression. Our work is very related to the work of Tu and Roth (2011), in that they have also particularly considered the problem of in-context analysis of light verb construction (as a specific type of MWEs) using both statistical and contextual features. Their approach is also supervised, but it requires parsed data from English. Their contextual features include POS tags of the words in context as well as information from Levin's classes of verb components. Our approach requires little pre-processing and is best suited for languages that lack ample tagged resources. The present study is in the same vein as the approach taken by Gharibeh et al. (2016). Here, we have specifically analysed expressions that have more ambiguous usages, running separate experiments on partitions of the dataset.

4 Methodology

Our goal is to classify tokens of Verb + Noun expressions into literal and idiomatic categories. To this end, we exploit the information contained in the concordance of each occurrence of an expression. Given each concordance, we extract vector representations for several of its words to act as syntactic and lexical features. Compared to literal Verb + Noun combinations, idiomatic combinations are expected to appear in more restricted lexical and syntactic forms (Fazly et al., 2009). One traditional approach in quantifying lexical restrictions is to use statistical measures. (Ramisch et al., 2010).

We target syntactic features by extracting vectors for the verb and the noun contained in the expression. Here we extract the vectors of the verb and the noun components in their raw form hoping to indirectly learn lexical and syntactic features for each occurrence of an expression. We believe that the structure of the verb component is important in extracting fixedness information for an expression. Also, the distributional representation of the noun component is informative since Verb + Noun expressions are known to have some degrees of semi-productivity (Stevenson et al., 2004).

Additionally, we extract vectors for co-occurring words around a target expression. Specifically, we focus on the two words immediately following the Verb + Noun expression. We expect the arguments of the verb and the noun components that occur following the expression to play a distinguishing role in these kinds of so-called complex predicates[2] (Samek-Lodovici, 2003).

The word vectors in this study come from the Italian word2vec embedding which is available online[3]. The generated word embedding approach has applied Gensim's skipgram word2vec model with the window size of 10 to extract vectors of size 300 for Italian words from Wikipedia corpus.

In order to construct our context features, given each occurrence of a Verb + Noun combination we concatenate four different word vectors corresponding to the verb, noun, and their two following adjacent words while preserving the original order. In other words, given each expression, the context feature consists of a combined vector with the dimension of $4 * 300 = 1200$.

Concatenated feature vectors are fed into a logistic regression classifier. The details with regards to training the classifier are explained in Section 6.

5 Experiments

5.1 Experimental Data

The data used in this study is taken from an Italian language resource for Verb + Noun expressions (Taslimipoor et al., 2016). The resource focuses on four most frequent Italian verbs: *fare*, *dare*, *prendere* and *trovare*. It includes all the concordances of these verbs when followed by any noun, taken from the itWaC corpus (Baroni and Kilgarriff, 2006) using SketchEngine (Kilgarriff et al., 2004).

The concordances include windows of ten words before and after an expression; hence, there are contexts around each Verb + Noun expression to be used for the classification task[4]. $30,094$ concordances are annotated by two native speakers and can be used as the gold-standard for this research. The Kappa measure of inter-annotator agreement between the two annotators on the whole list of concordances is 0.65 with the observed agreement of 0.85 (Taslimipoor et al., 2016). Since the agreement is substantial, we continue with the first annotator's annotated data for evaluation.

5.2 Partitioning the Dataset

The idea is to evaluate the effect of context features to identify the literal/idiomatic usages of expressions, particularly for the type of expressions that are likely to occur in both senses. In our specialised data, around 32% of expression types have been annotated in both idiomatic and literal form in different contexts. For this purpose, we divide the data into two groups:

(1) Expressions with a skewed division of the two senses (e.g., with more than 70% of instances having either a literal or idiomatic sense).[5]

(2) Expressions with a more balanced division of instances (e.g., with less than or equal to 70% of instances having either a literal or idiomatic sense).

We develop different baselines to evaluate our approach on these two groups as explained in the following section.

5.3 Baseline

5.3.1 Majority baseline

We devise a very informed and supervised baseline based on the idiomatic/literal usages of ex-

---

[2]Most of the Verb + Noun expressions that we investigate belong to the category of complex predicates which is the focus of Samek-Lodovici (Samek-Lodovici, 2003)

[3]http://hlt.isti.cnr.it/wordembeddings/

[4]Cases where components of a potential MWE occur with in-between gaps (intervening words) are not considered.

[5]Expressions such as *dare inizio* 'to start' and *trovare cose* 'to find things' which most of the times occur as MWE and non-MWE respectively.

pressions in the gold-standard data. According to this baseline a target instance vn_{ins}, of a test expression type vn, gets the label that it has received in the majority of vn occurrences in the gold-standard set. The baseline approach labels all instances of an expression with a fixed label (1 for MWE and 0 for non-MWE). This is a high precision model when working with Group 1, due to the more consistent behaviour of instances there. However, its results are suitable for evaluating the results of our developed model over expressions of Group 2.

5.3.2 Association measures as a baseline

The data in Group 1 include the expressions that mostly occur in either idiomatic or literal forms. These expressions are commonly categorised as being MWE or non-MWE using association measures. Association measures are computed by statistical analysis through the whole corpus, hence the values are the same for all instances of an expression. In other words, these methods are blind to the contexts in which different instances of an expression could occur.

To evaluate our model over data in Group 1, these association measures are used as features to develop a baseline. We focus on two widely used association measures, log-likelihood and Salience as defined in SketchEngine. We also use frequency of occurrence as a statistical measure to rank MWEs. The statistical measures are computed using SketchEngine on the whole of itWac. The statistical measures are then given to an SVM classifier to identify MWEs.

6 Evaluation

6.1 Evaluation Setup

There are $1,480$ types of expressions with $28,483$ occurrences in Group 1 and 169 types of expressions with $1,611$ occurrences in Group 2. For each group, we extract context features to train logistic regression classifiers.

Our proposed context features are vector representations of the raw form of the verb component, the raw form of the noun component and a window of two words after the target expression. We refer to the combination of these vectors as the Context feature. We apply a 5-fold cross validation approach to compute accuracies for each classifier. We split the dataset into five separate folds so that no instance of the same expression could occur in more than one fold. This is to make sure that the test data is blind enough to the training data. The classifiers are compared against the baselines using different features. The results are reported in Tables 1 and 2.

6.2 Results and Analyses

Table 2 shows the results of our model over data in Group 2 compared to the majority baseline. Recall that the data instances in Group 2 are highly unpredictable in their occurrence as MWE or non-MWE. We expect that our supervised model using context features (Context) be able to disambiguate between different instances of an expression. Here, our model performs slightly better than the informed majority baseline.

Table 1: Classification accuracies (%) using different features over Group 1 and the whole data.

Features	all data	Group 1
Freq	70.77	69.20
Likelihood	72.11	70.64
Salience	73.83	72.81
Likelihood+Salience+Freq	73.90	73.29
Context (word2vec)	**75.42**	74.13
Salience + Context	**78.40**	**80.13**
Likelihood+Salience+Freq+Context	**76.95**	**80.07**

Table 2: Classification accuracies (%) over data in Group 2 compared to the majority baseline.

Model	Group 2
Majority Baseline	59.52
Logistic regression with Context features	**63.21**
Logistic regression with Context+Salience	54.37

Statistical measures are expected to be promising features when identifying MWEs among expressions with consistent behaviour. However, the results in Table 1 show that our Context features are more effective in MWE classification even when applied over Group 1 and also over the whole data.

The good performance when using word context features leads us to think that their usefulness can be attributed to the information obtained from external arguments of the verb and the noun constituents of expressions. More experiments need to be done to confirm this and also to find the best suitable window size for the word context around a target expression[6].

We have also trained the logistic regression model with the combination of the `Context` features and the association measures in Table 1. According to these results, the combination of features improves the accuracies of our model in identifying idiomatic expressions specially when applied over the consistent data in Group 1. The results lead us to believe that context features are even more useful in cases where we expect the best result from statistical measures due to the more consistent behaviour of the data. The better performance when using `Context` and statistical measures together, compared with when we use `Context` features alone is also a remarkable observation visible at Table 1.

Our experiment using the combination of Context and Salience (as the best statistical measure) for training over Group 2 expressions (Table 2), shows that the statistical measure is not helpful for the class of ambiguous expressions.

7   Conclusions and Future Work

We investigate the inclusion of concordance as part of the feature set used in supervised classification of MWEs. We have shown that context features have discriminative power in detecting literal and idiomatic usages of expressions both for the group of expressions with high potential of occurring in both literal/idiomatic senses or otherwise. Our results suggest that, when used in combination with traditional features, context can improve the overall performance of a supervised classification model in identifying MWEs.

In future, we intend to consider incorporating linguistically motivated features into our model. We will also experiment with constructing features that would consider long-distance dependencies in cases of MWEs with gaps in between their components.

Acknowledgments

The authors would like to thank Manuela Cherchi and Anna Desantis for their annotations and input on Italian examples.

---

[6]We have realised through trial-and-error that a window size of two after a target expression leads to better results compared with no context or contexts of bigger size.

References

Timothy Baldwin and Su Nam Kim. 2010. Multiword expressions. In *Handbook of Natural Language Processing, second edition.*, pages 267–292. CRC Press.

Marco Baroni and Adam Kilgarriff. 2006. Large linguistically-processed web corpora for multiple languages. In *Proceedings of the Eleventh Conference of the European Chapter of the Association for Computational Linguistics: Demonstrations*, EACL '06, pages 87–90, Stroudsburg, PA, USA. Association for Computational Linguistics.

Julia Birke and Anoop Sarkar. 2006. A clustering approach for nearly unsupervised recognition of non-literal language. In *In Proceedings of EACL-06*, pages 329–336.

Julian Brooke, Vivian Tsang, Graeme Hirst, and Fraser Shein. 2014. Unsupervised multiword segmentation of large corpora using prediction-driven decomposition of n-grams. In *COLING 2014, 25th International Conference on Computational Linguistics, Proceedings of the Conference: Technical Papers, August 23-29, 2014, Dublin, Ireland*, pages 753–761.

Stefan Evert and Brigitte Krenn. 2005. Using small random samples for the manual evaluation of statistical association measures. *Computer Speech & Language*, 19(4):450–466.

Meghdad Farahmand and Ronaldo Martins. 2014. A supervised model for extraction of multiword expressions, based on statistical context features. In *Proceedings of the 10th Workshop on Multiword Expressions (MWE)*, pages 10–16, Gothenburg, Sweden, April. Association for Computational Linguistics.

Afsaneh Fazly, Paul Cook, and Suzanne Stevenson. 2009. Unsupervised type and token identification of idiomatic expressions. *Computational Linguistics*, 35(1):61–103.

Waseem Gharbieh, Virendra Bhavsar, and Paul Cook. 2016. A word embedding approach to identifying verb-noun idiomatic combinations. In *Proceedings of the 12th Workshop on Multiword Expressions, MWE@ACL 2016, Berlin, Germany, August 11, 2016*.

Sylviane Granger and Fanny Meunier. 2008. *Phraseology: an interdisciplinary perspective*. John Benjamins Publishing Company.

Graham Katz and Eugenie Giesbrecht. 2006. Automatic identification of non-compositional multiword expressions using latent semantic analysis. In *Proceedings of the Workshop on Multiword Expressions: Identifying and Exploiting Underlying Properties*, MWE '06, pages 12–19, Stroudsburg, PA, USA. Association for Computational Linguistics.

Adam Kilgarriff, Pavel Rychl, Pavel Smrz, and David Tugwell. 2004. The sketch engine. In *EURALEX 2004*, pages 105–116, Lorient, France.

Tomas Mikolov, Ilya Sutskever, Kai Chen, Greg S Corrado, and Jeff Dean. 2013. Distributed representations of words and phrases and their compositionality. In *Advances in neural information processing systems*, pages 3111–3119.

Johanna Monti, Federico Sangati, and Mihael Arcan. 2015. TED-MWE: a bilingual parallel corpus with mwe annotation. In *Proceedings of the Second Italian Conference on Computational Linguistics (CLiC-it 2015)*.

Carlos Ramisch, Aline Villavicencio, and Christian Boitet. 2010. mwetoolkit: a Framework for Multiword Expression Identification. In *Proceedings of the Seventh International Conference on Language Resources and Evaluation (LREC 2010)*, Valetta, Malta, May. European Language Resources Association.

Alexandre Rondon, Helena Caseli, and Carlos Ramisch. 2015. Never-ending multiword expressions learning. In *Proceedings of the 11th Workshop on Multiword Expressions*, pages 45–53, Denver, Colorado, June. Association for Computational Linguistics.

Bahar Salehi and Paul Cook. 2013. Predicting the compositionality of multiword expressions using translations in multiple languages. *Second Joint Conference on Lexical and Computational Semantics (* SEM)*, 1:266–275.

Vieri Samek-Lodovici. 2003. The internal structure of arguments and its role in complex predicate formation. *Natural Language & Linguistic Theory*, 21(4):835–881.

Nathan Schneider, Emily Danchik, Chris Dyer, and Noah A. Smith. 2014. Discriminative lexical semantic segmentation with gaps: Running the MWE gamut. *TACL*, 2:193–206.

Suzanne Stevenson, Afsaneh Fazly, and Ryan North. 2004. Statistical measures of the semi-productivity of light verb constructions. In *Proceedings of the Workshop on Multiword Expressions: Integrating Processing*, MWE '04, pages 1–8, Stroudsburg, PA, USA. Association for Computational Linguistics.

Shiva Taslimipoor, Anna Desantis, Manuela Cherchi, Ruslan Mitkov, and Johanna Monti. 2016. Language resources for italian: towards the development of a corpus of annotated italian multiword expressions. In *Proceedings of Third Italian Conference on Computational Linguistics (CLiC-it 2016) & Fifth Evaluation Campaign of Natural Language Processing and Speech Tools for Italian (EVALITA 2016)*, Napoli, Italy.

Yuancheng Tu and Dan Roth. 2011. Learning english light verb constructions: Contextual or statistical. In *Proceedings of the Workshop on Multiword Expressions: from Parsing and Generation to the Real World*, pages 31–39, Portland, Oregon, USA, June. Association for Computational Linguistics.

Aline Villavicencio. 2005. The availability of verb–particle constructions in lexical resources: How much is enough? *Computer Speech & Language*, 19(4):415–432.

Compositionality in Verb-Particle Constructions

Archna Bhatia[1], Choh Man Teng[2], and James F. Allen[2,3]

[1]Florida Institute for Human and Machine Cognition, 15 SE Osceola Ave, Ocala, FL 34471
[2]Florida Institute for Human and Machine Cognition, 40 S Alcaniz St, Pensacola, FL 32502
[3]Department of Computer Science, University of Rochester, Rochester, NY 14627
{abhatia, cmteng, jallen}@ihmc.us

Abstract

We are developing a broad-coverage deep semantic lexicon for a system that parses sentences into a logical form expressed in a rich ontology that supports reasoning. In this paper we look at verb-particle constructions (VPCs), and the extent to which they can be treated compositionally vs idiomatically. First we distinguish between the different types of VPCs based on their compositionality and then present a set of heuristics for classifying specific instances as compositional or not. We then identify a small set of general sense classes for particles when used compositionally and discuss the resulting lexical representations that are being added to the lexicon. By treating VPCs as compositional whenever possible, we attain broad coverage in a compact way, and also enable interpretations of novel VPC usages not explicitly present in the lexicon.

1 Introduction

Toward the goal of Natural Language Understanding of full interpretation of a text fragment (or a sentence), we want to produce a good semantic representation of the sentence. This involves combining rich grammatical information with information about specific lexical items in the sentence, such as word senses, among other things. Since multiword expressions (MWEs) constitute a significant proportion of the lexicon in any natural language (Moreno-Ortiz et al., 2013), in fact, Jackendoff (1997) estimated the number of MWEs in a speaker's lexicon to be of the same order of magnitude as the number of single words, it is important to get a good interpretation of MWEs.

For this paper, we focus on a specific type of MWEs, namely verb-particle constructions (VPCs). These consist of a verb and an adverbial or prepositional particle, e.g., *eat up, fade out, go on, show off* and *walk down*.[1] Adding every single occurrence of such verb particle combinations in a lexicon is possible but not ideal as, for example, some VPCs may be interpretable compositionally, i.e., the verb and the particle contribute their simplex meanings, e.g. *fly up*. Other compositional VPCs include cases such as *finish up* and *made away* for which either the verb or the particle, respectively, seems to contribute its simplex meaning (Bannard et al., 2003).[2] However, other VPCs indeed are noncompositional and require special interpretation, and hence need to be added into the lexicon, e.g., *bake off* 'contest' and *egg on* 'urge someone for an action that might not be a good idea'.

For an interpretation of the compositional types above, we need to determine the best senses for the verb and the particle in the VPCs. There are many lexical resources for an inventory of senses for verbs, such as WordNet (Miller, 1995), (Fellbaum, 1998) and VerbNet (Kipper-Schuler, 2005). But there is not much for the particles except for a few attempts at the semantics for a few particles, such as *up* (Cook and Stevenson, 2006) and *out* (Tyler and Evans, 2003). Our investigation of hundreds of VPCs has shown that the semantics of particles is also important, as can also be gathered from others' proposals for similar classifications of VPCs as mentioned above involving VPC types where particles contribute to the meaning, see Section 3 for details. Particles are not just the vacuous entities structurally required by the verbs in VPCs, they also have their own semantics which is found to be general across verbs

---

[1]Note we focus on the particle usage in this paper, not on the prepositional usage, i.e., a verb followed by a particle not a prepositional phrase. However, there may be an overlap in lexical semantic content (i.e., senses) of the homophonous particles and prepositions, see Section 4.1.

[2]However, refer to Section 3 for our take on such cases.

Proceedings of the 13th Workshop on Multiword Expressions (MWE 2017), pages 139–148,
Valencia, Spain, April 4. ©2017 Association for Computational Linguistics

in specific verb classes. For example, particle *up* has a *Direction* sense when it appears in resultative VPCs with verbs of motion, such as *wander/stroll/go/run up* (Villavicencio, 2006). Hence, in this paper, we provide a set of senses that particles in VPCs display across many verbs in a verb class.

To make use of these senses, we encode semantics of particles in an ontology, namely TRIPS (Allen et al., 2007) LF ontology which is designed to be linguistically informed.[3] The ontology encodes semantic types, the set of word senses and semantic relations that can be used in logical form (LF) graphs. Word senses are defined based on subcategorization patterns and selectional restrictions driven by linguistic considerations. The semantic types in the ontology are, to a large extent, compatible with FrameNet (Johnson and Fillmore, 2000). The ontology uses a rich semantic feature set, the features used are an extended version of EuroWordNet (Vossen, 1997). Unlike Word-Net, the TRIPS ontology does not attempt to capture all possible word senses but rather focuses on the level of abstraction that affects linguistic processing. We use TRIPS, a broad coverage deep semantic parser (driven by the ontology) to combine semantic, ontological and grammatical information to produce semantic representation. For a more detailed overview of the TRIPS system, refer Allen & Teng (2017) and Allen et al. (2008).[4]

The paper is organized as follows: Previous work on VPCs is discussed in Section 2. In Section 3, classification of VPCs is discussed based on their compositionality. A set of heuristics are presented to identify different classes of VPCs in Section 3.1. In Section 4, we discuss the semantics of particles in VPCs. An inventory of general sense classes for particles used in VPCs is provided in Section 4.1. In Section 5, we present various generalizations corresponding to the identified sense classes for the particles, and briefly discuss how a computational lexicon (including a lexicon for particles) is built for the computation of meaning for VPCs. This also includes a discussion of phenomena we cannot handle currently. In Section 6, we demonstrate the procedure to compute meaning of sentences involving compositional VPCs. Finally, in Section 7, we present our conclusions.

---

[3]The TRIPS ontology can be accessed at:`http://www.cs.rochester.edu/research/cisd/projects/trips/lexicon/browse-ont-lex-ajax.html`

[4]The TRIPS parser can be accessed at: `http://trips.ihmc.us/parser/cgi/parse`

2   Related work

A lot of computational literature on VPCs focuses on identification or extraction of VPCs, or on compositionality of VPCs, as discussed below. There are a few articles dealing with different senses of particles but they usually focus on only one or two specific particles rather than on a broader coverage of particles.

Vincze (2011) presents the Wiki50 corpus that has 446 VPCs (342 unique types) annotated. Bannard (2002) makes an attempt to identify different types of VPCs in terms of compositionality and builds a (decision tree) classifier to identify the four types. Bannard et al. (2003) also adopt a similar approach for compositionality. As an annotation experiment, they investigate various VPCs to see whether the sense is contributed by the verb and/or the particle. They build four classifiers for automatic semantic analysis of VPCs. Patrick and Fletcher (2004) also have a similar approach but focus on automatic classification of different types of compositionality. Unlike our work, in all these works, the focus is on compositionality only, not on actual senses of the particles.

Cook and Stevenson (2006) discuss various senses for the particle *up* in cognitive grammar framework and annotate a dataset and perform some classification experiments to identify the senses of *up* in unseen data. As a linguistic study, Jackendoff (2002) provides a very nice discussion of various types of VPCs involving particles such as directional particles, aspectual particles, time-AWAY constructions, and some idiomatic constructions. Our work differs from theirs in having a broader coverage of particles and/or strong emphasis on ontology with respect to the sense classes of the particles and how different particle sense classes relate to verbal ontological classes.

Fraser (1976) mentions semantic properties of verbs affecting patterns of verb particle combinations, e.g. semantically similar verbs *bolt/cement/clam/glue/paste/nail* all can combine with the particle *down* and specify the objects that can be used to join material. Our approach is also based on the similar assumption that there are generalizations, such as combinations of particles with specific verb classes or ontological classes result in specific sense classes for the particles. Villavicencio (2003) also adopts the same approach where she tries to encode the information in terms of lexical rules and restrictions etc, however her focus is on obtaining productive patterns in VPCs rather than on their interpretation.

Our work also differs from the previous works mentioned above in the following respect: we emphasize on building complete semantic representations of the sentences, not just on particles' semantics or just classification of VPCs. Similar to our criteria for compositionality, McCarthy et al. (2003), Baldwin et al. (2003), Bannard et al. (2003) have looked at distributional similarity as a measure of compositionality of VPCs. In contrast to the approaches focusing on statistical classification based on word/syntax features, we present our heuristics for classification of VPCs based on WordNet and discuss how we compute the semantics of the compositional classes.

3 Classification of VPCs

VPCs have often been classified in terms of their compositionality/decomposability (i.e., whether all constituents of a VPC, the verb and the particle, contribute their simplex meanings to the overall semantic content of the VPC or not), the classes following somewhere between the fully compositional and fully idiomatic VPCs, e.g., see Fraser (1976), Chen (1986), O'Dowd (1998), Dehé (2002) and Jackendoff (2002).[5]

In Figure 1, we present our classification of VPCs which also mainly consists of two types, the compositional and the noncompositional VPCs. We further identify the compositional VPCs into three subtypes, the symmetrically compositional VPCs, the light particle compositional VPCs (LP-compositional VPCs) and the light verb compositional VPCs (LV-compositional VPCs). The symmetrically compositional VPCs refer to the VPCs where both the constituents, the verb and the particle, contribute their lexical-semantic content. For example, in *The plane flew up in no time*, the senses for the verb *fly* (e.g., in WordNet, sense fly%2:38:00) as well as the particle *up* (e.g., in WordNet, sense up%4:02:00) combine together to

provide the meaning of the VPC *fly up*. We distinguish the other two compositional VPC types from the symmetrically compositional VPCs only in the aspect that in the other two types, the particle or the verb have a relatively lighter contribution[6] than the other constituent which adds its regular lexical-semantic content.

1. **Compositional VPCs:**

   (a) **Symmetrically compositional:** Both verb and the particle contribute their simplex meanings.
   The plane flew up in no time.

   (b) **Light particle compositional (LP-compositional):** Verb contributes most of the semantic content. Particle contributes aspectual information.
   Susan finished up her paper.

   (c) **Light verb compositional (LV-compositional):** Particle contributes most of the semantic content. The verb is generally a light verb contributing a bleached meaning such as BECOME or CAUSE etc.
   The thief made away with the cash.

2. **Noncompositional VPCs:**

   (a) **Noncompositional with certain generalizations:** Neither verb nor particle contribute their literal senses but certain generalizations are involved in interpretation of the VPCs.
   She took up photography/swimming [activities]. vs. She took up her position [responsibility/position].

   (b) **Idiosyncratic Noncompositional:** Idiomatic usages
   John wouldn't have done the dangerous experiment if his brother hadn't egged him on.

Figure 1: Classification of VPCs

The LP-compositional VPCs involve particles which, instead of contributing a preposition like lexical semantic content, contribute aspectual information to the VPC. For example, in *Susan finished up her paper*, the verb *finish* contributes its

---

[5]Based on Hawkins' (2000) classification, Lohse et al (2004) provide another classification of VPCs, also related to compositionality, in terms of whether the constituents of a VPC are independently processable or if one or both of them are dependent on the other for appropriate lexical-semantic content. For example, in *They turned off the lights*, how *off* is interpreted is independent of it appearing in the VPC, note this sentence entails *The lights are off*, however the verb is not independent of the particle in the VPC for its semantic content, the sentence does not entail *They turned the lights*.

Their categories can also be largely mapped to the compositional and the noncompositional cases.

[6]The term "light particle" is used in analogy with the term "light verb" which is commonly used in the literature for verbs with bleached content.

regular lexical content (e.g., in WordNet, sense finish%2:30:02), however, the particle *up*, instead of contributing its regular lexical-semantic content (e.g., WordNet sense up%4:02:00) adds aspectual information that the action was completed (i.e., the *Completely* sense in our sense inventory). See Section 4.1 for the specific senses of particles.

Similarly, the LV-compositional VPCs involve particles with their regular lexical-semantic content but have light verbs which carry bleached meaning than the regular verbs, e.g., CAUSE, BE-COME, etc. For example, in *The thief **made away** with the cash*, the particle *away* contributes its regular meaning (e.g., WordNet sense away%4:02:00) but the verb *make*, instead of contributing its regular meaning (e.g., WordNet sense make%2:36:01), adds a bleached meaning (e.g., cause to be). For details on the procedure to compute meanings of sentences with compositional VPCs, see Section 6.

The noncompositional VPCs also seem to have at least two subtypes based on whether their interpretation involves certain generalizations or if it is completely idiosyncratic. However, for the rest of this paper, we focus on the compositional VPCs.

3.1 Heuristics for compositionality of VPCs

As a first step toward interpretation of VPCs, we need to determine whether a given VPC is compositional or not. For this task, we employ a number of heuristics that make use of the rich inventory of hierarchically organized word senses (i.e., synsets) in WordNet which contains over 100,000 words including 64188 multi-words. Heuristics 1-7 below are used to identify compositional VPCs, whereas heuristic 8 indicates a noncompositional VPC.[7]

1. If the verb is among the list of light verbs, and WordNet does not have an entry for the VPC, it most likely is LV-compositional. For example, the VPC *make away* uses the light verb *make* and the VPC does not have an entry in WordNet.

2. If a VPC exists and WordNet has an entry for the verb as well as for the particle but no entry for the VPC, VPC is (symmetrically) compositional. For example, *fly* with the sense key **fly%2:38:01** as well as *up* with the sense key **up%4:02:00** appears in WordNet but *fly up* does not appear in any synset in WordNet.

3. If WordNet has the VPC as well as the verb in the same synset, VPC is LP-compositional. For example, *sort out* (**sort_out%2:31:00**) and *sort* (**sort%2:31:00**) both appear in the same synset in WordNet.

4. If WordNet has verb as a hypernym for the VPC, VPC is likely either symmetrically compositional or LP-compositional. For example, compositional VPC *go up* (**go_up%2:38:00**) has the verb *go* (**go%2:38:00**) as its direct hypernym.

5. If WordNet has the verb in the definition in the synset where VPC appears, VPC is either symmetrically compositional or LP-compositional. For example, the compositional VPC *move up* (**move_up%2:38:00**) has the verb *move* in its definition *move upwards*.

6. If WordNet has the relevant VPC as well as another VPC with the particle replaced with another particle in the same synset, VPC is either symmetrically compositional or LP-compositional (with the two particles in the same sense class). For example, *pull up* (**pull_up%2:35:00**) as well as *pull out* (**pull_out%2:35:00**) are in the same synset. In these VPCs, the particles *up* as well as *out* have the same general sense *Direction* (see Section 4.1 for an inventory of particle sense classes).

7. If WordNet has the relevant VPC as well as another VPC with the verb replaced with another verb in the same synset, VPC is compositional (either symmetrically compositional or LP-compositional or LV-compositional). For example, the compositional VPCs *pull out* (**pull_out%2:35:00**) and *rip out* (**rip_out%2:35:00**) appear in the same WordNet synset.

8. If none of the above are true and the VPC in WordNet does not have any other item in its synset, the VPC is likely idiomatic. For example, the idiomatic VPC *catch up* (**catch_up%2:38:00**) does not have any other item in its synset.

---

[7]Note that we do not claim that these heuristics cover the VPCs exhaustively.

3.2 An evaluation of heuristics for compositionality of VPCs

We conducted an evaluation of the heuristics 3-8 which is described as follows. From among all the VPCs for which WordNet has an entry, we automatically extracted 25 random VPCs such that each of the 12 particles (that we investigated, see Section 4) was represented in the extracted VPCs. These test VPCs were manually annotated by three annotators for the compositionality labels, *Compositional* and *Noncompositional*. Since a VPC may have both compositional and noncompositional usages in different contexts, we restricted assignment of the annotation label for a specific VPC to only one label by considering the first synset/definition each of the VPCs had in WordNet. In case of disagreement among the three annotations, the annotators discussed reasons for their decisions and arrived at a consensus to create the Gold annotations for the VPCs. One of the VPCs was dropped from the test set as the annotators could not reconcile with respect to the VPC.

A python implementation of the heuristics was applied to the remaining 24 test VPCs. Like the manual annotations mentioned above, for the heuristics also, only those annotations were considered which were based on the first synset/definition of the VPC in WordNet. The VPCs that heuristics 3-7 identified as representative of their category were annotated as *Compositional*, whereas the VPCs identified by heuristic 8 were annotated as *Noncompositional*. These annotations were tested against the Gold annotations for the VPCs.

As mentioned earlier, our heuristics do not cover all the VPCs. Out of the 24 VPCs, the heuristics did not assign a label to four VPCs. Also additional two VPCs had to be disregarded due to assignment of labels to them based on synsets/definitions other than the first synset/definition in WordNet. For the remaining 18 VPCs, the heuristics achieved an overall accuracy of 72%. For compositional cases specifically, the heuristics got 82% correct labels, and for the noncompositional cases, the heuristics achieved an accuracy of 57%.

One of the cases that the heuristics misidentified, namely *fly by*, was merely due to the current implementation of the heuristic not involving inflectional variations of the verb. Note WordNet definition includes the verb *fly* but in its inflected form *flying*. The heuristic 5 could capture it if the

implementation is refined to cover inflected forms of verbs.

Finally, note heuristics 1 and 2 could not be evaluated using the same procedure by extracting VPCs from WordNet randomly since heuristics 1 and 2 identify VPCs that are not included in WordNet.

4 Semantics of particles in VPCs

As mentioned in Section 3, particles contribute to the overall semantics of compositional VPCs. In order to study the contribution of particles in VPCs, we conducted an investigation of VPCs consisting of verbs in the ontology class ONT::EVENT-OF-CAUSATION in the TRIPS ontology. Currently, there are 1383 words with verb senses in this class (and a total of 1784 verb senses of those words). Our investigation consisted of combinations of these verbs with the following particles (wherever the combinations were possible as VPCs): *across*, *away*, *by*, *down*, *in*, *into*, *off*, *on*, *out*, *over*, *through*, and *up*. We searched for examples for each of the combinations using Google and manually went through each of the examples to test various things. For example, we checked if any of the verb or the particle contributed to the overall meaning of the VPC, identified the senses particles had in the VPCs if any, checked if the particle could be taken out without a major change in meaning, if the particle expressed RESULT or could be replaced with a RESULT-Prepositional Phrase,[8] if a corresponding VPC consisting of the particle with the opposite polarity was also possible, e.g., *take in* vs *take out*, if specific argument types, e.g., MANNER, RESULT, LOCATION, AFFECTED etc were instantiated in the sentence, etc. In the rest of this section, we present the sense classes particles in compositional VPCs tend to fall into.

4.1 Sense classes for particles in VPCs

While, on the one hand, particles may encode subtle nuances of meanings in each of their occurrences in (compositional) VPCs, on the other hand, they may display some general senses across many VPCs. WordNet attempts to capture the nuances by storing each of the VPCs as a separate

---

[8]RESULT is one of the argument roles identified in TRIPS ontology. The argument roles signal different argument positions for predicates as well as have their own inferential import, some other examples are AGENT, AFFECTED, MANNER, LOCATION, and FIGURE.

lexical item. However, this approach results in having as many sense categories as there are VPCs and we lose information about the common contributions made by the particles in VPC semantics which can be useful while producing semantic representation of sentences with new VPCs not stored in WordNet or another lexical resource. Hence, we focus on the general senses particles display across VPCs.

We identified three sense classes for the particles in compositional VPCs, namely *Direction*, *Ready/Active* and *Aspectual*, as illustrated in Figure 2. These sense classes also correspond to the VPC classes based on their compositionality mentioned in Section 3. For example, the *Direction* sense class is generally instantiated by the symmetrically compositional and LV-compositional VPCs. The *Ready/Active* sense class is instantiated by the LV-compositional VPCs, and the *Aspectual* sense class by the LP-compositional VPCs.

1. **Direction:**

    (a) **Away:** *Can Modi unlock $1 trillion worth of gold stashed AWAY in India's lockers?*

    (b) **Out:** *My mom never threw it OUT.*

    (c) **Up:** *The magic ketchup should sink when you squeeze the bottle and float UP when you release it.*

2. **Ready/Active [+/-]:**

    (a) **Ready:** *That won't take DOWN "the internet" though, just DNS resolution.*

    (b) **Active:** *Baby was having a good sleep and mom woke him UP.*

3. **Aspectual:**

    (a) **Completely:** *He sorted OUT every scrap of manuscript, every map, and the native letters, he looked THROUGH the files.*

    (b) **Continuing:** *Day after day she worked AWAY remaking the old Granville house into a home.*

    (c) **Starting:** *Ask AWAY the question.*

Figure 2: Sense classes for particles in VPCs

The *Direction* sense class has a number of sub-classes, each instantiated by a specific directional particle, such as *away, down, in, into, off, on, out, up* denoting a specific direction sense.[9]

The *Ready/Active* sense class also is a broad class of senses for the particles ranging from usages such as *Take DOWN the internet* to *Wake him UP*. We consider these VPC usages compositional since the particles display the same senses independently of the VPC usages. For example, one could say *The network is DOWN* where the particle *down* appears outside of a VPC with the same *Ready* sense as in the VPC usage *Take DOWN the internet*. Similarly, for *Active* sense, compare *I'm UP* with *Wake him UP*. More examples for this class of senses include: *Bring UP the internet/browser, Set UP an expertiment, Get UP, He had passed OUT from an apparent drug overdose* and *Turn ON/OFF the switch*. The common theme across these senses seems to be that these usages involve as AFFECTED arguments cognitive entities or processes/machines which may become more ready/active or less ready/active.[10]

The *Aspectual* sense class has three subclasses, namely *Completely*, *Continuing*, and *Starting*, where the particle modifies the verb by providing aspectual information.

We can employ certain heuristics to identify some of these particle senses. Since, in the symmetrically compositional and LV-compositional VPCs, particles contribute significantly in the lexical-semantic content of the VPCs, if they are removed from the construction, part of the meaning is also lost or the meaning changes drastically, as can be observed in the case of the *Direction* sense particle *out* in the following: *Then I can move OUT* vs. *Then I can move*, and in the case of the *Ready/Active* sense particle *Down* in the following: *That won't take DOWN "the internet" though* vs. *That won't take "the internet" though*.

Also, if a particle has a *Direction* sense, then replacing the particle with another directional particle should result in a VPC with just a change in the direction in the sense, e.g., *pull UP-/DOWN the screen*. The directional particles share their senses with the corresponding prepositional usages.[11] Hence, the directional particles

---

[9]All of the sense subclasses of *Direction* are not illustrated in Figure 2 to avoid redundancy.

[10]Even though we have identified *Ready* and *Active* as two separate subclasses for this class of senses, there seems to be more grey area for it to be difficult to always distinguish between the two subclasses.

[11]The difference seems to be that in the directional parti-

are replaceable with corresponding Prepositional Phrases (directional-PPs). For example, the particle *down* in *I walked DOWN* can be replaced with a corresponding directional-PP, as in *I walked DOWN THE STREET*.

Similarly, for LP-compositional cases, which include all the *Aspectual* sense classes, we check if the particle can be dropped without a major change in meaning in VPCs. For example, for *Completely* sense, the particle seems to enhance/emphasize the meaning of the verb or indicates completion of the activity denoted by the verb and can be dropped without a major change in meaning, e.g., *clean (UP) the room, EC is preparing to arrange (UP) elections in party lines as well, Techstars has acquired (UP) Global*. Also, the particle can generally be replaced with MANNER adverbials *completely* and *thoroughly*. For the other two senses also, there is only a slight loss of aspectual information in the VPC when the particle is dropped.

5 Building the computational lexicon (for semantic parsing of VPCs)

In this section, we discuss our findings in regard to the above mentioned sense classes. We find that there are complicated interactions between the verb ontology types and particles as well as arguments of the VPCs. We first present some of these interactions and discuss how corresponding information is encoded in the TRIPS lexicon. This is followed by the interactions which cannot be encoded in the ontology currently and are left for future work.

Particles can express one or more of the senses listed in Figure 2 in different VPCs. This information is encoded in TRIPS ontology by adding ontology types corresponding to these senses in the particle's lexicon. For example, the lexical entry for the particle *up* lists sense ontology types ONT::DIRECTION, ONT::COMPLETELY and ONT::READY among other possible senses.[12] Simultaneously, WordNet sense keys corresponding to the particle *up* may be added in the ontology entries for these sense ontology types.

Starting with the observation that the particle's sense may depend on the verb it combines with in a VPC, further generalizations are possible. Our investigation demonstrated that the sense of the particle in a VPC may be conditioned by the type of verb it appears with (rather than just a single verb) in most of the cases. That is, particles may convey the same sense when they appear with any of the verbs in a specific verb ontology class.[13] For example, the particle *down* exhibits *Completely* sense with the verbs in the TRIPS' ontology class ONT::PURSUE, as can be seen in *The internet **tracked** DOWN this guy's stolen car ...* and *A motorist **chased** DOWN, slapped and threatened a boy ...* .

In addition, we observed an interesting fact that particles *up* and *out* seem to be in complementary distribution with respect to various verb ontology classes for the *Completely* sense. That is, for *Completely* sense, either *up* or *out* is used but not both with verbs from a specific verb ontology class.[14] For example, with verb ontology class ONT::ACQUIRE, *up* is used with *Completely* sense, *out* cannot be used with the verbs in this ontology class with the same sense. Notice *Completely* sense in the VPC *acquire UP* in *Techstars has **acquired** UP Global* but we do not observe a VPC *acquire OUT* with the same sense. Similarly, with the verb ontology class ONT::EVOKE-TIREDNESS, *out* is used with *Completely* sense, but *up* cannot be used. Notice *Someone's a bit **tuckered** OUT* but not ***tuckered** UP*.

There are certain other generalizations observed for specific senses of particles corresponding to the semantic relation labels. For example, the verb takes a particle with an *Aspectual* sense as its MANNER argument and the *Aspectual* sense particle takes the verb as a FIGURE.

Such information is encoded in the ontology as restrictions on the relevant arguments for the relevant sense ontology types as well as relevant verb ontology types. For simplification for demonstration, we use the three example cases men-

---

cle usage, there is an implicit argument which is explicitly present in the prepositional usage.

[12]For a better idea of what information the lexical entries and semantic/ontology classes carry in TRIPS lexicon, browse http://www.cs.rochester.edu/research/cisd/projects/trips/lexicon/browse-ont-lex-ajax.html

[13]We find that different verb ontology types that were distinguished for other reasons in TRIPS (Allen et al., 2007) ontology also line up with the particles.

[14]This observation about the complementary distribution of usage between *up* and *out* may not be accidental. The Law of Differentiation (Paul, 1890), (Bréal, 1900), and the Avoid Synonymy principle (Kiparsky, 1983), (Clark, 1987) have been proposed in the lexico-semantic sphere which suggest that languages prefer to not have a given semantic slot be filled by two distinct lexical items.

tioned above and show how such information is encoded in the ontology. First of all, as mentioned above, the lexical entry for the particle lists the senses it can convey. Hence, *down*, *up* and *out* would include ONT::COMPLETELY in their lexical entry. Also the entry for the sense ontology type ONT::COMPLETELY would include Word-Net sense keys for particles *down*, *up* and *out*. The sense ontology type ONT::COMPLETELY specifies for its FIGURE argument all the verb ontology types with which a particle gets this sense. Note here we list all the verb ontology types with which we get the *Completely* sense irrespective of the specific particles with which we get the sense.[15] Hence, ONT::COMPLETELY would specify for its FIGURE argument ontology types ONT::PURSUE, ONT::ACQUIRE as well as ONT::EVOKE-TIREDNESS. The restriction with regard to specific particle is captured in the verb ontology type. Each of the verb ontology types specify for their MANNER argument all the particles that can take that role (i.e., they can get *Completely* sense). Hence, verb ontology type ONT::PURSUE would specify for its MANNER argument particle *down*, verb ontology type ONT::ACQUIRE would specify particle *up* and verb ontology type ONT:EVOKE-TIREDNESS would specify particle *out*.

Similar generalizations are available for various Direction senses and a similar approach is taken to encode corresponding information. The main difference lies in the semantic roles, e.g., for *Direction* sense class particles, the verb assigns a RESULT argument role instead of the MANNER argument role and the verb ontology types specify a less restricted set of particles for the RESULT argument (since many of the direction particles can constitute VPCs with the verbs in a specific verb ontology class). One of the classic examples for VPCs with direction sense particles is with verb ontology types corresponding to motion verbs.

5.1 Difficult cases

We describe below a few interactions between the verb ontology classes, particles, their senses and the verb arguments which the ontology does not have a way to handle currently. We leave these for future work.

We observe that the object (possibly the AFFECTED or AFFECTED-RESULT argument)[16] of the VPC may have an impact on the sense a particle gets. For example, in *I cleaned OUT **the desk***, the particle *out* is interpreted as having *Completely* sense whereas in *I cleaned OUT **the dirt***, it seems to have the *Direction* sense.

The order of the particle and the object may also affect the interpretation the particle gets. For example, in *help OUT **a friend***, the particle only gets the *Completely* sense. But in the reverse order for the particle and the object, e.g., in *help **a friend** OUT* as in "help a friend out of a difficult/unsafe situation", *Direction* sense is also possible.[17]

While ontology can specify semantic features for the verbal arguments for correct assignment of semantic roles to them, it cannot currently restrict senses that the particles may get in VPCs based on the semantic features of the verbal arguments. Similarly, the link between the argument position and the particle sense cannot be handled currently.

6 Procedure to compute meaning of sentences with VPCs

For the task of interpreting sentences with VPCs, we first need to determine if the VPC is compositional or not. We use heuristics mentioned in Section 3.1 to determine the compositionality of VPC. For the compositional cases, we get the senses for the verb and the particle from the ontology and/or WordNet. In the rest of this section, we walk through the process of computing the semantics of a sentence containing a compositional VPC using a broad coverage deep semantic parser driven by ontology.

Let's say the sentence we want to interpret is *She cleaned up her room*. The sentence involves the VPC *clean up* with the verb *clean* and the particle *up*. Let's say, the particle *up* has the following senses encoded in the ontology: *Direction*, *Completely*, and *Ready*. As mentioned in Section 5, there are certain constraints on verb ontology types (as well as verb/VPC arguments) for the parser to pick one of these senses of the particle when co-occurring with the verb. Depending on

---

[15]However, note since the ontology is hierarchical, there is no need to list all the children ontology types as well if the parent ontology types are included.

[16]AFFECTED-RESULT is a semantic role our ontology uses for entities that undergo a change at the end of the event. The AFFECTED role is used for entities that changed over the course of the event in some way.

[17]In fact, this seems to be a relatively general pattern as is pointed out by Fraser (1976) that a directional adverbial tends to follow the construction.

compliance or violations of all such constraints, the parser assigns scores for various parse options involving these senses. The parse with the highest score is selected as a semantic representation of the sentence involving the VPC.

In the sentence *She cleaned up her room*, the verb *clean* (ONT::CLEAN which appears under ONT::CHANGE-STATE in the ontology) is not among the list of relevant verb ontology types with which a *Direction* sense is licensed for the particle *up*. Additionally, a restriction on the verb argument for the *Direction* sense is that the argument have a semantic feature [+moveable] which is also violated in the given sentence, *the room* is generally not a moveable entity. Hence, the parser assigns a low score to the parse which involves the *Direction* sense for the particle *up* in this sentence.

The *Ready/Active* sense requires restrictions on the verbs that they take cognitive entities or processes as their AFFECTED arguments. The AFFECTED argument for the verb *clean*, namely *the room*, does not satisfy this restriction. Hence, the parser assigns a low score for the parse involving a *Ready/Active* sense for the particle *up* in the given sentence.

The constraints for the *Completely* sense of the particle *up* are satisfied for this sentence, the verb *clean* is among the set of verbs in the ontology type (ONT::CHANGE-STATE) with which the relevant particle has been identified in the ontology to get this sense. Hence, the parser assigns a higher score to the parse for the sentence with the *Completely* sense for the particle *up*. Among the three parses involving each of the above-mentioned senses of the particle, since the parse with the *Completely* sense gets the highest score, the parse is selected as the semantic representation of the sentence.

7 Conclusion

In order to attain broad coverage understanding, a system need not only identify multi-word expressions such as verb-particle constructions, but must compute their meaning. It is not plausible to hand enumerate all the possible combinations, although WordNet is an admirable start. We have described an approach where the meaning of a wide range of VPCs are computed compositionally, with the large advantage that VPCs not explicitly found in the lexicon can be both identified and semantically interpreted. To accomplish this, we identified the core senses of particles that have broad application across verb classes. This information is used while building computational lexicons. We also discussed some difficult cases involving interesting interactions between verb ontology classes, particles, their senses and the verb arguments which the ontology does not have a way to handle currently. We leave these for future work. Finally, we demonstrated through an example how grammatical/semantic/ontological information, that enables compositional parsing, is used to obtain full semantic representation of sentences.

Acknowledgments

This work has been partially supported by the DARPA Big Mechanism program under ARO grant W911NF-14-1-0391 and the DARPA CwC program under ARO grant W911NF-15-1-0542. We would also like to thank anonymous reviewers for their useful feedback. Also we thank William de Beaumont for technical support.

References

James F. Allen and Choh Man Teng. 2017. Broad coverage, domain-generic deep semantic parsing. In *Proceedings of the AAAI Spring Symposium, Computational Construction Grammar and Natural Language Understanding 2017*.

J. Allen, M. Dzikovska, M. Manshadi, and M. Swift. 2007. Deep linguistic processing for spoken dialogue systems. In *Proceedings of the ACL 2007 Workshop on Deep Linguistic Processing*, pages 49–56. Association for Computational Linguistics.

J. Allen, M. Swift, and W. de Beaumont. 2008. Deep semantic analysis of text. In *Symposium on Semantics in Systems for Text Processing (STEP)*.

Timothy Baldwin, Colin Bannard, Takaaki Tanaka, and Dominic Widdows. 2003. An empirical model of multiword expression decomposability. In *Proceedings of the ACL 2003 Workshop on Multiword Expressions: Analysis, Acquisition and Treatment - Volume 18*, MWE '03, pages 89–96, Stroudsburg, PA, USA. Association for Computational Linguistics.

Colin Bannard, Timothy Baldwin, and Alex Lascarides. 2003. A statistical approach to the semantics of verb-particles. In *Proceedings of the ACL 2003 Workshop on Multiword Expressions: Analysis, Acquisition and Treatment - Volume 18*, MWE '03, pages 65–72, Stroudsburg, PA, USA. Association for Computational Linguistics.

Colin Bannard. 2002. Statistical techniques for automatically inferring the semantics of verb-particle constructions. Technical report.

M. Bréal. 1900. *Semantics*. Translated by Mrs. H. Cust. Henry Holt, New York.

Ping Chen. 1986. Discourse and particle movement in english. *Studies in Language*, 10:79–95.

E. V. Clark. 1987. The principle of contrast. In B. MacWhinney, editor, *Mechanisms of Language Acquisition*, pages 1–33. Academic Press.

Paul Cook and Suzanne Stevenson. 2006. Classifying particle semantics in english verb-particle constructions. In *Proceedings of the Workshop on Multiword Expressions: Identifying and Exploiting Underlying Properties*, pages 45–53.

Nicole Dehé. 2002. *Particle verbs in English: Syntax, information structure and intonation*. John Benjamins.

Christiane Fellbaum. 1998. *WordNet: An Electronic Lexical Database*. MIT Press.

B. Fraser. 1976. *The Verb-Particle Combination in English*. Academic Press.

John A. Hawkins. 2000. The relative order of prepositional phrases in english: Going beyond manner-place-time. *Language Variation and Change*, 11:231–266.

Ray Jackendoff. 1997. *The Architecture of the Language Faculty*. MIT Press.

Ray Jackendoff. 2002. English particle constructions, the lexicon, and the autonomy of syntax. In *Verb-Particle Explorations*. Mouton de Gruyter.

C. Johnson and C. J. Fillmore. 2000. The framenet tagset for frame-semantic and syntactic coding of predicate-argument structure. In *Proceedings of the first conference on North American chapter of the Association for Computational Linguistics*, pages 56–62. Morgan Kaufmann Publishers Inc.

P. Kiparsky. 1983. Word-formation and the lexicon. In F. Ingemman, editor, *Proceedings of the 1982 Mid-America Linguistics Conference*, pages 47–78. University of Kansas, Dept. of Linguistics.

Karin Kipper-Schuler. 2005. *VerbNet: A broad-coverage, comprehensive verb lexicon*. Ph.D. thesis, Computer and Information Science Dept., University of Pennsylvania, Philadelphia, PA, 6.

Barbara Lohse, John A. Hawkins, and Thomas Wasow. 2004. Domain minimization in english verb-particle constructions. *Language*, 80:238–261.

Diana McCarthy, Bill Keller, and John Carroll. 2003. Detecting a continuum of compositionality in phrasal verbs. In *Proceedings of the ACL 2003 Workshop on Multiword Expressions: Analysis, Acquisition and Treatment - Volume 18*, MWE '03, pages 73–80, Stroudsburg, PA, USA. Association for Computational Linguistics.

George A. Miller. 1995. Wordnet: A lexical database for english. 38(11):39–41.

Antonio Moreno-Ortiz, Chantal Pérez-Hernández, and M. Ángeles Del-Olmo. 2013. Managing multiword expressions in a lexicon-based sentiment analysis system for spanish. In *Proceedings of the 9th Workshop on Multiword Expressions (MWE 2013)*, pages 1–10. Association for Computational Linguistics.

Elizabeth M. O'Dowd. 1998. *Prepositions and particles in English: A discourse-functional account*. Oxford University Press.

J. Patrick and J. Fletcher. 2004. Differentiating types of verb particle constructions. In *Proc. of Australasian Language Technology Workshop 2004 (ALTW2004)*.

H. Paul. 1890. *Principles of the History of Language*. Translated by H. A. Strong from the 2nd German Edition. McGrath, Reprinted College Park, MD. 1970.

Andrea Tyler and Vyvyan Evans. 2003. *The Semantics of English Prepositions: Spatial Scenes, Embodied Meaning, and Cognition*. Cambridge University Press, New York.

Aline Villavicencio. 2003. Verb-particle constructions and lexical resources. In *Proceedings of the ACL 2003 Workshop on Multiword Expressions: Analysis, Acquisition and Treatment - Volume 18*, MWE '03, pages 57–64, Stroudsburg, PA, USA. Association for Computational Linguistics.

Aline Villavicencio. 2006. Verb-particle constructions in the world wide web. In P. Saint-Dizier, editor, *Computational Linguistics Dimensions of the Syntax and Semantics of Prepositions*, pages 115–130. Springer.

Veronika Vincze, Nagy T. István, and Gábor Berend. 2011. Multiword expressions and named entities in the wiki50 corpus. In *Proceedings of Recent Advances in Natural Language Processing*, pages 289–295.

P. Vossen. 1997. Eurowordnet: a multilingual database for information retrieval. In *Proceedings of the DELOS workshop on Cross-language Information Retrieval*.

Rule-Based Translation of Spanish Verb+Noun Combinations into Basque

Uxoa Iñurrieta, Itziar Aduriz*, Arantza Díaz de Ilarraza, Gorka Labaka, Kepa Sarasola
IXA NLP group, University of the Basque Country
University of Barcelona
usoa.inurrieta@ehu.eus, itziar.aduriz@ub.edu
a.diazdeilarraza|gorka.labaka|kepa.sarasola@ehu.eus

Abstract

This paper presents a method to improve the translation of Verb-Noun Combinations (VNCs) in a rule-based Machine Translation (MT) system for Spanish-Basque. Linguistic information about a set of VNCs is gathered from the public database Konbitzul, and it is integrated into the MT system, leading to an improvement in BLEU, NIST and TER scores, as well as the results being significantly better according to human evaluators.

1 Introduction

Multiword Expressions (MWEs) constitute a challenging phraseological phenomenon for Natural Language Processing (NLP). They are formed by more than one word, but the whole expression has to be taken into account in order to understand its meaning (Sag et al., 2002). They are very frequent in natural language, but their processing is not straightforward, especially due to their morphosyntactic variability. Furthermore, difficulties multiply when it comes to Machine Translation (MT), since MWEs are not usually translated word for word and, hence, sophisticated processing methods are needed.

In this paper, we will deal with Verb-Noun Combinations (VNCs), and we will explain how MWE-specific linguistic information can be used to improve a rule-based MT system which translates Spanish into Basque, namely Matxin (Mayor et al., 2011). After discussing some related work (Section 2), a brief explanation about Matxin and the way it handles MWEs will be given (Section 3). Then, the experimental setup will be presented (Section 4), and results will be shown (Section 5).

2 Related Work

MWEs are word combinations that need to be treated as a whole in order to get good results in lexically-sensitive NLP tasks (Sag et al., 2002). Not all MWEs are morphosyntactically fixed –there are also semi-fixed and flexible combinations–, which makes their processing a complex task. Some kinds of MWEs, like VNCs, are specially tricky, as they are more likely to have multiple morphosyntactic variants.

Over the last decades, quite a lot of research has been done on MWE identification and extraction (Gurrutxaga and Alegria, 2011; Ramisch, 2015), which is relevant not only for NLP applications but also for other disciplines like Lexicography (Vincze et al., 2011). MWE-specific resources are being developed in a number of languages, as reported by Losnegaard *et al.* (2016) in a survey carried out within the PARSEME COST Action (IC1207).

However, not so much work has been undertaken concerning the multilingual aspects of this phraseological phenomenon, although challenges get bigger when multiple languages are involved. One of the reasons why this happens is that MWEs are not usually translated word for word from one language to another, especially when these languages are from very different typologies (Baldwin and Kim, 2010; Simova and Kordoni, 2013), as with Basque and Spanish[1].

Joint efforts are also being made towards improving Machine Translation systems, for example, within the european QTLeap project (Agirre et al., 2015). Although statistical MT systems already integrate some phraseological knowledge as a consequence of training their models on large

---

[1]Whereas Spanish is a romance language, Basque is a non-indoeuropean language which belongs to no known family. More details about the main differences between both languages are given in Section 3.

Proceedings of the 13th Workshop on Multiword Expressions (MWE 2017), pages 149–154,
Valencia, Spain, April 4. ©2017 Association for Computational Linguistics

corpora (Ren et al., 2009; Bouamor et al., 2012; Kordoni and Simova, 2014), rule-based systems often get bad results when MWEs are involved, as they tend to translate each word separately. Thus, this kind of expression being so frequent in natural language, MT systems benefit greatly from including phraseological knowledge, and several studies have shown that even the simplest method to process MWEs makes a difference in the system's translation quality (Wehrli et al., 2009; Seretan, 2014).

3 Matxin: Rule-based MT from Spanish into Basque

Matxin (Mayor et al., 2011) is an MT system which translates Spanish into Basque, two long-distance families. As opposed to Spanish, which uses prepositions, Basque is a morphologically rich language where postpositions and cases are used and word order is free. The system is rule-based, mainly because of the scarcity of parallel corpora available in these languages.

Matxin's general architecture is divided into three phases:

1. **Analysis**. The source text is analysed using the FreeLing parser (Padró and Stanilovsky, 2012), which gives morphological information, chunking information, and determines the dependency relationship between words.

2. **Transfer**. The deep syntactic representation of the Spanish sentence is transferred into an equivalent representation in Basque. During this phase, on the one hand, the lexical components in the source language are replaced with their corresponding elements in the target language, and, on the other hand, the structure is also transferred. Specific modules for Spanish-Basque translation are included in this phase, like the one to change prepositions into postpositional information.

3. **Generation**. Firstly, the nodes in each chunk and the chunks themselves are reordered in the sentence from scratch, and postpositional information is added to the chunks when needed. Then, the forms of the words in Basque are created from the labelled lexical elements. The morphological processor used for this purpose is *Morfeus* (Alegría et al., 1996).

3.1 Current MWE handling

At the moment, Matxin uses a very simple method to process MWEs. When an entry in the system's bilingual dictionary is formed by more than one word, the whole expression is treated as a fixed sequence, that is, as if it was a single word. During the transfer phase, the Spanish MWE is replaced by its corresponding Basque word(s), as shown in example (1)[2].

(1) 'A vacancy was filled.'
ES: Se *cubrió_una_plaza*.
    Refl covered a vacancy
MT: *Plaza_bat_bete* zen.
    vacancy a fill AuxV

In the case of verbal MWEs (including VNCs), verb inflection is taken into account, but the rest of the words have to follow the verb exactly like they appear in the entry. This means that morphosyntactic variation is not processed correctly, neither when identifying the MWE in the source language, nor when translating it into the target language. More details about this are given in Sections 4.1 and 4.2.

(2) 'They filled all vacancies.'
ES: *Cubrieron* todas las *plazas*.
    they-covered all the vacancies
MT: *Plaza* guztiak *estali* zituzten.
    vacancy all.abs cover AuxV
CT: *Plaza* guztiak *bete* zituzten.
    vacancy all.abs fill AuxV

(3) 'He doesn't pay me attention.'
ES: No me *hace_caso*.
    not me.IndObj he-does attention
MT: Ez nau *kasu_egiten*.
    not AuxV.DObj attention do
CT: Ez dit *kasu(rik) egiten*.
    not AuxV.IndObj attention.part do

In example (2), the VNC *cubrir plazas* is not identified as a MWE and, as a consequence, the wrong lexical choice is done when translating it into Basque. In example (3), on the other hand, the VNC is identified well, but the grammatical information of its Basque translation is incorrect, because the system ignores that the Basque VNC needs an indirect object instead of a direct one.

---

[2]In examples, we use ES for the Spanish text to be translated, MT for the result of the MT system, and CT for the correct Basque translation.

4 Experimental setup

The VNC set used for the experiment consisted of 92 combinations taken from the Konbitzul database[3], where a number of Spanish VNCs and their Basque translations are collected along with linguistic data. The combinations in Konbitzul were gathered from several sources; the set we used here originally came from the Elhuyar Spanish-Basque dictionary[4] and was then analysed and tailored to meet the requirements of the database. According to the information in Konbitzul, 57 out of the 92 combinations were morphosyntactically semi-fixed, while the resting 26 were completely flexible.

Concerning the corpus, 4,991 sentences were selected from a bigger parallel corpus made of cross-domain texts collected by web-crawling and automatically aligned between Spanish and Basque. It was expressly crafted for this experiment, meaning that it did not consist of random sentences but of selected sentences containing: either instances of the Spanish VNCs in our set (Example 4), or both the verb and the noun of a given VNC in our set, but not being part of the VNC in this context (Example 5). This allowed us to test the performance of the MT system both when the VNC needed to be processed as a whole and when the verb and the noun needed to be translated separately.

> (4) Iban *dando voces* por la calle.
> they-went giving voices on the street
> 'They were shouting on the street.'

> (5) Aquellas *voces* le *dieron* una pista.
> those voices her.IndObj gave a clue
> 'Those voices gave her a clue.'

The information in Konbitzul was first used to help to identify instances of the VNCs when analysing the source text (Section 4.1), and then to transfer the source sentence into the target language (Section 4.2). Therefore, the identification of VNCs was done within the Analysis phase of the translation procedure, and their translation was done within the Transfer phase, the Generation phase not needing any special adaptation for MWE handling (Section 3).

4.1 Identifying the Spanish VNCs

In Konbitzul, comprehensive linguistic information is specified for the VNC set we use here, including some features specifically analysed for NLP purposes. The morphosyntactic classification is first used, according to which the VNCs can be of three types: fixed, semi-fixed or flexible.

When a given VNC is classified as flexible, it means that, concerning morphosyntax, the noun and the verb work as any other noun and verb in the sentence, that is, they can have as many variants as any non-phraseological VNC.

> (6) Me *da* muchísimo *miedo*.
> me.IndObj gives very-much fear
> 'It scares me very much.'
> ¡Qué *miedo* me *da*!
> what fear me.IndObj gives
> 'How scary (I find it)!'

On the other hand, when the VNC is classified as semi-fixed, some restrictions are needed in order to distinguish occurrences of the VNC from other sentences where the verb and the noun are present but should not be treated as an MWE.

> (7) *Estoy* muy *de acuerdo*.
> I-am very of agreement
> 'I agree very much.'
> *Estoy* harta *del acuerdo*.
> I-am fed-up of-the agreement
> 'I'm fed up with the agreement.'

In example (7), two sentences are shown, both of which contain the verb *estar* and the noun *acuerdo* preceded by the preposition *de*. In the first sentence, those words constitute a MWE (*estar de acuerdo*, 'agree'), but not in the second one, where the noun phrase (NP) has a determiner. By restricting determiners from the NP in the VNC, the system identifies a MWE in the first sentence but not in the second one[5].

For the identification task, we followed the same procedure as the one used in (Iñurrieta et al., 2016). First of all, the method currently used by Matxin is run, that is: word sequences are searched for against entries in the database, taking verb infletion into acount, but not considering the potential variability of the rest of the elements.

---

[3] http://ixa2.si.ehu.eus/konbitzul
[4] http://hiztegiak.elhuyar.eus/

[5] All restrictions are collected and explained in (Iñurrieta et al., 2016).

Then, automatically-produced chunking information and syntactic dependencies are used, and morphosyntactic restrictions specified in Konbitzul are applied (Example 7).

4.2 Translating the VNCs into Basque

Concerning translation, Konbitzul classifies the Spanish VNCs according to what needs to be changed when translating them into Basque: lexicon, grammar, or both lexicon and grammar.

For the VNCs needing lexical treatment, Basque equivalents are specified for the verb and the noun in Spanish. This information is integrated into Matxin, so that, when a VNC is identified, the system does not translate it regularly (Example 8).

> (8) 'The topic aroused interest.'
> ES: El tema *despertó interés*.
>   the topic awakened interest
> MT: Gaiak *interesa esnatu* zuen.
>   topic.erg interest awaken AuxV
> CT: Gaiak *interesa piztu* zuen.
>   topic.erg interest turn-on AuxV

On the other hand, for the VNCs needing special grammatical treatment, the features that need to be taken into account are specified. For those cases, exceptional rules are added within the Transfer phase, so that the specified feature(s) is/are not translated regularly.

The features specified in the database are:

- Cases or postposition marks of the NPs
- Determiner irregularities
- Number and definiteness of the NPs
- Syntactic relations of the verbs and the NPs
- Postpositions of open slots

In example (9), for instance, the Basque NP needs a postposition other than the one automatically given as a translation of the Spanish preposition. Furthermore, it needs to be indefinite, but it would be translated as definite if no special rule was applied.

> (9) 'She treats me with respect.'
> ES: Me *trata con respeto*.
>   she-me.DObj treats with respect
> MT: *Errespetuarekin tratatzen* nau.
>   respect.soc treat AuxV
> CT: *Errespetuz tratatzen* nau.
>   respect.ins treat AuxV

When it comes to example (10), the noun in the Spanish VNC is preceded by a preposition, and this prepositional phrase works as a modifier of the verb. On the other hand, the combination has an object which works as an open slot, that is, an element which is always present but can be filled with any NP. In the Basque translation, the object of the verb in the VNC is actually the noun in the VNC, and the open slot is a postpositional phrase which works as a modifier. Therefore, both the syntactic relation and the postposition of the open slot need special rules to be processed correctly.

> (10) 'They miss him.'
> ES: Lo *echan en falta*.
>   him.IndObj throw in lack
> MT: *Faltan botatzen* dute.
>   lack.ine throw AuxV
> CT: Haren *falta sumatzen* dute.
>   his lack.abs feel AuxV

5 Results

After integrating all the linguistic information into Matxin, the system was evaluated using three automatic evaluation metrics: BLEU (Papineni et al., 2002), NIST (Doddington, 2002) and TER (Snover et al., 2006). Evaluation was carried out without casing, and two systems were compared: (a) the original one, Matxin, and (b) the same system with VNC-specific information.

System	BLEU	NIST	TER
Matxin	7.28	3.88	84.36
Matxin-VNC	7.50	3.90	84.27

Table 1: BLEU, NIST and TER scores obtained by Matxin with and without VNC-specific information

As shown in Table 1, all scores improve when VNC-specific information is used. The greatest improvement is obtained in BLEU score (0.22 points), and results are statistically significant according to paired bootstrap resampling ($p>0.05$). It must be noted that BLEU scores are low for Spanish-Basque, and this result means a relative increase of 3.02%.

5.1 Human evaluation

Apart from using automatic evaluation metrics, three human evaluators were also given a representative sample of the sentences translated differently by both systems and were asked to compare them. All evaluators were Spanish and Basque native speakers: two of them (A and B) were linguists, whereas the third one (C) had no linguistic background.

System	A	B	C
Matxin-VNC	77.50%	77.50%	46.50%
Matxin	6.50%	8%	40.50%
No preference	16%	14.50%	13%

Table 2: Scores by three human evaluators

Although scores clearly show that the system with VNC-specific information gets better results, they also suggest that improvements are much more evident for linguists than for native speakers with no linguistic background (Table 2). In fact, 43.52% of the evaluation set led to disagreements among annotators, but 78.57% of these (33% of the whole set) were cases in which both linguists said the new system performed better while annotator C chose the other translation.

Taking into account that only a few combinations were tested and the corpus used was specifically prepared based on those combinations, it can be foreseen that the overall improvement this method would produce on large corpora would not be as significant. However, as the kind of linguistic information we chose is proved to have a positive effect on the system's output, we conclude that this methodology is relevant and useful for further investigation.

6 Conclusion

In the experiment presented in this paper, linguistic information was used to improve the translation of VNCs in Matxin, a rule-based MT system for Spanish-Basque. MWE-specific linguistic information was gathered from Konbitzul, a database collecting data about a list of VNCs, and this information was then used both for the identification of idiomatic VNCs in Spanish and for their translation into Basque.

After integrating information about 92 VNCs into Matxin, the system was evaluated on a 4,991-sentence cross-domain corpus, using three automatic metrics: BLEU, NIST and TER. The score that raised the most was BLEU, with an increase of 0.22 points (3.02%). A human evaluation was also carried out, where the improvement became even more evident, even if it also suggested that linguists are more likely to notice improvements than native speakers with no linguistic background.

It must also be noted that the corpus we used here was specifically crafted for this experiment, which means that the improvement would probably not be as significant in a bigger general corpus. However, results are positive as a start, and we intend to keep investigating how this methodology can be enhanced. The next step will be to add more VNCs and test them in bigger corpora, so that conclusions can be drawn at a greater scale.

Acknowledgments

Uxoa Iñurrieta's doctoral research is funded by the Spanish Ministry of Economy and Competitiveness (BES-2013-066372). The work was carried out in the context of the SKATeR (TIN2012-38584-C06-02), EXTRECM (TIN2013-46616-C2-1-R) and TADEEP (TIN2015-70214-P) projects.

References

Eneko Agirre, Iñaki Alegría, Nora Aranberri, Mikel Artetxe, Ander Barrena, António Branco, Arantza Díaz de Ilarraza, Koldo Gojenola, Gorka Labaka, Arantxa Otegi, et al. 2015. Lexical semantics, Basque and Spanish in QTLeap: Quality Translation by Deep Language Engineering Approaches. *Procesamiento del Lenguaje Natural*, 55:169–172.

Iñaki Alegría, Xabier Artola, Kepa Sarasola, and Miriam Urkia. 1996. Automatic morphological analysis of basque. *Literary and Linguistic Computing*, 11(4):193–203.

Timothy Baldwin and Su Nam Kim. 2010. Multiword expressions. In *Handbook of Natural Language Processing, Second Edition*, pages 267–292. Chapman and Hall/CRC.

Dhouha Bouamor, Nasredine Semmar, and Pierre Zweigenbaum. 2012. Identifying bilingual multiword expressions for statistical machine translation. In *Proceedings of the 8th International Conference on Language Resources and Evaluation (LREC 2012)*, pages 674–679.

George Doddington. 2002. Automatic evaluation of machine translation quality using n-gram co-occurrence statistics. In *Proceedings of the second international conference on Human Language Technology Research*, pages 138–145. Morgan Kaufmann Publishers Inc.

Antton Gurrutxaga and Iñaki Alegria. 2011. Automatic extraction of nv expressions in basque: basic issues on cooccurrence techniques. In *Proceedings of the Workshop on Multiword Expressions: from Parsing and Generation to the Real World*, pages 2–7. Association for Computational Linguistics.

Uxoa Iñurrieta, Arantza Díaz de Ilarraza, Gorka Labaka, Kepa Sarasola, Itziar Aduriz, and John Carroll. 2016. Using linguistic data for english and spanish verb-noun combination identification. In *The 26th International Conference on Computational Linguistics (COLING 2016): Technical Papers*, pages 857–867.

Valia Kordoni and Iliana Simova. 2014. Multiword expressions in machine translation. In *Proceedings of the 9th International Conference on Language Resources and Evaluation (LREC 2014)*, pages 1208–1211.

Gyri Losnegaard, Federico Sangati, Carla Parra Escartín, Agata Savary, Sacha Bargmann, and Johanna Monti. 2016. Parseme survey on MWE resources. In *Proceedings of the 10th International Conference on Language Resources and Evaluation (LREC 2016), Paris, France. European Language Resources Association (ELRA)*.

Aingeru Mayor, Iñaki Alegría, Arantza Díaz De Ilarraza, Gorka Labaka, Mikel Lersundi, and Kepa Sarasola. 2011. Matxin, an open-source rule-based machine translation system for basque. *Machine translation*, 25(1):53–82.

Lluís Padró and Evgeny Stanilovsky. 2012. Freeling 3.0: Towards wider multilinguality. In *Proceedings of the 8th International Conference on Language Resources and Evaluation (LREC 2012)*, pages 2473–2479.

Kishore Papineni, Salim Roukos, Todd Ward, and Wei-Jing Zhug. 2002. BLEU: a method for automatic evaluation of machine translation. In *Proceedings of the 40th Annual Meeting of the Association for Computational Linguistics*, pages 311–318.

Carlos Ramisch. 2015. *Multiword Expressions Acquisition*. Springer.

Zhixiang Ren, Yajuan Lü, Jie Cao, Qun Liu, and Yun Huang. 2009. Improving statistical machine translation using domain bilingual multiword expressions. In *Proceedings of the Workshop on Multiword Expressions: Identification, Interpretation, Disambiguation and Applications (ACL 2009*, pages 47–54. Association for Computational Linguistics.

Ivan A Sag, Timothy Baldwin, Francis Bond, Ann Copestake, and Dan Flickinger. 2002. Multiword expressions: A pain in the neck for nlp. In *International Conference on Intelligent Text Processing and Computational Linguistics*, pages 1–15. Springer.

Violeta Seretan. 2014. On collocations and their interaction with parsing and translation. In *Informatics*, volume 1, pages 11–31. Multidisciplinary Digital Publishing Institute.

Iliana Simova and Valia Kordoni. 2013. Improving English-Bulgarian statistical machine translation by phrasal verb treatment. In *Proceedings of MT Summit XIV Workshop on Multi-word Units in Machine Translation and Translation Technology*.

Matthew Snover, Bonnie Dorr, Richard Schwartz, Linnea Micciulla, and John Makhoul. 2006. A study of translation edit rate with targeted human annotation. In *Proceedings of association for machine translation in the Americas*, volume 200.

Orsolya Vincze, Estela Mosqueira, and Margarita Alonso Ramos. 2011. An online collocation dictionary of Spanish. In *Proceedings of the 5th International Conference on Meaning-Text Theory*, pages 275–286.

Eric Wehrli, Violeta Seretan, Luka Nerima, and Lorenza Russo. 2009. Collocations in a rule-based mt system: A case study evaluation of their translation adequacy.

Verb-Particle Constructions in Questions

Veronika Vincze[1,2]
[1]University of Szeged
Institute of Informatics
[2]MTA-SZTE Research Group on Artificial Intelligence
`vinczev@inf.u-szeged.hu`

Abstract

In this paper, we investigate the behavior of verb-particle constructions in English questions. We present a small dataset that contains questions and verb-particle construction candidates. We demonstrate that there are significant differences in the distribution of WH-words, verbs and prepositions/particles in sentences that contain VPCs and sentences that contain only verb + prepositional phrase combinations both by statistical means and in machine learning experiments. Hence, VPCs and non-VPCs can be effectively separated from each other by using a rich feature set, containing several novel features.

1 Introduction

Multiword expressions (MWEs) contain more than one tokens but the whole unit exhibits syntactic, semantic or pragmatic idiosyncracies (Sag et al., 2002). Verb–particle constructions (VPCs), a specific type of MWEs, consist of a verb and a preposition/particle (like *set up* or *come in*). They often share their surface structures with compositional phrases, e.g. the phrases *to set up the rules* and *to run up the road* look similar but the first one contains a multiword expression while the other one is just a compositional phrase. This fact makes it hard to identify them on the basis of surface patterns. However, there are some syntactic or semantic processes that can be used to distinguish MWEs from compositional phrases. For instance, question formation (WH-movement), passivization and pronominalization are often listed among the distinctive tests (see e.g. (Kearns, 2002)). Phrasal-prepositional verbs usually employ the WH-words *what* or *who*, leaving the preposition at the end of the sentence as

in *What did you set up?* In contrast, questions formed from compositional phrases usually contain the WH-words *where* or *when* as in *Where did you run?* However, the questions **Where did you set?* and **What did you run up?* are unacceptable.

In this study, we aim at investigating the behavior of verb-particle constructions in English questions. As a first step of our study, a database of questions will be created that contains verb-particle constructions and verb – prepositional phrase pairs. We will analyze these data from a quantitative point of view. This dataset will also constitute the training and test datasets for machine learning experiments. A rich feature set including morphological, semantic, syntactic and lexical features will be employed to learn the difference between verb-particle constructions and verb – prepositional phrase pairs in questions.

2 Related Work

Verb-particle constructions have been paid considerable attention in natural language processing. Baldwin and Villavicencio (2002) detected verb-particle constructions in raw texts on the basis of POS-tagging, chunking, statistical and lexical information. Kim and Baldwin (2006) relied on semantic information when detecting verb-particle constructions. Nagy T. and Vincze (2011) introduced a rule-based system using morphological features to detect VPCs in texts. Tu and Roth (2012) used syntactic and lexical features to classify VPCs candidates on a crowdsourced corpus. Nagy T. and Vincze (2014) implemented VPC-Tagger, a machine learning-based tool that selects VPC candidates on the basis of syntactic information and then classifies them as VPCs or not, based on lexical, syntactic and semantic features. Smith (2014) extracted VPCs from an English–Spanish parallel subtitles corpus.

Proceedings of the 13th Workshop on Multiword Expressions (MWE 2017), pages 155–160,
Valencia, Spain, April 4. ©2017 Association for Computational Linguistics

Here, we differ from earlier approaches in that we focus on just questions and we examine how linguistic features of questions may help in identifying VPCs in texts.

3 Data Collection

For data collection, we used three English corpora. First, we made use of the Google Web Treebank (Bies et al., 2012), which contains texts from the web annotated for syntactic (dependency) structures. Second, we used QuestionBank (Judge et al., 2006), which contains 4000 questions from two different sources: a test set for question-answering systems and a collection of question-answer type pairs. Each sentence in the treebank is assigned their constituency structures. Third, we used the Tu & Roth dataset (Tu and Roth, 2012), which contains verb-particle constructions and verb-prepositional phrase combinations.

From all three sources of data, we automatically filtered the sentences and selected questions from them. Furthermore, we also selected sentences that ended in a preposition or a particle (based on morphological information) and we grouped them into two classes: positive examples (questions with VPC) and negative examples (questions where the last token was a preposition due to preposition stranding). After these filtering steps, we got 280 questions out of which 227 were negative examples and the remaining 53 were positive examples. We parsed these sentences with the Bohnet dependency parser (Bohnet, 2010) in order to get a unified syntactic representation of the data. We will analyze these data from a quantitative point of view and report some statistics on them. This dataset will also be exploited by a machine learning system that aims at classifying each VPC candidate as a positive or negative one, which will be described in Section 5.

4 Statistical data

Here we will show some statistical data on the distribution of verbs, particles and WH-words in our dataset. We emphasize that our dataset is small and thus our results should be interpreted as showing only particular tendencies, and they should not be generalized.

4.1 Verbs

We first investigated what the distribution of the most frequent verbs are in the data. Table 1 shows

	positive	negative	total
be	0	36	36
come	5	18	23
get	10	2	12
go	3	2	5
grow	3	0	3
look	1	2	3
make	6	19	25
set	1	0	1
stand	0	32	32
take	2	2	4
turn	1	1	2
other	21	113	134

Table 1: Distribution of verbs.

the results, which are significant (χ^2-test, p = 6.72297E-12).

The data reveal that there are some interesting differences in the distribution of verbs. For instance, it is a small set of verbs that can occur in positive examples (i.e. as part of a VPC), and there are verbs that occur exclusively as negative examples in the data such as *be* or *stand*.

4.2 Prepositions

We also analyzed the distribution of prepositions in positive and negative sentences. The results are shown in Table 2. Again, the results are significant (χ^2-test, p = 5.50637E-30). As can be seen, a small set of prepositions is responsible for most of the positive data. On the other hand, there are prepositions that do not occur in verb-particle constructions (at least in this dataset). Thus, the preposition itself seems to be a good indicator whether the construction is a genuine VPC or not.

Having a closer look at directional prepositions (marked with bold in Table 2), i.e. prepositions the meaning of which is related to spatial movement, a similar picture can be drawn. The prepositions *down*, *out* and *up* usually occur as parts of VPCs while *in* and *into* usually occur as parts of prepositional phrases. Results are significant (χ^2-test, p = 3.16905E-15).

The dependency labels of the prepositions are shown in Table 3. Results are significant here as well (χ^2-test, p = 9.58168E-09). Table 4 illustrates whether the preposition had any dependents in the syntactic tree and if yes, what its label was. Results are significant (χ^2-test, p = 0.0234).

	positive	negative	total
about	2	3	5
along	0	1	1
by	1	3	4
down	3	0	3
for	0	61	61
in	5	72	77
into	0	6	6
off	4	1	4
on	8	12	20
out	15	2	17
over	0	1	1
through	1	0	1
to	0	4	4
up	12	1	13
other	2	61	63

Table 2: Distribution of (**directional**) prepositions.

	positive	negative	total
ADV	12	110	122
PRT	37	59	96
other	4	58	62

Table 3: Dependency labels of prepositions. ADV: adverbial modifier, PRT: particle.

	positive	negative	total
COORD	1	0	1
PMOD	7	57	64
no child	45	170	215

Table 4: Dependency labels of the dependents of prepositions. COORD: coordination, PMOD: prepositional modifier.

	positive	negative	total
how	9	3	12
what	10	193	203
when	8	1	9
where	6	14	20
whom	1	0	1
why	2	0	2
which	0	3	3
who	0	5	5
other	17	8	25

Table 5: WH-words.

	positive	negative	total
WDT	4	8	12
WP	10	194	204
WRB	24	18	42
other	15	7	22

Table 6: POS codes of WH-words. WDT: WH-determiner, WP: WH-pronoun, WRB: WH-adverb.

4.3 WH-words

We also investigated the distribution of WH-words in the data. As can be seen from Tables 5 and 6, both WH-words and their morphological codes show significant differences between positive and negative sentences (χ^2-test, p = 2.89581E-25 for WH-words, p = 4.45435E-22 for codes). As for their dependency labels (see Table 7), question words functioning as adverbials of manner (MNR) and time (TMP) occur almost exclusively in sentences containing VPCs while when they function as subjects (SBJ), objects (OBJ) or arguments of prepositions (PMOD), the sentence usually does not contain a VPC. Results are significant (χ^2-test, p = 1.42263E-10).

5 Machine Learning experiments

We also carried out some machine learning experiments on the data. We implemented some of the features used by Nagy T. and Vincze (2014) and based on their results, we trained a J48 model (Quinlan, 1993) and an SVM model (Cortes and Vapnik, 1995) on the data (using Weka's (Hall et al., 2009) default settings) applying ten fold cross validation. As an evaluation metric, we used accuracy score. We use majority labeling as a baseline result, which yields an accuracy score of 81.07%.

	positive	negative	total
ADV	3	0	3
LOC	2	1	3
MNR	7	0	7
OBJ	2	9	11
PMOD	0	56	56
SBJ	8	51	59
TMP	8	1	9
other	15	56	71

Table 7: Dependency labels of WH-words. ADV: adverbial modifier, LOC: adverbial modifier of location, MNR: adverbial modifier of manner, OBJ: direct object, PMOD: prepositional modifier, SBJ: subject, TMP: adverbial modifier of time.

5.1 Feature Set

We made use of the following simple features:

WH-features: the WH-word; its POS code; whether it is sentence initial or not; its distance from the previous verb; its distance from the previous noun; its dependency label.

Verbal features: we investigated whether the lemma of the verb coincides with one of the most frequent English verbs since the most common verbs occur most typically in VPCs; we investigated whether the verb denotes motion as many verbs typical of VPCs express motion.

Prepositional features: whether the preposition coincides with one of the most frequent English prepositions; whether the preposition denotes direction; whether the preposition starts with *a* since etymologically, the prefix *a* denotes motion (like in *across*); its position within the sentence; its dependency label; whether the preposition has any children in the dependency tree.

Sentence-level features: the length of the sentence; we noted if the verb and the preposition both denoted motion or direction since these combinations usually have compositional meaning (as in *go out*); whether the verb had an object in the sentence; whether a pronominal object occurred in the sentence; whether a pronominal subject occurred in the sentence.

We note that WH-features and the last three of prepositional features are novel, which means that to the best of our knowledge, they have not been implemented in VPC detection yet.

5.2 Results

First, we trained our system with all the features, which resulted in an accuracy score of 90.36% with decision trees and 92.5% with SVM. Both results are well above our baseline (81.07%). Then we wanted to examine what the effect of the features that show significant differences can be on the results. Thus, we relied on the statistical results (see Section 4), and we retrained the system with only the statistically significant features, which are listed below:

1. the length of the sentence;

2. whether the verb and the preposition both denoted motion or direction;

3. the WH-word;

4. the POS code of the WH-word;

5. the dependency label of the WH-word;

6. whether the preposition coincides with one of the most frequent English prepositions;

7. whether the preposition denotes direction;

8. the position of the preposition within the sentence;

9. the dependency label of the preposition;

10. the dependency label of the preposition's child (if any);

11. whether the lemma of the verb coincides with one of the most frequent English verbs;

12. whether the verb and the preposition both denoted motion or direction.

With these settings, we could achieve an accuracy of 90% with decision trees and 92.14% with SVM, which is slightly worse than the previous results. Thus, the contribution of non-significant features is also important to the overall performance.

With further experiments, we found that the lexical features are the most important features for the system, as using only these features, accuracy scores of 89.64% and 93.93% can be obtained. Although our dataset is small, these results indicate that VPC detection can be relatively well performed with only a handful of features. All of our results are shown in Table 8.

	SVM	**J48**
baseline	81.07	81.07
all features	92.5	90.36
only significant features	92.14	90
only lexical features	93.93	89.64

Table 8: Results of machine learning experiments.

In order to test whether the same features can be applied to other datasets, we also experimented on the entire Tu & Roth dataset (i.e. we did not carry out any filtering steps). For the sake of comparability with previous results obtained for this corpus (Tu and Roth, 2012; Nagy T. and Vincze, 2014), here we applied an SVM model (Cortes and Vapnik, 1995) with 5 fold cross validation and obtained an accuracy score of 80.05%. On the same data, Tu and Roth (2012) obtained an accuracy score of 78.6%, which was outperformed by Nagy T. and Vincze (2014) with a score of 81.92%. Thus, our results can outperform those of Tu & Roth, but are below the one reported in Nagy T. and Vincze (2014). Thus, we can argue that our algorithm is capable of identifying VPCs effectively in a bigger dataset as well.

6   Discussion

Both our statistical investigations and machine learning experiences confirmed that the most important features in VPC detection are lexical features: i.e. the lemma of the verb, the preposition/particle and the WH-word can predict highly accurately whether the candidate is a VPC or not. Furthermore, semantic properties of the preposition – like denoting direction – also play a significant role. All these facts illustrate that relying on simple lexical features, VPC detection can be carried out effectively.

However, additional features that go behind a simple morphological analysis can also contribute to performance. For instance, investigating the dependency labels of the WH-word and the preposition reveals that there are significant differences among the positive and negative examples. It should be nevertheless noted that the dependency parser applies a separate label for VPCs, i.e. the particle is attached to the verb with the PRT relation, that is, the parser itself would also be able to identify VPCs (cf. Nagy T. and Vincze (2014)). However, as we can see from Table 3, the parser's performance is not perfect as it could achieve only

an accuracy of 73.21% on our dataset and 58.13% on the Tu & Roth dataset. Thus, other features are also necessary to be included in the system.

Applying new features also contributed to the overall performance. We retrained our model on the Tu & Roth dataset without features that were implemented by us, in other words, we just applied features that had been introduced in earlier studies. In this way, we obtained an accuracy score of 77.46%, which means a gap of 3.81 percentage points. Thus, the added value of new features is also demonstrated.

7   Conclusions

In this paper, we investigated how verb-particle constructions behave in questions. We constructed a small dataset that contains questions and carried out statistical analyses of the data and also some machine learning experiments. From a statistical point of view, we found that there are significant differences in the distribution of WH-words, verbs and prepositions/particles in sentences that contain VPCs and sentences that contain only verb + prepositional phrase combinations. Dependency parsing also revealed some interesting facts, e.g. investigating whether the preposition has any children in the dependency tree proved also to be a significant factor. All these features proved useful in our machine learning settings, which demonstrated that VPCs and non-VPCs can be effectively separated from each other by using a rich feature set, containing several novel features. Our results achieved on a benchmark dataset are also very similar to those reported in the literature, thus the value of relying on additional features based on WH-words was also shown.

In the future, we would like to extend our database with additional examples and we plan to improve our machine learning system.

Acknowledgments

The work described in this paper has been supported by the IC1207 PARSEME COST action[1] and has been carried out during a Short Term Scientific Mission at Stanford University. The author is grateful to Dan Flickinger for his helpful comments and remarks on this paper.

---

[1] http://www.parseme.eu

References

Timothy Baldwin and Aline Villavicencio. 2002. Extracting the unextractable: A case study on verb-particles. In *Proceedings of the 6th Conference on Natural Language Learning - Volume 20*, COLING-02, pages 1–7, Stroudsburg, PA, USA. Association for Computational Linguistics.

Ann Bies, Justin Mott, Colin Warner, and Seth Kulick. 2012. English Web Treebank. Technical report, Linguistic Data Consortium, Philadelphia. LDC2012T13.

Bernd Bohnet. 2010. Top accuracy and fast dependency parsing is not a contradiction. In *Proceedings of Coling 2010*, pages 89–97.

Corinna Cortes and Vladimir Vapnik. 1995. *Support-vector networks*, volume 20. Kluwer Academic Publishers.

Mark Hall, Eibe Frank, Geoffrey Holmes, Bernhard Pfahringer, Peter Reutemann, and Ian H. Witten. 2009. The WEKA data mining software: an update. *SIGKDD Explorations*, 11(1):10–18.

John Judge, Aoife Cahill, and Josef Van Genabith. 2006. Questionbank: Creating a corpus of parse-annotated questions. In *Proceedings of the 21st International Conference on Computational Linguistics and 44th Annual Meeting of the ACL (COLING-ACL-06)*, pages 497–504.

Kate Kearns. 2002. *Light verbs in English.* Manuscript.

Su Nam Kim and Timothy Baldwin. 2006. Automatic identification of English verb particle constructions using linguistic features. In *Proceedings of the Third ACL-SIGSEM Workshop on Prepositions*, pages 65–72.

István Nagy T. and Veronika Vincze. 2011. Identifying Verbal Collocations in Wikipedia Articles. In *Proceedings of the 14th International Conference on Text, Speech and Dialogue*, TSD'11, pages 179–186, Berlin, Heidelberg. Springer-Verlag.

István Nagy T. and Veronika Vincze. 2014. VPC-Tagger: Detecting Verb-Particle Constructions With Syntax-Based Methods. In *Proceedings of the 10th Workshop on Multiword Expressions (MWE)*, pages 17–25, Gothenburg, Sweden, April. Association for Computational Linguistics.

Ross Quinlan. 1993. *C4.5: Programs for Machine Learning.* Morgan Kaufmann Publishers, San Mateo, CA.

Ivan A. Sag, Timothy Baldwin, Francis Bond, Ann Copestake, and Dan Flickinger. 2002. Multiword Expressions: A Pain in the Neck for NLP. In *Proceedings of the 3rd International Conference on Intelligent Text Processing and Computational Linguistics (CICLing-2002*, pages 1–15, Mexico City, Mexico.

Aaron Smith. 2014. Breaking bad: Extraction of verb-particle constructions from a parallel subtitles corpus. In *Proceedings of the 10th Workshop on Multiword Expressions (MWE)*, pages 1–9, Gothenburg, Sweden, April. Association for Computational Linguistics.

Yuancheng Tu and Dan Roth. 2012. Sorting out the Most Confusing English Phrasal Verbs. In *Proceedings of the First Joint Conference on Lexical and Computational Semantics - Volume 1: Proceedings of the Main Conference and the Shared Task, and Volume 2: Proceedings of the Sixth International Workshop on Semantic Evaluation*, SemEval '12, pages 65–69, Stroudsburg, PA, USA. Association for Computational Linguistics.

Simple Compound Splitting for German

Marion Weller-Di Marco
Institut für Maschinelle Sprachverarbeitung, Universität Stuttgart
Centrum für Informations- und Sprachverarbeitung, LMU München
`dimarco@ims.uni-stuttgart.de`

Abstract

This paper presents a simple method for German compound splitting that combines a basic frequency-based approach with a form-to-lemma mapping to approximate morphological operations. With the exception of a small set of hand-crafted rules for modeling transitional elements, our approach is resource-poor. In our evaluation, the simple splitter outperforms a splitter relying on rich morphological resources.

1 Introduction

In German, as in many other languages, two (or more) words can be combined to form a compound, leading to an infinite amount of new compounds. For many NLP applications, this productive word formation process presents a problem as compounds often do not appear at all or only infrequently in the training data. A typical NLP application that benefits from compound handling is statistical machine translation (SMT). For example, a compound that does not occur in the training data cannot be translated. However, the components of a compound often occur in the training data and can be used to translate a previously unseen compound. Thus, making the parts of a compound accessible through compound splitting when training an SMT system leads to a better lexical coverage and, consequently, to improved translation quality. Similarly, in an information retrieval scenario, information about the individual parts of a compound helps to generalize and can thus lead to improved performance.

The basis for successful compound handling in NLP applications is the decomposition of a complex compound into its components. This is not a trivial task, as the compound parts are not always just concatenated as in *Reis|feld* ('rice field'), but are often subject to morphological modifications. For example, the components can be connected with a transitional element, as the *-er* in *Bild<u>er</u>|buch* ('picture book'); or parts of the modifier can be deleted, for example *Kirch|turm* ('church tower'), where the final *-e* of the lemma *Kirch<u>e</u>* is deleted. Furthermore, the modifier components can undergo non-concatenative morphological modifications such as changing a vowel in the word stem ("Umlautung"), for example *Buch* → *Büch-* in *B<u>ü</u>cher|regal* ('book shelf').

To split compounds into meaningful parts, and in particular to obtain a lemmatized representation of the modifier, all these morphological operations need to be considered and modeled accordingly.

There are many approaches for compound splitting, ranging from simple substring operations (e.g. Koehn and Knight (2003)) to linguistically sound splitting approaches relying on high-quality morphological resources (e.g. Fritzinger and Fraser (2010)). This paper aims at the "middle ground" of this spectrum by combining a minimum amount of linguistic information with corpus-derived statistics. We present a simple method for compound splitting that makes linguistically informed splitting decisions, but requires only minimal resources. It relies on a small set of handcrafted rules to model transitional elements, but all other morphological operations (such as "Umlautung") are induced from a mapping of inflected word forms to the word lemma – this can be easily obtained from large part-of-speech tagged corpora. Our approach makes use of the fact that many of the forms that are taken on by compound modifiers are equal to inflected forms (typically plural or genitive forms) and thus can be observed in corpora. Thus, an explicit modeling of morphological operations for the modifier is often not necessary. Furthermore, we make use of part-of-speech information for a flat analysis of the compound, as illustrated below:

Proceedings of the 13th Workshop on Multiword Expressions (MWE 2017), pages 161–166,
Valencia, Spain, April 4. ©2017 Association for Computational Linguistics

Häuserfassade   →   haus_NN fassade_NN
house front

Abfüllanlage   →   abfüllen_V anlage_NN
filling facility

In contrast to morphological resources, which typically involve a large amount of manual work, part-of-speech taggers are easily available and cheap to use even for very large corpora. We thus consider the presented splitting approach as essentially resource-poor.

In the remainder of the paper, we first outline the splitting method, and then evaluate the splitting quality on a set of more than 51,000 German nominal compounds. In a comparison with the splitting results obtained with a well-acclaimed splitter relying on a high-quality morphological resource, our simple splitter obtains competitive results.

2 Related Work

Koehn and Knight (2003) present a frequency-based approach to compound splitting for German. They use word frequencies derived from corpus data to identify compound parts. Different splitting analyses are then ranked based on the geometric mean of subword frequencies. They allow two linking elements (*-s* and *-es*), as well as the deletion of characters. Their basic approach is extended by part-of-speech tags and a bilingual lexicon to restrict the selection of splitting options. Despite the simplicity of the basic approach, they report imrovements in translation quality for German–English translation. Stymne (2008) extends the algorithm by Koehn and Knight (2003) with the 20 most frequent morphological transformations and explores the effect on factored machine translation.

Macherey et al. (2011) present an unsupervised method to compound splitting that does not rely on any handcrafted rules for transitional elements or morphological operations. Their method uses a bilingual corpus to learn morphological operations. Ziering and van der Plas (2016) take this idea a step further, but avoid relying on parallel corpora and instead learn "morphological operation patterns" based on inflectional information derived from lemmatized monolingual corpora. Phenomena such as "Umlautung" are learned as a replacement operation between lemma and inflected form. Riedl and Biemann (2016) present a method based on the assumption that a compound's components are semantically similar, to identify valid splitting points. Their method is based on a distributional thesaurus

and a set of "atomic word units" obtained from corpus data. It does not include normalization of the modifier, but only identifies the splitting points of a compound. Fritzinger and Fraser (2010) use the morphological resource SMOR (Schmid et al., 2004) to obtain splitting points. Multiple splitting options are ranked according to the geometric mean of the subword frequencies.

The approach presented in this paper is based on a splitting method outlined in Weller and Heid (2012) where it is used as a basis for term alignment of bilingual vocabulary in a scientific domain. With the main focus on alignment, the paper does not provide much information on the splitting technique itself. We re-implemented and extended the splitting approach, and present it in more detail with a comparison to a state-of-the-art splitter by Fritzinger and Fraser (2010).

3 Simple Compound Splitting via Form-to-Lemma Mapping

The splitting approach presented in this paper is similar to the frequency-based approach by Koehn and Knight (2003), but is extended with a mapping from inflected forms to lemmas to approximate compounding morphology. Assuming that the components of a compound also occur as inflected forms, a frequency list of lemmatized word forms serves as training data, in combination with a small set of possible transitional elements. In the splitting process, this allows to map a modifier such as *Häuser*, which is also a plural form, to the lemma *Haus* ('house')[1]. Additionally, we also use part-of-speech tags in order to restrict splitting possibilities to content words only (e.g. adjectives, nouns, verbs) and to avoid incorrect splits into short, but highly frequent inflected words, such as splitting the simple word *Gründer* ('founder') into *grün|der* ('green|the'), where *der* is a definite article. At the same time, the part-of-speech tags allow to label the components and thus to provide a flat analysis. In the splitting process, the part-of-speech-tags of the modifier(s) can vary between all tags available in the training data, whereas the tag of the compound head is equal to the tag of the entire compound

---

[1]Lemmatizing the modifier is not possible with the splitting algorithm by Koehn and Knight (2003), which outputs the observed modifier form minus potential transitional elements, leading to different representations for different modifier realizations of the same lemma, e.g. *länderspiel → länder|spiel* ('country match': international match) vs. *landeswährung → land|währung* ('country currency': national currency).

(which is part of the input to the splitting process).

The splitting process begins with partitioning the compound into two substrings, which can then be split again in two substrings, respectively[2]. To be accepted as a valid substring, the substring must be found in the list of lemmas (via form-to-lemma mapping), after being modified for transitional elements, if necessary (cf. section 4). In this first splitting step, it is however possible to keep an "intermediate substring" that is to be split into valid substrings at the next splitting step, as illustrated by the word *Breitflügelfledermaus* ('wide wing bat: serotine bat')

comp.	Breitflügelfledermaus
input	breitflügelfledermaus_NN
split-1	breitflügel_XX fledermaus_NN
split-2	breit_ADJ flügel_NN fledermaus_NN

The part *breitflügel* does not exist as an individual word, and thus cannot be found in the lemma and part-of-speech lists; in the second step, it is split into the adjective *breit* and the noun *flügel*, resulting in a correct analysis.

After having determined all possible splitting points and subwords, the resulting splitting possibilities are scored by the *geometric mean* of the lemma frequencies of the parts p_i of the respective splitting. If two splitting analyses have the same score, analyses with fewer explicit morphological operations to model transitional elements are preferred.

4 Modeling Transitional Elements

While many compounds can be formed seamlessly by concatenating two ore more words, some contain transitional elements linking the components. Many transitional elements are part of the inflectional inventory, and sometimes indicate a syntactic function such as *genitive* (e.g. *Tageslicht*; 'light of the day: daylight') or a plural (e.g. *Katzenfutter*; 'food for cats: cat food '). This is, however, not always the case. The grammar *Duden* (Eisenberg et al. (1998), §879 ff.) lists the following transitional elements for noun compounds:

Noun+Noun This category has the most transitional rules, but many are part of the inflection inventory as either plural (pl) or genitive (gen) form and thus do not need to be modeled explicitly,

but are covered by the form-to-lemma mapping:

add -en	Tat**en**drang	Tat|Drang	pl
add -n	Hase**n**braten	Hase|Braten	pl
add -ens	Herz**ens**güte	Herz|Güte	gen
add -ns	Glaube**ns**frage	Glaube|Frage	gen
add -es	Kind**es**wohl	Kind|Wohl	gen
add -er	Büch**er**regal	Buch|Regal	pl
add -e	Hunde**hütte**[3]	Hund|Hütte	pl
add -s	Museum**s**leiter	Museum|Leiter	gen
	Ansicht**s**karte	Ansicht|Karte	∅
rem. -e	Kirchturm	Kirche|Turm	∅

From this set, only modifier forms resulting from the last two rules (*add -s*, *remove -e*) are not (entirely) covered by existing inflected forms: while *-s* often marks genitive forms, this transitional element can also occur in modifiers that do not have *-s* as inflection, including the group of nouns ending with frequent nominalization suffixes such as *-ung*, *-keit* or *-ion*. Similarly, the deletion of *-e* results in forms not covered by the inflectional inventory[4].

Verb+Noun There are only two modifications for compounds with a verbal modifier:

add -en	Schreibmaschine	schreib**en**|Maschine
add -n	Wanderweg	wander**n**|Weg

For verbal modifiers containing a nasal (m, n), an additional deletion of *-e-* might be required, for example *Rechengerät* → *rechnen\|Gerät*.

Other+Noun For all other modifiers (adjective, adverb, preposition), no modification is required.

Implemented Rules Based on the enumeration above, the morphological operations applied to the modifier are modeled as follows:

- Noun: *remove -s*
- Noun: *add -e*
- Noun: *remove -s, add -e*
- Verb: *add -en* (including deletion of *-e* in the context of *n,m*)
- Verb: *add -n*

All other morphological modifications are covered by mapping an inflected (plural or genitive) form to the lemma; this includes the phenomenon of

---

[2]This limits the number of splits to 4 components in total, which is sufficient for most applications, even though the number of components in a compound can be infinite.

[3]There can be some exceptions to this rule where the modifier form is not a plural form, e.g. *Mauseloch – Maus\|Loch*.

[4]Both *add -s* and *remove -e* can actually only be applied to feminine nouns. However, as we only use basic POS-tags, this restriction is not used in the splitting process.

"Umlautung" which changes a vowel in the word stem when building the plural form, e.g. *Buch – Bücher*. Modeling more transitional elements is not necessary, and can even be harmful: for example, a *remove rule* for *-er* can result in incorrect analyses, as *-er* is not only a plural suffix, but can also represent a nominalization suffix that is part of the lemma, such as *Fischerboot → Fischer|boot* ('fisherman boat') vs. **Fisch|boot* ('fish|boat').

5 Restricting Splitting Operations

In some cases, the selection of components or the application of particular transitional rules leads to incorrect splits. We employ two strategies to prevent some systematically occurring problems.

First, the splitting allows to define stop-words that should not be used as compound components. This concerns, for example, high-frequent verb prefixes, such as *ge-, be-, ver-* or similar items, that cannot stand alone, but nonetheless occur in the training data. Alternatively, such entries can be excluded from the word/lemma lists used to estimate the splitting statistics, cf. section 6.

Furthermore, it is possible to forbid specific operations for particular nouns: this concerns words that are identical to other, unrelated words after removing or adding transitional elements. In contrast to the stop-word list, such words cannot be completely excluded; instead, the list specifies the word in combination with the forbidden operation.

For example, adding an *e* to the word *Reis* ('rice') changes the word to *Reise* ('journey') – thus, the *add -e* operation should not be performed for this word. In the current implementation, there are 17 entries (of which 4 restrict the removal of *-s* and 13 restrict the addition of *-e*, corresponding to the two implemented modifier modifications for nouns). The list of restricted operations does not have a big impact on the overall performance: using the 17 entries results in 121 more correct splitting analyses in a test set of more than 51,000 nouns. However, it is useful to avoid systematic mis-splittings and can be easily extended.

6 Training Data and Categories

The training data consists of two lists: a mapping of inflected forms to lemmas with indication of the part-of-speech tag, and a lemma-POS-frequency list. Such lists can easily be derived from tagged corpora. Since the splitting routine relies on word frequencies, some simple cleaning steps help to im-

prove splitting results: in particular high-frequent "non-words" can harm the splitting quality. Filtering the training data in order to remove such words is likely to be rewarded by better splitting outputs.

Since not all POS-tags make sense as modifier, the tags for this category are restricted to

- **adverbs** *wieder|Aufforstung* 're|forestation'
- **adjectives** *alt|Bestand* 'old|stock'
- **particles** *auf|Preis* 'sur|charge'
- **verbs** *wandern|Weg* 'hiking track'
- **nouns** *Apfel|Kuchen* 'apple cake')
- **proper nouns** *Adam|Apfel* 'adam's apple'

There is an additional "other" tag that can be used to add further categories if necessary, for example neoclassical items such as *hydro* to analyze terms of scientific domains.

As training data, we use a large German web-corpus (1.5 Mrd tokens, based on Baroni et al. (2009)), tagged with TreeTagger (Schmid, 1994). The corpus cleaning steps contain a mapping from old to new German orthography, as well as filtering out bad "short" words (up to length 3) using a dictionary [5]. All data is lowercased for splitting.

7 Evaluation

To evaluate our splitting method, we analyze the splitting analyses obtained for a gold standard and compare them with a state-of-the-art splitter (Fritzinger and Fraser, 2010) relying on the morphological resource SMOR (Schmid et al., 2004). SMOR is a comprehensive German finite-state morphology covering inflection, derivation and compounding. As gold standard, we use the binary split compound set developed for GermaNet (Henrich and Hinrichs, 2011), containing 51,230 noun compounds. For this task, all words in the test-set should be split into two parts.

To evaluate the splitting results, we use the measures *precision* and *recall* as defined in (Fritzinger and Fraser, 2010), adapted to the simpler setting of only rating correct vs. wrong splits, without deciding whether a word should be split or not:

- **precision**: $\frac{correct\ split}{correct\ split + wrong\ split}$

- **recall**: $\frac{correct\ split}{correct\ split + wrong\ split + not\ split}$

---

[5] Dictionary obtained from `dict.cc`

	correct split	wrong split	not split	P	R	F
SMOR Split	45,054	2,914	3,262	93.93	87.94	90.84
Simple Split	46,905	4,012	313	92.12	91.56	91.84

Table 1: Comparison of splitting results for "SMOR Split" and the presented method.

Without the need to decide whether a word should be split, the *accuracy* of splitting results corresponds to the *recall*. Furthermore, we compute the F-score as

$$F = 2 \frac{precision * recall}{precision + recall} \qquad (1)$$

Table 1 shows the results of the two systems for the respective best split into two parts. A splitting analysis is counted as correct if both head and modifier are correct (i.e. exact string-match with the reference set). Part-of-speech tags are not part of the test-set and can thus not be evaluated.

The simple splitting system has a higher total number of correct splittings, and is thus better at recall/accuracy. However, the SMOR-based splitting system has a higher precision. In the combined measure F-score, the simple split system is slightly better.

Looking at the number of *unsplit* compounds, it becomes clear that the SMOR-based system employs a much more conservative splitting approach. This is due to several factors: First, some word forms are lexicalized in SMOR and thus remain unsplit, for example *Abend|Land* ('evening country: Occident'). This is often the case for non-compositional compounds, the splitting of which can turn out to be harmful in subsequent applications as their meaning cannot be derived from the parts as is the case with compositional compounds. Additionally, compounds containing a proper noun as modifier are likely not covered by SMOR's lexicon. Furthermore, the splitting approach itself is not designed to cover certain types of splittings, for example *auf_PART fahrt_NN* ('up|drive: driveway'), as particles cannot occur on their own, as opposed to nouns or verbs. The decision whether to split or not in such cases depends entirely on the application. In SMT applications, for example, it is generally assumed that over-splitting does not harm the translation quality, as the system can recover from this by translating split words as a phrase.

Summarizing, we can say that the presented simple splitting approach is competitive with a method relying on a high-quality morphological tool, despite being based only on tagged and lemmatized corpus data in combination with a small set of rules to cover transitional elements. The results show that the system is robust and nearly always produces a splitting analysis. This is due to the fact that it is independent of a hand-crafted lexicon, but rather relies on statistics derived from large corpora. As a result, even compounds containing proper names can be split, for example *Beaufort|skala* ('Beaufort scale') or *Bennett|känguru* ('Bennett kangaroo'). Furthermore, by choosing appropriate corpus data, the splitter can be easily adapted to a new domain.

8 Conclusion

We presented a simple compound splitter for German that relies on form–lemma mappings derived from POS-tagged data to approximate morphological operations. The use of part-of-speech tags restricts the splitting points, and furthermore provides a flat structure of the compounds. To model transitional elements, a small set of hand-crafted rules is defined, that can be extended with a list of words for which certain operations are forbidden.

In an evaluation of splitting performance using a gold standard of bipartite noun compounds, the presented approach performs better than a state-of-the-art splitter relying on a high-quality morphological resource. While the SMOR-based approach might be at a slight disadvantage due its different splitting philosophy, the comparison shows that the relatively resource-poor simple approach is competitive, if not better, than a method using rich linguistic information.

9 Download

The compound splitter can be found at `www.ims.uni-stuttgart.de/data/ SimpleCompoundSplitter`

Acknowledgments

This project has received funding from the European Union's Horizon 2020 research and innovation programme under grant agreement No 644402 (HimL), from the European Research Council (ERC) under grant agreement No 640550, from the DFG grants *Distributional Approaches to Semantic Relatedness* and *Models of Morphosyntax for Statistical Machine Translation (Phase Two)*.

References

Marco Baroni, Silvia Bernardini, Adriano Ferraresi, and Eros Zanchetta. 2009. The WaCky wide web: a collection of very large linguistically processed web-crawled corpora. *Language Resources and Evaluation*, 43:209–226.

Peter Eisenberg, Herrmann Gelhaus, Hans Wellmann, Helmut Henne, and Horst Sitta. 1998. *Duden – Grammatik der Deutschen Gegenwartssprache*, volume 4. Dudenverlag, Mannheim, Germany, 6th edition.

Fabienne Fritzinger and Alexander Fraser. 2010. How to Avoid Burning Ducks: Combining Linguistic Analysis and Corpus Statistics for German Compound Processing. In *Proceedings of the Fifth Workshop on Statistical Machine Translation (WMT)*, pages 224–234, Uppsala, Sweden. Association for Computational Linguistics.

Verena Henrich and Erhard Hinrichs. 2011. Determining Immediate Constituents of Compounds in GermaNet. In *Proceedings of Recent Advances in Natural Language Processing (RANLP)*, pages 420–426, Hissar, Bulgaria.

Philipp Koehn and Kevin Knight. 2003. Empirical methods for compound splitting. In *Proceedings of the 10th Conference of the European Chapter of the Association for Computational Linguistics (EACL)*, pages 187–193, Budapest, Hungary.

Klaus Macherey, Andrew M. Dai, David Talbot, Ashok C. Popat, and Franz Och. 2011. Language-independent Compound Splitting with Morphological Operations. In *Proceedings of the 49th Annual Meeting of the Association for Computational Linguistics: Human Language Technologies*, pages 1395–1404, Portland, Oregon.

Martin Riedl and Chris Biemann. 2016. Unsupervised Compound Splitting With Distributional Semantics Rivals Supervised Methods. In *Proceedings of the 2016 Conference of the North American Chapter of the Association for Computational Linguistics: Human Language Technologies*, pages 617–622, San Diego, California.

Helmut Schmid, Arne Fitschen, and Ulrich Heid. 2004. SMOR: A German Computational Morphology Covering Derivation, Composition, and Inflection. In *Proceedings of the 4th International Conference on Language Resources and Evaluation (LREC)*, pages 1263–1266, Lisbon, Portugal.

Helmut Schmid. 1994. Probabilistic part-of-speech tagging using decision trees. In *Proceedings of the International Conference on New Methods in Language Processing*, pages 44–49, Manchester, UK.

Sara Stymne. 2008. German compounds in factored statistical machine translation. In *GoTAL '08: Proceedings of the 6th International Conference on Natural Language Processing*, pages 464–475, Gothenburg, Sweden.

Marion Weller and Ulrich Heid. 2012. Analyzing and aligning german compound nouns. In *Proceedings of the the 8th International Conference on Language Resources and Evaluation (LREC)*, pages 2395–2400, Istanbul, Turkey.

Patrick Ziering and Lonneke van der Plas. 2016. Towards unsupervised and language-independent compound splitting using inflectional morphological transformations. In *Proceedings of the 2016 Conference of the North American Chapter of the Association for Computational Linguistics: Human Language Technologies*, pages 644–653, San Diego, California.

Identification of Ambiguous Multiword Expressions
Using Sequence Models and Lexical Resources

Manon Scholivet and **Carlos Ramisch**
Aix Marseille Univ, CNRS, LIF, Marseille, France
`manon.scholivet@etu.univ-amu.fr`
`carlos.ramisch@lif.univ-mrs.fr`

Abstract

We present a simple and efficient tagger capable of identifying highly ambiguous multiword expressions (MWEs) in French texts. It is based on conditional random fields (CRF), using local context information as features. We show that this approach can obtain results that, in some cases, approach more sophisticated parser-based MWE identification methods without requiring syntactic trees from a treebank. Moreover, we study how well the CRF can take into account external information coming from a lexicon.

1 Introduction

Identifying multiword expressions (MWEs) in running text with the help of a lexicon is often considered as a trivial task. In theory, one could simply scan the text once and mark (e.g. join with an underscore) all sequences of tokens that appear in the MWE lexicon. Direct matching and projection of lexical entries onto the corpus can be employed as a preprocessing step in parsing and MT (Nivre and Nilsson, 2004; Carpuat and Diab, 2010). Afterward, MWEs can be retokenized and treated as words with spaces, improving parsing and MT quality.

However, this simple pipeline does not work for many categories of MWEs, since variability and inflection may pose problems. For instance, if a lexicon contains the idiom *to make a face*, string matching will fail to identify it in *children are always making faces*. Since lexicons contain canonical (lemmatized) forms, matching must take inflection into account. This can be carried out by (a) pre-analysing the text and matching lemmas and POS tags instead of word forms (Finlayson

and Kulkarni, 2011) or (b) using lexicons of inflected MWEs (Silberztein et al., 2012).

Things get more complicated when the target MWEs are ambiguous, though. An MWE is *ambiguous* when its member words can cooccur without forming an expression. For instance, *to make a face* is an idiom meaning 'to show a funny facial expression', but it can also be used literally when someone is making a snowman (Fazly et al., 2009). Additionally, the words of the expression can cooccur by chance, not forming a phrase (Boukobza and Rappoport, 2009; Shigeto et al., 2013). For example, *up to* is an MWE in *they accepted up to 100 candidates* but not in *you should look it up to avoid making typos*.

This paper focuses on a specific category of highly frequent and ambiguous MWEs in French. Indeed, in French some of the most recurrent function words are ambiguous MWEs. For instance, some conjunctions are formed by combining adverbs like *ainsi* (*likewise*) and *maintenant* (*now*) with subordinate conjunctions like *que* (*that*). However, they may also cooccur by chance when the adverb modifies a verb followed by a subordinate clause, as in the example taken from Nasr et al. (2015) :

1. *Je mange* **bien que** *je n'aie pas faim*
   I eat **although** *I am not hungry*

2. *Je pense* **bien** **que** *je n'ai pas faim*
   I think **indeed that** *I am not hungry*

The same happens for determiners like *de la* (partitive *some*), which coincides with preposition *de* (*of*) and determiner *la* (*the*).

3. *Il boit* **de la** *bière*
   He drinks **some** *beer*

4. *Il parle* **de la** *bière*
   He talks **about the** *beer*

As showed by Nasr et al. (2015), recognizing

Proceedings of the 13th Workshop on Multiword Expressions (MWE 2017), pages 167–175,
Valencia, Spain, April 4. ©2017 Association for Computational Linguistics

these MWEs automatically requires quite high-level syntactic information such as access to a verbal subcategorization lexicon. Our hypothesis is that this information can be modeled without the use of a parser by choosing an appropriate data encoding and representative features.

The main reason why we are interested in these particular constructions is that they are frequent: in the frWaC corpus, containing 1.6 billion words, 2.1% of the sentences contain at least one occurrence of adverb+*que* construction, and 48.6% contain at least one occurrence of *de*+determiner construction. For example, the word *des* is the 7th most frequent word in this corpus. Even if some of these constructions (*bien que, ainsi que*) are more frequent in formal registers, all the others are really pervasive and register-independent.

We propose a simple, fast and generic sequence model for tagging ambiguous MWEs using a CRF. One of the main advantages of the CRF is that we do not need a syntactic tree to train our model, unlike methods based on a parser. Moreover, for expressions that are not very syntactically flexible, it is natural to ask ourself if we really need a parser for this task. Parsers are good for discontiguous MWEs, but contiguous ones in theory can be modelled by sequence models that take ambiguity into account (such as CRFs). Regardless of the syntactic nature of these ambiguities, we expect that the CRF's highly lexicalised model compensates for the lack of structure. We focus on grammatical MWEs in French, which are prototypical examples of ambiguous MWEs. Our CRF-based approach pre-identifies MWEs without resorting to syntactic trees, and results are close to those obtained by state-of-the-art parsers (Green et al., 2013; Nasr et al., 2015). We also study the influence of features derived from an external lexicon of verb valence. We believe that our approach can be useful (a) when no treebank is available to perform parsing-based MWE identification and (b) as a preprocessing step to parsing which can improve parsing quality by reducing attachment ambiguities (Nivre and Nilsson, 2004).

2 Related Work

Token identification of ambiguous MWEs in running text can be modelled as a machine learning problem that learns from MWE-annotated corpora and treebanks. To date, it has been carried out using mainly two types of models: sequence taggers and parsers. Sequence taggers, like conditional random fields (CRFs), structured support vector machines and structured perceptron, allow disambiguating MWEs using local feature sets such as word affixes and surrounding word and POS n-grams. Parsers, on the other hand, can take longer-distance relations and features into account when building a parse tree, at the expense of using more complex models.

Sequence taggers have been proven useful in identifying MWEs. MWE identification is also sometimes included into part-of-speech (POS) taggers in the form of special tags. Experiments have shown the feasibility of sequence tagging for general expressions and named entities in English and Hungarian (Vincze et al., 2011), verb-noun idioms in English (Diab and Bhutada, 2009) and general expressions in French (Constant and Sigogne, 2011) and in English (Schneider et al., 2014). Shigeto et al. (2013) tackle specifically English function words and build a CRF from the Penn Treebank, additionally correcting incoherent annotations. We develop a similar system for French, using the MWE annotation of the French Treebank as training data.

Parsing-based MWE identification requires a treebank annotated with MWEs. Lexicalized constituency parsers model MWEs as special non-terminal nodes included in regular rules (Green et al., 2013). In constituency parsers, it is possible to employ a similar approach, using special dependency labels to identify relations between words that make up an expression (Candito and Constant, 2014). This technique has shown good performance in identifying ambiguous grammatical MWEs in French (Nasr et al., 2015).

Our paper adapts a standard CRF model like the ones proposed by Constant and Sigogne (2011) and Shigeto et al. (2013) to deal with ambiguous contiguous MWEs. Our hypothesis is that sophisticated techniques like the ones described by Green et al. (2013) and Nasr et al. (2015) are not required to obtain good performances on these expressions.

3 CRF-Based MWE Tagger

We trained a CRF tagger using CRFSuite[1] (Okazaki, 2007). We used a modified version of the French Treebank (Abeillé et al., 2003) as train-

---

[1] `http://www.chokkan.org/software/crfsuite/`

i:	-2	-1	0	1	2	3
w_i:	*Il*	*jette*	*de*	*la*	*nourriture*	*périmée*
	He	*discards*	*some*		*food*	*expired*
MWE:	O	O	B	I	O	O

Figure 1: Example of BIO tagging of a sentence containing a *de*+determiner MWE.

ing data and the MORPH dataset[2] (Nasr et al., 2015) as development and test data. We also include features from an external valence lexicon, Dicovalence[3] (van den Eynde and Mertens, 2003). Since our focus is on function words, our evaluation covers adverb+*que* and *de*+determiner constructions present in the MORPH dataset.

Training Corpus The training corpus is an adaptation of the French Treebank (FTB) in CONLL format that we have transformed into the CRFsuite format. For each word, the corpus contains its wordform, lemma, POS (15 different coarse POS tags), and syntactic dependencies (that were ignored). In the original corpus, MWE information is represented as words with spaces. We have added an extra column containing MWE annotation using a Begin-Inside-Outside (BIO) encoding, as in Figure 1.

The MWE-BIO tags were generated using the following transformation heuristics:

- For adverb+*que* pairs (AQ):

    1. We scan the corpus looking for the lemmas *ainsi_que*, *alors_que*, *autant_que*, *bien_que*, *encore_que*, *maintenant_que* and *tant_que*.
    2. We split them in two new words and tag the adverb as B and *que* as I.

- For *de*+determiner pairs (DD):

    1. We scan the corpus looking for the wordforms *des*, *du*, *de_la* and *de_l'*. Due to French morphology, *de* is sometimes contracted with the articles *les* (determinate plural) and *le* (determinate singular masculine). Contractions are mandatory for both partitive and preposition+determiner uses. Therefore, we systematically separate these pairs into two tokens.

    2. If a sequence was tagged as a determiner (D), we split the tokens and tag *de* as B and the determiner as I.

    3. Contractions (*des*, *du*) tagged as P+D (preposition+determiner) were split in two tokens, both tagged as O.

- All other tokens are tagged as O, including some other types of MWEs.

The expressions under study in this paper are strictly continuous. In unreported experiments, we use the method described in (Schneider et al., 2014) to treat discontinuous MWEs (more informations in Section 5).

For the newly created tokens, we assign individual lemmas and POS tags. The word *de* is systematically tagged as P (preposition), not distinguishing partitives from prepositions at the POS level. The input to the CRF is a file containing one word per line, BIO tags as targets, and `featureName=value` pairs including n-grams of wordforms, lemmas and POS tags.

Development and Test Corpora To create our test and development (dev) corpora, we used the MORPH dataset. It contains a set of 1,269 example sentences of 7 ambiguous adverb+*que* constructions and 4 ambiguous *de*+determiner constructions. For each target construction, around 100 sentences extracted from the frWaC corpus were manually annotated as to whether they contain a multiword function word (MORPH) or accidental cooccurrence (OTHER). We have preprocessed the raw sentences as follows:

1. We have automatically POS tagged and lemmatized all sentences using an off-the-shelf POS tagger and lemmatizer independently trained on the FTB.[4] This information is used as features for our CRF.

2. We have located the target construction in the sentence and added BIO tags according to the manual annotation provided: target pairs in

---

[2] `http://pageperso.lif.univ-mrs.fr/~carlos.ramisch/?page=downloads/morph`
[3] `http://bach.arts.kuleuven.be/dicovalence/`

[4] `http://macaon.lif.univ-mrs.fr/`

MORPH sentences were tagged B + I, target pairs in OTHER sentences were tagged O.

3. For each target construction, we have taken the first 25 sentences as development corpus (dev, 275 sentences).

4. We created four targeted datasets: DEV_{AQ}, DEV_{DD}, FULL_{AQ} and FULL_{DD}, where the different construction classes are separated, in order to perform feature selection.

External Lexicon The verbal valence dictionary Dicovalence specifies the allowed types of complements per verb sense in French. For each verb, we extract two binary flags:

- queCompl: one of the senses of the verb has one object that can be introduced by *que*.[5]

- deCompl: one of the senses of the verb has a locative, temporal or prepositional paradigm that can be introduced by *de*.[6]

CRF Features We selected 37 different features (referred to as ALL) inspired on those proposed by Constant and Sigogne (2011):

- Single-token features (t_i):[7]

  - w_0 : wordform of the current token.
  - l_0 : lemma of the current token.
  - p_0 : POS tag of the current token.
  - w_i, l_i and p_i: wordform, lemma or POS of previous ($i \in \{-1, -2\}$) or next ($i \in \{+1, +2\}$) tokens.

- N-gram features ($t_{i-1}t_i$ and $t_{i-1}t_it_{i+1}$):

  - $w_{i-1}w_i$, $l_{i-1}l_i$, $p_{i-1}p_i$: wordform, lemma and POS bigrams of previous-current ($i = 0$) and current-next ($i = 1$) tokens.

  - $w_{i-1}w_iw_{i+1}$, $l_{i-1}l_il_{i+1}$, $p_{i-1}p_ip_{i+1}$: wordform, lemma and POS trigrams of previous-previous-current ($i = -1$), previous-current-next ($i = 0$) and current-next-next ($i = 1$) tokens.

- Orthographic features (orth):

  - hyphen and digits: the current word contains a hyphen or digits.
  - f-capital: the first letter of the current word is uppercase.
  - a-capital: all letters of the current word are uppercase.
  - b-capital: the first letter of the current word is uppercase, and it is at the beginning of a sentence.

- Lexicon features/Subcat features (SF):[8]

  - queV: the current word is *que*, and the closest verb to the left accepts a queCompl.
  - deV: the current word is *de*, and the closest verb to the left accepts a deCompl.

In our evaluation, we report precision (P), recall (R) and F-measure (F_1) of MWE tags. In other words, instead of calculating a micro-averaged scores over all BIO tags, we only look at the proportion of correctly guessed B tags. Since all our target expressions are composed of exactly 2 contiguous words, we can use this simplified score because all B tags are necessarily followed by exactly 1 I tag. As a consequence, the measured precision, recall and F-measure scores on B and I tags are identical.

4 Evaluation

We evaluate our approach in two experimental setups. First, we perform feature selection using the dev/test split of the MORPH dataset, both regarding coarse groups (4.1) and individual features (4.2). Then, we apply the best configuration to the whole MORPH dataset in order to compare our results with the state of the art (4.3).

4.1 Feature Selection: Coarse

Our first evaluation was performed on the dev sets for adverb+*que* (DEV_{AQ}, 175 sentences) and *de*+determiner (DEV_{DD}, 100 sentences). It includes all features described in Section 3 (ALL), and obtains an F_1 score of 75.47 for AQ and 69.7 for DD constructions, as shown in the first row of Table 1. The following rows of this table show the results of a first ablation study, conducted to identify coarse groups of features that are not discriminant and hurt performance.

---

[5]In Dicovalence, an object P1, P2 or P3 licenses a complementizer qpind

[6]In Dicovalence, the paradigm is PDL, PT or PP.

[7]t_i is a shortcut denoting the group of features w_i, l_i and p_i for a token. The same applies to n-grams.

[8]This is the same as the *subcat feature* proposed by Nasr et al. (2015).

Feature set	DEV$_{AQ}$			DEV$_{DD}$		
	P	R	F_1	P	R	F_1
`ALL`	89.55	65.22	75.47	92.00	56.10	69.70
`ALL − orth`	90.28	70.65	79.27	95.83	56.10	70.77
`ALL − W`	90.79	75.00	82.14	87.10	65.85	75.00
`ALL − SF`	91.18	67.39	77.50	88.89	58.54	70.59
`ALL −` $t_{\pm2}$	87.67	69.57	77.58	88.00	53.66	66.67
`ALL −` $t_{i-1}t_it_{i+1}$	87.84	70.65	78.31	91.67	53.66	67.69
`ALL −` $t_{i-1}t_i$	**93.55**	63.04	75.32	95.83	56.10	70.77
`ALL −` $t_{i-1}t_i - t_{i-1}t_it_{i+1}$	88.57	67.39	76.54	**96.00**	58.54	72.73
`ALL − orth − W`	90.24	**80.43**	**85.06**	87.10	65.85	75.00
`ALL − orth − W −` $t_{\pm2}$ `(REF)`	89.74	76.09	82.35	85.29	**70.73**	**77.33**

Table 1: First feature selection, removing coarse-grained feature groups.

Features	DEV$_{AQ}$			DEV$_{DD}$		
	P	R	F_1	P	R	F_1
`REF`	89.74	76.09	82.35	85.29	70.73	77.33
`REF − SF`	90.00	78.26	83.72	75.76	60.98	67.57
`REF −` $t_{-1}t_0$	90.54	72.83	80.72	85.29	70.73	77.33
`REF −` t_0t_{+1}	89.87	77.17	83.04	84.85	68.29	75.68
`REF −` $t_0t_{+1}t_{+2}$ `(BEST)`	87.36	82.61	84.92	83.78	75.61	79.49

Table 2: Second feature selection, removing fine-grained feature groups.

When we ignore orthographic features (`ALL − orth`), all scores increase for DEV$_{AQ}$ and DEV$_{DD}$, showing that MWE occurrences are not correlated with orthographic characteristics. F_1 also increases when we remove all wordform-level features, including single words and n-grams (represented by `W`). We hypothesize that the use of lemmas and POS is more adequate, since it reduces sparsity by conflating variants, so wordforms only introduce noise.

Then, we try to remove the subcat features (`ALL − SF`). This information seems important to us, because it allows assigning O tags to conjunctions and prepositions that introduce verbal complements. Surprisingly, though, the system performs better without them. We suppose that this happens because, since there are many features, the CRF disregards `SF` features anyway because they are not frequent enough. These features will be analyzed individually later (see Table 3).

Single tokens located 2 words apart from the target token should not provide much useful information, so we try to remove their corresponding features (`ALL −` $t_{\pm2}$). While this is true for DEV$_{AQ}$, it does not hold for DEV$_{DD}$. Next, we try to remove all trigram, and then all bigram features at once. When we remove trigrams, F_1 de-

creases by 2.01 absolute points in DEV$_{DD}$ and increases by 2.84 absolute points in DEV$_{AQ}$. Bigrams are somehow included in trigrams, and their removal has little impact on the tagger's performance. When we remove bigram and trigram features altogether, scores are slightly better even though a large amount of information is ignored. Since these results are inconclusive, we perform a more fine-grained selection considering specific n-grams in Table 2.

Finally, we try to remove several groups of features at the same time. When we remove both orthographic and wordform features, F_1 increases to 85.06 for DEV$_{AQ}$ and 75.00 for DEV$_{DD}$. When we remove also tokens located far away from the current one, performance increases for DEV$_{DD}$ but not for DEV$_{AQ}$. Unreported experiments have shown, however, that further feature selection (Table 2) also has better results for DEV$_{AQ}$ when we ignore $t_{\pm2}$ features. Therefore, our reference (`REF`) for the fine-grained feature selections experiments will be this set of features, corresponding to the last row of Table 1.

4.2 Feature Selection: Fine

In the second row of Table 2, we try to remove subcat features again from `REF`, because on Table 1 these features seem to hurt performance. However, this is not the case anymore. We assume that these features can be better taken into account now that there are less noisy features in the whole system.

The last three rows of the table show our experiments in trying to remove individual n-gram features that seemed not very informative or redundant to us. First, we delete the two types of bigram features independently, including wordforms, POS and lemmas. We can see that bigrams seem useful and their removal causes the scores to drop. The only exception are the results on DEV_{AQ} for the bigram t_0t_{+1}.

Finally, we remove all trigram features of the form $t_0t_{+1}t_{+2}$, . We can see that performance increases in both datasets. This makes sense because MWE identification generally does not depend on the next tokens, but on the previous ones. This is the best configuration obtained on the development datasets, and we will refer to it as BEST in the next experiments.

Our last feature selection experiments study the influence of subcategorization features individually, as shown in Table 3. We observe that deV is an important feature, because when we remove it, F_1 decreases by almost 7 absolute points on the DEV_{DD} set. The feature queV, however, seems less important, and its absence only slightly decreases the F_1 score on the DEV_{AQ} set. This is in line with what was observed by Nasr et al. (2015) for the whole dataset. In sum, these features seem to help but the system could benefit more from them with a more sophisticated representation.

Features	Dataset	P	R	F_1
BEST	DEV_{AQ}	87.36	82.61	84.92
	DEV_{DD}	83.78	75.61	79.49
BEST−queV	DEV_{AQ}	91.25	79.35	84.88
BEST−deV	DEV_{DD}	77.78	68.29	72.73

Table 3: Impact of subcat features (SF) on separate dev sets per construction.

4.3 Comparison with State of the Art

The best system obtained after feature selection was then compared with the results reported by Nasr et al. (2015) in Table 4. We include two versions of their systems since they also report experiments on including subcategorization features coming from Dicovalence.

We report the performance on the full MORPH dataset split in two parts: sentences containing adverb+*que* constructions (FULL_{AQ}) and sentences containing *de*+determiner constructions (FULL_{DD}). Even though the use of the full datasets is not ideal, given that we performed feature selection on part of these sentences, it allows direct comparison with related work.

We also report results of a simple baseline:

1. We extract from the French Treebank the list of all adverb+*que* and *de*+determiner pairs.

2. We calculate the proportion of times that they were annotated as MWEs (B-I tags) with respect to all their occurrences.

3. We keep in the list only those constructions annotated 50% of the time or more.

4. We systematically annotate these constructions as MWEs (B-I) in all sentences of the MORPH dataset, regardless of their context.

Table 4 shows that this baseline reaches 100% recall, covering all target constructions, but precision is very low due to the lack of context. Our BEST system can identify the target ambiguous MWEs much better than the baselines for both FULL_{AQ} and FULL_{DD}.

We did not expect our system to outperform parsing-based approaches, which were trained on a full treebank, have access to more sophisticated models of a sentence's syntax, and handle long-distance relations and grammatical information. Nonetheless, for some constructions we obtain results that are near to those obtained by the parsers. For FULL_{AQ}, our BEST system obtains an F_1 score that is 1.2 absolute points lower than the best parser. For FULL_{DD}, however, our best system, which includes subcategorization features, is comparable with a parser without subcategorization features. When the parser has access to the lexicon, it beats our system a significant margin of 7.99 points, indicating that the accurate disambiguation of DD constructions indeed requires syntax-based methods rather than sequence taggers.

Despite the different performances depending on the nature of the target constructions, these results are encouraging, as they prove the feasibility of using sequence taggers for the identification of highly ambiguous MWEs. Our method has mainly

	FULL$_{AQ}$			FULL$_{DD}$		
System	P	R	F_1	P	R	F_1
Baseline	56.08	100.00	71.86	34.55	100.00	51.35
Nasr et al. (2015)$-$SF	88.71	82.03	85.24	77.00	73.09	75.00
Nasr et al. (2015)$+$SF	91.57	81.79	86.41	86.70	82.74	84.67
BEST	91.08	78.31	84.21	79.14	74.37	76.68

Table 4: Comparison with baseline and state of the art.

two advantages over parsing-based MWE identification: (a) it is fast and only requires a couple of minutes on a desktop computer to be trained and (b) it does not require the existence of a treebank annotated with MWEs.

Expression	P	R	F_1
ainsi que	94.44	93.15	93.79
alors que	84.00	97.67	90.32
autant que	93.48	51.81	66.67
bien que	100.00	91.43	95.52
encore que	76.19	94.12	84.21
maintenant que	97.62	64.06	77.36
tant que	100.00	60.00	75.00
de la	67.74	72.41	70.00
de les	92.41	71.57	80.66
de le	78.05	71.11	74.42
de l'	61.11	95.65	74.58

Table 5: Performance of the BEST configuration broken down by expression.

Table 5 shows the detailed scores for each expression in the MORPH dataset. We notice that some expressions seem to be particularly hard, specially if we look at precision, whereas for others we obtain performances well above 90%. When we compare our results to those reported by Nasr et al. (2015), we can see that they are similar to ours: *ainsi*, *alors* and *bien* have F_1 higher than 90%, while *autant* and *tant* are less than 80%. The adverb+*que* constrictions with *encore* and *maintenant* are the only ones which behave differently: our system is better for *encore*, but worse for *maintenant*. Likewise, for *de*+determiner expressions, our system obtains a performance that is near to their system without subcategorization features: both approaches are more efficient to identify the plural article *de les* than the partitive constructions.

5   Conclusions and Future Work

We have described and evaluated a simple and fast CRF tagger that is able to identify highly ambiguous multiword expressions in French[9]. We have reported a feature selection study and shown that, for adverb+*que* constructions, our results are near those obtained by parsers, even though we do not use syntactic trees. While these experiments shed some light on the nature of this frequent phenomenon in French, the methodology is highly empirical and cannot be easily adapted to other contexts. Therefore, we would like to experiment different techniques for generic automatic feature selection and classifier tuning (Ekbal and Saha, 2012). This could be performed on a small development set and ease the adaptation of the tagger to other contexts.

We also think it could be interesting to test more sophisticated baselines. For instance, we could learn simple conditional rules from the training corpus depending on the lemma of the preceding verb.

Another idea for future work is to study the interplay between automatic POS tagging and MWE identification. We recall that our results were obtained using an off-the-shelf POS tagger and lemmatizer. Potentially, performing both tasks jointly could help obtaining more precise results (Constant and Sigogne, 2011).

Moreover, we are not fully satisfied with the representation of subcategorization features. We would like to study why SF features are not very useful by looking at the verbs preceding the MWEs and their feature values, performing error analysis. Furthermore, we would like to try implementing a threshold on the distance between the verb and the MWE to tag: only verbs close enough to the target construction generate subcategorization features for the MWE candidate.

We would also like to perform a cross validation

---

[9]The system described in this paper is publicly available `http://mwetoolkit.sourceforge.net`

experience, training the system on the MORPH dataset itself instead of using the French Treebank. This would allow us to quantify to what extent the CRF is able to generalize from the training data, even if it has never seen a particular expression before but only similar ones.

Finally, we would also like to experiment with other sequence tagging models such as recurrent neural networks. In theory, such models are very efficient to perform feature selection and can also deal with continuous word representations, which can include semantic information. Moreover, distributed word representations are helpful in building cross-lingual MWE identification systems.

Acknowledgments

This work has been partly funded by projects PARSEME (Cost Action IC1207), PARSEME-FR (ANR-14-CERA-0001), and AIM-WEST (FAPERGS-INRIA 1706-2551/13-7).

References

Anne Abeillé, Lionel Clément, and François Toussenel. 2003. Building a treebank for french. In Anne Abeillé, editor, *Treebanks: building and using parsed corpora*, pages 165–168. Kluwer academic publishers, Dordrecht, The Netherlands.

Ram Boukobza and Ari Rappoport. 2009. Multi-word expression identification using sentence surface features. In *Proceedings of the 2009 Conference on Empirical Methods in Natural Language Processing*, pages 468–477, Singapore, August. Association for Computational Linguistics.

Marie Candito and Matthieu Constant. 2014. Strategies for contiguous multiword expression analysis and dependency parsing. In *Proc. of the 52nd ACL (Volume 1: Long Papers)*, pages 743–753, Baltimore, MD, USA, Jun. ACL.

Marine Carpuat and Mona Diab. 2010. Task-based evaluation of multiword expressions: a pilot study in statistical machine translation. In *Proc. of HLT: The 2010 Annual Conf. of the NAACL (NAACL 2003)*, pages 242–245, Los Angeles, California, Jun. ACL.

Matthieu Constant and Anthony Sigogne. 2011. MWU-aware part-of-speech tagging with a CRF model and lexical resources. In Kordoni et al. (Kordoni et al., 2011), pages 49–56.

Mona Diab and Pravin Bhutada, 2009. *Proceedings of the Workshop on Multiword Expressions: Identification, Interpretation, Disambiguation and Applications (MWE 2009)*, chapter Verb Noun Construction MWE Token Classification, pages 17–22. Association for Computational Linguistics.

Asif Ekbal and Sriparna Saha. 2012. Multiobjective optimization for classifier ensemble and feature selection: an application to named entity recognition. *International Journal on Document Analysis and Recognition (IJDAR)*, 15(2):143–166.

Afsaneh Fazly, Paul Cook, and Suzanne Stevenson. 2009. Unsupervised type and token identification of idiomatic expressions. *Comp. Ling.*, 35(1):61–103.

Mark Finlayson and Nidhi Kulkarni. 2011. Detecting multi-word expressions improves word sense disambiguation. In Kordoni et al. (Kordoni et al., 2011), pages 20–24.

Spence Green, Marie-Catherine de Marneffe, and Christopher D. Manning. 2013. Parsing models for identifying multiword expressions. *Comp. Ling.*, 39(1):195–227.

Valia Kordoni, Carlos Ramisch, and Aline Villavicencio, editors. 2011. *Proc. of the ACL Workshop on MWEs: from Parsing and Generation to the Real World (MWE 2011)*, Portland, OR, USA, Jun. ACL.

Alexis Nasr, Carlos Ramisch, José Deulofeu, and André Valli. 2015. Joint dependency parsing and multiword expression tokenization. In *Proceedings of the 53rd Annual Meeting of the Association for Computational Linguistics and the 7th International Joint Conference on Natural Language Processing (Volume 1: Long Papers)*, pages 1116–1126. Association for Computational Linguistics.

Joakim Nivre and Jens Nilsson. 2004. Multiword units in syntactic parsing. In *MEMURA 2004 – Methodologies and Evaluation of Multiword Units in Real-World Applications (LREC Workshop)*, pages 39–46.

Naoaki Okazaki. 2007. Crfsuite: a fast implementation of conditional random fields (crfs).

Nathan Schneider, Emily Danchik, Chris Dyer, and A. Noah Smith. 2014. Discriminative lexical semantic segmentation with gaps: Running the mwe gamut. *Transactions of the Association of Computational Linguistics – Volume 2, Issue 1*, pages 193–206.

Yutaro Shigeto, Ai Azuma, Sorami Hisamoto, Shuhei Kondo, Tomoya Kouse, Keisuke Sakaguchi, Akifumi Yoshimoto, Frances Yung, and Yuji Matsumoto. 2013. Construction of English MWE dictionary and its application to POS tagging. In Valia Kordoni, Carlos Ramisch, and Aline Villavicencio, editors, *Proc. of the 9th Workshop on MWEs (MWE 2013)*, pages 139–144, Atlanta, GA, USA, Jun. ACL.

Max Silberztein, Tamás Váradi, and Marko Tadić. 2012. Open source multi-platform NooJ for NLP. In *Proc. of COLING 2012: Demonstration Papers*, pages 401–408, Mumbai, India, Dec. The Coling 2012 Organizing Committee.

Karel van den Eynde and Piet Mertens. 2003. La valence: l'approche pronominale et son application au lexique verbal. *Journal of French Language Studies*, (13):63–104.

Veronika Vincze, István Nagy T., and Gábor Berend. 2011. Detecting noun compounds and light verb constructions: a contrastive study. In Kordoni et al. (Kordoni et al., 2011), pages 116–121.

Comparing Recurring Lexico-Syntactic Trees (RLTs) and Ngram Techniques for Extended Phraseology Extraction: a Corpus-based Study on French Scientific Articles

Agnès Tutin and **Olivier Kraif**
Univ. Grenoble Alpes, LIDILEM
CS40700
38058 Grenoble cedex 9, France
`agnes.tutin,olivier.kraif@univ-grenoble-alpes.fr`

Abstract

This paper aims at assessing to what extent a syntax-based method (Recurring Lexico-syntactic Trees (RLT) extraction) allows us to extract large phraseological units such as prefabricated routines, e.g. *as previously said* or *as far as we/I know* in scientific writing. In order to evaluate this method, we compare it to the classical ngram extraction technique, on a subset of recurring segments including speech verbs in a French corpus of scientific writing. Results show that the RLT extraction technique is far more accurate for extended MWEs such as routines or collocations but performs more poorly for surface phenomena such as syntactic constructions or fully frozen expressions.

1 Introduction

Multiword expressions are diverse. They include frozen expressions such as grammatical words (e.g. *as far as*, *in order to*), non compositional idioms (e.g. *kick the bucket*), but also less frozen expressions which belong to the "extended phraseology": collocations (e.g. *pay attention*), pragmatemes (e.g. *see you later, how do you do?*) or clichés and routines (*as far as I know, as previously said* in scientific writing). Given this diversity, we think that MWE extraction techniques should be tuned according to specific kinds of MWEs. Syntax-based MWE extraction techniques produce very interesting results for collocation extraction (e.g. (Evert, 2008), (Seretan, 2011)) and are now widely used in NLP, in particular to deal with binary collocations such as *pay attention* or *widely used*. In this paper, we wish to assess to what extent a syntax-based method (Recurring Lexico-syntactic Trees (RLT) extraction)

is accurate to extract larger phraseological units such as prefabricated routines. In order to evaluate this method, we compare it to the classical ngram extraction technique on a subset of recurring segments including speech verbs in a French corpus of scientific writing. We will first present the syntax-based extraction technique and will present the methodology (corpus and linguistic typology). We will then provide some first results on a quantitative and a qualitative analysis.

2 Recurring Lexico-syntactic Trees: a syntax-based extraction technique for extended MWEs

In a dependency parsed treebank, one may be interested in identifying recurring sub-trees. From a sequence of words, it is easy to extract all the subsequences of 2..n words (for a given value of n, e.g. 8), with their frequencies (what (Salem, 1987) calls "repeated segments", also called "ngrams"). Similarly, it is possible to extract from a treebank all the sub-trees containing 2..n nodes. But combinatorics is much more larger in the case of trees: theoretically, for a tree that includes t nodes, one may have up to

$$\sum_{k=2}^{n} \binom{t-1}{k}$$

subtrees with 2..n nodes (Corman, 2012). For instance, with a sentence of 20 tokens we obtain a total of 54 ngrams of length 2 to 4, and up to 704 subtrees of 2 to 4 nodes (ibid.). To solve the computational problem due to this combinatorial explosion, we simplify it by focusing on the binary co-occurrences between nodes connected by syntactic relations (in this case dependency relations). The RLT method was developed within a software architecture centered on the notion of "syntactic co-occurrence", in the words of (Evert, 2008),

Proceedings of the 13th Workshop on Multiword Expressions (MWE 2017), pages 176–180,
Valencia, Spain, April 4. ©2017 Association for Computational Linguistics

which characterizes a significant statistical association between two words syntactically related, for example (play-OBJ->role). We used a tool called Lexicoscope ((Kraif and Diwersy, 2012); (Kraif and Diwersy, 2014)), which extracts, for a given node-word, a table that records its most significant syntactic collocates (for all or only a subset of syntactic relationships). This table is called *lexicogram*, and presents significant collocates in a way analogous to the *Sketch Engine* ((Kilgarriff and Tugwell, 2001)), except that all the involved relationships are merged into a single table. Including frequency statistics and association measures, this lexicogram contains information about the syntactic relations, and about the *dispersion*, which indicates the number of sub-corpora where the co-occurrence has been identified. This latter clue is useful to highlight general phenomena, shared by all the sub-corpora, because some recurring associations may be very prominent locally, in a small part of the corpus (even in a single document), without having general scope. The architecture of Lexicoscope allows to study the collocates for simple node-words, but also for trees, comparable to what (Rainsford and Heiden, 2014) call *keynodes*. As an example, for the sub-tree <présenter+article>we obtain the collocates of Figure 1:

We see that these collocates, when clustered two by two, may be used to reconstruct the full tree of the routine <nous + proposer + dans + cet + article>. Starting from these binary co-occurrence scheme, including a sub-tree and a single word, we developed an iterative method to extract complete recurring trees with an arbitrary number of nodes. This method is fully automated, and operates in the following manner:

1. start from an initial keynode (single word or subtree) ;

2. extract the lexicogram ;

3. expand the keynode with any collocate that exceed a given threshold of association measure ;

4. repeat step 2 for all the newly expanded keynodes.

The process is repeated as long as there are new collocates that exceed the significance threshold, and until the extracted trees have not exceeded a certain length (in the following, the maximum length will be set to 8 elements). We call "Recurring Lexico-syntactic Trees" (RLT) the recurring trees yielded by this process. These steps are illustrated in Figure 2, for the RLT corresponding to <proposer + dans + ce + article>:

This method assumes that most interesting recurring expressions have at least two adjacent nodes that are strongly associated, which allows to start the iterative process. Once the first two nodes are merged into one tree, the association measure with other nodes is usually high, even though the pairwise association measure between words is initially low (because the frequency of the initial subtree is generally much lower than the frequency of its individual words). The analysis of the results in a corpus-based study will make it possible to determine whether this hypothesis is valid.

3 Comparison of Ngrams and RLTs of Speech Verbs in Scientific Writing

3.1 Aims of the study

This study aims at comparing through concrete examples different kinds of segments extracted by the syntax-based *RLT method* and a conventional method widely used in phraseology and stylistics, the *repeated segments method* (or *n-grams*) which identify recurrent sequences of words, lemmas or contiguous punctuation ((Salem, 1987), (Biber et al., 2004)). We focused on particular recurring segments associated with 25 speech verbs, selected among several semantic subfields[1] and used to extract segments such as *comme on l'a dit* ('as previously said') or *article propose* (lit. 'article proposes'). Among these segments, the routines associated with the rhetorical and discourse functions in scientific writing are of particular interest (see also (Teufel and Moens, 2002); (Sándor, 2007); (Tutin and Kraif, 2016)). The corpus used for this experiment includes 500 scientific articles of about 5 million words in 10 fields of human science, syntactically annotated using the XIP dependency parser ((Aït-Mokhtar et al., 2002)). We evaluated qualitatively and quantitatively the segments extracted with both methods.

---

[1] e.g. 'mention', 'emphasis', 'discussion', 'formulation'...

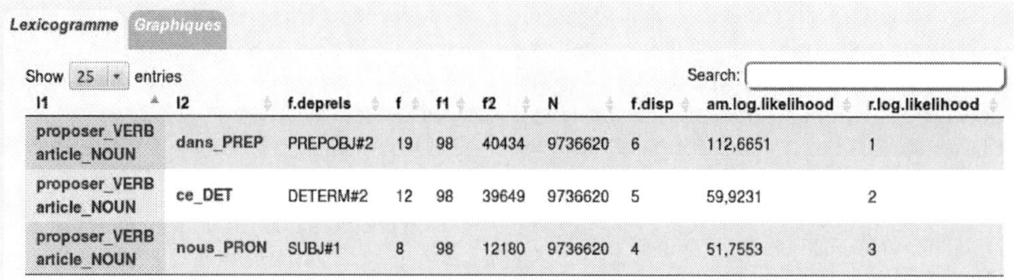

Figure 1: Extracting a lexicogram for a given subtree (<proposer+article>))

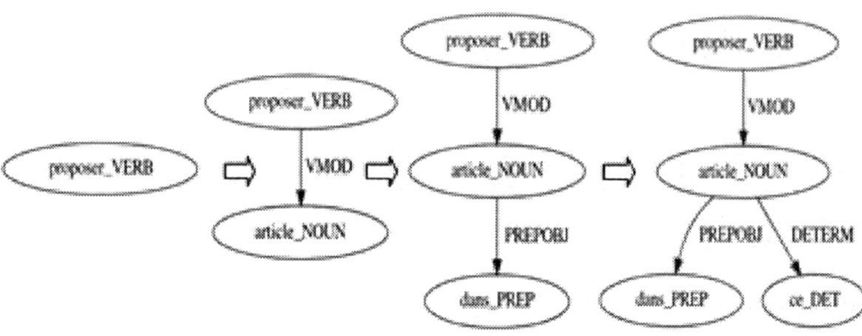

Figure 2: A three steps extraction to get the RLT <proposer + dans + ce + article>)

3.2 Extraction methods and linguistic typology of segments

Both extraction methods use the lemmatized corpus. Ngrams were extracted with the help of a homemade script, which identifies contiguous words and punctuation marks (essentially commas) occurring at least 8 times in at least 3 disciplines, and including at least 3 words. Similarly, we extracted RLTs occurring at least 8 times at each iteration (with a likelihood ratio >10.81) in at least three disciplines, including at least 3 words. The dispersion measure has proved useful for targeting cross-disciplinary expressions, and therefore the routines specific within the genre of scientific articles rather than within a specific discipline. We further characterized the extracted segments, relying on a linguistic typology in order to better understand the complementarity of both methods. A close look at the text was often necessary in order to characterize the segments more accurately.

a. Routines are sentence patterns which fulfill a rhetorical function in scientific writing, such as performing a demonstration, providing a proof, guiding the reader, etc. The following segments are routines: *comme nous le avoir souligner*(lit. 'as we have pointed it out'), *il falloir dire que* (lit. 'it must be said').

b. Collocations, unlike routines, are considered as plain binary recurring associations (cf. (Hausmann, 1989)), as in *formuler le hypothèse* (lit. formulate a hypothesis).

c. Specific syntactic constructions deal with specific alternations, e.g. passive constructions, impersonal or modal constructions, which are often characteristic of the scientific genre, e.g. *avoir être souligner* (lit. 'have been pointed out'), *permettre de préciser* (lit. 'allows to specify')

d. Frozen expressions include non compositional multiword expressions, close to idioms (see (Sag et al., 2002)), e.g. *c'est-à-dire* ('that is to say'), or *cela va sans dire* ('it goes without saying').

e. Non relevant expressions are segments which do not belong to the previous typology and are considered as irrelevant since they have no phraseological function, e.g. *avoir dire que il* (lit. 'have say that he/it'), *dire que ce ltre* (lit. 'say what this be').

4 Results

4.1 Quantitative comparison

The extractions performed with the ngram techniques produced a large set of sequences. To limit noise, we removed ngrams ending with a determiner (which proved to be redundant with segments without determiners). After filtering, there is a total of 435 ngrams to be examined. Extrcated RLTs are much less numerous (276 elements), slightly more than half of the ngrams. 124 segments are extracted by both techniques (45 % of extracted RLTs also extracted with ngram techniques). In order to assess the interest of both methods, we considered the relevance of the extracted segments according to the above linguistic typology. Figure 3 shows the results of this analysis, using raw data, while Figure 4 and Figure 5 show the relative distribution for each method.

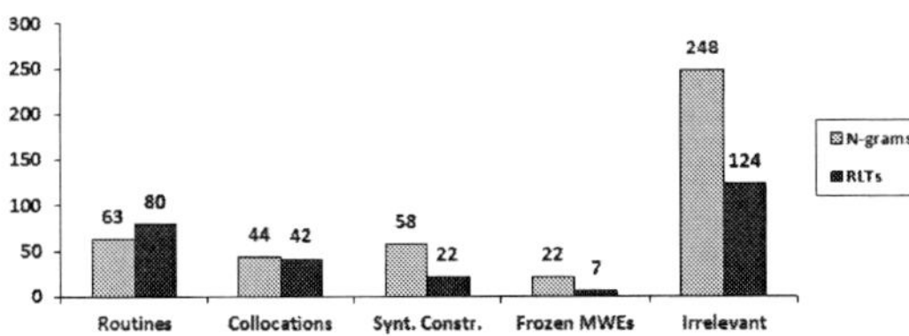

Figure 3: Comparison of results by type (raw data)

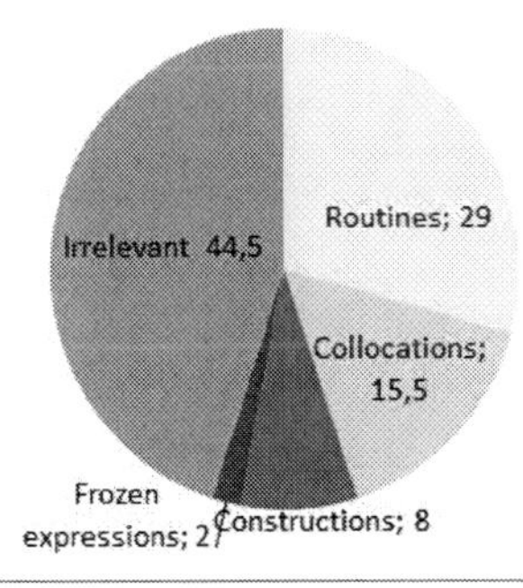

Figure 4: Distribution of results for RLTs (in %)

In general, the results broadly confirm our expectations. Regarding raw results, the RLT technique extracts less elements than the ngram technique, but a larger number of routines and a comparable number of collocations. On the other hand, for fixed expressions and constructions, which can be considered as surface phenomena among multiword expressions, the recall of the ngram technique is better. The contrast between

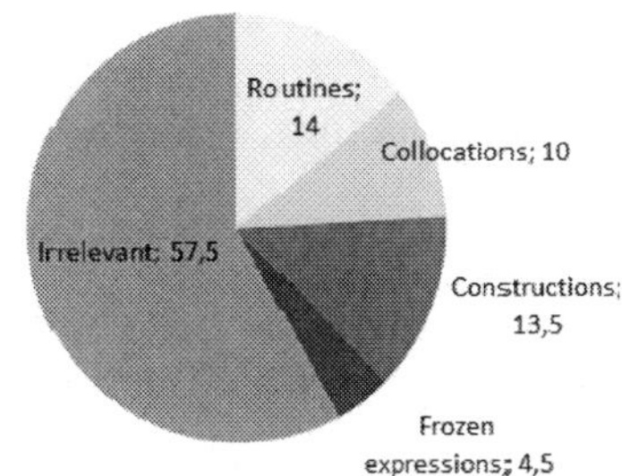

Figure 5: Distribution of results for ngrams (in %)

both approaches is even more striking when looking at the distribution of the linguistic MWE types in percentage terms (see Figures 4 and 5). The RLT technique undoubtedly produces more satisfactory results for the "extended" phraseological phenomena, such as collocations or routines, since almost half results fall into these two categories, but proves to be disappointing for fixed expressions and constructions. As regards precision rate now, the overall precision rate of the RLT technique is 55.5 %, 13 points ahead of ngram techniques, but given the complexity of RLT method, we expected a better accuracy.

4.2 Qualitative comparison

A qualitative comparison is essential to better understand the specificity of both approaches. The observation of **routines** extracted by both methods shows that expressions with contiguous elements are unsurprisingly well identified by both techniques, but frequencies are in general higher with the RLT method. Among the routines only identified by the RLT technique, we observed routines whose elements are often distant, occur in syntactic alternations or have variable determiners. Interestingly, some routines were best identified by ngram techniques than by RLT extraction techniques, e.g. routines such as 'ce + article + se + proposer + de' ('this article aims at'), due to the fact that in the dependency syntactic model used, prepositions and conjunctions are not directly related to the verb but to their arguments. This information could, however, be integrated within the RLTs with a syntactic post-treatment. Concerning **collocations**, both methods appear to be complementary. While the RLT method is more accurate with variable determiners in Verb Prep N structures (e.g. *insister sur aspect* 'insist on aspect'), it often fails to detect verb-adverb collocations due to parsing errors (e.g. *voir plus haut/plus bas* 'see above/below'. Surface phenomena (**syntactic constructions** and **fully frozen MWEs** are better extracted by ngram techniques. Again, these poor results appear to be partly related to syntactic analysis, since some dependency relations do not relate adjacent words. For example, in an expression such as *s'exprimer par, par* ('lit. to be expressed with'), the preposition *par* is not attached to the verb, but to the noun which is the prepositional complement of the verb. This kind of syntactic representation is however not specific to XIP parser and is very common among dependency models.

5 Conclusion

Our comparison of RLT and ngram extraction techniques shows clearly that the first method is more suited to extract sentence patterns and routines, which have a hierarchical structure rather than a sequential nature. The RLT technique also performs well on collocation extraction, but does not produce good results on surface phenomena such as syntactic constructions or fully frozen MWEs, where grammatical words (preposition, conjunctions, adverbs) are not sufficiently taken into account. In future work, we would like to develop the multidimensional aspect of the LRT method, by using morphosyntactic categories or semantic classes rather than lexical units. The hierarchical representation makes it possible to substitute the lemmas to more general classes, more likely to explain the abstract structure of many linguistic patterns.

References

Salah Aït-Mokhtar, J-P Chanod, and Claude Roux. 2002. Robustness beyond shallowness: incremental deep parsing. *Natural Language Engineering*, 8(2-3):121–144.

Douglas Biber, Susan Conrad, and Viviana Cortes. 2004. If you look at: Lexical bundles in university teaching and textbooks. *Applied linguistics*, 25(3):371–405.

Julien Corman. 2012. *Extraction d'expressions polylexicales sur corpus arboré*. Mémoire de master recherche Industries de la langue, Univ. Stendhal Grenoble 3.

Stefan Evert. 2008. Corpora and collocations. *Corpus linguistics. An international handbook*, 2:1212–1248.

Franz Josef Hausmann. 1989. Le dictionnaire de collocations. *Wörterbücher, Dictionaries, Dictionnaires*, 1:1010–1019.

Adam Kilgarriff and David Tugwell. 2001. Word sketch: Extraction and display of significant collocations for lexicography.

Olivier Kraif and Sascha Diwersy. 2012. Le lexicoscope: un outil pour l'étude de profls combinatoires et l'extraction de constructions lexico-syntaxiques. In *Actes de la conférence TALN 2012*, pages 399–406.

Olivier Kraif and Sascha Diwersy. 2014. Exploring combinatorial profiles using lexicograms on a parsed corpus: a case study in the lexical field of emotions. *Blumenthal P., Novakova I., Siepmann D.(éd). Les émotions dans le discours. Emotions in discourse. Peter Lang*, pages 381–394.

Thomas M Rainsford and Serge Heiden. 2014. Key node in context (knic) concordances: Improving usability of an old french treebank. In *SHS Web of Conferences*, volume 8, pages 2707–2718. EDP Sciences.

Ivan A Sag, Timothy Baldwin, Francis Bond, Ann Copestake, and Dan Flickinger. 2002. Multiword expressions: A pain in the neck for nlp. In *International Conference on Intelligent Text Processing and Computational Linguistics*, pages 1–15. Springer.

André Salem. 1987. Pratique des segments répétés. essai de statistique textuelle. *Lexicométrie et textes politiques*.

Ágnes Sándor. 2007. Modeling metadiscourse conveying the authors rhetorical strategy in biomedical research abstracts. *Revue française de linguistique appliquée*, 200(2):97–109.

Violeta Seretan. 2011. *Syntax-based collocation extraction*, volume 44. Springer Science & Business Media.

Simone Teufel and Marc Moens. 2002. Summarizing scientific articles: experiments with relevance and rhetorical status. *Computational linguistics*, 28(4):409–445.

Agnès Tutin and Olivier Kraif. 2016. Routines sémantico-rhétoriques dans lécrit scientifique de sciences humaines: lapport des arbres lexico-syntaxiques récurrents. *Lidil. Revue de linguistique et de didactique des langues*, (53):119–141.

Benchmarking Joint Lexical and Syntactic Analysis on Multiword-Rich Data

Matthieu Constant
Université de Lorraine, ATILF, CNRS
Nancy, France
`Mathieu.Constant@univ-lorraine.fr`

Héctor Martinez Alonso
Inria (ALMAnaCH)
Paris, France
`hector.martinez-alonso@inria.fr`

Abstract

This article evaluates the extension of a dependency parser that performs joint syntactic analysis and multiword expression identification. We show that, given sufficient training data, the parser benefits from explicit multiword information and improves overall labeled accuracy score in eight of the ten evaluation cases.

1   Introduction

In this paper, we expand the work of Constant and Nivre (2016) —henceforth CN16— by evaluating their system more extensively, representing Multiword Expressions (MWEs) in different ways that are linguistically motivated. Their transition-based system jointly performs lexical analysis and syntactic dependency parsing, using special transitions for MWE identification. In particular, these special transitions generate new lexical nodes for MWEs, that can also serve as nodes of the syntactic dependency trees. Their system is based on the classical split between fixed and free MWEs. Fixed MWEs defined by Sag et al. (2002) are contiguous. They are considered syntactically non-decomposable and are represented as a single syntactic node that requires a part of speech (POS) tag like all other tokens. Free MWEs are the remaining MWEs, that usually display regular internal structure and variations. The system predicts their internal syntactic structure, and their MWE status. The hypothesis behind this approach is that such a specialized extension of a standard transition-based parser to capture lexical relation for MWEs is a better option than using a regular transition based parser that relies on distributed annotation for MWEs as it is used for example in Universal Dependencies [UD] (Nivre et al., 2016).

In our experiments, we used UD, which we believe is an interesting playground because it provides different lexical-association labels such as MWEs. Nonetheless, we encounter an important drawback regarding MWEs, i.e. they are not provided with an overall POS, which plays a key role in our parsing systems. We have therefore proposed a common filler principle in order to automatically assign a POS to each MWE. Our other hypothesis is that enriching treebanks with explicit annotation of MWE status and MWE POS should help parsing accuracy. In addition, since UD treebanks may be non-projective, we have improved the parsing algorithm to account for non-projective trees, which the original work in CN16 could not provide. In the setup of CN16, only projective sentences could be used for training.

2   Joint lexical and syntactic analysis

The system by Constant and Nivre (2016) is based on a factorized lexical and syntactic representation, that consists of a graph over lexical nodes. Every lexical node corresponds to a lexical unit: either a simple unit or an MWE. It incorporates linguistic attributes (unit form, POS tag). MWE nodes may be of two sorts: fixed and free MWEs.

The representation can be decomposed into a lexical and a syntactic layer. The lexical layer is a forest of trees over lexical nodes. Every MWE is represented as a tree whose root is the lexical node of the MWE and its children are its (potentially non-adjacent) components. For instance, the verb-particle construction (VPC) *gave up* is a verbal lexical node which child nodes are *give* and *up*. The syntactic layer is a dependency tree over syntactic nodes. A syntactic node is either a simple lexical unit or a fixed MWE.

These two layers share the syntactic nodes because these nodes correspond to lexical ones. Con-

181

Proceedings of the 13th Workshop on Multiword Expressions (MWE 2017), pages 181–186,
Valencia, Spain, April 4. ©2017 Association for Computational Linguistics

Initial:	$([\,],[\,],[0,\ldots,n],\{\,\},\{\,\})$		
Terminal:	$([x],[\,],[\,],A,L)$		
Shift:	$(\sigma_l,\sigma_s,i\|\beta,A,L)$	$\Rightarrow$	$(\sigma_l\|i,\sigma_s\|i,\beta,A,L)$
Right-Arc(k):	$(\sigma_l\|x\|y,\sigma_s,\beta,A,L)$	$\Rightarrow$	$(\sigma_l\|x,\sigma_s,\beta,A\cup\{(x,k,y)\},L)$
Left-Arc(k):	$(\sigma_l\|x\|y,\sigma_s,\beta,A,L)$	$\Rightarrow$	$(\sigma_l\|y,\sigma_s,\beta,A\cup\{(y,k,x)\},L)$
Merge$_F(t)$:	$(\sigma_l\|x\|y,\sigma_s\|x\|y,\beta,A,L)$	$\Rightarrow$	$(\sigma_l\|t(x,y),\sigma_s\|t(x,y),\beta,A,L)$
Merge$_N(t)$:	$(\sigma_l,\sigma_s\|x\|y,\beta,A,L)$	$\Rightarrow$	$(\sigma_l,\sigma_s\|t(x,y),\beta,A,L)$
Complete:	$(\sigma_l,\sigma_s\|x,\beta,A,L)$	$\Rightarrow$	$(\sigma_l,\sigma_s,\beta,A,L\cup\{x\})$
Swap:	$(\sigma_l,\sigma_s\|x\|y,\beta,A,L)$	$\Rightarrow$	$(\sigma_l,\sigma_s\|y,x\|\beta,A,L)$

Figure 1: Transition system for joint syntactic and lexical analysis handling non-projectivity. This schema simply extends (Constant and Nivre, 2016) system by adding a **Swap** transition.

versely, lexical nodes are not necessarily syntactic ones: the light verb construction *make decision* is an MWE node, but is not part of the syntactic tree; only its components *make* and *decision* are. The fixed MWE *at least* is a syntactic node, but its child nodes *at* and *least* are not.

2.1 A transition-based system

The proposed transition system is a mild extension of an arc-standard system (Nivre, 2004), as schematized in Figure 1. It iteratively builds a graph over lexical nodes by applying a sequence of actions (namely transitions) from an initial parser state (namely **Initial** configuration) to a terminal state (namely **Terminal** configuration). Every parsing state is a 5-uple made of two stacks (a lexical stack σ_l and a syntactic stack σ_s), one buffer (β), a set of already predicted syntactic arcs (A) and a set of already predicted lexical trees (L). We use only one buffer in order to synchronize the prediction of the two layers, as they share elements, namely syntactic nodes. Each element popped from the buffer via the **Shift** transition is put on top of the two stacks.

The set of transitions also includes standard transitions devoted to create syntactic arcs (**Right-Arc** and **Left-Arc**) from the syntactic stack. MWE lexical trees are constructed by applying either **Merge**$_F$ for fixed MWEs or **Merge**$_N$ for free MWEs. Both transitions take the two top elements x and y on the lexical stack (and on the syntactic stack for fixed MWEs since they are shared by the two layers) and creates a new lexical node which children are x and y on top of the stack(s). The **Complete** transition is applied to complete the lexical unit on top of the lexical stack, i.e. it is moved to the set of predicted lexical trees.

The system proposed by Constant and Nivre

(2016) only works for predicting projective syntactic trees. A classical way to deal with non-projectivity is to add a **Swap** transition, permuting the two top elements on the syntactic stack, the second element being pushed back to the buffer (Nivre, 2009). This simple integration in our joint system is not as straightforward as in a classical arc-standard system. One needs to add more conditions to apply the **Shift** transition. If the buffer is not empty, the first element x is moved onto the syntactic stack. It is also pushed onto the lexical stack if the following condition holds: x must not have been already pushed on the lexical stack in order to avoid it being processed multiple times during lexical analysis.

In our experiments, we also used a partial system that predicts the syntactic layer only. For this, the lexical stack is deactivated as well as the **Merge**$_N$ and **Complete** transitions. This partial system is equivalent to the one in Nivre (2014).

3 Multiword-aware treebanks

We use the Universal Dependencies treebanks or UD (Nivre et al., 2016) to obtain data for our experiments. UD has different labels that indicate different kinds of lexical associations, some of them more apt for a treatment as fixed or free.

For fixed MWE labeled as *mwe*, UD proposes a flat, first-headed analysis. While this simplifies our task of choosing fixed MWEs for our experiments, we do not have explicit information on the part of speech that a given fixed mwe would have if it were treated as a single lexical unit.

Since the parser in Section 2 treats MWEs as single units for attachment purposes after a **Merge** transition, it is desirable to have access to the factual part of speech of that MWE, given that POS information is the most important feature to determine a word's attachment.

Incorporating POS information of MWEs in our parsers requires enriching the labels of treebanks with the POS of the overall function of the MWE, and indicating whether it is free or fixed.[1]

Fixed MWEs have a factual part of speech when treated as a unit, which need not be the part of speech of any of its parts, e.g. 'by and large' is an adverb, unlike any of its parts. However, factual part of speech of a MWE can be approximated from the MWE's syntactic label, e.g. if the overall label for 'by and large' is *advmod*, its most plausible part of speech is adverb. We refer to the most frequent POS that satisfies a certain label as **most-common filler**.

This heuristic is geared towards completing fixed-MWE information, but we also apply it to free MWEs to give account for the potential particularities in MWEs of the different treebanks.

3.1 Multiword definition scope

The *mwe* label is not the only MWE indicator. For instance, the *name* relation also encodes MWEs, often treated as named entity spans. Different languages have different extensions of the *compound* relation. In English a regular *compound* is something like 'phone **book**' while a *compound:prt* would be '**fall** off'. We use five different variants of the definition of MWE, both free and fixed, for our experiments. These variants aim at capturing semantic and syntactic variation.[2]

Variant A: *mwe* labels are fixed; *compound* (and its extensions), *cc:preconj*, *auxpass:reflex*, and *name* are free. This variant represents a fairly standard view of multiword expressions, where fixed multiwords are only the ones that are grammaticalized, and the other relations that represent multiword-related lexical association like compounds or reflexive pronouns of verbs are treated as free multiwords.

Variant B is similar to A, but also includes all verb auxiliaries as members of free multiwords, namely *aux*, *auxpass* and *cop*. This variant aims at giving account for the pragmatic preference of certain verbs to appear in specific periphrastic tenses or their lexical preference for one kind of auxiliary or modal verb.

Variant C uses the inventory of variant A, but all labels correspond to free multiwords. This variant intends to relax the hard constrain for fixed multiwords to form an uninterrupted span.

Variant D only contemplates the *mwe* label as fixed, and no free expressions. This span aims at measuring the contribution of only focusing on grammaticalized multiwords.

Variant E Same as variant D, except it is a strict variant where discontinuous spans with the *mwe* label are ignored during training.

4 Experiments

Each of the competing systems in our experiments is a combination of one of the five data variants (Section 3.1), and one of the three parsers: the full (FULL) or partial (PART) parsers in Section 2.1, or a standard transition-based parser (STD) without a lexical stack or **Merge/Complete** transitions. For instance, the FULL$_C$ system uses the FULL parser on Variant C of the multiword inventory.

We compare these systems to a baseline without special data transformations for MWEs, and that depends on the standard transition-based parser. The aim of our experiments is not to optimize a parser for UD, but to benefit from the amount and variety of data offered by it to benchmark the possibilities of joint lexical and syntactic prediction.

Data: We have chosen treebanks where the *mwe* label constitutes at least 1% of the labels in the development section, and where the support is of at least 100 instances, cf. Table 1. Note that two of these treebanks are not the canonical treebank for their respective language.

Language	Treebank	Train	Test	Dev
Catalan	*UD_Catalan*	429.2k	59.5k	58.0k
Dutch	*UD_Dutch-LassySmall*	88.9k	4.5k	4.6k
Persian	*UD_Persian*	121.0k	16.0k	15.8k
Spanish	*UD_Spanish-Ancora*	453.2k	53.6k	53.4k
Swedish	*UD_Swedish*	66.6k	20.4k	9.8k

Table 1: Treebank properties.

The only variable parameter in our experiments is the choice of system, namely of parser and data variant. We replicate the remaining parameters with the choices in (Constant and Nivre, 2016), namely 6 training iterations, static oracle, greedy perceptron learning and the same feature templates, which we do not tune for any language. Using no language tuning allows us to evaluate equally on the test and development data.

---

[1] Parser is freely available at https://github.com/MathieuConstant/lgtools

[2] Conversion code is available at https://github.com/hectormartinez/mweparse

Language	LAS_{BL}	LAS_{sys}	System	fixed LAS	fixed head	#O
Catalan	86.09	86.38	FULL_C	94.95 (+1.56)	73.60 (0)	11
Dutch	78.05	78.22	FULL_C	61.82 (+6.47)	52.17 (-0.37)	7
Persian	79.01	—	—	—	—	0
Spanish	85.56	85.77	STD_B	90.13 (-0.15)	70.95 (+7.44)	7
Swedish	81.93	82.25	STD_B	55.59 (-2.67)	50.55 (+4)	8
Catalan	86.16	86.48	PART_F	93.76 (+1.16)	78.13 (+8.11)	12
Dutch	78.83	—	—	—	—	0
Persian	78.79	79.41	FULL_C	82.26 (+2.15)	71.53 (+11.87)	6
Spanish	85.88	85.93	PART_F	87.71 (+0.89)	69.27 (+5.39)	2
Swedish	78.32	79.14	FULL_E	56.92 (+5.43)	50.28 (+12.11)	9

Table 2: Language-wise best system scores for the test (above) and development (below) sections.

5 Results

After prediction, we evaluate each parser-variant combination. Table 2 shows the results for each language for the test (above) and development (below) sections, for which we provide the Labeled Attachment Score of the baseline (LAS_{BL}), the Labeled Attachment Score of the best system above the baseline (LAS_{sys}) as well as the system's descriptor. We also provide the attachment score for the *mwe* label, which corresponds to the accuracy of identifying fixed MWEs, and the labeled accuracy of the first token of fixed MWEs, which corresponds to correctly finding the head of MWEs. For these two metrics, we provide the difference with regard to the baseline. Moreover, we provide the amount of systems out of 12 which outperform the baseline for a given language.

While using any of the variants A–D which contemplate MWEs aids syntactic prediction in general, there is no general preference. We attribute this variation to differences in corpus and linguistic properties, but also in how the UD principles are annotated on each treebank. We do observe, however, that certain parsers lend themselves better for certain data variants. For instance, variant C is best combined with the FULL parser.

The FULL parser yields an average test-section improvement of 4.7% on MWE accuracy across all treebanks and data variants with respect to the baseline, while it gives 3.6% with respect to PART system. This improvement is not only local to MWE labels. We observe a small but consistent improvement of about 0.20 both in root labeled accuracy and in the accuracy of the nominal roles for subject, direct object and nominal modifier.

Larger treebanks have more stable results and aid the learning system. Indeed, the FULL transition system, which has more operations will need more data to converge. This argument is supported by the irregularity of behavior of Dutch and Persian, which only yield improvements in one of the evaluation sections. We attribute this instability to the size of the training set and the sensitivity to sampling bias of the small evaluation sections.

We have also assessed the usefulness of the most common filler heuritistic. If during the label-enriching operation (Sec. 3) we mark the label of each part of a MWE with its original POS—instead of giving all parts of a MWE the most-common filler POS—, the LAS drops on 1-2% for all treebanks and variants. Moreover, even for the E variant using the standard parser, the system presents improvements, which is a consequence of the multiword labels, both free and fixed, containing also POS information. We consider this improvement as support evidence for our initial hypothesis.

6 Related Work

MWE processing is an ever growing research topic since Sag et al. (2002), as it has been shown in (Ramisch, 2015). On the side of MWE-aware dependency parsing, the main line of research for joint approaches is to use standard dependency parsers using special arc labels and flat structures for MWEs (Nivre and Nilsson, 2004; Eryiğit et al., 2011; Seddah et al., 2013; Nasr et al., 2015). Vincze et al. (2013) and Candito and Constant (2014) integrate richer arc labels and non-flat structures to predict internal MWE structure. Truly joint approaches incorporating special parsing mechanisms to handle MWE recognition is a recent line of research (Constant and Nivre, 2016).

On the side of UD, Silveira and Manning (2015) explore whether the UD treebank formalism needs an additional representation to improve parsing. Salehi et al. (2016) identify MWE in a surprise target language with no prior knowledge of MWE patterns, using training on a UD MWE-aware treebank of a source language.

7 Conclusions and Further Work

We have expanded the CN16 system to a more thorough evaluation, using different variants of multiword inventories. We show that, given sufficient data, the parser benefits from explicit multiword information and improves overall labeled accuracy score in eight of the ten evaluation cases.

Further work includes devising more refined strategies to generate full lexical entries for joined MWE tokens. The most-common filler can also be used to calculate their prototypical morphological features. Moreover, if the treebank is lemmatized we can create pseudolemmas for the MWEs by concatenating the lemmas of the formants. While these pseudolemmas might differ from the actual reference forms, they would have the same distribution as the overall MWEs, thereby contributing to parsing to the same extend than the other lemmas in the treebank.

We also intend to perform a more thorough evaluation of the improvements of non-projective parsing against the increased complexity of the parser, and how it relates to the effect on projectivity of the flat, projective subtrees enforced by fixed MWEs.

The overall system should also be evaluated on the, as per February 2017, upcoming version 2.0 of Universal Dependencies, where the treatment of MWEs has been redefined and the new label inventory provides, besides the *fixed* label for grammaticalized MWEs, a *flat* label for named entities. Ideally, further versions of UD will present a more homogeneous and streamlined treatment of both fixed and free multiwords.

References

Marie Candito and Matthieu Constant. 2014. Strategies for contiguous multiword expression analysis and dependency parsing. In *Proceedings of the 52nd Annual Meeting of the Association for Computational Linguistics (Volume 1: Long Papers)*, pages 743–753, Baltimore, Maryland, June. Association for Computational Linguistics.

Matthieu Constant and Joakim Nivre. 2016. A transition-based system for joint lexical and syntactic analysis. In *Proceedings of the 54th Annual Meeting of the Association for Computational Linguistics (Volume 1: Long Papers)*, pages 161–171,
Berlin, Germany, August. Association for Computational Linguistics.

Gülşen Eryiğit, Tugay Ilbay, and Ozan Arkan Can. 2011. Multiword expressions in statistical dependency parsing. In *Proceedings of the Second Workshop on Statistical Parsing of Morphologically Rich Languages*, pages 45–55, Dublin, Ireland, October. Association for Computational Linguistics.

Alexis Nasr, Carlos Ramisch, José Deulofeu, and André Valli. 2015. Joint dependency parsing and multiword expression tokenization. In *Proceedings of the 53rd Annual Meeting of the Association for Computational Linguistics and the 7th International Joint Conference on Natural Language Processing (Volume 1: Long Papers)*, pages 1116–1126, Beijing, China, July. Association for Computational Linguistics.

Joakim Nivre and Jens Nilsson. 2004. Multiword units in syntactic parsing. In *Proceedings of Methodologies and Evaluation of Multiword Units in Real-World Applications (MEMURA)*.

Joakim Nivre, Marie-Catherine de Marneffe, Filip Ginter, Yoav Goldberg, Jan Hajič, Christopher D. Manning, Ryan McDonald, Slav Petrov, Sampo Pyysalo, Natalia Silveira, Reut Tsarfaty, and Dan Zeman. 2016. Universal Dependencies v1: A Multilingual Treebank Collection. In *Proceedings of the 10th International Conference on Language Resources and Evaluation*.

Joakim Nivre. 2004. Incrementality in deterministic dependency parsing. In Frank Keller, Stephen Clark, Matthew Crocker, and Mark Steedman, editors, *Proceedings of the ACL Workshop Incremental Parsing: Bringing Engineering and Cognition Together*, pages 50–57, Barcelona, Spain, July. Association for Computational Linguistics.

Joakim Nivre. 2009. Non-projective dependency parsing in expected linear time. In *Proceedings of the Joint Conference of the 47th Annual Meeting of the ACL and the 4th International Joint Conference on Natural Language Processing of the AFNLP*, pages 351–359, Suntec, Singapore, August. Association for Computational Linguistics.

Joakim Nivre. 2014. Transition-Based Parsing with Multiword Expressions. In 2nd *PARSEME General Meeting, Athens, Greece*.

Carlos Ramisch. 2015. *Multiword Expressions Acquisition: A Generic and Open Framework*, volume XIV of *Theory and Applications of Natural Language Processing*. Springer.

Ivan A. Sag, Timothy Baldwin, Francis Bond, Ann Copestake, and Dan Flickinger. 2002. Multiword Expressions: A Pain in the Neck for NLP. In Alexander Gelbukh, editor, *Computational Linguistics and Intelligent Text Processing*, volume 2276 of *Lecture Notes in Computer Science*, pages 1–15. Springer Berlin Heidelberg.

Bahar Salehi, Paul Cook, and Timothy Baldwin. 2016. Determining the multiword expression inventory of a surprise language. In *Proceedings of COLING 2016, the 26th International Conference on Computational Linguistics: Technical Papers*, pages 471–481, Osaka, Japan, December. The COLING 2016 Organizing Committee.

Djamé Seddah, Reut Tsarfaty, Sandra Kübler, Marie Candito, Jinho D. Choi, Richárd Farkas, Jennifer Foster, Iakes Goenaga, Koldo Gojenola Galletebeitia, Yoav Goldberg, Spence Green, Nizar Habash, Marco Kuhlmann, Wolfgang Maier, Joakim Nivre, Adam Przepiórkowski, Ryan Roth, Wolfgang Seeker, Yannick Versley, Veronika Vincze, Marcin Woliński, Alina Wróblewska, and Eric Villemonte de la Clergerie. 2013. Overview of the SPMRL 2013 shared task: A cross-framework evaluation of parsing morphologically rich languages. In *Proceedings of the Fourth Workshop on Statistical Parsing of Morphologically-Rich Languages*, pages 146–182, Seattle, Washington, USA, October. Association for Computational Linguistics.

Natalia Silveira and Christopher Manning. 2015. Does universal dependencies need a parsing representation? an investigation of english. In *Proceedings of the Third International Conference on Dependency Linguistics (Depling 2015)*, pages 310–319, Uppsala, Sweden, August. Uppsala University, Uppsala, Sweden.

Veronika Vincze, János Zsibrita, and István Nagy T. 2013. Dependency parsing for identifying hungarian light verb constructions. In *Proceedings of the Sixth International Joint Conference on Natural Language Processing*, pages 207–215, Nagoya, Japan, October. Asian Federation of Natural Language Processing.

Semi-Automated Resolution of Inconsistency for a Harmonized Multiword Expression and Dependency Parse Annotation

King Chan, Julian Brooke, and Timothy Baldwin

Department of Computing and Information Systems, The University of Melbourne

`chanking@gmail.com, julian.brooke@unimelb.edu.au, tb@ldwin.net`

Abstract

This paper presents a methodology for identifying and resolving various kinds of inconsistency in the context of merging dependency and multiword expression (MWE) annotations, to generate a dependency treebank with comprehensive MWE annotations. Candidates for correction are identified using a variety of heuristics, including an entirely novel one which identifies violations of MWE constituency in the dependency tree, and resolved by arbitration with minimal human intervention. Using this technique, we identified and corrected several hundred errors across both parse and MWE annotations, representing changes to a significant percentage (well over 10%) of the MWE instances in the joint corpus.

1 Introduction

The availability of gold-standard annotations is important for the training and evaluation of a wide variety of NLP tasks, including the evaluation of dependency parsers (Buchholz and Marsi, 2006). In recent years, there has been a focus on multi-annotation of a single corpus, such as joint syntactic, semantic role, named entity, coreference and word sense annotation in Ontonotes (Hovy et al., 2006) or constituency, semantic role, discourse, opinion, temporal, event and coreference (among others) annotation of the Manually Annotated Sub-Corpus of the ANC (Ide et al., 2010). As part of this, there has been an increased focus on harmonizing and merging existing annotated data sets as a means of extending the scope of reference corpora (Ide and Suderman, 2007; Declerck, 2008; Simi et al., 2015). This effort sometimes presents an opportunity to fix conflicting annotations, a worthwhile endeavour since even a

small number of errors in a gold-standard syntactic annotation can, for example, result in significant changes in downstream applications (Habash et al., 2007). This paper presents the results of a harmonization effort for the overlapping STREUSLE annotation (Schneider et al., 2014) of multiword expressions ("MWEs": Baldwin and Kim (2010)) and dependency parse structure in the English Web Treebank ("EWT": Bies et al. (2012)), with the long-term goal of building reliable resources for joint MWE/syntactic parsing (Constant and Nivre, 2016).

As part of merging these two sets of annotations, we use analysis of cross-annotation and type-level consistency to identify instances of potential annotation inconsistency, with an eye to improving the quality of the component and combined annotations. It is important to point out that our approach to identifying and handling inconsistencies does not involve re-annotating the corpus; instead we act as arbitrators, resolving inconsistency in only those cases where human intervention is necessary. Our three methods for identifying potentially problematic annotations are:

- a cross-annotation heuristic that identifies MWE tokens whose parse structure is incompatible with the syntactic annotation of the MWE;
- a cross-type heuristic that identifies n-grams with inconsistent token-level MWE annotations; and
- a cross-type, cross-annotation heuristic that identifies MWE types whose parse structure is inconsistent across its token occurrences.

The first of these is specific to this harmonization process, and as far as we aware, entirely novel. The other two are adaptions of an approach to improving syntactic annotations proposed by Dickinson and Meurers (2003). After applying these heuristics and reviewing the candidates, we identified hundreds of errors in MWE annotation and

Proceedings of the 13th Workshop on Multiword Expressions (MWE 2017), pages 187–193,
Valencia, Spain, April 4. ©2017 Association for Computational Linguistics

about a hundred errors in the original syntactic annotations. We make available a tool that applies these fixes in the process of joining the two annotations into a single harmonized, corrected annotation, and release the harmonized annotations in the form of HAMSTER (the HArmonized Multiword and Syntactic TreE Resource): `https://github.com/eltimster/HAMSTER`.

2   Related Work

Our long-term goal is in building reliable resources for joint MWE/syntactic parsing. Explicit modelling of MWEs has been shown to improve parser accuracy (Nivre and Nilsson, 2004; Finkel and Manning, 2009; Korkontzelos and Manandhar, 2010; Green et al., 2013; Vincze et al., 2013; Candito and Constant, 2014; Constant and Nivre, 2016). Treatment of MWEs has typically involved parsing MWEs as single lexical units (Nivre and Nilsson, 2004; Eryiğit et al., 2011; Aggeliki Fotopoulou, 2014), however this flattened, "words with spaces" (Sag et al., 2002) approach is inflexible in its coverage of MWEs where components have some level of flexibility.

The English Web Treebank (Bies et al., 2012) represents a gold-standard annotation effort over informal web text. The original syntactic constituency annotation of the corpus was based on hand-correcting the output of the Stanford Parser (Manning et al., 2014); for our purposes we have converted this into a dependency parse using the Stanford Typed Dependency converter (de Marneffe et al., 2006). We considered the use of the Universal Dependencies representation (Nivre et al., 2016), however we noted that several aspects of that annotation (in particular the treatment of all prepositions as case markers dependent on their noun) make it inappropriate for joint MWE/syntactic parsing since it results in large numbers of MWEs that are non-contiguous in their syntactic structure (despite being contiguous at the token-level). As such, the Stanford Typed Dependencies are the representation which has the greatest currency for joint MWE/syntactic parsing work (Constant and Nivre, 2016).

The STREUSLE corpus (Schneider et al., 2014) is based entirely on the Reviews subset of the EWT, and comprises of 3,812 sentences representing 55,579 tokens. The annotation was completed by six linguists who were native English speakers. Every sentence was assessed by at least two annotators, which resulted in an average inter-annotator F1 agreement of 0.7. The idiosyncratic nature of MWEs lends itself to challenges associated with their interpretation, and this was readily acknowledged by those involved in the development of the STREUSLE corpus (Hollenstein et al., 2016). Two important aspects of the MWE annotation are that it includes both contiguous and non-contiguous MWEs (e.g. *check * out*), and that it supports both weak and strong annotation; both of these are considered in scope for our inconsistency analysis. A variety of cues are employed to determine this associative strength. The primary factor relates to the degree in which the expression is semantically opaque and/or morphosyntactically idiosyncratic. An example of a strong MWE would be *top notch*, as used in the sentence: *We stayed at a top notch hotel.* The semantics of this expression are not immediately predictable from the meanings of *top* and *notch*. On the other hand, the expression *highly recommend* is considered to be a weak expression as it is largely compositional — one can *highly recommend a product* — as indicated by the presence of alternatives such as *greatly recommend* which are also acceptable though less idiomatic. A total of 3,626 MWE instances were identified in STREUSLE, across 2,334 MWE types.

Other MWE-aware dependency treebanks include the various UD treebanks (Nivre et al., 2016), the Prague Dependency Treebank (Bejček et al., 2013), and others (Nivre and Nilsson, 2004; Eryiğit et al., 2011; Candito and Constant, 2014). The representation of MWEs, and the scope of types covered by these treebanks, can vary significantly. For example, the internal syntactic structure may be flattened (Nivre and Nilsson, 2004), or in the case of Candito and Constant (2014), allow for distinctions in the granularity of syntactic representation for regular vs. irregular MWE types.

The identification of inconsistencies in annotation requires comparisons to be made between similar instances that are labeled differently. Boyd et al. (2007) employed an alignment-based approach to assess differences in the annotation of n-gram word sequences in order to establish the likelihood of error occurrence. Other work in the syntactic inconsistency detection domain includes those related to POS tagging (Loftsson, 2009; Eskin, 2000; Ma et al., 2001) and parse structure (Ule and Simov, 2004; Kato and Mat-

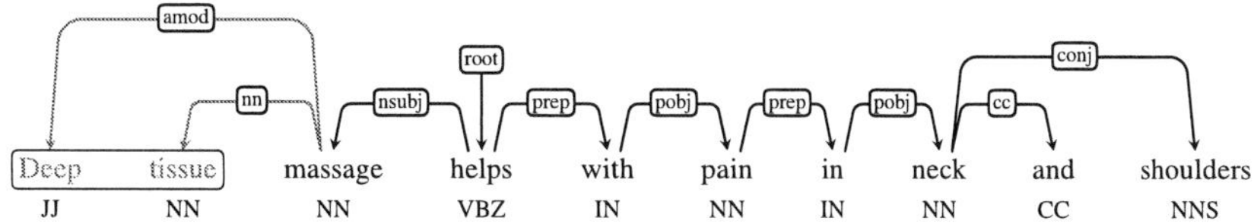

Figure 1: An example where the arc count heuristic is breached. *Deep tissue* has been labeled in the sentence here as an MWE in STREUSLE. *Deep* and *tissue* act as modifiers to *massage*, a term that has not been included as part of the MWE.

subara, 2010). Dickinson and Meurers (2003) outline various approaches for detecting inconsistencies in parse structure within treebanks.

In general, inconsistencies associated with MWE annotation fall under two categories: (1) *annotator error* (i.e. false positives and false negatives); and (2) ambiguity associated with the assessment of *hard cases*. While annotation errors apply to situations where a correct label can be applied but is not done so, hard cases are those where the correct label is inherently difficult to assign, and can be particularly relevant to certain classes of MWEs. For example, there may be considerable differences in inter-annotator agreement associated with assessing the relative transparency and associative strength of a non-fixed MWE.

3 Error Candidate Identification

3.1 MWE Syntactic Constituency Conflicts

The hypothesis that drives our first analysis is that for nearly all MWE types, the component words of the MWE should be syntactically connected, which is to say that every word is a dependent of another word in the MWE, except one word which connects the MWE to the rest of the sentence (or the root of the sentence). We can realise this intuition by using an arc count heuristic: for each labeled MWE instance we count the number of incoming dependency arcs that are headed by a term outside the MWE, and if the count is greater than one, we flag it for manual analysis. Figure 1 gives an example where the arc count heuristic is breached since both terms of the MWE *deep tissue* act as modifiers to the head noun that sits outside the MWE.

3.2 MWE Type Inconsistency

Our second analysis involves first collecting a list of all MWE types in the STREUSLE corpus, corresponding to lemmatized n-grams, possibly with gaps. We then match these n-grams across the same corpus, and flag any MWE type which has at least one inconsistency with regards to the annotation. That is, we extract as candidates any MWE types where there were at least two occurrences of the corresponding n-gram in the corpus that were incompatible with respect to their annotation in STREUSLE, including discrepancies in weak/strong designation. For non-contiguous MWE types, matches containing up to 4 words of intervening context between the two parts of the MWE type were included as candidates for further assessment.

3.3 MWE Type Parse Inconsistency

The hypothesis that drives our third analysis is that we would generally expect the internal syntax of an MWE type to be consistent across all its instances.[1] For each MWE type, we extracted the internal dependency structure of all its labeled instances, and flagged for further assessment any type for which the parse structure varied between at least two of those instances. Note that although this analysis is aimed at fixing parse errors, it makes direct use of the MWE annotation provided by STREUSLE to greatly limit the scope of error candidates to those which are most relevant to our interest.

4 Error Arbitration

Error arbitration was carried out by the authors (all native English speakers with experience in MWE identification), with at least two authors looking at each error candidate in most instances, and for certain difficult cases, the final annotation being based on discussion among all three authors. One advantage of our arbitration approach over a traditional token-based annotation was that we could enforce consistency across similar error can-

---

[1]Noting that we would not expect this to occur between MWE instances of a given combination of words, and non-MWE combinations of those same words.

didates (e.g. *disappointed with* and *happy with*) and also investigate non-candidates to arrive at a consensus; where at all possible, our changes relied on precedents that already existed in the relevant annotation.

Arbitration for the MWE syntax conflicts usually involved identifying an error in one of the two annotations, and in most cases this was relatively obvious. For instance, in the candidate *... the usual lady called in sick hours earlier*, *called in sick* was correctly labeled as an MWE, but the parse incorrectly includes *sick* as a dependent of *hours*, rather than *called in*. An example of the opposite case is *... just to make the appointment ...*, where *make the* had been labeled as an MWE, an obvious error which was caught by our arc count heuristic. There were cases where our arc count heuristic was breached due to what we would view as a general inadequacy in the syntactic annotation, but we decided not to effect a change because the impact would be too far reaching; examples of this were certain discourse markers (e.g. *as soon as*), and infinitives (e.g. *have to complete* where the *to* is considered a dependent of its verb rather than of the other term in the MWE *have to*). The most interesting cases were a handful of non-contiguous MWEs where there was truly a discontinuity in the syntax between the two parts of the MWE, for instance *no amount of * can*. This suggests a basic limitation in our heuristic, although the vast majority of MWEs did satisfy it.

For the two type-level arbitrations, there were cases of inconsistency upheld by real usage differences (e.g. *a little house* vs. *a little tired*). We identified clear differences in usage first, and divided the MWE types into sets, excluding from further analysis non-MWE usages of MWE type n-grams. For each consistent usage of an MWE type, the default position was to prefer the majority annotation across the set of instances, except when there were other candidates that were essentially equivalent: for instance, if we had relied on majority annotation for *job * do* (e.g. *the job that he did*) it would have been a different annotation than *do * job* (e.g. *do a good job*), so we considered these two together. We treated contiguous and non-contiguous versions of the same MWE type in the same manner.

In the MWE type consistency arbitration, for cases where majority rules did not provide a clear answer and there was no overwhelming evidence

for non-compositionality, we introduced a special internal label called *hard*. These correspond to cases where the usage is consistent and the inconsistency seems to be a result of the difficulty of the annotation item (as discussed earlier in Section 2), which extended also to our arbitration. Rather than enforce a specific annotation without strong evidence, or allow the inconsistency to remain when there is no usage justification for it, the corpus merging and correction tool gives the user the option to treat *hard* annotated MWEs in varying ways: the annotation may be kept unchanged, removed, converted to weak, or covered to *hard* for the purpose of excluding it from evaluation. Examples of hard cases include *go back, go in, more than, talk to, speak to, thanks guys, not that great, pleased with, have * option, get * answer, fix * problem*. On a per capita basis, inconsistencies are more common for non-contiguous MWEs relative to their contiguous counterparts, and we suspect that this is partially due to their tendency to be weaker, in addition to the challenges involved in correctly discerning the two parts, which are sometimes at a significant distance from each other.

Table 1 provides a summary of changes to MWE annotation at the MWE type and token levels. *Mixed* refer to MWEs that are heterogeneous in the associative strength between terms in the MWE (between `weak` and `strong`). Most of the changes in Table 1 (98% of the types) were the result of our type consistency analysis. Almost half of the changes involved the use of the `hard` label, but even excluding these (since only some of these annotations required actual changes in the final version of the corpus) our changes involve over 10% of the MWE tokens in the corpus, and thus represent a significant improvement to the STREUSLE annotation.

Relative to the changes to the MWE annotation, the changes to the parse annotation were more modest, but still not insignificant: for 181 MWE tokens across 157 types, we identified and corrected a dependency and/or POS annotation error. The majority of these (61%) were identified using the arc count heuristic. Note we applied the parse relevant heuristics after we fixed the MWE type consistency errors, ensuring that MWE annotations that were added were duly considered for parse errors.

		No MWE	Weak	Strong	Mixed	Hard	TOTAL
Token	**No MWE**	—	56	134	6	148	344
	Weak	33	—	22	5	46	106
	Strong	41	43	—	9	70	163
	Mixed	0	4	5	14	2	25
	TOTAL	74	103	161	34	266	638
Type	**No MWE**	—	31	72	5	63	171
	Weak	29	—	13	4	35	81
	Strong	32	28	—	7	43	110
	Mixed	0	4	4	9	2	19
	TOTAL	61	63	89	25	143	381

Table 1: Summary of changes to MWE annotation at the MWE type and token level

5 Discussion

Our three heuristics are useful because they identify potential errors with a high degree of precision. For the MWE type consistency analysis 77% of candidate types were problematic, and for parse type consistency, 79%. For the arc count heuristic, 45% of candidate types were ultimately changed: as mentioned earlier, some of the breaches involved systematic issues with annotation schema that we felt uncomfortable changing in isolation. By bringing these candidate instances to our attention, we were able to better focus our manual analysis effort, including in some cases looking across multiple related types, or even searching for specialist knowledge which could resolve ambiguities: for instance, in the example shown in Figure 1, though a layperson without reference material may be unsure whether it is *tissue* or *massage* which is considered to be *deep*, a quick online search indicates that the original EWT syntax is in error (*deep* modifies *tissue*).

However, it would be an overstatement to claim to have fixed all (or even almost all) the errors in the corpus. For instance, our type consistency heuristics only work when there are multiple instances of the same type, yet it is worth noting that 82% of the MWE types in the corpus are represented by a singleton instance. Our arc count heuristic can identify issues with singletons, but its scope is fairly limited. We cannot possibly identify missing annotations for types that were not annotated at least once. We might also miss certain kinds of systematic annotation errors, for instance those mentioned in De Smedt et al. (2015), though

that work focused on the use of mwe dependency labels which are barely used in the EWT, one of the reasons a resource like STREUSLE is so useful.

6 Conclusion

We have proposed a methodology for merging multiword expression and dependency parse annotations, to generate HAMSTER: a gold-standard MWE-annotated dependency treebank with high consistency. The heuristics used to enforce consistency operate at the type- and cross-annotation level, and affected well over 10% of the MWEs in the new resource.

References

Voula Giouli Aggeliki Fotopoulou, Stella Markantonatou. 2014. Encoding MWEs in a conceptual lexicon. In *Proceedings of the 10th Workshop on Multiword Expressions (MWE 2014)*.

Timothy Baldwin and Su Nam Kim. 2010. Multiword expressions. In Nitin Indurkhya and Fred J. Damerau, editors, *Handbook of Natural Language Processing, Second Edition*. CRC Press, Taylor and Francis Group, Boca Raton, FL.

Eduard Bejček, Eva Hajičová, Jan Hajič, Pavlína Jínová, Václava Kettnerová, Veronika Kolářová, Marie Mikulová, Jiří Mírovský, Anna Nedoluzhko, Jarmila Panevová, et al. 2013. Prague dependency treebank 3.0.

Ann Bies, Justin Mott, Colin Warner, and Seth Kulick. 2012. English web treebank. technical report ldc2012t13. Technical report, Linguistic Data Consortium.

Adriane Boyd, Markus Dickinson, and Detmar Meurers. 2007. Increasing the recall of corpus annotation error detection. In *Proceedings of the Sixth Workshop on Treebanks and Linguistic Theories (TLT 2007)*, Bergen, Norway.

Sabine Buchholz and Erwin Marsi. 2006. Conll-x shared task on multilingual dependency parsing. In *Proceedings of the Tenth Conference on Computational Natural Language Learning*, CoNLL-X '06, pages 149–164, Stroudsburg, PA, USA. Association for Computational Linguistics.

Marie Candito and Matthieu Constant. 2014. Strategies for contiguous multiword expression analysis and dependency parsing. In *The 52nd Annual Meeting of the Association for Computational Linguistics (ACl '14)*.

Matthieu Constant and Joakim Nivre. 2016. A transition-based system for joint lexical and syntactic analysis. In *the 54th Annual Meeting of the Association for Computational Linguistics (ACL '16)*, pages 161–171.

Marie-Catherine de Marneffe, Bill MacCartney, and Christopher D. Manning. 2006. Generating typed dependency parses from phrase structure parses. In *Proceedings of the 5th International Conference on Language Resources and Evaluation (LREC '06)*, Genova, Italy.

Koenraad De Smedt, Victoria Rosén, and Paul Meurer. 2015. Studying consistency in ud treebanks with iness-search. In *Proceedings of the Fourteenth Workshop on Treebanks and Linguistic Theories (TLT14)*, pages 258–267.

Thierry Declerck. 2008. A framework for standardized syntactic annotation. In *Proceedings of the 2008 Language Resource and Evaluation Conference (LREC 08)*.

Markus Dickinson and W. Detmar Meurers. 2003. Detecting inconsistencies in treebanks. In *Proceedings of the Second Workshop on Treebanks and Linguistic Theories (TLT 2003)*.

Gülşen Eryiğit, Tugay İlbay, and Ozan Arkan Can. 2011. Multiword expressions in statistical dependency parsing. In *Proceedings of the Second Workshop on Statistical Parsing of Morphologically Rich Languages*, SPMRL '11, pages 45–55, Stroudsburg, PA, USA. Association for Computational Linguistics.

Eleazar Eskin. 2000. Detecting errors within a corpus using anomaly detection. In *Proceedings of the 1st North American Chapter of the Association for Computational Linguistics Conference*, NAACL 2000, pages 148–153, Stroudsburg, PA, USA. Association for Computational Linguistics.

Jenny Rose Finkel and Christopher D. Manning. 2009. Joint parsing and named entity recognition. In *Proceedings of Human Language Technologies: The 2009 Annual Conference of the North American Chapter of the Association for Computational Linguistics*, NAACL '09, pages 326–334, Stroudsburg, PA, USA. Association for Computational Linguistics.

Spence Green, Marie-Catherine de Marneffe, and Christopher D. Manning. 2013. Parsing models for identifying multiword expressions. *Computational Linguistics*, 39(1):195–227, March.

Nizar Habash, Ryan Gabbard, Owen Rambow, Seth Kulick, and Mitchell P Marcus. 2007. Determining case in arabic: Learning complex linguistic behavior requires complex linguistic features. In *EMNLP-CoNLL*, pages 1084–1092.

Nora Hollenstein, Nathan Schneider, and Bonnie Webber. 2016. Inconsistency detection in semantic annotation. In *Proceedings of the 2016 Langauage Resources and Evaluation Conference (LREC '16)*.

Eduard Hovy, Mitchell Marcus, Martha Palmer, Lance Ramshaw, and Ralph Weischedel. 2006. OntoNotes: The 90% solution. In *Proceedings of the Main Conference on Human Language Technology Conference of the North American Chapter of the Association of Computational Linguistics*, pages 57–60, New York City, USA.

Nancy Ide and Keith Suderman. 2007. Graf: A graph-based format for linguistic annotations. In *Proceedings of the Linguistic Annotation Workshop*, LAW '07, pages 1–8, Stroudsburg, PA, USA. Association for Computational Linguistics.

Nancy Ide, Collin Baker, Christiane Fellbaum, and Rebecca Passonneau. 2010. The manually annotated sub-corpus: A community resource for and by the people. pages 68–73.

Yoshihide Kato and Shigeki Matsubara. 2010. Correcting errors in a treebank based on synchronous tree substitution grammar. In *Proceedings of the ACL 2010 Conference Short Papers*, pages 74–79. Association for Computational Linguistics.

Ioannis Korkontzelos and Suresh Manandhar. 2010. Can recognising multiword expressions improve shallow parsing? In *Human Language Technologies: The 2010 Annual Conference of the North American Chapter of the Association for Computational Linguistics*, HLT '10, pages 636–644, Stroudsburg, PA, USA. Association for Computational Linguistics.

Hrafn Loftsson. 2009. Correcting a pos-tagged corpus using three complementary methods. In *Proceedings of the 12th Conference of the European Chapter of the Association for Computational Linguistics*, pages 523–531. Association for Computational Linguistics.

Qing Ma, Bao-Liang Lu, Masaki Murata, Michnori Ichikawa, and Hitoshi Isahara. 2001. On-line error detection of annotated corpus using modular neural networks. In *International Conference on Artificial Neural Networks*, pages 1185–1192. Springer.

Christopher D. Manning, Mihai Surdeanu, John Bauer, Jenny Finkel, Steven J. Bethard, and David Mc-Closky. 2014. The Stanford CoreNLP natural language processing toolkit. In *Proceedings of 52nd Annual Meeting of the Association for Computational Linguistics: System Demonstrations*, pages 55–60.

Joakim Nivre and Jens Nilsson. 2004. Multiword units in syntactic parsing. In *Methodologies and Evaluation of Multiword Units in Real-World Applications (MEMURA)*.

Joakim Nivre, Marie-Catherine de Marneffe, Filip Ginter, Yoav Goldberg, Jan Hajic, et al. 2016. Universal dependencies v1: A multilingual treebank collection.

Ivan A. Sag, Timothy Baldwin, Francis Bond, Ann Copestake, and Dan Flickinger. 2002. Multiword expressions: A pain in the neck for NLP. In *Proceedings of the 3rd International Conference on Intelligent Text Processing and Computational Linguistics (CICLing '02)*.

Nathan Schneider, Spencer Onuffer, Nora Kazour, Emily Danchik, Michael T. Mordowanec, Henrietta Conrad, and Noah A. Smith. 2014. Comprehensive annotation of multiword expressions in a social web corpus. In *Proceedings of the Ninth International Conference on Language Resources and Evaluation*, pages 455–461, Reykjavík, Iceland.

Maria Simi, Simonetta Montemagni, and Cristina Bosco. 2015. Harmonizing and merging italian treebanks: Towards a merged italian dependency treebank and beyond. In *Harmonization and Development of Resources and Tools for Italian Natural Language Processing within the PARLI Project*, pages 3–23.

Tylman Ule and Kiril Simov. 2004. Unexpected productions may well be errors. In *Proceedings of the 2004 Language Resources and Evaluation Conference (LREC '04)*.

Veronika Vincze, Janos Zsibrita, and István Nagy T. 2013. Dependency parsing for identifying hungarian light verb constructions. In *Proceedings of International Joint Conference on Natural Language Processing (IJCNLP '13)*.

Combining Linguistic Features for the Detection of
Croatian Multiword Expressions

Maja Buljan and **Jan Šnajder**
University of Zagreb, Faculty of Electrical Engineering and Computing
Text Analysis and Knowledge Engineering Lab
Unska 3, 10000 Zagreb, Croatia
`{maja.buljan,jan.snajder}@fer.hr`

Abstract

As multiword expressions (MWEs) exhibit a range of idiosyncrasies, their automatic detection warrants the use of many different features. Tsvetkov and Wintner (2014) proposed a Bayesian network model that combines linguistically motivated features and also models their interactions. In this paper, we extend their model with new features and apply it to Croatian, a morphologically complex and a relatively free word order language, achieving a satisfactory performance of 0.823 F1-score. Furthermore, by comparing against (semi)naïve Bayes models, we demonstrate that manually modeling feature interactions is indeed important. We make our annotated dataset of Croatian MWEs freely available.

1 Introduction

Multiword expressions (MWEs) have attracted a great deal of attention in the natural language processing community. While MWEs span a wide range of types, common to all is the idiosyncrasy at the lexical, syntactic, semantic, pragmatic, or statistical level (Baldwin and Kim, 2010). A variety of models has been proposed for the automatic identification of MWE in corpora, including statistical (Church and Hanks, 1990; Lin, 1999; Pecina, 2010) and linguistic-based approaches (Cook et al., 2007; Baldwin, 2005; Green et al., 2011); see (Ramisch, 2015) for a recent overview. Sag et al. (2002) argued for a combination of the two approaches.

Recently, Tsvetkov and Wintner (2014) proposed an approach for the detection of MWE candidates that combines a number of statistical and linguistic features. The most interesting aspect of their work is that they explicitly model the linguistically motivated interactions between the features

using a Bayesian network (BN). The advantages of BNs lie in their interpretability and the possibility to encode linguistic knowledge in the form of the network structure. Furthermore, unlike most previous work, Tsvetkov and Wintner address MWE of various types and flexible syntactic constructions. They show that the manually-designed BN outperforms a number of strong baselines, including an SVM model, on English, French, and Hebrew datasets. Another advantage of their model is that it is in principle language-independent, aside from a few language-specific features.

In this paper, we address the task of MWE detection (type-level MWE classification) for Croatian, a South Slavic language with a rich morphology and a relatively free word order. The starting point of our work is the model of Tsvetkov and Wintner (2014), which we extend with a number of features, including language-specific ones that account for the relatively free word order. Our main research question is whether modeling the interactions between features is important, and whether these can be learned automatically. Tsvetkov and Wintner (2014) showed that a manually-designed BN substantially outperforms the one whose structure is learned automatically, hypothesizing that the cause for this might be the increased model complexity. We conduct a similar experiment using a structure-learning algorithm, but also model the interactions using a simpler, semi-naive Bayes classifier, for which the number of parameters is restricted. Finally, we compare these models against a structure-free counterpart, a naïve Bayes classifier.

For the experiments, we compile a new manually annotated dataset of Croatian MWEs. Unlike Tsvetkov and Wintner (2014), who only consider bigrams, we consider MWEs of up to five words in length. We make the dataset freely available, along with all feature sets needed to replicate the experiments.

Proceedings of the 13th Workshop on Multiword Expressions (MWE 2017), pages 194–199,
Valencia, Spain, April 4. ©2017 Association for Computational Linguistics

2 Model

We adopt the BN model of Tsvetkov and Wintner (2014), but extend it with language-specific as well as semantically motivated features. Most newly added features were inspired by the analysis of Croatian MWEs of Blagus Bartolec (2008), and a sample-based analysis of a MWE from a dictionary of Croatian MWEs (Kovačević, 2012) and their occurrences in the hrWaC corpus (Ljubešić and Erjavec, 2011). The MWE candidates were POS-tagged using the tagger from (Pinnis et al., 2012).

2.1 Features

Original features. The model of Tsvetkov and Wintner (2014) uses nine statistically and linguistically motivated features, computed for each MWE candidate and designed to discriminate between MWEs and ordinary word sequences. We adopted eight of these features:[1] (1) *capitalization* (indicating which MWE constituents are capitalized), (2) *hyphenation* (which constituents are hyphenated), (3) *fossil word* (whether constituents also occur outside of the MWE), (4) *frozen form* (whether the MWE is morphologically frozen), (5) *partial morphological inflection* (whether MWE admits only limited inflection), (6) *syntactic pattern* (the MWE's part-of-speech pattern), (7) *semantic context*, and (8) *association measure*.

The values of statistical features were computed from hrWaC, a 1.2B-token Croatian web corpus compiled by Ljubešić and Erjavec (2011). All numeric features were discretized into five reference levels based on their average values in the corpus.

Interesting MWE examples from the corpus that showcase the above-mentioned statistical properties are *curriculum vitae*, which is made of fossil words, *hodati po jajima* (*to walk on eggshells*), which is a frozen form, and *zlatno doba* (*golden age*), which almost exclusively appears in the nominative and locative singular (partial inflection).

Modified features. In the original model, the semantic context feature computes the lexical variety of the words following a MWE candidate vary, the idea being that MWEs have a more restricted context. In our sample-based analysis of Croatian MWEs, we concluded that in many cases this restriction is not limited to the right context. Thus,

we introduced two additional features: one for the left context and another considering a 5-word window around the MWE. Likewise, we used the Dice coefficient association measure, rather than PMI as used in the original model, as the former turned out to be more discriminative.

New features. We introduced six new features, four of which were inspired by our analysis of Croatian MWEs. The *simile* feature is motivated by the observation that many Croatian similes are MWEs, e.g., *plakati kao ljuta godina*, (*to cry like a bitter year* – to cry heavily). We consider a MWE to be a simile if it contains a preposition *kao* (*like*) or *poput* (*as*). We furthermore observe many Croatian MWEs contain loanwords. The *foreign word* feature indicates, for each MWE constituent, whether it has been tagged as a foreign word by the POS tagger.

We also introduced two features to account for the relatively free word order of Croatian: *constituent adjacency* and *constituent permutation*. The former is turned on if there are more contiguous than discontinuous MWE candidate occurrences, while the latter is turned on if the corpus contains five or more word permutations of the MWE candidate. While most MWEs in Croatian nominally do not allow intervening words between its components, in fact most types of MWEs will allow the insertion of copula and pronoun enclitics; e.g., *zadnji [je] čas* (*[is] last moment*). When searching for discontinuous MWE candidates of length n, we only consider n-grams for which the number of tokens between the first and final constituent is less than or equal to $2n$. On the other hand, permutation of MWE constituents is much less frequent, even for a relatively free word order language such as Croatian. Thus, there may be a benefit to capturing which types of MWE – presumably mostly characterized by their POS patterns – allow for permutations; e.g., *jednim udarcem ubiti dvije muhe / dvije muhe ubiti jednim udarcem, etc.* (*to kill two flies with one stone*).

Finally, inspired by a growing body of research on semantic non-compositionality of MWEs (Baldwin et al., 2003; Kim and Baldwin, 2006; Biemann and Giesbrecht, 2011; Krčmář et al., 2013), we introduced a simple *semantic opacity* feature. We opted for a simple approach proposed by (Mitchell and Lapata, 2008), and computed this feature by deriving distributional vectors from hrWaC for the MWE and the additive composition of its con-

---

[1]We omitted a feature that indicates the existence of a translation equivalent. Namely, Tsvetkov and Wintner (2014) use parallel bilingual corpora for acquiring the initial MWE candidates.

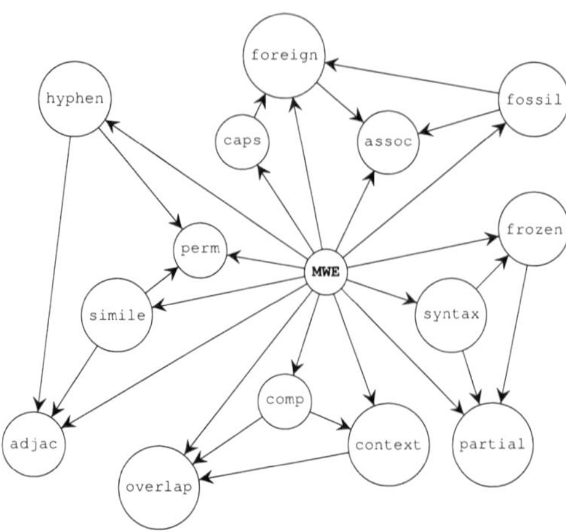

Figure 1: Bayesian network for MWE classification

stituents, and then computing the cosine between the two vectors. For opaque MWEs, we expect the cosine to be lower than for semantically transparent MWEs. Similarly as with other numeric features, we discretized the cosine scores into five levels.

2.2 Feature Interactions

The structure of a BN defines feature interactions by means of conditional independence assumptions between the variables. When constructed manually, the structure of the network essentially models our knowledge about the causal links between the features.

We extended the structure of the original BN model by introducing additional links for the newly added features. We primarily based our design choices on linguistic intuition, but also on experimental validation. To this end, we compiled a small validation set of 33 MWEs and 33 non-MWEs, for which we computed the features over 50K sentences from hrWaC. We used this dataset to verify whether adding an interaction link improves the accuracy of the model.

The resulting BN is shown in Fig. 1. All nodes depend on the MWE node, which is the label to be predicted.[2] We introduced feature interaction between the caps and foreign node, given that a high number of loanwords pertain to proper names. Additionally, we defined interactions between comp, context, and overlap, as the semantic opacity influences the general context of an expression, and the ratio of overlapping context

---

[2] When using the BN model for MWE detection, we simply run a maximum a posteriori query on the MWE variable with all feature variables set to the observed values.

words depends upon both features. Finally, since similes and hyphenated expressions signal a strict word order, we defined interactions between perm, adjac, hyphen, and simile.

3 Dataset

MWE definition. As there is no publicly available annotated datasets of Croatian MWEs, we decided to create one. We first established a working definition of Croatian MWEs, starting out from the taxonomy proposed by Blagus Bartolec (2008), and adopted it to the universal classification of Sag et al. (2002). We identified five major groups of MWEs: (1) *idioms*, semantically opaque expressions; (2) *fixed expressions*, common phrases whose meaning can clearly be gleaned from its constituents, but whose constituents are rarely replaced with synonyms in practice; (3) *technical terms*, expressions pertaining to the technical language of a particular profession; (4) *foreign terms*, any expression adopted from another language, as well as imaginary and nonsensical phrases; and (5) *proper names*, names of persons, institutions, geographical terms, etc., composed of two or more words.

Annotation. As a source of data for our dataset, we use hrMWELex, a lexicon of Croatian MWEs candidate n-grams compiled by Ljubešić et al. (2015). The lexicon was obtained by matching parse trees from hrWaC against a set of predefined syntactic patterns (POS patterns) for Croatian, yielding a high-recall, low-precision MWE lexicon. The resulting lexicon contains 12M n-grams with matching POS patterns.

We next sorted the n-grams by corpus frequency, and made a balanced 2-, 3-, and 4-gram selection from the most frequent candidates, selecting 4000 MWE candidates. We then asked four native speakers of Croatian to label the dataset. Each annotated all 4000 instances, presented in random order to minimize the effect of a context bias. We also included 124 gold positive MWEs, extracted from (Anić, 2003), to serve as a control set.

To measure the inter-annotator agreement, we calculated the Cohen's coefficient (Cohen, 1960) between all pairs of annotations (Table 1). The agreement ranges between 0.413 and 0.578, which, according to Landis and Koch (1977), is considered a moderate agreement.

Gold dataset. For the final dataset, we adjudicated the annotations by considering a MWE can-

$\kappa(x, y)$	A	B	C	D
A	–	0.499	0.505	0.578
B	0.499	–	0.420	0.466
C	0.505	0.420	–	0.413
D	0.578	0.466	0.413	–

Table 1: Inter-annotator agreement on the MWE classification

		n-gram length			
	2	3	4	5	Total
Positive	338	76	44	3	461
Negative	233	150	78	–	461
Total	571	226	122	3	**922**

Table 2: Dataset breakdown by n-gram length

didate to be a true MWE if at least three annotators have labeled it as positive. Out of 4124 MWE candidates, 111 MWEs were labeled as positive by all four annotators, while 163 were labeled as positive by three annotators. To this set we add 187 positive MWEs extracted from a standard Croatian dictionary (Anić, 2003) and a dictionary of multiword expressions (Kovačević, 2012), yielding a total of 461 positive MWEs.[3] Finally, we add an equal number of n-grams annotated as negative MWE instances by at least three annotators, yielding a perfectly-balanced dataset of 922 n-grams. Table 2 shows a breakdown of positive and negative examples by n-gram length. For each n-gram from this dataset, we computed the feature values on a random sample of the hrWaC corpus comprising 200K sentences ($\sim$5M tokens). We make the dataset and the precomputed features publicly available.[4]

4 Evaluation

We compare the BN model from Section 2 against two commonly used statistical baselines: Dice and PMI association measures. Furthermore, we compare the BN model to three variants of Bayes classifiers, differing in their ability to model feature interactions: a Naive Bayes classifier (NB), a tree-augmented Naive Bayes classifier (TAN) (Friedman et al., 1997), and a Bayesian network classifier trained using the K2 structure learning algorithm (BN-K2) (Cooper and Herskovits, 1992). The NB and TAN allow for no feature interaction or limited feature interaction, respectively. More precisely, a TAN cannot model circular feature dependencies,

---

[3] We took care not to select any MWEs from the samples we used for designing the features or feature interactions.

[4] `http://takelab.fer.hr/cromwe`

	Acc	P	R	F_1
Dice	0.735	0.788	0.788	0.788
PMI	0.717	0.777	0.769	0.773
NB	0.783	0.795	0.761	0.778
TAN	0.804	0.808	**0.796**	0.805
BN-K2	0.809	0.850	0.751	0.797
BN	**0.832**	**0.867**	0.783	**0.823**

Table 3: Performance of Bayes classifiers and the baselines (scores averaged over ten folds)

such as those among the `syntax`, `frozen`, and `partial` features in Fig. 1. The NB is even simpler, as it does not model any feature interactions at all, i.e., it assumes all feature pairs are conditionally independent within the MWE and non-MWE classes. In contrast, the BN and BN-K2 models can model (undirected) circular dependencies. The difference between them is that for the BN model the feature interactions were designed manually, based on linguistic insights, whereas in case of BN-K2 the interactions are learned from the train set.

Table 3 shows the MWE classification accuracy, precision, recall, and F1-scores of the two baselines and the four Bayes classifiers. All models were trained and tested using 10-fold cross-validation on the gold dataset. The threshold of the two baseline models was optimized on the train sets. We observe that all four Bayes classifiers outperform the baselines in terms of accuracy and F1-score, except for the NB model which performs worse than Dice in terms of F1-score. On the other hand, the BN model outperforms all considered models in terms of both accuracy and F1-score by a considerable margin. This demonstrates that manual modeling of feature interactions is indeed important for MWE detection, and that BN does a reasonably good job in modeling these interactions. The more simple NB and TAN models even out in terms of F1-score, but differ in precision and recall scores, while the BN-K2 model performs comparably to TAN.

5 Conclusion

We described the experiments on using a combination of linguistically motivated features for MWE detection in Croatian. We adopted the Bayesian network model of Tsvetkov and Wintner (2014) and extended it with new features and manually-designed feature interactions, inspired by an analysis of Croatian MWEs. To train and evaluate the model, we built a manually annotated dataset of Croatian MWEs. On this dataset, our model substantially outperforms statistical baselines, reaching a satisfactory performance of 0.823 F1-score on our dataset. The model also outperforms the (semi)naïve Bayes models, which limit the feature interactions, as well as a Bayesian network model with automatically learned feature interactions. Thus, the main finding of our work is that the model benefits from the linguistically motivated, manually-designed feature interactions, which proves that MWE features interact in rather intricate ways.

Acknowledgments

This work has been supported by the Croatian Science Foundation under the project UIP-2014-09-7312. We thank the annotators for their work and the anonymous reviewers for their insightful comments. We thank Nikola Ljubešić for his help with the hrMWELex lexicon.

References

V. Anić. 2003. *Veliki rječnik hrvatskoga jezika*. Novi Liber.

Timothy Baldwin and Su Nam Kim. 2010. Multiword expressions. In *Handbook of Natural Language Processing, Second Edition*, pages 267–292. Chapman and Hall/CRC.

Timothy Baldwin, Colin Bannard, Takaaki Tanaka, and Dominic Widdows. 2003. An empirical model of multiword expression decomposability. In *Proceedings of the ACL 2003 workshop on Multiword expressions: analysis, acquisition and treatment-Volume 18*, pages 89–96. Association for Computational Linguistics.

Timothy Baldwin. 2005. Deep lexical acquisition of verb–particle constructions. *Computer Speech & Language*, 19(4):398–414.

Chris Biemann and Eugenie Giesbrecht. 2011. Distributional semantics and compositionality 2011: Shared task description and results. In *Proc. of the Workshop on Distributional Semantics and Compositionality*, pages 21–28. Association for Computational Linguistics.

Goranka Blagus Bartolec. 2008. Kolokacijske sveze u hrvatskom jeziku (s posebnim osvrtom na leksikografiju).

Kenneth Ward Church and Patrick Hanks. 1990. Word association norms, mutual information, and lexicography. *Computational linguistics*, 16(1):22–29.

Jacob Cohen. 1960. A coefficient of agreement for nominal scales. *Educational and psychological measurement*, 20(1):37–46.

Paul Cook, Afsaneh Fazly, and Suzanne Stevenson. 2007. Pulling their weight: Exploiting syntactic forms for the automatic identification of idiomatic expressions in context. In *Proceedings of the workshop on a broader perspective on multiword expressions*, pages 41–48. Association for Computational Linguistics.

Gregory F Cooper and Edward Herskovits. 1992. A bayesian method for the induction of probabilistic networks from data. *Machine learning*, 9(4):309–347.

Nir Friedman, Dan Geiger, and Moises Goldszmidt. 1997. Bayesian network classifiers. *Machine learning*, 29(2-3):131–163.

Spence Green, Marie-Catherine De Marneffe, John Bauer, and Christopher D Manning. 2011. Multiword expression identification with tree substitution grammars: A parsing tour de force with french. In *Proceedings of the Conference on Empirical Methods in Natural Language Processing*, pages 725–735. Association for Computational Linguistics.

Su Nam Kim and Timothy Baldwin. 2006. Automatic identification of English verb particle constructions using linguistic features. In *Proc. of the Third ACL-SIGSEM Workshop on Prepositions*, pages 65–72. Association for Computational Linguistics.

Barbara Kovačević. 2012. *Hrvatski frazemi od glave do pete*. Institut za hrvatski jezik i jezikoslovlje.

Lubomír Krčmář, Karel Ježek, and Pavel Pecina. 2013. Determining compositionality of word expresssions using various word space models and methods. In *Proc. of the Workshop on Continuous Vector Space Models and their Compositionality*, pages 64–73. Association for Computational Linguistics.

J Richard Landis and Gary G Koch. 1977. The measurement of observer agreement for categorical data. *biometrics*, pages 159–174.

Dekang Lin. 1999. Automatic identification of non-compositional phrases. In *Proceedings of the 37th annual meeting of the Association for Computational Linguistics on Computational Linguistics*, pages 317–324. Association for Computational Linguistics.

Nikola Ljubešić and Tomaž Erjavec. 2011. hrWaC and slWaC: Compiling web corpora for Croatian and Slovene. In *International Conference on Text, Speech and Dialogue*, pages 395–402. Springer.

Nikola Ljubešić, Kaja Dobrovoljc, and Darja Fišer. 2015. MWELex – MWE lexica of Croatian, Slovene and Serbian extracted from parsed corpora. *Informatica*, 39(3):293.

Jeff Mitchell and Mirella Lapata. 2008. Vector-based models of semantic composition. In *ACL*, pages 236–244.

Pavel Pecina. 2010. Lexical association measures and collocation extraction. *Language resources and evaluation*, 44(1-2):137–158.

Marcis Pinnis, Nikola Ljubešić, Dan Stefanescu, Inguna Skadina, Marko Tadic, and Tatiana Gornostay. 2012. Term extraction, tagging, and mapping tools for under-resourced languages. In *Proceedings of the 10th Conference on Terminology and Knowledge Engineering (TKE 2012), June*, pages 20–21.

Carlos Ramisch. 2015. State of the art in mwe processing. In *Multiword Expressions Acquisition*, pages 53–102. Springer.

Ivan A Sag, Timothy Baldwin, Francis Bond, Ann Copestake, and Dan Flickinger. 2002. Multiword expressions: A pain in the neck for nlp. In *International Conference on Intelligent Text Processing and Computational Linguistics*, pages 1–15. Springer.

Yulia Tsvetkov and Shuly Wintner. 2014. Identification of multiword expressions by combining multiple linguistic information sources. *Computational Linguistics*, 40(2):449–468.

Complex Verbs are Different: Exploring the Visual Modality in Multi-Modal Models to Predict Compositionality

Maximilian Köper and **Sabine Schulte im Walde**
Institut für Maschinelle Sprachverarbeitung
Universität Stuttgart, Germany
{maximilian.koeper,schulte}@ims.uni-stuttgart.de

Abstract

This paper compares a neural network DSM relying on textual co-occurrences with a multi-modal model integrating visual information. We focus on nominal vs. verbal compounds, and zoom into lexical, empirical and perceptual target properties to explore the contribution of the visual modality. Our experiments show that (i) visual features contribute differently for verbs than for nouns, and (ii) images complement textual information, if (a) the textual modality by itself is poor and appropriate image subsets are used, or (b) the textual modality by itself is rich and large (potentially noisy) images are added.

1 Introduction

Distributional semantic models (DSMs) rely on the *distributional hypothesis* (Harris, 1954), that words with similar distributions have related meanings. They represent a well-established tool for modelling semantic relatedness between words and phrases (Bullinaria and Levy, 2007; Turney and Pantel, 2010). In the last decade, standard DSMs using bag-of-words or syntactic co-occurrence counts have been enhanced by integration into neural networks (Baroni et al., 2014; Levy et al., 2015; Nguyen et al., 2016), or by integrating perceptual information (Silberer and Lapata, 2014; Bruni et al., 2014; Kiela et al., 2014; Lazaridou et al., 2015). While standard DSMs have been applied to a variety of semantic relatedness tasks such as word sense discrimination, selectional preferences, relation distinction (among others), multi-modal models have predominantly been evaluated on their general ability to model semantic similarity as captured by *SimLex* (Hill et al., 2015), *WordSim* (Finkelstein et al., 2002), etc.

In this paper, we compare a neural network DSM relying on textual co-occurrences with a multi-modal model extension integrating visual information. We focus on the prediction of compositionality for two types of German multi-word expressions: noun-noun compounds and particle verbs. Differently to most previous multi-modal approaches, we thus address a semantically specific task that was traditionally addressed by standard DSMs, mainly for English and German (Baldwin, 2005; Bannard, 2005; Reddy et al., 2011; Salehi and Cook, 2013; Schulte im Walde et al., 2013; Salehi et al., 2014; Bott and Schulte im Walde, 2014; Bott and Schulte im Walde, 2015; Schulte im Walde et al., 2016a). Furthermore, we zoom into factors that might influence the quality of predictions, such as lexical and empirical target properties (e.g., ambiguity, frequency, compositionality); and filters to optimise the visual space, such as dispersion and imageability filters (Kiela et al., 2014), and a novel clustering filter.

Our experiments demonstrate that the contributions of the textual and the visual models differ for predictions across the nominal vs. verbal compositions. The visual modality adds complementary features in cases where (a) the textual modality performs poorly, and images of the most imaginable targets are added, or (b) the textual modality performs well, and all available –potentially noisy– images are added. In addition, we demonstrate that perceptual features of verbs, such as abstractness and imageability, have a different influence on multi-modality than for nouns, presumably because they are more difficult to grasp.

2 Data

Target Multi-Word Expressions (MWEs) German noun-noun compounds represent two-part multi-word expressions where both con-

Proceedings of the 13th Workshop on Multiword Expressions (MWE 2017), pages 200–206,
Valencia, Spain, April 4. ©2017 Association for Computational Linguistics

(a) Complete set of images.

(b) Images in largest cluster.

Figure 1: Clustering filter for *abzupfen* 'to pick'.

stituents are nouns, e.g., *Feuerwerk* 'fire works' is composed of the nominal constituents *Feuer* 'fire' and *Werk* 'opus'. German particle verbs are complex verbs such as *anstrahlen* 'beam/smile at' which are composed of a separable prefix particle (such as *an*) and a base verb (such as *strahlen* 'beam/smile'). Both types of German MWEs are highly frequent and highly productive in the lexicon. In addition, the particles are notoriously ambiguous, e.g., *an* has a partitive meaning in *anbeißen* 'take a bite', a cumulative meaning in *anhäufen* 'pile up', and a topological meaning in *anbinden* 'tie to' (Springorum, 2011). We rely on two existing gold standards annotated with compositionality ratings: GS-NN, a set of 868 German noun-noun compounds (Schulte im Walde et al., 2016b), and GS-PV, a set of 400 particle verbs across 11 particle types (Bott et al., 2016).

Multi-Modal Vector Space Models For the textual representation we used two sets of embeddings. Based on *word2vec* (Mikolov et al., 2013), we obtained both representations using the skip-gram architecture with negative sampling. The sets differ with respect to window size (5 vs. 10) and dimensionality (400 vs. 500). As corpus resource we relied on the lemmatized version of the *DECOW14AX*, a German web corpus containing 12 billion tokens (Schäfer and Bildhauer, 2012).

The visual features rely on images downloaded from the *bing* search engine, following Kiela et al. (2016). We queried 25 images per word, and con-

verted all images into high-dimensional numerical representations by using the caffe toolkit (Jia et al., 2014) and pre-trained models. In the default setting, a word is represented in the visual space by the mean vector of its 25 image representations. As image-recognition neural network models, we used: (i) GoogLeNet (Szegedy et al., 2015), a 22-layer deep network; we obtained vectors by using the value of the last layer before the final softmax, containing 1024 elements (= dimensionality). (ii) AlexNet (Krizhevsky et al., 2012), a neural network with five convolutional layers (4,096-dim).

The multi-modal representations were combined by applying mid-fusion between textual and visual representation, i.e., concatenation of the L2-normalized representations (Bruni et al., 2014)[1]

3 Experiments

Predicting Compositionality For the prediction of compositionality, we represented the meanings of the multi-word expressions and their constituent words by textual, visual and textual+visual (i.e., multi-modal) vectors. The similarity of a compound–constituent vector pair as measured by the *cosine* was taken as the predicted degree of compound–constituent compositionality, and the overall ranking of pair similarities was compared to the gold standard compositionality ratings using Spearman's Rank-Order Correlation Coefficient ρ (Siegel and Castellan, 1988).

---

[1]Experiments with other fusion techniques showed that mid-fusion performs best.

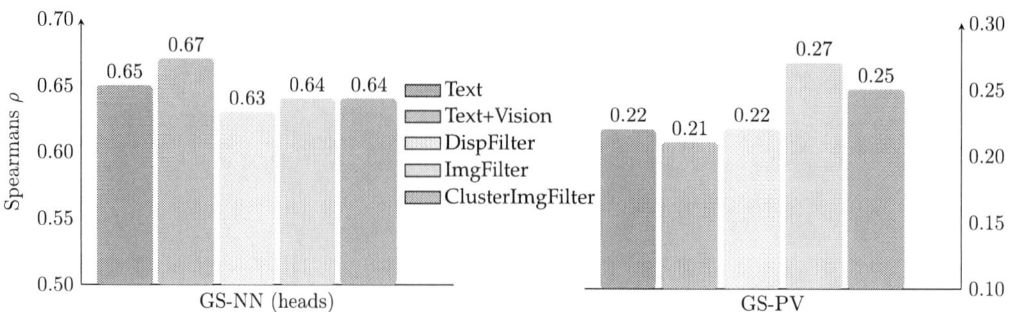

Figure 2: Overall prediction of compositionality for GS-NN (heads) and GS-PV.

Lexical, Empirical and Visual Filters The experiments compare the predictions of compositionality across all targets in the gold standards.[2] Furthermore, we zoom into factors that might influence the quality of predictions: (A) the *impact of lexical and empirical target properties*, i.e., ambiguity (relying on the DUDEN dictionary[3], frequency (as provided by the gold standards), abstractness and imageability (as taken from Köper and Schulte im Walde (2016)); (B) *optimisation of the visual space*: (i) In accordance with human concept processing (Paivio, 1990), including image representations should be more useful for words which are visual. We therefore apply the *dispersion-based filter* suggested by Kiela et al. (2014). The filter decides whether to include perceptual information for a specific word or not, relying on a pairwise similarity between all images of a concept. The underlying idea is that highly visual concepts are visualised by similar pictures and thus trigger a high average similarity between the word's images. Abstract concepts, on the other hand, are expected to provide a lower dispersion. For a given word, the filter decides about using only the textual representation, or both the textual and visual representations, depending on the dispersion value and a predefined threshold (set to the median of all the dispersion values). (ii) We apply an *imageability filter* based on external imageability norms (Köper and Schulte im Walde, 2016), to successively include only images for the most imaginable target words. This filter is applied in the same way as dispersion. (iii) We suggest a novel *clustering filter*, that performs a clustering of the 25 images for a given concept, using the algorithm from Apidianaki (2010), and includes only images from the largest image cluster, cf. Figure 1.

Results and Discussion Figure 2 present the prediction results for the two gold standards, GS-NN and GS-PV. For GS-NN, we focus on predicting the compositionality for compound–head pairs (ignoring compound–modifier pairs), in order to have a more parallel setup to GS-PV, where the particle verb compositionality focuses on the contribution of the base verb. The figures show the results across all targets. Note that the vertical axis, showing the range of Spearman's ρ are different for both results.

Figures 3 and 4 zoom into target subsets regarding target ambiguity (one sense vs. multiple senses), frequency, abstractness vs. concreteness, imageability, and compositionality. The bars refer to the textual model, the multi-modal model (including all images for all targets), and the best results obtained when using the dispersion/imageability/clustering[4] filters.

The plots demonstrate that overall the multi-modal model provides only a tiny gain for GS-NN in comparison to the text-only model, which is however significant using *Steiger*'s test ($p < 0.001$) (Steiger, 1980). All filters worsen the results. For GS-PV, we also obtain a significant improvement by the multi-modal model, but only when applying the imageability or the clustering filter to the visual information. The main differences in the overall noun and verb results are emphasised in Figure 5, comparing the successive increase of images to the multi-modal model in comparison to the textual model, based on the dispersion and imageability filters. Note that the textual

---

[2]We focus on the model with window 5 and 500 dimensions, and GoogLeNet as the overall best approach.

[3]www.duden.de

[4]For the clustering filter, we focus on a combination with the imageability filter, which provided the best results.

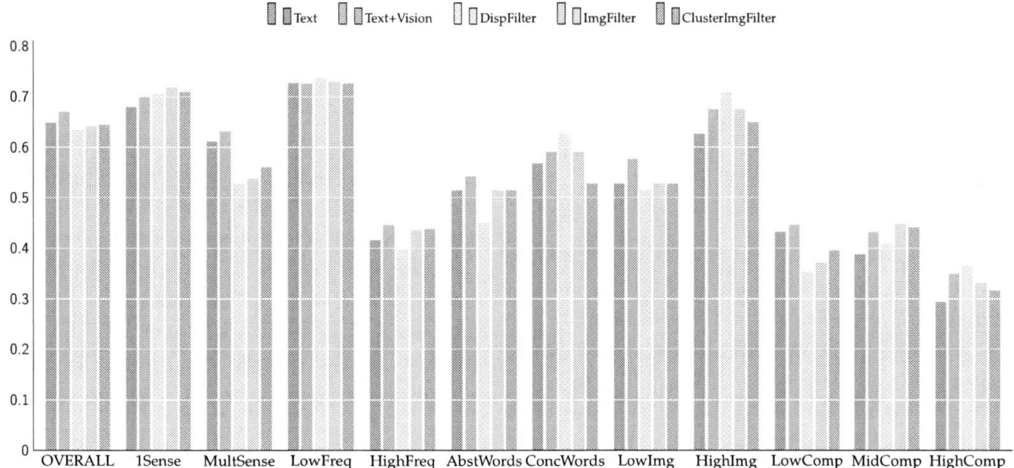

Figure 3: Prediction of compositionality for GS-NN heads.

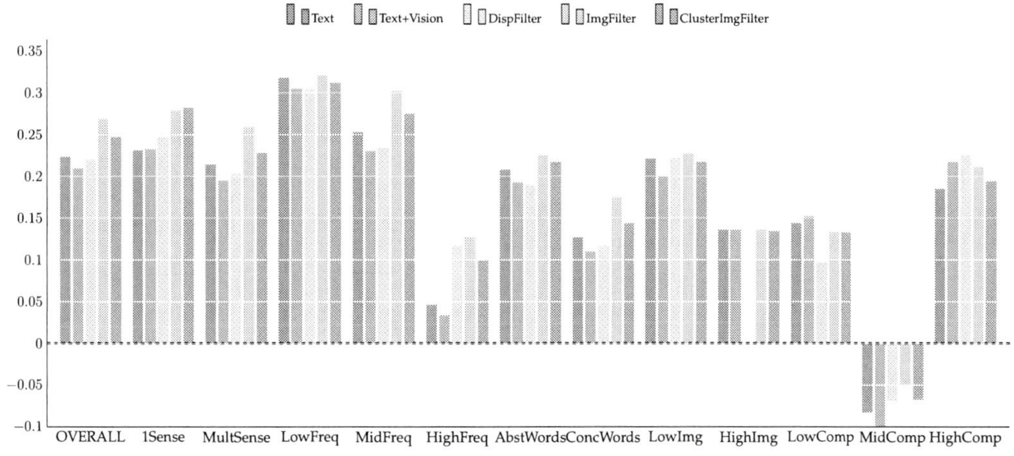

Figure 4: Prediction of compositionality for GS-PV.

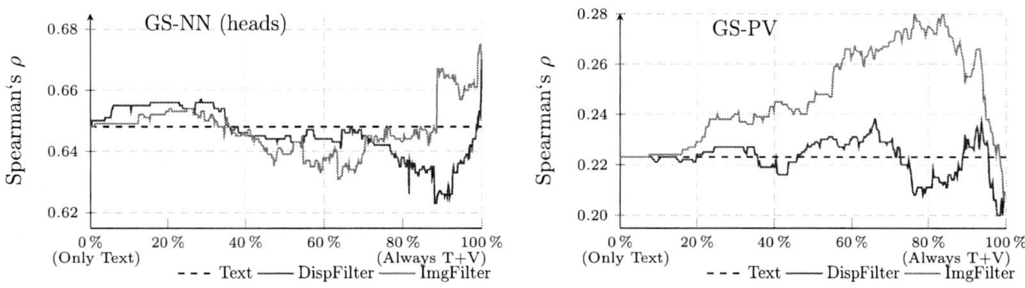

Figure 5: Prediction of compositionality: effect of dispersion and imageability filters.

model baselines are very different for the two gold standards, $\rho = .65$ for GS-NN and $\rho = .22$ for GS-PV. Regarding the nouns, the multi-modality improves the textual modality when adding the images for the $\approx 35\%$ most imaginable words, and when adding all images. Regarding the verbs, the multi-modality improves the textual modality in most proportions, reaching its maximum when adding images for $\approx 80\%$ of the most imaginable verbs; when adding the $\approx 10\%$ of the least imaginable verbs, the model strongly drops in its performance. For the dispersion filter, the tendencies are less clear. We conclude that the visual information adds to the textual information either by adding all (potentially noisy) images because the textual information is rich by itself; or by adding a selection of images (unless they are overly dissimilar to each other, or for non-imaginable targets), because the textual information by itself is poor.

Zooming into target subsets, the predictions for monosemous targets are better than those for ambiguous targets (significant for GS-NN), see Figure 3; ditto for low-frequency vs. high-frequency targets. Taking frequency as an indicator of ambiguity, these differences are presumably due to the difficulty of distinguishing between multiple senses in vector spaces that subsume the features of all word senses within one vector, which applies to our textual and multi-modal models.

The gold standard predictions strongly differ regarding the influence of target abstractness, imageability and compositionality. For GS-NN, the compositionality of concrete and imaginable targets is predicted better than for abstract and less imaginable targets, as one would expect and has been shown by Kiela et al. (2014); for GS-PV, the opposite is the case. Similarly, while for GS-NN highly compositional targets are predicted worse than low- and mid-compositional targets, for GS-PV mid-compositional targets are predicted much worse than low- and high-compositional targets. These differences in results point to questions that have still been unsolved across research fields: while humans can easily grasp intuitions about the abstractness, imageability and compositionality of nouns, the categorisations are difficult to define for verbs (Glenberg and Kaschak, 2002; Brysbaert et al., 2014). Particle verbs add to this complexity, especially since compositionality (rating) is typically reduced to the semantic relatedness between the complex verb and the base verb, ignoring the particle that however contributes a considerable portion of meaning to the complex verb.

4 Conclusion

The paper demonstrated strong differences in the effect of adding visual information to a textual neural network model, when predicting the compositionality for nominal vs. verbal MWE targets. The visual modality adds complementary features in cases where (a) the textual modality performs poorly, and images of the most imaginable targets are added, or (b) the textual modality performs well, and all available –potentially noisy– images are added. Image filters relying on imageability and a novel clustering filter positively affect the verbal but not the nominal perceptual feature spaces.

Acknowledgments

The research was supported by the DFG Collaborative Research Centre SFB 732 (Maximilian Köper) and the DFG Heisenberg Fellowship SCHU-2580/1 (Sabine Schulte im Walde).

References

Marianna Apidianaki. 2010. An Algorithm for Cross-lingual Sense Clustering tested in a MT Evaluation Setting. In *Proceedings of the 7th International Workshop on Spoken Language Translation*, pages 219–226, Paris, France.

Timothy Baldwin. 2005. Deep Lexical Acquisition of Verb–Particle Constructions. *Computer Speech and Language*, 19:398–414.

Collin Bannard. 2005. Learning about the Meaning of Verb–Particle Constructions from Corpora. *Computer Speech and Language*, 19:467–478.

Marco Baroni, Georgiana Dinu, and Germán Kruszewski. 2014. Don't count, predict! A Systematic Comparison of Context-counting and Context-predicting Semantic Vectors. In *Proceedings of the 52nd Annual Meeting of the Association for Computational Linguistics*, pages 238–247, Baltimore, MD.

Stefan Bott and Sabine Schulte im Walde. 2014. Optimizing a Distributional Semantic Model for the Prediction of German Particle Verb Compositionality. In *Proceedings of the 9th International Conference on Language Resources and Evaluation*, pages 509–516, Reykjavik, Iceland.

Stefan Bott and Sabine Schulte im Walde. 2015. Exploiting Fine-grained Syntactic Transfer Features to Predict the Compositionality of German Particle Verbs. In *Proceedings of the 11th Conference on Computational Semantics*, pages 34–39, London, UK.

Stefan Bott, Nana Khvtisavrishvili, Max Kisselew, and Sabine Schulte im Walde. 2016. G$_h$ost-PV: A Representative Gold Standard of German Particle Verbs. In *Proceedings of the 5th Workshop on Cognitive Aspects of the Lexicon*, pages 125–133, Osaka, Japan.

Elia Bruni, Nam Khanh Tran, and Marco Baroni. 2014. Multimodal Distributional Semantics. *Journal of Artificial Intelligence Research*, 49(1):1–47.

Marc Brysbaert, Amy Beth Warriner, and Victor Kuperman. 2014. Concreteness Ratings for 40 Thousand generally known English Word Lemmas. *Behavior Research Methods*, 64:904–911.

John A. Bullinaria and Joseph P. Levy. 2007. Extracting Semantic Representations from Word Co-Occurrence Statistics: A Computational Study. *Behavior Research Methods*, 39(3):510–526.

Lev Finkelstein, Evgeniy Gabrilovich, Yossi Matias, Ehud Rivlin, Zach Solan, Gadi Wolfman, and Eytan Ruppin. 2002. Placing Search in Context: The Concept Revisited. *ACM Transactions on Information Systems*, 20(1):116–131.

Arthur M. Glenberg and Michael P. Kaschak. 2002. Grounding Language in Action. *Psychonomic Bulletin & Review*, 9(3):558–565.

Zellig Harris. 1954. Distributional structure. *Word*, 10(23):146–162.

Felix Hill, Roi Reichart, and Anna Korhonen. 2015. SimLex-999: Evaluating Semantic Models With (Genuine) Similarity Estimation. *Computational Linguistics*, 41(4):665–695.

Yangqing Jia, Evan Shelhamer, Jeff Donahue, Sergey Karayev, Jonathan Long, Ross Girshick, Sergio Guadarrama, and Trevor Darrell. 2014. Caffe: Convolutional architecture for fast feature embedding. In *Proceedings of the International Conference on Multimedia*, pages 675–678, New York, NY, USA.

Douwe Kiela, Felix Hill, Anna Korhonen, and Stephen Clark. 2014. Improving Multi-Modal Representations Using Image Dispersion: Why Less is Sometimes More. In *Proceedings of the 52nd Annual Meeting of the Association for Computational Linguistics*, pages 835–841, Baltimore, MA.

Douwe Kiela, Anita L. Verő, and Stephen Clark. 2016. Comparing Data Sources and Architectures for Deep Visual Representation Learning in Semantics. In *Proceedings of the Conference on Empirical Methods in Natural Language Processing*, Austin, TX.

Maximilian Köper and Sabine Schulte im Walde. 2016. Automatically Generated Affective Norms of Abstractness, Arousal, Imageability and Valence for 350 000 German Lemmas. In *Proceedings of the 10th International Conference on Language Resources and Evaluation*, pages 2595–2598, Portoroz, Slovenia.

Alex Krizhevsky, Ilya Sutskever, and Geoffrey E. Hinton. 2012. ImageNet Classification with Deep Convolutional Neural Networks. In F. Pereira, C. J. C. Burges, L. Bottou, and K. Q. Weinberger, editors, *Advances in Neural Information Processing Systems 25*, pages 1097–1105.

Angeliki Lazaridou, Nghia The Pham, and Marco Baroni. 2015. Combining Language and Vision with a Multimodal Skip-gram Model. In *Proceedings of the Conference of the North American Chapter of the Association for Computational Linguistics: Human Language Technologies*, pages 153–163, Denver, Colorado, USA.

Omer Levy, Yoav Goldberg, and Ido Dagan. 2015. Improving Distributional Similarity with Lessons Learned from Word Embeddings. *Transactions of Computational Linguistics*, 3:211–225.

Tomas Mikolov, Ilya Sutskever, Kai Chen, Greg S. Corrado, and Jeff Dean. 2013. Distributed Representations of Words and Phrases and their Compositionality. In *Advances in Neural Information Processing Systems 26*, pages 3111–3119.

Kim-Anh Nguyen, Sabine Schulte im Walde, and Thang Vu. 2016. Integrating Distributional Lexical Contrast into Word Embeddings for Antonym-Synonym Distinction. In *Proceedings of the 54th Annual Meeting of the Association for Computational Linguistics*, pages 454–459, Berlin, Germany.

A. Paivio. 1990. *Mental Representations: A Dual Coding Approach*. Oxford Psychology Series. Oxford University Press.

Siva Reddy, Diana McCarthy, and Suresh Manandhar. 2011. An Empirical Study on Compositionality in Compound Nouns. In *Proceedings of the 5th International Joint Conference on Natural Language Processing*, pages 210–218, Chiang Mai, Thailand.

Bahar Salehi and Paul Cook. 2013. Predicting the Compositionality of Multiword Expressions Using Translations in Multiple Languages. In *Proceedings of the 2nd Joint Conference on Lexical and Computational Semantics*, pages 266–275, Atlanta, GA.

Bahar Salehi, Paul Cook, and Timothy Baldwin. 2014. Using Distributional Similarity of Multi-way Translations to Predict Multiword Expression Compositionality. In *Proceedings of the 14th Conference of the European Chapter of the Association for Computational Linguistics*, pages 472–481, Gothenburg, Sweden.

Roland Schäfer and Felix Bildhauer. 2012. Building Large Corpora from the Web Using a New Efficient Tool Chain. In *Proceedings of the 8th International Conference on Language Resources and Evaluation*, pages 486–493, Istanbul, Turkey.

Sabine Schulte im Walde, Stefan Müller, and Stephen Roller. 2013. Exploring Vector Space Models to Predict the Compositionality of German Noun-Noun Compounds. In *Proceedings of the 2nd Joint Conference on Lexical and Computational Semantics*, pages 255–265, Atlanta, GA.

Sabine Schulte im Walde, Anna Hätty, and Stefan Bott. 2016a. The Role of Modifier and Head Properties in Predicting the Compositionality of English and German Noun-Noun Compounds: A Vector-Space Perspective. In *Proceedings of the 5th Joint Conference on Lexical and Computational Semantics (*SEM)*, pages 148–158, Berlin, Germany.

Sabine Schulte im Walde, Anna Hätty, Stefan Bott, and Nana Khvtisavrishvili. 2016b. $G_h$ost-NN: A Representative Gold Standard of German Noun-Noun Compounds. In *Proceedings of the 10th International Conference on Language Resources and Evaluation*, pages 2285–2292, Portoroz, Slovenia.

Sidney Siegel and N. John Castellan. 1988. *Nonparametric Statistics for the Behavioral Sciences*. McGraw-Hill, Boston, MA.

Carina Silberer and Mirella Lapata. 2014. Learning Grounded Meaning Representations with Autoencoders. In *Proceedings of the Annual Meeting of the Association for Computational Linguistics*, pages 721–732, Baltimore, Maryland.

Sylvia Springorum. 2011. DRT-based Analysis of the German Verb Particle *"an"*. *Leuvense Bijdragen*, 97:80–105.

James H Steiger. 1980. Tests for Comparing Elements of a Correlation Matrix. *Psychological Bulletin*.

Christian Szegedy, Wei Liu, Yangqing Jia, Pierre Sermanet, Scott Reed, Dragomir Anguelov, Dumitru Erhan, Vincent Vanhoucke, and Andrew Rabinovich. 2015. Going Deeper with Convolutions. In *Computer Vision and Pattern Recognition*.

Peter D. Turney and Patrick Pantel. 2010. From Frequency to Meaning: Vector Space Models of Semantics. *Journal of Artificial Intelligence Research*, 37:141–188.

Author Index